POVERTY, MENTAL HEALTH, AND SOCIAL INCLUSION

POVERTY, MENTAL HEALTH, AND SOCIAL INCLUSION

Edited by Cheryl Forchuk and Rick Csiernik

CANADIAN SCHOLARS
Toronto | Vancouver

Poverty, Mental Health, and Social Inclusion
Edited by Cheryl Forchuk and Rick Csiernik

First published in 2021 by
Canadian Scholars, an imprint of CSP Books Inc.
425 Adelaide Street West, Suite 200
Toronto, Ontario
M5V 3C1

www.canadianscholars.ca

Library and Archives Canada Cataloguing in Publication

Title: Poverty, mental health, and social inclusion / edited by Cheryl Forchuk and Rick Csiernik.
Names: Forchuk, Cheryl, editor. | Csiernik, Rick, editor.
Description: Includes bibliographical references and index.
Identifiers: Canadiana (print) 20200398857 | Canadiana (ebook) 20200399101 |
ISBN 9781773382234 (softcover) | ISBN 9781773382241 (PDF) |
ISBN 9781773382258 (EPUB)
Subjects: LCSH: Marginality, Social—Canada. | LCSH: Poor—Canada—Social conditions. |
LCSH: Mentally ill—Canada—Social conditions. | LCSH: Poor—Mental health—Canada. |
LCSH: Mentally ill—Canada—Economic conditions. | LCSH: Poor—Services for—Canada. |
LCSH: Mentally ill—Services for—Canada.
Classification: LCC HN110.Z9 M26 2021 | DDC 305.5/60971—dc23

Page layout by S4Carlisle Publishing Services
Cover design by Em Dash

Printed and bound in Ontario, Canada

Canada

Contents

SECTION III BECOMING SOCIALLY EXCLUDED

SECTION IV CREATING SOCIAL INCLUSION

Preface

This book provides highlights from a five-year Canadian Community University Research Alliance (CURA) funded through the Social Sciences and Humanities Research Council of Canada. The focus of this CURA was on poverty and social inclusion as it relates to mental health consumer-survivors. Our team had worked together on a previous CURA, focusing on housing, homelessness, and mental health. The challenges and successes of that project are summarized in an earlier book, *Homelessness, Housing, and Mental Health: Finding Truths—Creating Change*, edited by Cheryl Forchuk, Rick Csiernik, and Elsabeth Jensen that is also published by Canadian Scholars.

However, the origins of what actually inspired this project and the original CURA date back well over a decade, arising from concerns raised by individuals who would eventually become some of our community partners in London, Ontario. Representatives of a poverty support agency contacted our academic lead for both CURAs (Forchuk) and spoke of the increasing numbers of women with mental health issues who were suddenly accessing their services and how these women's dire financial situations were leading them into homelessness. In the same month, a homeless shelter also reached out to Forchuk regarding their concerns about the growing number of men with mental health issues who were increasingly using the programs that they provided. It was becoming evident, quickly, that the safety net in London was clearly changing. In a study examining psychiatric discharge models across several cities in Ontario, Canada, we also found that the number of people post-discharge in dire situations, including being discharged to no fixed address, a euphemism for being released without having any place to live, was growing. A group of researchers, community agencies, and people with the lived experience of mental illness began to meet monthly in attempting to develop a better understanding of what was happening and how to meaningfully address the changes being witnessed and documented. It was after a year of these meetings that we applied for and were successful in obtaining funding for the inaugural CURA. The inter-relationships of poverty and housing issues, as well as the complex questions related to social inclusion and exclusion, convinced us that our work was not complete after five years. We needed to continue to build on our new initiatives and the strong community partnerships that had been developed to further examine the intersection of these issues and to continue to explore solutions. Our current community partnerships have now developed across two decades, allowing for numerous projects to arise through a solid participatory action process. This current edited book highlights examples of our most recent work, integrating them with some of our past learnings.

Poverty, Mental Health, and Social Inclusion is divided into four sections with contributions from 59 researchers, direct practitioners, and mental health consumer-survivors. Section I offers an introduction to this complex issue, situating the reader on what we have previously learned. Chapter 1 provides the theoretical foundations and context that led us to shift our focus from housing and homelessness to explore the broader but related issues of poverty and social inclusion. Chapter 2 is an overview of the major policy changes that created the problems we were witnessing at the time of the first CURA and that have continued to affect this population. There was a huge disconnect between changes introduced to housing policy, income support policy, and mental health services policy that created the perfect storm we were witnessing and that continue to engulf this community. Chapter 3 uses a metaphor, based on the game of musical chairs, to understand the relationship between housing, poverty, and life transitions. The model drawn from this metaphor illustrates how policy and practices in these areas can contribute to homelessness, but also presents direction for interventions.

Section II focuses on methodological issues. The CURAs' processes were founded on engaging community members: doing with rather than to or just for. Both CURAs were based on participatory action research (PAR) principles, a description of which is provided in Chapter 4 to begin this section. Chapter 5 describes the Article Idea Chart, a concrete example of how PAR was enacted with regards to publications and academic information dissemination. Chapter 6 discusses, in depth, how we were able to retain a sample of transient homeless youth, and the section concludes with Chapter 7, on the application of the British-designed Stigma Scale to the Canadian context.

Section III, *Becoming Socially Excluded*, delves into how individuals with mental health issues became and become socially excluded. Chapter 8 provides a formal examination of poverty trajectories experienced by persons with mental illnesses, which is followed by a discussion of the relationship between poverty and social inclusion predictors in Chapter 9. The remainder of the third section highlights issues faced by specific populations, discussing what we learned regarding social exclusion and how it pertains to each group. The populations we engaged with were mothers with mental illness (Chapter 10), Indigenous women (Chapter 11), and veterans (Chapters 12 and 13). The interface between poverty and social exclusion is the central focus of the third section, highlighted by the lived realities of these different groups of individuals.

Section IV on *Creating Social Inclusion* presents solutions our research has documented over the course of the CURA. The function and utility of peer support (Chapter 14) and employment and social enterprises (Chapter 15) opens the section. This is followed by Chapter 16, which is perhaps the most unique chapter in the entire book—a look at the use of iris scanning, a biometric approach to address the issue of lost identification, to better enable individuals to readily access health and social services. The section concludes with chapters discussing means to prevent family homelessness (Chapter 17), discharge to homelessness from health care systems (Chapter 18), along with how to better and more actively support those with addiction issues (Chapter 19) and aid youth with mental health issues to avoid becoming homeless and thus breaking a cycle of homelessness before it even begins (Chapter 20).

We hope you find this book challenges your thinking regarding mental health and also challenges you to become actively involved in working to socially include not only individuals with mental health issues but all members of our civil society.

Cheryl Forchuk
Brantford, Ontario

Rick Csiernik
Hamilton, Ontario

December 2020

Acknowledgements

We would like to acknowledge the research participants, community partners, researchers, and students who support the Community University Research Alliance on poverty and social inclusion that was foundational to this book. In particular we acknowledge our many community partners:

Addiction Services of Thames Valley
Atlohsa Family Healing Services
Canadian Mental Health Association – Elgin
Canadian Mental Health Association – Middlesex
Canadian Mental Health Association – Sudbury
Canadian Mental Health Association – Ontario
Can-Voice
Centre of Hope, Salvation Army
City of London
Connect for Mental Health
Goodwill Industries
Homes for Special Care
John Howard Society of London and District
King's University College: Social Work
Laurentian University
London CAReS
London Child and Youth Network
London Health Science Centre
London Homeless Coalition
London Housing Advisory Committee
London InterCommunity Health Centre
London Police Services
Mental Health Support Network South East Ontario
Mission Services
Ontario Disability Support Program – London
Ontario Peer Development Initiative
Ontario Works Employment and Income Support – London
Pillar Nonprofit Network
Regional HIV/AIDS Connection

Simon Fraser University
Society of Saint Vincent de Paul London
South Western Alliance Network
St. Joseph's Healthcare
St. Leonard's Community Services
Support Over Stigma
United Way Elgin Middlesex
University of Manitoba
Western University
Wilfrid Laurier University
Youth Opportunities Unlimited

SECTION I

INTRODUCTION

People with mental illness routinely experience physical, psychological, and social challenges in various aspects of their lives. The book's opening chapter, "The Unspoken Intersection of Mental Illness and Poverty: Social Exclusion," highlights current global research that has established the close relationship between mental health issues and poverty. The concept of poverty among people with a history of mental illness is multidimensional in nature. This has led the United Nations to tout poverty as the most significant challenge facing humanity today. Chapter 1 examines the intersection of mental illness, poverty, and social exclusion. The authors begin by exploring the global and Canadian extant literature concerning poverty, and then elaborate on theoretical perspectives that link poverty to mental illness. Further discourse related to the intersections between mental illness, poverty, stigma, and social exclusion are next discussed. The chapter concludes by proposing approaches to address mental illness and poverty through a lens of emancipation and social inclusion.

The second chapter, entitled "Creating Social Exclusion: The Disconnection between Housing, Income Support, and Mental Health Policies," explores the lack of integration of policies in these three interconnected areas. While these policies intersect in the lives of many, there remains no coordination of service delivery that is provided through federal, provincial, and municipal levels of government. Canada is one of the few developed nations that has yet to formalize a national mental health policy, although, as for progress, we have had in recent years a mental health commission. Due to the federal government policy reforms of the 1970s, the provincial governments now oversee the process of deinstitutionalization from the hospital to the community level. During this same time period, the availability of affordable housing dramatically decreased as responsibility for social housing was transferred from the federal government to the provincial and/or municipal levels of government without sufficient funding to maintain an adequate housing supply. Canada likewise stands alone in terms of being a developed nation without a national housing policy for two decades, with a new national strategy ("A place to call home," https://www.placetocallhome.ca/) just introduced this past year. Instead, what is considered "affordable" housing is partially dependent upon each individual's personal economic resources. As well, since the beginning of the century, rates of income supports have been reduced in terms of real dollar value, despite increasing costs of living, further contributing to the risk of homelessness among mental health consumer-survivors.

Joe operates an elevator on the way to a job on the third floor of a CMHA social housing unit in the northwest end of London, Ontario, in February 2014.
Source: Photo by Justin Langille

The concluding chapter of the opening section, "Playing Musical Chairs: Understanding How to End Homelessness," uses this metaphor to help simplify the complexity of approaching the issue of homelessness. Attempting to address all the factors that contribute to homelessness, and in turn the social exclusion that arises from being homeless, can be overwhelming. However, by applying this metaphor, successful responses can be readily observed, as can methods to implement changes. Chapter 3 focuses upon two specific areas: housing interventions and the need for supports. Specific examples of how homelessness has been addressed in these two areas is discussed, allowing us to see how we need to both increase the number of chairs in the game but at the same time ensure individuals are able to keep their chair once they find one.

CHAPTER 1

The Unspoken Intersection of Mental Illness and Poverty: Social Exclusion

Sebastian Gyamfi, Cheryl Forchuk, and Rick Csiernik

1. INTRODUCTION

Globally, millions of people experience mental illness at some point in their lives, with the number of individuals who report mental health problems in care settings steadily increasing (World Health Organization [WHO], 2019). Recent WHO estimates indicate that nearly 450 million people worldwide suffer from either mental health– or neurobiology-related disorders. The WHO further reports that these disorders represent the fourth leading cause of disability worldwide. The incidence of mental illness in people's lives has the potential to plunge them into physical, social, and psychological suffering, with dire socioeconomic implications for individuals and their families arising from this change in their health status (Mental Health Foundation, 2016). Current global research has established a close link between mental health issues and poverty (Lund et al., 2010). Lund et al. (2010) reviewed 115 studies conducted in 33 countries across the world, including both developed and developing nations. Approximately 80% of the included studies identified a significant relationship between poverty and mental illness. This systematic review also established that among people living in poverty, the incidence of mental health issues is more common, more severe, and longer lasting, with poorer outcomes. Individuals with mental illness face numerous social problems, including lack of employment and limited income-generation opportunities, poor education, homelessness, and higher rates of incarceration (Funk, Drew, & Knapp, 2012). Individuals with mental illness can also experience reduced intellectual capacity owing to the cognitive decline that leaves them with limited attention or no alternative sources for performing other tasks

Joe paces along the front yard as the Impact Junk Solutions Crew slowly empties furniture from a home in the south end of London, Ontario, in April 2014.
Source: Photo by Justin Langille

(Mani, Mullainathan, Shafir, & Zhao, 2013). As well, there is extensive evidence demonstrating that poverty imposes significant limitations on the capacity and well-being of persons with mental illness in a range of life domains (Leventhal, & Brooks-Gunn, 2003; Funk, Drew, & Knapp, 2012).

Even though there has been a significant improvement in efforts aimed at reducing poverty globally by 2030, the number of people living in economic need remains substantive (World Bank, 2018). The Organisation for Economic Co-operation and Development (OECD), in its 2018 report, stated that one in seven children lives in extremely low income across the 36 OECD countries, which includes Canada, the United States, and the United Kingdom. Children in low-income families experience deprivation in several spheres of life, including sub-standard housing conditions, lack of educational opportunities (OECD, 2018), poor health, and food insecurity (Canada Without Poverty, 2019).

2. POVERTY AND ITS EFFECTS ON MENTAL ILLNESS

Poverty is a key social determinant of overall mental health, and when people live in chronic poverty over an extended period of time, they become more easily predisposed to risk factors for mental health problems. The concept of poverty among people with a history of mental illness is multidimensional in nature (Compton & Shim, 2015; Narayan et al., 2000), carrying diverse meanings based on social, economic, cultural, and political attributions within a society (Simon, Beder, & Manseau, 2018). Poverty impacts health, education, shelter, and employment, as well decreasing social involvement, with the United Nations (n.d.) stating that poverty is the most significant challenge facing humanity today. The Canadian Poverty Institute (CPI) equally conceive poverty as multidimensional, involving material, social, and spiritual perspectives (CPI, 2020). Material poverty refers to a lack of access or appropriate skills to acquire adequate material and financial resources to help one to thrive. Social poverty constitutes exclusionary activities that are characterized by lack of formal and informal supports required for coping in crisis situations. Spiritual poverty constitutes a lack of meaning or purpose in life as well as one's faith community that sustains them.

Various countries have different definitions of what constitutes poverty. Therefore, it is not surprising that literature pertaining to poverty is conceptualized distinctly in different jurisdictions. In Canada, poverty is viewed as a state where a person is deprived of resources, means, choices, and the power necessary to acquire and maintain a basic level of living standards to facilitate integration and participation in society (Government of Canada, 2018). Simon, Beder, and Manseau (2018) defined poverty as a state of low socioeconomic class that is measured by the social or income status, unemployment, or low levels of education of the individual. Bhuiya and colleagues (2007) define poverty as a state in which the consumption or income level of a person falls below a certain threshold necessary to meet basic needs.

A quintessential indicator of poverty is adequate and affordable housing with incidences of mental illness correlated with both individual and family homelessness. Jones-Rounds, Evans, and Braubach (2014) found that those requiring financial support to maintain their housing were more than twice as likely to develop mental health issues. The prevalence of mental illness among urban homeless populations is high. For instance, in Rio de Janeiro, Brazil, almost 50% suffer from mental health–related problems (Lovisi et al., 2003), with the lifetime prevalence of mental illness among the homeless being three times greater than among the general Brazilian population (Bresnahan et al., 2003; Lovisi et al., 2003). In Brazil, children living in extreme poverty are more than five times more likely to suffer from mental illness compared to their middle-class counterparts (Fleitlich & Goodman, 2001). Evidence from high-income countries likewise indicates a strong relationship between socioeconomic class and mental health outcomes, with people from lower socioeconomic backgrounds having a greater likelihood of developing mental health issues (WHO & Calouste Gulbenkian Foundation, 2014). A study from Great Britain found that children and adults living in the lowest income bracket had a two to three times greater prospect of developing mental health problems compared to the national average (Marmot et al., 2010). Similarly, British children in the lowest income quintile were 4.5 times more likely to experience severe mental health problems compared to children in the high-income groups (Gutman, Joshi, Parsonage, & Schoon, 2015).

Employment status is another factor that appears to significantly impact health and poverty trajectories of individuals diagnosed with mental illness. The influence of a person's employment status on mental health outcomes and social status has been established globally. Stansfeld et al. (2016), in their work conducted in Leeds, England, revealed that people who are unemployed or have low income are more easily predisposed to mental illness compared to their employed counterparts. When people engage in healthy and beneficial employment, they attain better mental health scores than unemployed peers. Nonetheless, when the work is of low quality, as in low pay and job insecurity, the individual stands a greater risk of experiencing mental health problems than individuals in more secure and better paid positions (Marmot et al., 2010).

The incidence of mental illness is a major barrier preventing individuals and their families from leaving poverty, creating a vicious cycle of intergenerational poverty and the associated state of poor health (McLoyd, 1998). A state of poverty has dire health consequences, with people who experience mental illness facing ongoing marginalization that further exacerbates socioeconomic inequalities. These inequalities cross many sectors: education, access to health care, employment, housing, community participation, and ultimately social inclusion. Literature from around the world identifies income inequality as a critical predictor of mental health outcomes with associated greater incidences of adverse child educational achievements, childhood mental illness, depression, drug-related deaths, and juvenile homicides (Melchior et al., 2018; Simon et al., 2018; Yoshikawa, Aber, & Beardslee, 2012; Zimmerman & Bell, 2006). In turn, generational poverty can perpetuate mental illness and low socioeconomic status of families. Simon and colleagues (2018) assert that when people experience poverty in early life for long periods, they become predisposed to various adverse health and developmental sequels. Experiences of childhood poverty have been linked with lower school achievement, deficits in executive brain cognitive functioning, behavioural and attention-related deficits, such as higher rates of delinquency, and mental illness during adulthood (Moore, 2015; Simon et al., 2018; Yoshikawa et al., 2012; Zimmerman & Bell, 2006). Family-level poverty experiences also lead to parental relationship stress, parental mental illness, and low parental family investment. Family poverty is also characterized by inconsistent parenting, a low-stimulating home environment, child abuse, and neglect, all of which impacts a child's mental health (Canadian Mental Health Association [CMHA], 2007; Heflin & Iceland, 2009; Labella et al., 2019; Simon et al., 2018; Stavinoha, 2018).

Poverty also affects the mental health of people through social, psychological, and biological mechanisms acting at individual, familial, institutional, community, and national levels. Individual poverty leads to chronic and acute stressful life events along with hypothalamic-pituitary-adrenal (HPA) axis changes. Exposure to low socioeconomic conditions, especially during childhood, leads to stress that disrupts neuroendocrine system development (Holochwost, Towe-Goodman, Rehder, Wang, & Mills-Koonce, 2020). During chronic stress, changes occur to the neurons in the hypothalamus, leading to increased and sustained activation of the HPA axis. The hypothalamus increases the release of corticotropin-releasing hormone (CRH) in response to stress. The CRH in turn acts on the pituitary gland, causing it to release adrenocorticotrophic hormone (ACTH), which then causes the adrenal cortex to release cortisol. Stress causes increased cortisol output from the adrenal cortex. Dysfunction of the HPA axis activity may cause a buildup of cortisol in the body in response to chronic stress linked to poor socioeconomic state of the individual (Brewer, 2019). A dysfunctional HPA axis (due to prolonged or intense stressors) may lead to outcomes of increased HPA reactivity (such as suppressed immunity, anxiety, depression, social withdrawal among others), which can lead to psychopathology or mental illness (Brewer, 2019; Busso, McLaughlin, & Sheridan, 2017; Koss, & Gunnar, 2018; LeMoult, Ordaz, Kircanski, Singh, & Gotlib, 2015; Nelson & Sheridan, 2011).

Poverty also results in poor pre- and postnatal health outcomes and inadequate nutrition (Simon et al., 2018). Hudson (2005) examined data from 34,000 persons with a history of multiple admissions into acute psychiatric units in the United States. The study revealed a positive correlation between poor socioeconomic conditions and risk of mental illness and hospitalization readmissions over time. Anakwenze and Zuberi (2013) corroborated Hudson's finding by attributing individual post-illness impoverishment to higher health care costs, poor physical health, and decreased productivity. Poverty forces people to settle in disadvantaged urban areas, which are generally characterized by adverse psychosocial and physical

The last belongings of a family evicted from their south-end apartment lie on the kitchen floor before the Impact Junk Solutions crew removes them in February 2014.
Source: Photo by Justin Langille

conditions that cause further distress, diminish well-being, and undermine positive mental health–promotional activities (Chow, Johnson, & Austin, 2005; Chung & Steinberg, 2006) that affect both the physical and mental health of an entire family (McSilver Institute for Poverty Policy and Research, 2019). Children and adults experiencing poverty are more likely to be exposed to violence and trauma in low-income neighbourhoods, which contributes to the cyclical nature of poverty, trauma, and mental illness (Anakwenze, & Zuberi, 2013; Collins et al., 2010; McKay, Lynn, & Bannon, 2005; McSilver Institute for Poverty Policy and Research, 2019).

3. POVERTY ISSUES IN CANADA

The Ontario Human Rights Commission (OHRC, 2017) states that poverty is a human rights violation of the vulnerable in society and may be caused by systemic discrimination. This compels us to engage in a discourse of what leads to and/or sustains poverty as well as the associated health implications at the micro (individual), mezzo (community), and macro (national and global) levels. In 2015, one in eight Canadians lived in poverty (Government of Canada, 2018). In response to the United Nations' call for country-specific approaches in eradicating poverty, Canada put in place its first national poverty reduction strategy Opportunity for All. This initiative sought to reduce poverty in Canada by 20% by the end of 2020 and by 50% by 2030. Despite these recent efforts towards fighting socioeconomic hardships, poverty rates remain substantive.

In Canada, poverty is measured through varying levels of material and social deprivation of basic life necessities relative to a combination of educational, economic, and occupational criteria (Canadian Institute for Health Information, 2008; Williamson & Reutter, 1999). A standard definition of poverty is expressed primarily as a relationship of income to expenses that results in the inability to meet one's basic needs. Key poverty indicators used by Statistics Canada (2019) are the Low-Income Measure (LIM) and the Market Basket Measure (MBM). The LIM defines an individual as low income if their adjusted after-tax income falls below 50% of the median adjusted after-tax income for all households of the same size. In comparison, the MBM assesses poverty based on the cost of basic goods and services, such as food, clothing, footwear, transportation, and shelter, and in relation to disposable income of a family to determine whether or not they fall below the poverty line.

Statistics Canada reported that in 2017 there was a 3.3% increase in median income, to $59,800, for Canadian families and unattached individuals. This meant that any individual or family with an after-tax income of less than $29,900 would be considered poor. That figure was estimated to be 3.4 million Canadians, or 9.5% of the population, who had an income that placed them below the poverty line. However, the 2018 poverty trends report (Tables 1.1 and 1.2) indicated that approximately 5.8 million people, representing 16.8% of Canada's population, or 75% more Canadians, actually lived in poverty (Citizens for Public Justice, 2018). However, what also needs to be factored in is geography, as costs in urban centres (Toronto, Vancouver), rural centres (Winkler, Truro), and northern communities (Cambridge Bay, Yellowknife) also impact cost-based definitions of poverty.

As discussed, poverty has a negative impact on a person's physical and mental health, personal dignity, ability to care for one's family, and the ability to be recognized and accepted to fully participate in community activities. There is a strong link between poverty and homelessness among people with mental health problems, due to a lack of affordable housing in Canada (Ontario Human Rights Commission [OHRC], 2009) with almost half (45%) of individuals experiencing

Table 1.1: Poverty Trends in Canada

Poverty Trends Nationwide[1]	Rate in Percentages
5.8 million people in Canada (1 in every 6 people)	16.8%
Children (CFLIM-AT[2])	19.6%
Children in lone-parent families (CFLIM-AT)	47.4%
Single-parent families (CFLIM-AT)	36.0%
Single adults (CFLIM-AT)	37.7%
Single seniors (CFLIM-AT)	25.7%
Single persons with disabilities (LIM-AT[3])	23.0%
Indigenous people (LIM-AT)	23.6%
Racialized people (LIM-AT)	20.8%

Notes: 1. Poverty trends in Canada as reported by Citizens for Public Justice (2018); 2. CFLIM-AT = Census Family Low Income Measure, after tax; 3. LIM-AT = Low Income Measure, after tax

Table 1.2: Provincial Poverty Trends in Canada

Poverty Trends across Provinces of Canada	Rate in Percentages: Current (previous)[1]
Alberta	13.6% (13.0%)
British Columbia	18.7% (19.3%)
Manitoba	20.7% (21.1%)
New Brunswick	17.1% (18.1%)
Newfoundland and Labrador	14.6% (15.4%)
Northwest Territories	18.0% (18.3%)
Nova Scotia	18.5% (18.8%)
Nunavut	29.0% (31.2%)
Ontario	17.0% (17.7%)
Prince Edward Island	16.2% (16.9%)
Quebec	16.1% (16.8%)
Saskatchewan	18.1% (17.7%)
Yukon	12.1% (12.9%)

Note: 1. Provincial poverty rates depicting current (2016) and previous (2015) reports (Citizens for Public Justice, 2018)

homelessness living with some form of disability or mental illness (Canada Without Poverty, 2019). A recent longitudinal study by Statistics Canada (Wall, 2017) suggests that 26.6% of individuals with a mental-cognitive disability, which includes both intellectual and psychiatric disabilities, live in poverty, compared with 8.6% of non-disabled persons.

4. DRIFTING INTO POVERTY

Poverty and mental illness intersect (McSilver Institute for Poverty Policy and Research, 2019). When people suffer from mental illness, it increases their chances of becoming and remaining poor. The poverty people with mental illness experience also exacerbates additional symptoms in many instances (Anakwenze & Zuberi, 2013; Hudson, 2005; Lederbogen et al., 2011). The relationship between mental illness and poverty is argued to be bidirectional, with poverty predisposing individuals to mental illness, and in turn, mental illness leading to a greater risk of living in poverty. While researchers have predicted positive relationships between lower social class and incidence of mental illness (Eaton et al., 2001; Fox, 1990), the debate remains in relation to the causal pathways of what leads to this "double jeopardy" of mental illness and poverty.

Two prominent theories dominate the literature in this area. Hoffmann, Kröger, and Geyer (2019) argue that socioeconomic status (SES) affects health (social causation) and, in turn, health affects socioeconomic status through drifting, which is also referred to as either social selection or health selection. Conversely, supporters of the social drift or health selection theory put forward that constitutional (genetic) and other environment-related influences underwrite incidences of mental illness, which in turn cause individuals to experience downward drift from a high socioeconomic status to a lower level, causing them to stagnate into poverty (Wender, Rosenthal, Kety, Schulsinger, & Welner, 1973). The debate has centred on the relative role of social causation and drifting theories with regards to the illness-poverty pathway.

Proponents of the social causation theory posit that environmental adversities, other social-related disadvantages, as well as stress associated with low socioeconomic status contribute to incidences of mental illness (American Psychological Association, 2014; Finegan, Firth, Wojnarowski, & Delgadillo, 2018; Hoffmann, Kröger, & Geyer, 2019; Hollingshead & Redlich, 1958; McLaughlin, Costello, Leblanc, Sampson, & Kessler, 2012; Santiago, Wadsworth, & Stump, 2011). Previous longitudinal studies (Dodge, Pettit, & Bates, 1994; Hamilton, Broman,

Hoffman, & Renner, 1990; Link & Phelan, 1995; Shaw, Winslow, Owens, & Hood, 1998) and some quasi-experimental findings (Dohrenwend et al., 1992) have all supported the social causation theory indicating that loss of income and low socioeconomic status account for incidences of mental health problems. However, findings from cross-sectional and quasi-experimental studies have also shown consistency by predicting associations between social selection (drift) theory and incidences of low socioeconomic status after occurrences of mental illness (Kessler et al., 1995; Miech et al., 1999; Wender et al., 1986).

Hoffman et al. (2019) identified eight previous studies that not only compared social causation and drifting, but also traced different dimensions of socioeconomic status from a life course viewpoint of childhood to adulthood. Of the eight articles, three gave preference to a relationship between low socioeconomic status (poverty) and social causation, with two giving preference to a relationship between socioeconomic status and drifting (health selection). Only one study gave equal weight to both mechanisms, while one study concluded that neither social causation nor drift was important, while yet another study did not draw any direct conclusions concerning the two concepts.

Though there is no definitive theory explaining the phenomena, both social causation and social drift are bidirectional, supporting the belief that causation in relation to the incidence of mental illness and change in socioeconomic status is a vicious cycle. Dohrenwend and Dohrenwend (1969) and Plomin (1990) previously stated that both social causation and drift theories complement each other in accounting for the association between the dynamics of socioeconomic status and incidences of mental health–related problems. Contemporary researchers seem to corroborate these views. Hoffmann, Kröger, and Geyer (2019) used retrospective survey data from ten European countries (n = 18,734) and applied structural equation models in determining the relative explanatory power of social causation and health selection through childhood, adulthood, and old age. They found social causation and drifting (health selection) equally important in determining socioeconomic status from childhood to adulthood. Hoffman and colleagues also asserted that social causation theories are relevant in explaining childhood transitions through adulthood to old age, compared to the drift hypothesis. This makes the social causation concept a dominant mechanism in old age when it comes to intragenerational mobility outcomes along the health–poverty continuum. Despite the competing approaches, the implications are the same, reinforcing the importance of health-care providers to also address social problems during screening and assessment procedures.

A CMHA supported unit rendered uninhabitable by an individual suffering from mental illness was challenging for the Impact Junk Solutions to de-clutter in February 2014.

Source: Photo by Justin Langille

5. MENTAL ILLNESS AND SOCIAL EXCLUSION

Social exclusion is a widespread phenomenon that is inadequately examined and incompletely explored in the literature. The exclusion of people with mental illness is historically rooted and continues to pose global public health and human rights concerns. Social exclusion is a behavioural consequence entailing dynamic and multifaceted mechanisms, which are embedded in unequal power relations across economic, political, social, and cultural dimensions (Popay et al., 2008; World Health Organization [WHO], 2019). Social exclusion of individuals with mental health issues occurs at the individual, household, group, community, country, and global levels. The segregation of people with mental illness occurs in a continuum of circumstances characterized by inclusion/exclusion attitudes of unequal access to resources, and reduced rights that leads to health inequalities (WHO, 2019). Exclusion and inclusion sometimes exist as an interface, where an individual may feel included in one instance and yet is excluded in other domains of social life. Micro-level exclusion affects the income, occupational status, social networks, and religion of the individual. In contrast, macro-level exclusions are embedded in policy development and legislation in relation to access to affordable education and equal employment opportunity, along with societal, cultural, and gender norms.

Social exclusion can be regarded as both process and outcome of complex interactions of factors that represent visible (direct or physical) and invisible (indirect) forces in society. Freedman, Williams, and Beer (2006) posited that exclusion is a complex interactive process that occurs between a source and target. Their Responsive Theory of Social Exclusion categorized exclusion into three areas: explicit rejection, ostracism, and ambiguous rejection. Explicit rejection connotes a clear statement of no communication from the source to the target, while ostracism is characterized by ignoring or neglecting the target without a direct response of no. Ambiguous rejection comes in the form of unclear communication from the source to the target. This kind of exclusion is literally blurred, creating confusion and much more stress to the target. Inferring from the Responsive Theory of Social Exclusion, exclusion feeds on power relations, allowing power imbalances to perpetuate in social systems, leading to exclusionary behaviours against the powerless, highlighted by people with mental health issues.

The concept of social exclusion helps to delineate various actions that deprive people of their basic human rights and increasing inequities through marginalizing attitudes across the social fabric of society. Exclusionary behaviours result in reduced public participation, social integration, access to social amenities, social influence, public recognition, and acceptance (Taket et al., 2009). The continued neglect and rejection faced by people with mental health issues in society has negative implications, including lower skill levels, unemployment, low incomes, poor housing, living in high crime environments, poor health, and family breakdown (Jehoel-Gijsbers & Vrooman, 2007).

Arguments have been forwarded that one does not need to have low income or be unemployed to experience social exclusion (Bailey, 2006; Levitas, 2006). While this is certainly true, prevailing mental health literature reveals that most people with mental illness face widespread exclusion due to these exact factors. Poverty certainly influences outcomes of prolonged social exclusionary patterns through negative societal attitudes and behaviours, which produce stigma. Like poverty, social exclusion is a multidimensional phenomenon that is characterized by economic, structural, social, and cultural aspects of life (CMHA, 2007; Hall et al., 2019; Jehoel-Gijsbers & Vrooman, 2007; Popay et al., 2008; WHO, 2019).

Jehoel-Gijsbers and Vrooman (2007) conceptualized social exclusion from the perspectives of economic and structural dimensions in association with sociocultural realms after completing a large European study. They referred to the economic-structural domain as a disturbed distributional process of material-related income, goods, and basic needs deprivation in connection with the abuse of a non-material aspect of the social rights of a person. They classified lifestyle deprivation, problems with debt servicing as well as credit, and housing as aspects of material deprivation that further fuel social exclusion. They also identified human rights issues relating to lack of access to government and quasi-governmental provisions as risk factors for continued social exclusion. They catalogued several examples of structural inequalities that normalize social exclusion, including impediments in accessing health care, education of children, housing, legal aid, social services, debt assistance, and being placed on waiting lists by employment agencies, social security, and financial and commercial services such as banks. Jehoel-Gijsbers and Vrooman's exclusion framework implies that poverty and social exclusion result from structural factors that are based in specific social settings and subcultures.

An owl is seen through the window of the apartment of a Connect group participant, Anthony, in December 2014.
Source: Photo by Justin Langille

6. MENTAL ILLNESS, STIGMA, DISCRIMINATION, AND EXCLUSION

Social stigma attached to mental illness is reported to be a major predictor of social exclusionary attitudes and behaviours globally (Hall et al., 2019; Hunting, Grace, & Hankivsky, 2015; Mathias et al., 2015; Popay et al., 2008). Stigma is a major stressor impacting many with mental health issues. Personal encounters with discriminating acts and microaggressions affect the psychological and physiological activities of stigmatized persons in several ways, including self-esteem, academic performance, and physical health. Stigma attached to mental illness emanates from both public and personal attitudes, with a potentially destructive impact on individuals, their families, as well as national development (Ahmedani, 2011; Campo-Arias & Herazo, 2015; Corrigan & Watson, 2002; Goepfert et al., 2019; Koschorke et al., 2017). Stigmatizing attitudes have also been associated with negative perceptions leading to reduced social acceptance (Goffman, 1963). Perceptions of stigma motivate efforts by the stigmatized individual to hide any characteristic of mental illness as much as possible. Crabb and colleagues (2012) stated that stigma creates guilt, concealment, isolation, and exclusion. The exclusionary behaviours that people with mental illness face in society account for more stress and frequent relapse, leading to prolonged treatment duration, and can further exacerbate existing mental health issues (Fikreyesus, Soboka, & Feyissa, 2016; Alphs et al., 2016; Shrivastava et al., 2012; WHO, 2019).

Public discriminatory attitudes that accompany stigmatized persons lead to those individuals restricting social contacts even during significant life events, thereby further negatively impacting their social status in community social settings. Negative societal treatment of people with mental illness likewise impacts on their psychological and physical well-being (Major & O'Brien, 2005). According to the Identity Threat Model of Stigma, "stigma directly affects the stigmatized via mechanisms of discrimination, expectancy confirmation, and automatic stereotype activation, and indirectly via threats to personal and social identity" (Major & O'Brien, 2005, p. 393). The model proposes that individuals who experience social identity threat are at high risk for stress and personal identity threat. Personal reactions to identity threat have the potential to lead to involuntary emotional, cognitive, physiological, and overt behavioural reactions, such as extreme anxiety states and increased working memory load, further negatively impacting social engagement (Major & O'Brien, 2005).

Research has clearly demonstrated that stigma is a relationship- and context-specific issue fuelled mostly by the social context rather than from the individual standpoint (Ahmedani, 2011; Eriksson, 2019; Major & O'Brien, 2005). Goffman's

(1963) pioneering work described stigma as a serious form of dishonour directed towards individuals whom the public perceived as different and less human. This erroneous perception that people with mental illness are less human permits "normals," the majority of society, to marginalize and exclude those with mental health issues through socioeconomic, health, and institutional means.

Since Goffman's (1963) seminal work, the concept of stigma has been defined in more robust ways. For instance, Stafford and Scott (1986) defined stigma as a characteristic of persons that is contrary to a social norm. Jones et al. (1984) viewed stigma as an attribute that links an individual to undesirable characteristics (stereotypes). Link and Phelan (2001) define stigma as a construct that is characterized by five inter-related components of labelling, stereotyping (negative attributes), separation, status loss, and discrimination. The stigma attached to mental health problems appears to be both source and consequence of socio-political and economic exclusion that people with mental illness face on an ongoing basis. This occurs because members of the public regard stigma as something within the individual rather than a label or tag that others, the "normals," attach to the person. Therefore, the term *stigma* directs public attention towards a state of unwholesomeness, warranting ill-treatment due to the negative connotations given to the stereotypes in relation to the person's health and social status.

Link and Phelan's 2001 conceptualization of stigma further delineates social separation as a power-based activity that is both social and cognitive in nature, producing an "us" and "them" dichotomy. Such judgemental attitudes are based on a philosophy of social selection of human differences through labels, with social separation characterized by power-related inequalities that lead to the status loss. Status loss always tilts to the side of the powerless, with powerful normal, the majority, prevailing and either pushing or creating an impression of dominance over the powerless, who quickly become and remain stigmatized and marginalized. With the support of policy frameworks, legal documents, and socio-political influences, such power imbalances infiltrate social and institutional arrangements of how everyone ought to be treated based on social status. By this, the normals who have already perceived the stigmatized as low in social status reinforce an attitude of "we have the right to decide the fate of these low-social-class occupants." The ensuing ascribed status loss of people with mental illness leads to discrimination, rejection, and exclusion from social events and social life.

Research points to labelling as the beginning point of mental illness stigma (Hansson, Stjernswärd, & Svensson, 2014; Sorsdahl, Stein, & Myers 2012; Yuksel, Bingol, & Oflaz, 2014). The public use various negative tags to describe or identify people with a history of mental illness, such as dangerous (Sorsdahl, Stein, & Myers, 2012), unpredictable (Henderson, Evans-Lacko, & Thornicroft, 2013; Poreddi,

Thimmaiah, & Math, 2015), and violent (Csiernik et al., 2007; Parcesepe & Cabassa, 2013). Some members of the public believe that persons with schizophrenia and other psychiatric illness are unintelligent (Csiernik et al., 2007; Kishore, Gupta, Jiloha, & Bantman, 2011) and incompetent (Szasz, 2005; Parcesepe & Cabassa, 2013) with others perceiving them as criminals (Parcesepe & Cabassa, 2013).

Individuals with mental health issues experience discrimination across the spectrum of social life: in the housing market (Centre for Equality Rights in Accommodation, 2009; Corrigan et al., 2003; Silva, Loureiro, & Cardoso, 2016), employment (Hipes, Lucas, Phelan, & White, 2016), and interpersonal relationships (Chan et al., 2015; Knaak, Mantler, & Szeto, 2017). Mental health consumer-survivors have claimed their loss of social connections and housing were related more to societal responses to mental illness than to the illness itself (Forchuk et al., 2006). There is a growing understanding of poverty, and the social processes responsible for poverty, as an influential and preventative factor to social exclusion (Labonté, Hadi, & Kauffmann, 2011; Sylvestre et al., 2018). The consequence of the social exclusion that people with mental illness face is enduring poverty that worsens social acceptance and leads to a cycle of events associated with further deterioration of existing mental health problems (Figure 1.1).

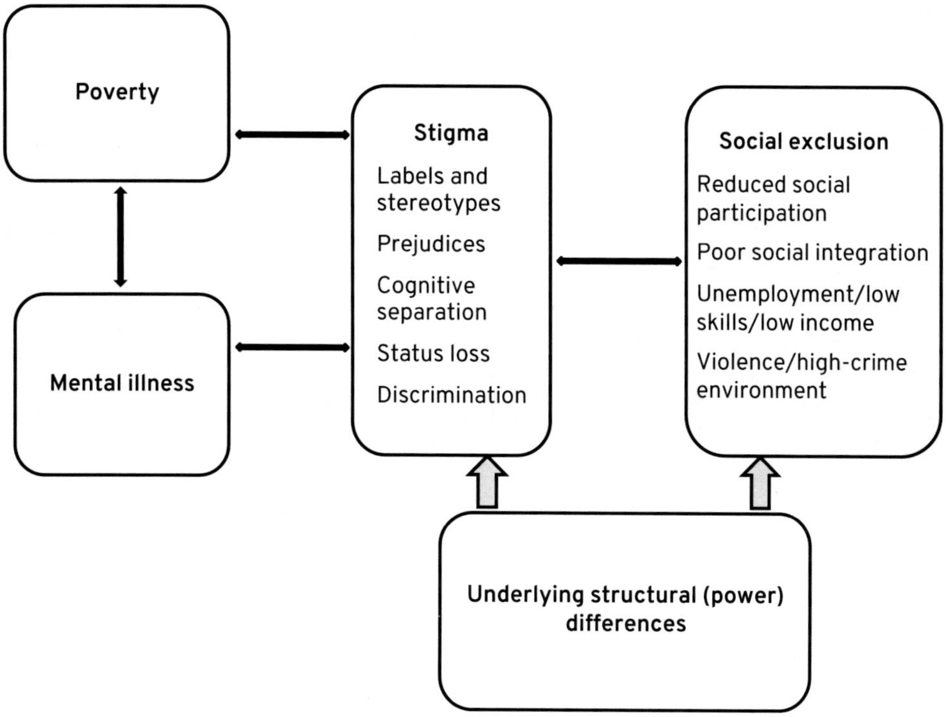

Figure 1.1: A Framework of the Poverty–Mental Illness Trajectory among Individuals with Mental Health Issues

7. ADDRESSING MENTAL ILLNESS AND POVERTY THROUGH SOCIAL INCLUSION

Even though the concepts of social exclusion and social inclusion appear to converge at a point when conceptualized along a continuum, they are different when viewed from a philosophical perspective. Social inclusion promotes the full participation of marginalized groups, such as mental health consumer-survivors. It does so by countering the systemic effects of poverty and promotes productivity for this population in our society. Hall et al. (2019) refer to social inclusion as instances of feeling accepted, having individual or collective right to determine participation, and the removal of structural and attitudinal barriers to social participation. It is

Les secures a load from a London-Middlesex Housing Corporation (LMHC) unit in the south end of London in September 2014. LMHC contracts the Impact crew to clean out units in a timely manner so that new residents can move into rent-geared-to-income housing.
Source: Photo by Justin Langille

an emancipatory-related conscious effort aimed at re-instating the basic rights that some people have been denied because of a personal attribute.

Inclusion is the equally dynamic and resource-oriented interventional process that helps to seek redress in instances of discrimination, social inequality, marginalization, or undue oppression. Social support interventions that encourage autonomy, self-accountability, and eventual self-reliance of people with mental health issues are likely to enhance the quality of life and ensure positive socio-relational outcomes for this marginalized group. Social exclusion appears to overlap with poverty in several jurisdictions. Therefore, policy efforts that aim at reducing social exclusion may indirectly improve social inclusion and the socioeconomic status of the marginalized in society.

Examining the themes discussed to this point in the chapter, it is not difficult to understand how mental health issues, stigma, and social exclusion intersect to influence low socioeconomic status and poverty in society. In order to break this cycle, equity and social justice–oriented interventions at all levels of society, including government policy, are required. The promotion of social inclusion of people with mental health issues needs to become a core component of both mental health and human rights initiatives across the world. Mental health strategic planning needs to have an increased focus upon people-centred programs (Hall et al., 2019; Patel et al., 2018). In a high-income country such as Canada, social inclusion strategies for marginalized persons have involved various schemes from the first admission through to discharge into the community and after. Community-based mental health interventional programs such as the Community Homes of Opportunity and the No Fixed Address initiative (Chapter 19) have shown promise towards the fight in eradicating poverty among people with mental health issues.

Given the interactive effects of mental illness and poverty on people with low socioeconomic status are multifaceted, Simon et al. (2018) suggested a multi-step approach to produce improved social accountability for this population. The first step is screening, which needs to be completed in conjunction with appropriate stakeholders at micro, mezzo, and macro levels in order to foster common ground for advocacy and action. Secondly, for intervention to be successful, client-driven measures are required that give voice and a sense of involvement, ownership, and accountability to those with mental health issues looking to gain greater social inclusion. In addition to the active participation of social and health-care providers at community-level interventions, persons who might need additional assistance should be linked with appropriate case management support teams coordinated by social workers for this type of individualized aid. Here too, clinicians need to be adequately resourced to undertake evidence-informed strategies for community engagement, education, and training. However, clinicians also need to be supported by policymakers in order to develop these person-centred outreach programs that bolster social inclusion. This helps to break systemic barriers while creating necessary upstream change for better social support and efficient service delivery in education, housing, income equality, access to care, adequate family support, and childcare (Simon et al., 2018).

Finally, research has firmly established that childhood poverty and chronic childhood stress negatively influence adult cognitive abilities, including shortfalls in academic achievement stemming from the impairment of executive functioning capacities (Evans & Fuller-Rowell, 2013; Evans, & Schamberg, 2009; Roze et al., 2018). According to WHO (2014), supportive family building and effective parenting are influential in children's mental and physical health and determine adult mental health on the growth and development trajectory. The WHO adds that offering and maintaining good support for parents in terms of housing, employment, and income influences successful parenting and reduces mental disorders in childhood through adolescence into adulthood. In addition, support must be appropriate to parental circumstances and to that of the child's developmental stage for optimum outcomes. The WHO further reiterates that effective social support will help disrupt intergenerational cycles of socioeconomic inequities that affect homeless families on chronic bases. Again, strategies that help to rehouse families are said to improve access to health services, thereby improving the mental health and social sequels of adult parents and their children (Roze et al., 2018).

8. CONCLUSION

Having established a relationship between mental health issues, poverty, and social exclusion, there is a need to expatiate how we can better address this debilitating societal occurrence in order to give hope among people with mental health issues. Even though the Canadian government has instituted various initiatives that support people with low income, more focused needs-based intervention is required to act as a catalyst for raising people with a history of mental health issues out of poverty and facilitating them onto a path of self-reliance and self-sustenance. The McSilver Institute for Poverty Policy and Research (2019) report revealed that the costs associated with burdens linked to mental illness and poverty continue to increase worldwide. This vicious cycle of mental illness, poverty, and social exclusion requires the development of pragmatic solutions, which is the ultimate intent of this book.

REFERENCES

Ahmedani, B. (2011). Mental health stigma: Society, individuals, and the profession. *Journal of Social Work Values and Ethics, 8*(2), 4-1–4-16.

Alphs, L., Nasrallah, H. A., Bossie, C. A., Dong-Jing, F., Gopal, S., Hough, D., & Turkoz, I. (2016). Factors associated with relapse in schizophrenia despite adherence to long-acting injectable antipsychotic therapy. *International Clinical Psychopharmacology, 31*(4), 202–209.

American Psychological Association. (2014). *Children, youth, families and socioeconomic status*. Retrieved from http://www.apa.org/pi/ses/resources/publications/factsheet-cyf.aspx

Anakwenze, U., & Zuberi, D. (2013). Mental health and poverty in the inner city. *Health & Social Work, 38*(3), 147–157.

Bailey, N. (2006). Does work pay? Employment, poverty and exclusion from social relations. In C. Pantazis, D. Gordon, & R. Levitas (Eds.), *Poverty and social exclusion in Britain: The millennium survey* (pp. 163–189). Bristol, UK: The Policy Press.

Bhuiya, A., Mahmood, S. S., Rana, A. K., Wahed, T., Ahmed, S. M., & Chowdhury, A. M. (2007). A multidimensional approach to measure poverty in rural Bangladesh. *Journal of Health, Population and Nutrition, 25*(2), 134–145.

Bingenheimer, J. B., Brennan, R. T., & Earls, F. J. (2005). Firearm violence exposure and serious violent behavior. *Science, 308*(5726), 1323–1326.

Bresnahan, M., Collins, P. Y., & Susser, E. (2003). Mental illness in an adult sample admitted to public hostels in the Rio de Janeiro metropolitan area, Brazil. *Social Psychiatry and Psychiatric Epidemiology, 38*(9), 499–501.

Brewer, S. K. (2019). *The roles of HPA axis activity and attentional bias in the development of anxiety symptoms in low-income Mexican-origin children* [Dissertation]. Loyola University Chicago. Retrieved from https://ecommons.luc.edu/luc_diss/2946/

Busso, D. S., McLaughlin, K. A., & Sheridan, M. A. (2017). Dimensions of adversity, physiological reactivity, and externalizing psychopathology in adolescence: Deprivation and threat. *Psychosomatic Medicine, 79*(2), 162–171. Retrieved from https://www.ncbi.nlm.nih.gov/pmc/articles/PMC5237627/

Campo-Arias, A., & Herazo, E. (2015). The stigma-discrimination complex associated with mental disorder as a risk factor for suicide. *Revista Colombiana de Psiquiatria, 44*(4), 243–250.

Canada Without Poverty. (2019). *Just the facts*. Retrieved from https://cwp-csp.ca/poverty/just-the-facts/

Canadian Institute for Health Information [CIHI]. (2008). *Reducing gaps in health: A focus on socio-economic status in urban Canada*. Ottawa, ON: Author.

Canadian Mental Health Association. (2007). *Poverty and mental illness.* Retrieved from http://ontario.cmha.ca/documents/poverty-and-mental-illness/

Canadian Poverty Institute [CPI]. (2020). *Poverty in Canada.* Retrieved April 21, 2020, from https://www.povertyinstitute.ca/poverty-canada

Centre for Equality Rights in Accommodation. (2009). *Annual report 2008–2009.* Retrieved from https://www.equalityrights.org/annual-reports

Chan, K., Evans, S., Chiu, M. Y., Huxley, P. J., & Yu-Leung, N. (2015). Relationship between health, experience of discrimination, and social inclusion among mental health service users in Hong Kong. *Social Indicators Research, 124*, 127–139.

Chow, J. C., Johnson, M. A., & Austin, M. J. (2005). The status of low-income neighborhoods in the post-welfare reform environment: Mapping the relationship between poverty and place. *Journal of Health & Social Policy, 21*(1), 1–32.

Chung, H. L., & Steinberg, L. (2006). Relations between neighborhood factors, parenting behaviors, peer deviance, and delinquency among serious juvenile offenders. *Developmental Psychology, 42*(2), 319–331.

Citizens for Public Justice. (2018). *Poverty trends 2018.* Retrieved from https://cpj.ca/poverty-trends-2018/

Collins, K., Connors, K., Davis, S., Donohue, A., Gardner, S., Goldblatt, E., … Thompson, E. (2010). *Understanding the impact of trauma and urban poverty on family systems: Risks, resilience and interventions.* Baltimore, MD: Family Informed Trauma Treatment Center.

Compton, M. T., & Shim, R. S. (2015). The social determinants of mental health. *Focus, 13*(4), 419–425.

Corrigan, P., Markowitz, F. E., Watson, A., Rowan, D., & Kubiak, M. (2003). An attribution model of public discrimination towards persons with mental illness. *Journal of Health and Social Behavior, 44*(2), 162–179.

Corrigan, P. K., & Watson, A. C. (2002). Understanding the impact of stigma on people with mental illness. *World Psychiatry, 1*(1), 16–20.

Crabb, J., Stewart, R. C., Kokota, D., Masson, N., Chabunya, S., & Krishnadas, R. (2012). Attitudes towards mental illness in Malawi: A cross-sectional survey. *BMC Public Health, 12*(1), 541. doi:10.1186/1471-2458-12-541

Csiernik, R., Forchuk, C., Speechly, M., & Ward-Griffin, C. (2007). De "myth" ifying mental health—findings from a Community University Research Alliance (CURA). *Critical Social Work, 8*(1), 1–15.

Dodge, K. A., Pettit, G. S., & Bates, J. E. (1994). Socialization mediators of the relation between socioeconomic status and child conduct problems. *Child Development, 65*(2), 649–665.

Dohrenwend, B. P., & Dohrenwend, B. S. (1969). *Social status and psychological disorder.* New York, NY: John Wiley & Sons.

Dohrenwend, B. P., Levav, I., Shrout, P. E., Schwartz, S., Naveh, G., Link, B. G., ... Stueve, A. (1992). Socioeconomic status and psychiatric disorders: The causation-selection issue. *Science, 255*(5047), 946–952.

Eaton, W. E., Muntaner, C., Bovasso, G., & Smith, C. (2001). Socioeconomic status and depressive syndrome: The role of inter- and intra-generational mobility, government assistance, and work environment. *Journal of Health and Social Behavior, 42*(3), 277–294.

Eriksson, K. (2019). Self-stigma, bad faith and the experiential self. *Human Studies, 42*(3), 391–405.

Evans, G. W., & Fuller-Rowell, T. E. (2013). Childhood poverty, chronic stress, and young adult working memory: The protective role of self-regulatory capacity. *Developmental Science, 16*(5), 688–696.

Evans, G. W., & Schamberg, M. A. (2009). Childhood poverty, chronic stress, and adult working memory. *Proceedings of the National Academy of Sciences of the United States of America, 106*(16), 6545–6549.

Fikreyesus, M., Soboka, M., & Feyissa, G. T. (2016). Psychotic relapse and associated factors among patients attending health services in Southwest Ethiopia: A cross-sectional study. *BMC Psychiatry, 16*, 354. doi:10.1186/s12888-016-1076-2

Finegan, M., Firth, N., Wojnarowski, C., & Delgadillo, J. (2018). Associations between socioeconomic status and psychological therapy outcomes: A systematic review and meta-analysis. *Depression and Anxiety, 35*(6), 560–573.

Fleitlich, B., & Goodman, R. (2001). Social factors associated with child mental health problems in Brazil: Cross sectional survey. *BMJ, 323*(7313), 599–600.

Forchuk, C., Russell, G., Kingston-MacClure, S., Turner, K., & Dill, S. (2006). From psychiatric ward to the streets and shelters. *Journal of Psychiatric and Mental Health Nursing, 13*(3), 301–308.

Fox, J. W. (1990). Social class, mental illness, and social mobility: The social selection-drift hypothesis for serious mental illness. *Journal of Health and Social Behavior, 31*(4), 344–353.

Freedman, G., Williams, K. D., & Beer, J. S. (2016). Softening the blow of social exclusion: The responsive theory of social exclusion. *Frontiers in Psychology, 7*, 1570. doi:10.3389/fpsyg.2016.01570

Funk, M., Drew, N., & Knapp, M. (2012). Mental health, poverty and development. *Journal of Public Mental Health, 11*(4), 166–185.

Goepfert, N. C., Conrad von Heydendorff, S., Dreßing, H., & Bailer, J. (2019). Effects of stigmatizing media coverage on stigma measures, self-esteem, and affectivity in persons with depression—an experimental controlled trial. *BMC Psychiatry, 19*(1), 138. doi:10.1186/s12888-019-2123-6

Goffman, E. (1963). *Stigma: Notes on the management of spoiled identity.* Englewood Cliffs, NJ: Prentice-Hall.

Government of Canada. (2018). *Canada's first poverty reduction strategy.* Retrieved from https://www.canada.ca/en/employment-social-development/programs/poverty-reduction/reports/strategy.html

Gutman, L. M., Joshi, H., Parsonage, M., & Schoon, I. (2015). *Children of the new century: Mental health findings from the Millennium Cohort Study.* London, UK: Centre for Mental Health.

Hall, T., Kakuma., R., Palmer, L., Minas, H., Martins, J., & Kermode, M. (2019). Social inclusion and exclusion of people with mental illness in Timor-Leste: A qualitative investigation with multiple stakeholders. *BMC Public Health, 19,* 702.

Hamilton, V. L., Broman, C. L., Hoffman, W. S., & Renner, D. S. (1990). Hard times and vulnerable people: Initial effects of plant closing on autoworkers' mental health. *Journal of Health and Social Behavior, 31*(2), 123–140.

Hansson, L., Stjernswärd, S., & Svensson, B. (2014). Perceived and anticipated discrimination in people with mental illness—an interview study. *Nordic Journal of Psychiatry, 68*(2), 100–106.

Heflin, C. M., & Iceland, J. (2009). Poverty, material hardship and depression. *Social Science Quarterly, 90*(5), 1051–1071.

Henderson, C., Evans-Lacko, S., & Thornicroft, G. (2013). Mental illness stigma, help seeking, and public health programs. *American Journal of Public Health, 103*(5), 777–780.

Hipes, C., Lucas, J., Phelan, J. C., & White, R. C. (2016). The stigma of mental illness in the labor market. *Social Science Research, 56*(1), 16–25.

Hoffmann, R., Kröger, H., & Geyer, S. (2019). Social causation versus health selection in the life course: Does their relative importance differ by dimension of SES? *Social Indicators Research, 141*(3), 1341–1367.

Hollingshead, A. B., & Redlich, F. C. (1958). *Social class and mental illness: A community study.* New York, NY: John Wiley & Sons.

Holochwost, S. J., Towe-Goodman, N., Rehder, P. D., Wang, G., & Mills-Koonce, W. R. (2020). Poverty, caregiving, and HPA-axis activity in early childhood. *Developmental Review, 56,* 100898.

Hudson, C. G. (2005). Socioeconomic status and mental illness: Tests of the social causation and selection hypotheses. *American Journal of Orthopsychiatry, 75*(1), 3–18.

Hunting, G., Grace, D., & Hankivsky, O. (2015). Taking action on stigma and discrimination: An intersectionality-informed model of social inclusion and exclusion. *Intersectionalities: A Global Journal of Social Work Analysis, Research, Polity, and Practice, 4*(2), 101–125.

Jehoel-Gijsbers, G., & Vrooman, J. C. (2007). *Explaining social exclusion: A theoretical model tested in the Netherlands.* The Hague, Netherlands: The Netherlands Institute for Social Research.

Jones, E., Farina, A., Hastorf, A., Markus, H., Miller, D., Scott, R., & de Sales-French, R. (1984). *Social stigma: The psychology of marked relationships.* New York, NY: W. H. Freeman.

Jones-Rounds, M. L., Evans, G. W., & Braubach, M. (2014). The interactive effects of housing and neighbourhood quality on psychological well-being. *Journal of Epidemiology and Community Health, 68*(2), 171–175.

Kessler, R. C., Foster, C. L., Saunders, W. B., & Stang, P. E. (1995). Social consequences of psychiatric disorders, I: Educational attainment. *American Journal of Psychiatry, 152*(7), 1026–1032.

Kishore, J., Gupta, A., Jiloha, R. C., & Bantman, P. (2011). Myths, beliefs and perceptions about mental disorders and health-seeking behavior in Delhi, India. *Indian Journal of Psychiatry, 53*(4), 324–329.

Knaak, S., Mantler, E., & Szeto, A. (2017). Mental illness-related stigma in healthcare: Barriers to access and care and evidence-based solutions. *Healthcare Management Forum, 30*(2), 111–116.

Koschorke, M., Padmavati, R., Kumar, S., Cohen, A., Weiss, H. A., Chatterjee, S., … Thornicroft, G. (2017). Experiences of stigma and discrimination faced by family caregivers of people with schizophrenia in India. *Social Science & Medicine, 178*(1), 66–77.

Koss, K. J., & Gunnar, M. R. (2018). Annual research review: Early adversity, the hypothalamic–pituitary–adrenocortical axis, and child psychopathology. *Journal of Child Psychology and Psychiatry, 59*(4), 327–346.

Labella, M. H., Narayan, A. J., McCormick, C. M., Desjardins, C. D., & Masten, A. S. (2019). Risk and adversity, parenting quality, and children's social-emotional adjustment in families experiencing homelessness. *Child Development, 90*(1), 227–244.

Labonté, R., Hadi, A., & Kauffmann, X. (2011). Indicators of social exclusion and inclusion: A critical and comparative analysis of the literature. *E/Exchange Working Papers, 2*(8). University of Ottawa, Institute of Population Health.

Lederbogen, F., Kirsch, P., Haddad, L., Streit, F., Tost, H., Schuch, P., … Meyer-Lindenberg, A. (2011). City living and urban upbringing affect neural social stress processing in humans. *Nature, 474*(7352), 498–501.

LeMoult, J., Ordaz, S. J., Kircanski, K., Singh, M. K., & Gotlib, I. H. (2015). Predicting first onset of depression in young girls: Interaction of diurnal cortisol and negative life events. *Journal of Abnormal Psychology, 124*(4), 850–859. doi:10.1037/abn0000087

Leventhal, T., & Brooks-Gunn, J. (2003). Moving to opportunity: An experimental study of neighborhood effects on mental health. *American Journal of Public Health, 93*(9), 1576–1582.

Levitas, R. (2006). The concept and measurement of social exclusion. In C. Pantazis, D. Gordon, & R. Levitas (Eds.), *Poverty and social exclusion in Britain: The millennium survey* (pp. 123–160). Bristol, UK: The Policy Press.

Link, B. G., & Phelan, J. (1995). Social conditions as fundamental causes of disease. *Journal of Health and Social Behavior, J6*(Extra issue), 80–94.

Link, B., & Phelan, J. (2001). Conceptualizing stigma. *Annual Review of Sociology, 27*, 363–385.

Lovisi, G. M., Mann, A. H., Coutinho, E., & Morgado, A. F. (2003). Mental illness in an adult sample admitted to public hostels in the Rio de Janeiro metropolitan area, Brazil. *Social Psychiatry and Psychiatric Epidemiology, 38*(9), 493–498.

Lund, C., Breen, A., Flisher, A. J., Kakuma, R., Corrigall, J., Joska, J. A., … Patel, V. (2010). Poverty and common mental disorders in low and middle income countries: A systematic review. *Social Science & Medicine, 71*(3), 517–528.

Major, B., & O'Brien, L. T. (2005). The social psychology of stigma. *Annual Review of Psychology, 56*, 393–421.

Mani, A., Mullainathan, S., Shafir, E., & Zhao, J. (2013). Poverty impedes cognitive function. *Science, 341*(6149), 976–980.

Marmot, M., Allen, J., Goldblatt, P., Boyce, T., McNeish, D., Grady, M., & Geddes, I. (2010). *Fair society, healthy lives: Strategic review of health inequalities in England post-2010.* Retrieved from instituteofhealthequity.org/projects/fair-society-healthy-lives-the-marmot-review

Mathias, K., Kermode, M., San Sebastian, M., Koschorke, M., & Goicolea, I. (2015). Under the banyan tree—exclusion and inclusion of people with mental disorders in rural North India. *BMC Public Health, 15*, 446. doi:10.1186/s12889-015-1778-2

McKay, M. M., Lynn, C. J., & Bannon, W. M. (2005). Understanding inner city child mental health need and trauma exposure: Implications for preparing urban service providers. *American Journal of Orthopsychiatry, 75*(2), 201–210.

McLaughlin, K. A., Costello, E. J., Leblanc, W., Sampson, N. A., & Kessler, R. C. (2012). Socioeconomic status and adolescent mental disorders. *American Journal of Public Health, 102*(9), 1742–1750. doi:10.2105/AJPH.2011.300477

McLoyd, V. C. (1998). Socioeconomic disadvantage and child development. *American Psychologist, 53*(2), 185–204.

McSilver Institute for Poverty Policy and Research. (2019). *Mental health and poverty.* Retrieved from http://mcsilver.nyu.edu/sites/default/files/reports/Mental_Health_and_Poverty_one-sheet.pdf

Melchior, M., Ziad, A., Courtin, E., Goldberg, M., Zins, M., & van der Waerden, J. (2018). Intergenerational socioeconomic mobility and adult depression: The CONSTANCES study. *American Journal of Epidemiology, 187*(2), 260–269.

Mental Health Foundation. (2016). *Fundamental facts about mental health 2016*. London, UK: Mental Health Foundation.

Miech, R. A., Caspi, A., Moffitt, T. E., Wright, B. R. E., & Silva, P. A. (1999). Low socioeconomic status and mental disorders: A longitudinal study of selection and causation during young adulthood. *American Journal of Sociology, 4*(4), 1096–1131.

Moore, M. (2015). Academic performance among homeless students: Exploring relationships of socio-economic and demographic variables. *Electronic Theses and Dissertations 2004–2019*, 700. Retrieved from http://stars.library.ucf.edu/etd/700

Narayan, D., Patel, R., Schafft, K., Rademacher, A., & Koch-Schulte, S. (2000). *Voices of the poor: Can anyone hear us?* New York, NY: Oxford University Press.

Nelson, C. A., & Sheridan, M. A. (2011). Lessons from neuroscience research for understanding causal links between family and neighborhood characteristics and educational outcomes. In G. J. Duncan & R. J. Murnane (Eds.), *Whither opportunity: Rethinking the role of neighborhoods and families on schools and school outcomes for American children* (pp. 25–46). New York, NY: Russell Sage Foundation Press.

Ontario Human Rights Commission [OHRC]. (2009). *Poverty, mental health and addiction*. Retrieved from http://www.ohrc.on.ca/en/policy-preventing-discrimination-based-mental-health-disabilities-and-addictions/8-poverty-mental-health-and-addiction

Ontario Human Rights Commission [OHRC]. (2017). A bold voice: *2016–2017 annual report*. Retrieved from http://www.ohrc.on.ca/sites/default/files/A%20bold%20voice_Annual%20report%202016-2017_accessible.pdf

Organisation for Economic Co-operation and Development. (2018). *Policy brief on child well-being—Poor children in rich countries: Why we need policy action*. Retrieved from www.oecd.org

Parcesepe, A. M., & Cabassa, L. J. (2013). Public stigma of mental illness in the United States: A systematic literature review. *Administration and Policy in Mental Health, 40*(5), 384–399.

Patel, V., Saxena, S., Lund, C., Thornicroft, G., Baingana, F., Bolton, P., … Unützer, U. (2018). The Lancet Commission on global mental health and sustainable development. *The Lancet, 392*(10157), 1553–1598.

Plomin, R. (1990). The role of inheritance in behavior. *Science, 248*(4592), 183–188.

Popay, J., Escorel, S., Hernández, M., Johnston, H., Mathieson, J., & Rispel, L. (2008). *Understanding and tackling social exclusion: Final report to the WHO Commission on social determinants of health from the Social Exclusion Knowledge Network*. Geneva, Switzerland: WHO.

Poreddi, V., Thimmaiah, R., & Math, S. B. (2015). Attitudes toward people with mental illness among medical students. *Journal of Neurosciences in Rural Practice, 6*(3), 349–354.

Roze, M., Vandentorren, S., van der Waerden, J., & Melchiora, M. (2018). Factors associated with depression among homeless mothers. Results of the ENFAMS survey. *Journal of Affective Disorders, 229*, 314–321.

Santiago, C. D., Wadsworth, M. E., & Stump, J. (2011). Socioeconomic status, neighborhood disadvantage, and poverty-related stress: Prospective effects on psychological syndromes among diverse low-income families. *Journal of Economic Psychology, 32*(2), 218–230.

Shaw, D. S., Winslow, E. B., Owens, E. B., & Hood, N. (1998). Young children's adjustment to chronic family adversity: A longitudinal study of low-income families. *Journal of the American Academy of Child and Adolescent Psychiatry, 37*(5), 545–553.

Shrivastava, A., Johnston, M., & Bureau, Y. (2012). Stigma of mental illness-1: Clinical reflections. *Mens Sana Monographs, 10*(1), 70–84.

Silva, M., Loureiro, A., & Cardoso, G. (2016). Social determinants of mental health: A review of the evidence. *European Journal of Psychiatry, 30*(4), 259–292.

Simon, K. M., Beder, M., & Manseau, M. W. (2018). Addressing poverty and mental illness. *Psychiatric Times, 35*(6), 7–9. Retrieved from https://www.psychiatrictimes.com/special-reports/addressing-poverty-and-mental-illness

Sorsdahl, K., Stein, D. J., & Myers, B. (2012). Negative attributions towards people with substance use disorders in South Africa: Variation across substances and by gender. *BMC Psychiatry*, 12, 101. doi:10.1186/1471–244x-12–101

Stafford, M. C., & Scott, R. R. (1986). Stigma deviance and social control: Some conceptual issues. In S. C. Ainlay, G. Becker, & L. M. Coleman (Eds.), *The dilemma of difference: A multidisciplinary view of stigma* (pp. 77–91). New York, NY: Plenum Press.

Stansfeld, S., Clark, C., Bebbington, P., King, M., Jenkins, R., & Hinchliffe, S. (2016). Common mental disorders. In S. McManus, P. Bebbington, R. Jenkins, & T. Brugha (Eds.), *Mental health and wellbeing in England: Adult psychiatric morbidity survey 2014* (pp. 37–68). Leeds, UK: NHS Digital.

Statistics Canada. (2019). *Canadian income survey, 2017.* Retrieved from https://www150.statcan.gc.ca/n1/daily-quotidien/190226/dq190226b-eng.htm

Stavinoha, P. (2018). 5 high-stress family situations & how to deal with them. *Psych Central.* Retrieved from https://psychcentral.com/lib/5-high-stress-family-situations-how-to-deal-with-them/

Sylvestre, J., Notten, G., Kerman, N., Polillo, A., & Czechowki, K. (2018). Poverty and serious mental illness: Toward action on a seemingly intractable problem. *American Journal of Community Psychology, 61*(1–2), 153–165.

Szasz, T. (2005). "Idiots, infants, and the insane": Mental illness and legal incompetence. *Journal of Medical Ethics, 31*(2), 78–81.

Taket, A., Crisp, B. R., Nevill, A., Lamaro, G., Graham, M., & Barter-Godfrey, S. (Eds.). (2009). *Theorising social exclusion.* New York, NY: Taylor & Francis.

United Nations. (n.d.). *About the sustainable development goals.* Retrieved from https://www.un.org/sustainabledevelopment/sustainable-development-goals/

Wall, K. (2017). *Low income among persons with a disability in Canada.* Retrieved from www.statcan.gc.ca

Wender, P. H., Kety, S. S., Rosenthal, D., Schulsinger, F., Ortmann, J., & Lunde, I. (1986). Psychiatric disorders in the biological and adoptive families of adopted individuals with affective disorders. *Archives of General Psychiatry, 43*(10), 923–929.

Wender, P. H., Rosenthal, D., Kety, S. S., Schulsinger, F., & Welner, J. (1973). Social class and psychopathology in adoptees: A natural experimental method for separating the roles of the genetic experimental factors. *Archives of General Psychiatry, 28*(3), 318–325.

Williamson, D. L., & Reutter, L. (1999). Defining and measuring poverty: Implications for the health of Canadians. *Health Promotion International, 14*(4), 355–364.

The World Bank. (2018). *Poverty.* Retrieved from https://www.worldbank.org/en/topic/poverty/overview

World Health Organization [WHO]. (2014). *Advocacy for mental health.* Geneva, Switzerland: Author.

World Health Organization [WHO]. (2019). *Mental disorders.* Retrieved from https://www.who.int/news-room/fact-sheets/detail/mental-disorders

World Health Organization [WHO]. (n.d.). *Social exclusion.* Retrieved from https://www.who.int/social_determinants/themes/socialexclusion/en/

World Health Organization & Calouste Gulbenkian Foundation. (2014). *Social determinants of mental health.* Geneva, Switzerland: WHO.

Yoshikawa, H., Aber, J. L., & Beardslee, W. R. (2012). The effects of poverty on the mental, emotional, and behavioral health of children and youth: Implications for prevention. *American Psychologist, 67*(4), 272–284.

Yuksel, C., Bingol, F., & Oflaz, F. (2014). "Stigma: The cul-de-sac of the double bind" the perspective of Turkiye; A phenomenological study. *Journal of Psychiatric and Mental Health Nursing, 21*(8), 667–678.

Zimmerman, F. J., & Bell, J. F. (2006). Income inequality and physical and mental health: Testing associations consistent with proposed causal pathways. *Journal of Epidemiology & Community Health, 60*(6), 513–521.

CHAPTER 2

Creating Social Exclusion: The Disconnection between Housing, Income Support, and Mental Health Policies

Rick Csiernik, Cheryl Forchuk, Katherine Turner, Libbey Joplin, Ruth Schofield, and Carolyn Gorlick

1. INTRODUCTION

The relationship between homelessness, increased rates of poverty, and mental illness has long been discussed (Draine et al., 2002; Fischer & Breakey, 1991; Forchuk et al., 2011; Scott, 1993). However, the exact dynamics of this relationship has remained unclear. While early literature suggested that increased rates of homelessness and unstable housing were due to the presence of a mental illness (Drake et al., 1989; Lamb & Lamb, 1990), subsequent research has suggested that these increased rates are more likely the result of an overall lack of affordable housing (Drake & Wallach, 1999; Gaetz et al., 2016; Leviten-Reid & Parker, 2018). In Canada, the lack of national housing, income support, and mental health policies has further added to the basic problems related to the issues of mental health and social inclusion.

2. HOUSING DEVELOPMENT

The definition of affordable housing, according to the Canada Mortgage and Housing Corporation (CMHC), is when a household spends less than 30% of its pre-tax income on adequate shelter (CMHC, 2018). Under section 92 of the *Constitution Act (1867)*, responsibility for development of social housing is with provincial governments, although the federal government retains the ability to unilaterally initiate programs under the "Peace, Order, and Good Government" clause of the act, as long as these programs are determined by the courts to be in the national interest. Until the 1990s, the federal government was actively involved with a variety of partners, including various provincial governments, in the development of social housing. However, at the close of the last century, the Canadian government transferred administrative responsibility for most of the existing housing stock to provincial governments.

Not surprisingly, each province responded differently to this added responsibility; however, no initiative was totally effective in responding to increasing demands for the creation of new affordable housing developments, which was evident in increasing levels of homelessness across Canada (Begin et al., 1999). This led to renewed federal focus on creating affordable housing stock, with the federal government initiating a federal-provincial partnership regarding the development of affordable housing in 2001. Individual agreements were struck with each province to leverage matching provincial dollars of $25,000 per unit to provide the upfront capital funds necessary for new affordable housing development.

During the tenure of the Stephen Harper government (2006–2015) housing policy did develop some evidence-informed programming, highlighted by support for Housing First policy and supporting local communities to gather better data on the chronically homeless through a nationally coordinated point-in-time count in January 2016. However, the federal government did not provide substantive financial support to address this major policy change. Housing policy during this era saw incremental changes to existing programs launched by prior federal governments, along with retrenchment in funding for the Homelessness Partnering Strategy (HPS). The Harper government's efforts on housing development have been characterized as a holding pattern that attempts to contain homelessness without making any meaningful progress towards ending it (Doberstein & Smith, 2015). By the end of the Harper government, it was estimated that on any given day there were 35,000 Canadians who were homeless, with over a quarter-million Canadians being without shelter during the course of the year—figures that do not take into account individuals living in substandard or inadequate shelter (Rech, 2019).

The framework for Canada's housing policy going forward was introduced by the Trudeau government just before the 2019 election campaign, which witnessed the Liberal majority government become a Liberal minority. Bill C-97 received royal assent on June 21, 2019. It was an omnibus budget bill, which included the *Housing Strategy Act*, whose intent was to make housing a right of Canadian citizenship. However, with the change in status to a minority government and with the economic costs of the COVID-19 pandemic, how this bill will be implemented remains unknown. However, what is known is that the economic crisis has placed even more Canadians at risk for losing their housing and could lead to a significant increase in the Canadian homeless population.

3. INCOME SUPPORTS

Each province is responsible for providing income security to its most vulnerable citizens, generally through two initiatives. General welfare assistance programs are intended as temporary stop-gap measures to provide a minimum income until an individual is able to find employment. If a physical or mental health issue makes permanent employment unlikely, provinces have established distinct social income supports at a higher income level. Table 2.1 summarizes these programs, while Table 2.2 provides a breakdown of the exact income support provided to a single person.

Provincial income support programs fall into two categories for individuals with mental health issues unable to work: a set shelter subsidy and a floating shelter subsidy. Taking into account differences in average rental costs that vary by the population of the community and province, only two provinces provide their citizens with long-term disabilities an income above the Canadian Low-Income Cut-Off (LICO) point: Saskatchewan and Alberta. Thus, in the majority of the country, individuals with chronic mental health issues will spend their lives living in government-sanctioned poverty (Csiernik et al., 2017).

4. MENTAL HEALTH CARE: DEINSTITUTIONALIZATION

Bachrach (1978) defined deinstitutionalization as a process having two main elements: the avoidance of traditional institutions/hospitals and the concurrent expansion of community-based facilities (p. 573). The deinstitutionalization of individuals diagnosed with a mental illness has been a process that has been evolving for decades. Goldman and Morrissey (1985) described cycles of institutional reforms such as the early 19th-century introduction of moral treatment through the use of asylums; the mental health hygiene movement and psychopathic hospitals; and the mid-20th-century community-focused mental health movement. They argue that the fourth cycle in this evolutionary process is the establishment of a broad network of both mental health and social welfare services. However, according to Goldman and Morrissey, the "failure to address the basic social problems themselves has resulted in a repeating cycle of policies which only partly accomplish the goals of their activist proponents" (p. 727). This has culminated in the 21st century with a disproportionate number of individuals with mental health issues being incarcerated rather than hospitalized or supported in the community (Slate, 2016; Slate et al., 2013).

Table 2.1: Summary of Provincial Social Assistance Programs

Province/ Territory	Program	Ministry	Legislation
Alberta	Assured Income for the Severely Handicapped (AISH)*	Disability Services	*Assured Income for the Severely Handicapped Act*
British Columbia	Employment and Assistance for Persons with Disabilities*	Ministry of Social Development and Social Innovation	*Employment and Assistance for Persons with Disabilities Act*
Manitoba	Employment and Income Assistance (EIA)	Jobs and the Economy	*The Manitoba Assistance Act*
New Brunswick	Social Assistance Program	Social Development	*Family Income Security Act*
Newfoundland and Labrador	Income Support Benefits	Department of Advanced Education and Skills	*The Income and Support Act* and Regulations
Nova Scotia	Income Assistance	Community Services	Employment Support and Income Assistance Regulations
Ontario	Ontario Disability Support Program (ODSP)*	Community and Social Services	*Ontario Disability Support Program Act*
Prince Edward Island	Social Assistance Program	Community Services and Seniors	*Social Assistance Act*
Quebec	Social Solidarity Program	Espace Citoyens (Citizens' space)	Individual and Family Assistance Regulation
Saskatchewan	Saskatchewan Assured Income for Disability (SAID)*	Income Assistance Service Delivery	*The Saskatchewan Assistance Act* and Regulations

Note: * Specific program developed for those with ability issues

Table 2.2: Social Assistance Income by Province for a Single Disabled Person

	Basic Monthly Benefit	Shelter Subsidy	Other Supplementary Benefits	Monthly Total	Yearly Income
Rank Province/ Territory	**(a) $**	**(b) $**	**(c) $**	**(a+b+c) $**	**(a+b+c) (12) $**
Set Shelter Subsidy					
1. Saskatchewan	993.00	221.50	312.08	1,526.58	18,318.96
2. Ontario	619.00	479.00	91.50	1,189.50	14,274.00
3. Newfoundland and Labrador	534.00	372.00	94.25	1,000.25	12,003.00
4. British Columbia	531.42	375.00	37.17	937.59	11,251.08
5. Nova Scotia	255.00	535.00	66.35	856.35	10,276.20
Average	586.48	396.50	120.27	1,102.05	13,224.65
Shelter Subsidy Top-Up					
1. Alberta	1,588.00	[1]	35.08	1,623.80	19,476.96
2. Prince Edward Island	1,200.00	[1]	41.25	1,241.25	14,895.00
3. Quebec	947.00	[1]	27.09	974.09	11,689.00
4. Manitoba	871.00	[1]	47.92	918.92	11,027.04
5. New Brunswick	663.00	[1]	73.00	736.00	8,832.00
Average	1,053.80		44.87	1,098.81	13,184.00

Note: 1. Shelter subsidies are provided in Alberta and New Brunswick when the rent exceeds 30% of the household's total income and in Quebec and Prince Edward Island when it exceeds 25%. In Manitoba, the rent supplement is the difference between the rent-geared-to-income and the approved market rent for the affordable housing unit.

Sussman (1998) described the evolution of psychiatric facilities across Canada as a process that has occurred with little in the way of communication or collaboration between the provinces. Sussman also differentiated between the process of deinstitutionalization and the process of dehospitalization and discovered that many so-called community programs were in actuality simply smaller institutions. The movement associated with making the community the focus of care instead of psychiatric hospitals began with the introduction of first-generation anti-psychotic drugs after the 1950s (Smith & Hart, 1975). In Ontario, the total number of patients in provincial psychiatric hospitals peaked in 1959–1961, with the largest decrease occurring between 1965 and 1968. In 1960, there were 19,501 hospitalized patients in Ontario; by 1982, there were 4,514 (Heseltine, 1983), and by 2016, there remained only 2,760 beds in 35 facilities across the province (Auditor General of Ontario, 2017). The newly elected Conservative government's major announcement upon election in 2018 was that 50 beds were to be added across 12 institutions, bringing the total to 14.4% of the number that existed at the beginning of the deinstitutionalization movement in Ontario.

The Ontario branch of the Canadian Mental Health Association (n.d.) has documented 23 provincial discussion papers and policy documents focused on mental health policy reform produced between 1983 and 2016. The process of deinstitutionalization and the corresponding movement to emphasize community-based care have served as the predominant focus of these initiatives. Since the Ontario Ministry of Health (1993) *Putting People First* report, this proposed recommendation has included an explicit shift in finances such that the majority of funding for mental health services would be distributed to community-based programs. In 1999, the Health Services Restructuring Committee recommended that the provincial psychiatric hospitals (PPHs) be transferred by the provinces to local community service centres and/or to community hospitals. The document called for a reduction in hospital beds and stated that the proposed hospital bed targets are achievable once the appropriate community services and supports are in place with a goal of reducing the need for hospital-based treatment services (Ontario Ministry of Health, 1999). However, all of these decreases in the total number of hospitalized service users occurred as the province's overall population steadily grew from 11.4 million in 1998 to 14.4 million in 2018, an increase of 26.3%.

Despite this dramatic decrease in the funding of psychiatric hospitals and the reduction of the number of available beds, a concurrent shift of resources to community-based mental health programs did not occur. In addition, given that psychiatric hospitals provided patients with housing as well as mental health services, the need for new homes has increased as the process of dehospitalization and bed reductions have also increased.

The rhetoric of mental health reform policy paper (Wasylenki et al., 1992) and the *Putting People First* policy document (Ontario Ministry of Health, 1993) both recognized the need to take into account recognized health determinants and to provide a more comprehensive vision of health rather than narrowly focusing on alleviating illness in the delivery of mental health services. The 1998 Ministry of Health policy document entitled *2000 and Beyond: Strengthening Ontario's Mental Health System* further recognized that one of the principles guiding the reform of mental health policies should be the adoption of a holistic approach that addresses broader determinants of health, including housing and income support. Unfortunately, in the subsequent policy document *Making It Happen—Implementation Plan for Mental Health Reform* (Ontario Ministry of Health, 1999), this holistic principle was rejected as a guiding value underlying mental health policy reform while, at the same time, the document stated that increasing the quality of life of those with mental illness must be a goal of all subsequent reforms. The Implementation Task Force that arose from this document focused on community-based initiatives, which ironically, given the earlier discussion, highlighted the need for adequate income support and providing safe and affordable housing.

This focus on community-based care was further solidified in 2004, under the newly elected provincial Liberal government, with the Ministry of Health and Long-Term Care increasing funding to the community mental health and addictions system by 52%. This project underwent extensive evaluation, leading to the creation of the Minister's Advisory Group on Mental Health and Addictions, which undertook extensive public consultation as part of the development of a new 10-year provincial strategy for mental health and addiction in Ontario. The major provincial policy initiative that arose from this process was entitled *Open Minds, Healthy Minds* (Ontario Ministry of Health and Long-Term Care, 2011). While this included additional funding and increased focus on mental health, leading to improvements in the child and youth mental health systems, it remained focused entirely on community-level interventions, such as tele-mental health, without directly addressing either income or affordable housing issues. During this era, acute care hospitals experienced a huge influx of mental health cases that contributed to crowded emergency rooms and the rise of hallway medicine as the norm in Ontario (Brien et al., 2015; Khan et al., 2016).

These circumstances influenced the second annual report of the Ontario Mental Health and Addictions Leadership Advisory Council (2016) such that addressing the chronic gap in supportive housing became one of its three strategic considerations. The Council recommended creating a minimum of 30,000 units of supportive housing over the following decade to address the chronic issue of inadequate housing that exacerbates mental health issues in the community, in part due to inadequate income provided to those with substantive mental health issues. However, with the election of a new fiscally conservative government in 2018, there remains grave uncertainty if this will remain a viable action plan moving forward.

5. IMPLICATIONS

There is a substantive area of disconnect existing between policies pertaining to housing, income support, and mental health care that contributes to the development of social exclusion. The intersection of these issues has been a documented concern for half a century. The question that then arises is how can the government expect the quality of life of the mentally ill to improve if such well-established determinants of health as housing and poverty (Raphael, 2016) are not taken into account in the implementation of relevant policies?

The move to shift the focus of care of mental health service users to community-based centres, away from the hospital and institutional setting, occurred while the availability of affordable housing was experiencing a decrease. The increased restrictions placed upon income support further reduced the availability of housing that could be considered affordable to this population. The disconnection existing between these policy areas has created a situation that has increased an already vulnerable population's risk of being reduced to a state of homelessness and further social exclusion. Since these policy changes have occurred simultaneously throughout multiple policy sectors, the resulting areas of disconnect are often poorly understood even by service providers within each policy sector. Solutions to the problems resulting from the existing areas of disconnect can only arise by re-establishing and strengthening the connections existing between these diverse policy arenas.

What is often neglected in the discussion of mental health policy and practice is the actual voice of service users. Service users have described the disconnect existing at the mental health service-provider level and their level as resembling a false ploy doubling as an art form in practice. In some circumstances, no matter how unhealthy a situation becomes, the service provider's credo remains essentially "don't worry dear, we have everything under control," even when circumstances clearly have passed beyond their control. Hence, the creation of policy disconnection and social exclusion is also achieved at the interpersonal level when fending off a service user's concerns. Given the disconnection existing between evolving policies in the areas of mental health, income support, and housing, it becomes evident why the term *mental health consumer-survivors* has become such an accurate descriptor of this group. Health-care and social service professionals, as well as policymakers, need to understand and acknowledge the areas of disconnect existing between the various policies related to housing, income maintenance, and mental health. Clearly, there is a role for advocacy to increase community awareness and to promote system-level change. However, proper acknowledgement of the disconnection includes working on a personal level with service users and avoiding the use of therapeutic euphemisms or pathologizing very real poverty-related fears. The disconnection existing between housing policy, income support policies, and mental health policies adversely impacts many of the lives these policies were meant to improve, excluding these individuals from being engaged citizens. It is this disconnect that causes many of these people to feel as though they've been disregarded by society, harmed even further, and had their experiences with mental health issues minimized. These disconnections bind people while holding them back and eroding their sense of dignity, worth, stability, security; in other words, their social inclusion. It effectively serves to re-victimize the already aggrieved, disenfranchised, and at-risk. It is our hope that through means of reforming the aforementioned practices, programs, and policies, we can reverse this trend and better serve those individuals these programs were intended to benefit and that the following chapters provide direction in doing so.

REFERENCES

Auditor General of Ontario. (2017). *2016 annual report. Office of the Auditor General of Ontario.* Toronto, ON: Auditor General of Ontario.

Bachrach, L. L. (1978). A conceptual approach to deinstitutionalization. *Hospital & Community Psychiatry, 29*(9), 573–578.

Begin, P., Casavant, L., Chenier, N. M., & Depuis, J. (1999). *Homelessness.* (Ottawa Library of Parliament PRB 99–1E). Ottawa, ON: Parliamentary Research Branch.

Brien, S., Grenier, L., Kapral, M., Kurdyak, P., & Vigod, S. (2015). *Taking stock: A report on the quality of mental health and addictions services in Ontario. An HQO/ICES report.* Toronto, ON: Health Quality Ontario and Institute for Clinical Evaluative Sciences.

Canadian Mental Health Association—Ontario. (n.d.). *History of mental health reform.* Retrieved from http://ontario.cmha.ca/provincial-policy/health-systems-transformation/history-of-mental-health-reform

Canadian Mortgage and Housing Corporation (CMHC). (2018). *About affordable housing in Canada.* Retrieved from https://www.cmhc-schl.gc.ca/en/developing-and-renovating/develop-new-affordable-housing/programs-and-information/about-affordable-housing-in-canada

Csiernik, R., Csiernik, B., & Brideau, M. (2017). A thirty year retrospective on the income adequacy of Canadian provincial social assistance payments to non-institutionalized disabled adults. *Canadian Review of Social Policy/Revue Canadienne de Politique Sociale, 77*(Summer/Fall), 95–119.

Doberstein, C., & Smith, A. (2015). Housing first, but affordable housing last: The Harper government and homelessness. In T. Healy & S. Trew (Eds.), *The Harper record: 2008–2015* (pp. 265–278). Ottawa, ON: Canadian Centre for Policy Awareness.

Draine, J., Salzer, M. S., Culhane, D. P., & Hadley, T. R. (2002). Role of social disadvantage in crime, joblessness, and homelessness among persons with serious mental illness. *Psychiatric Services, 53*(5), 565–573.

Drake, R. E., & Wallach, M. A. (1999). Homelessness and mental illness: A story of failure. *Psychiatric Services, 50*(5), 589.

Drake, R. E., Wallach, M. A., & Hoffman, J. S. (1989). Housing instability and homelessness among aftercare patients of an urban state hospital. *Hospital & Community Psychiatry, 40*(1), 46–51.

Fischer, P. J., & Breakey, W. R. (1991). The epidemiology of alcohol, drug, and mental disorders among homeless persons. *American Psychologist, 46*(11), 1115–1128.

Forchuk, C., Csiernik, R., & Jensen, E. (Eds.). (2011). *Homelessness, housing and mental health: Finding truths—creating change.* Toronto, ON: Canadian Scholars' Press.

Gaetz, S., Dej, E., Richter, T., & Redman, M. (2016). *The state of homelessness in Canada 2016.* Toronto, ON: Canadian Observatory on Homelessness Press.

Goldman, H. H., & Morrissey, J. P. (1985). The alchemy of mental health policy: Homelessness and the fourth cycle of reform. *American Journal of Public Health, 75*(7), 727–731.

Health Services Restructuring Commission. (1999). *Building a community mental health system in Ontario: Report of the Health Services Restructuring Commission.* Toronto, ON: Ministry of Health and Long-Term Care.

Heseltine, G. (1983). *Towards a blueprint for change: A mental health policy and program perspective: Discussion paper.* Toronto, ON: Ontario Ministry of Health.

Khan, S., Chiu, M., Simpson, A. I. F., Guttmann, A., Jembere, N., & Kurdyak, P. (2016). Use of mental health services by youths and young adults before and during correctional custody: A population-based study. *Psychiatric Services, 67*(7), 790–793.

Lamb, H. R., & Lamb, D. M. (1990). Factors contributing to homelessness among the chronically and severely mentally ill. *Hospital & Community Psychiatry, 41*(3), 301–305.

Leviten-Reid, C., & Parker, B. (2018). Left out? Housing insecurity for one-person, low-income, non-senior households in Cape Breton Regional Municipality. *The Canadian Geographer, 62*(4), 470–481.

Ontario Mental Health and Addictions Leadership Advisory Council. (2016). *Better mental health means better health—moving forward: Second annual report.* Toronto, ON: Author.

Ontario Ministry of Health. (1993). *Putting people first: The reform of mental health services in Ontario.* Toronto, ON: Author.

Ontario Ministry of Health. (1999). *Making it happen—implementation plan for mental health reform* (Cat. #2231504). Toronto, ON: Queen's Printer for Ontario.

Ontario Ministry of Health and Long-Term Care. (2011). *Open minds, healthy minds: Ontario's comprehensive mental health and addictions strategy.* Toronto, ON: Queen's Printer for Ontario.

Raphael, D. (2016). *Social determinants of health: Canadian perspective* (3rd ed.). Toronto, ON: Canadian Scholars' Press.

Rech, N. (2019). Homeless in Canada. *The Canadian Encyclopedia.* Retrieved from https://thecanadianencyclopedia.ca/en/article/homelessness-in-canada

Scott, J. (1993). Homelessness and mental illness. *British Journal of Psychiatry, 162*(3), 314–324.

Slate, R. (2016). Deinstitutionalization, criminalization of mental illness, and the principle of therapeutic jurisprudence. *Southern California Interdisciplinary Law Journal, 26*, 341–356.

Slate, R., Buffington-Vollum, J. K., & Johnson, W. W. (2013). *The criminalization of mental illness: Crisis and opportunity for the justice system* (2nd ed.). Durham, NC: Carolina Academic Press.

Smith, W. G., & Hart, D. W. (1975). Community mental health: A noble failure? *Hospital & Community Psychiatry, 26*(9), 581–583.

Sussman, S. (1998). The first asylums in Canada: A response to neglectful community care and current trends. *The Canadian Journal of Psychiatry, 43*(3), 260–264.

Wasylenki, D., Goering, P., & Macnaughton, E. (1992). Planning mental health services: 1. background and key issues. *The Canadian Journal of Psychiatry, 37*(3), 199–206.

CHAPTER 3

Playing Musical Chairs: Understanding How to End Homelessness

Cheryl Forchuk

1. INTRODUCTION

Issues like poverty and homelessness are complex. This complexity can be so overwhelming it creates a temptation to not even attempt to solve such issues. It is usually easier to address the consequences of the outcomes rather than the issues themselves. Food banks and homeless shelters are examples of services we have created to respond to homelessness, and while they can provide much-needed assistance, they do not solve the problems of poverty or housing instability. Where does one even start?

Poverty and homelessness are examples of society's "wicked problems" (Camillus, 2008; Rittel & Webber, 1973) that appear to have no immediate solution as they cross so many sectors. However, to understand such problems we need to appreciate how they develop and are maintained. This requires insight and knowledge of the relationships that cross the multiple sectors involved. In our work, we have found the analogy of musical chairs to be a particularly helpful metaphor. If we can better understand these issues, the solutions really may not be so difficult to identify.

Interestingly, we began thinking about the game of musical chairs after a set of focus groups at a family shelter during our first Community University Research Alliance (CURA), which examined housing, homelessness, and mental health. Adults would be unable to attend the focus groups without someone watching their children. This led us to establish three childcare areas: one for infants, one for toddlers, and one for primary-grade aged children. Each area had staff and university students providing support and offering activities. In the older group, we played musical chairs and, unlike all the other games, several children found this activity quite upsetting. (As a result, we stopped playing musical chairs with homeless children and will never do so again.) We quickly realized that losing chairs had an emotionally triggering effect for some of the older children. Fortunately, their distress was quickly resolved when other games were introduced to the group. When we spoke with the parents of the children who had cried while playing musical chairs and inquired why they may have responded in this manner, parents in general expressed surprise, mentioning that their children had played this game in the past without any reactions, typically, beyond enjoying the game, especially when they won. As a research team, we later talked through this experience and reflected on what had happened. Some of the children had no doubt literally lost chairs, as well as other furniture, when they became homeless. However, the idea of musical chairs as a metaphor for homelessness began to resonate for us as a team.

2. LITERATURE REVIEW

In examining the literature, the metaphor of musical chairs has been used many times. Intriguingly, from a research perspective, in most instances one discussion of the metaphor does not reference another. Table 3.1 summarizes publications we found using this construct.

3. MUSICAL CHAIRS

So how does the metaphor of musical chairs help us understand homelessness? The chairs in the game represent the housing that is available to those at the lowest income levels within the community. The people circling the chairs represent those at the lowest income levels. When the music stops playing, the difference between the number of chairs and the number of people circling will be the homeless population. Although simplistic, this model does provide us with several distinct intervention approaches to address homelessness.

One of the best approaches to ending homelessness is to simply increase the "chairs" in the game. Where average rent is high and rental property availability is low, the game is being played with too few chairs. There are many strategies that have been proven to increase affordable housing stock within a community, including increasing public housing and rent-geared-to-income housing. Strategies to assist and support individuals in accessing market housing are also needed. This can be as easy as mandating that some affordable housing be included within new multi-unit building sites.

Table 3.1: Publications Using the Metaphor of Musical Chairs to Help Understand Homelessness

Author	Title	Relevant Findings	Cross References to Other Publications
Apicello, J. 2010	A Paradigm Shift in Housing and Homeless Services: Applying the Population and High-Risk Framework to Preventing Homelessness	-Briefly explains the musical chairs analogy to prevalence of homelessness -It is difficult to prevent new cases of homelessness if overall context and social and environmental factors are not addressed -Increasing the supply of affordable housing means less competition among households for a scarce and limited resource	References: Sclar, 1990
Buckner, J. 2014	The Why and Who of Family Homelessness	-Discusses a simplifying model for homelessness -Musical chairs used as a metaphor to better understand homelessness	References: Sclar, 1990 Shinn, 1992
Christensen, H. 2009	How Psychologists Can Help to End Homelessness	-Utilizes the metaphor of musical chairs to explore relationships between homelessness risk factors -Individual risk factors amplify the longer an individual remains homeless -Crucial to quickly intervene and re-house people when they are homeless -Implications for psychologists: educating policymakers, designing and implementing programs for vulnerable populations, and evaluating programs with rigorous research designs	Citations: none References: none

Table 3.1: Continued

Author	Title	Relevant Findings	Cross References to Other Publications
McChesney, K. Y. 1990	Family Homelessness: A Systematic Problem	-Ratio of low-income households is higher than affordable housing units -Regardless of characteristics of households, mental health, or transitional housing interventions, homelessness will not be eradicated if the supply of affordable housing is not increased and poverty is not reduced	Citations: Johnston-Robledo, 2001 Rollins et al., 1992
Rollins, J. H., Saris, R. N., & Johnston-Robledo, I. 2001	Low-Income Women Speak Out about Housing: A High-Stakes Game of Musical Chairs	-Highlights women's experiences with homelessness and qualitative data in their attempt to "escape the game of musical chairs"	References: McChesney, 1990 Sclar, 1990 Shinn, 1992 Shinn & Gillespie, 1994
Sclar, E. D. 1990	Homelessness and Housing Policy: A Game of Musical Chairs	-Discusses how the individuals/players who are physically least adept are the ones who are left "chairless" when the music stops in the game of musical chairs -Compares musical chairs to the situation of homelessness, stating how too many poor people are asked to chase too few low-cost housing units	Citations: Apicello, 2010 Buckner, 2014 Rollins et al., 2001

Table 3.1: Continued

Author	Title	Relevant Findings	Cross References to Other Publications
Shinn, M. 1992	Homelessness: What Is a Psychologist to Do?	-The difference of individual problems and structural determinants of homelessness are explored using analogy of musical chairs -Individual-level analyses typically used in psychology are inadequate to fully understand the causes of homelessness -Difficult population to study; compromises in sampling and design of studies led to overestimates of individual deficits as causes of homelessness	Citations: Buckner, 1992 Rollins et al., 2001 References: McChesney, 1990
Shinn, M. 2000	Homelessness	-Causes of homelessness can be divided into psychological and sociopolitical perspectives -Individual pathology and victim-blaming of homeless individuals are inherent in research and policies -From a structural view, homelessness can be referred to as a game of musical chairs, whereby affordable housing units are chairs, and poor citizens are players	Citations: Zahniser, 2007

Table 3.1: Continued

Author	Title	Relevant Findings	Cross References to Other Publications
Shinn, M., & Gillespie, C. 1994	The Roles of Housing and Poverty in the Origins of Homelessness	-Low-income households are players and chairs are affordable housing -Cause of homelessness differs for families and single adults -Racism contributes to adverse living conditions of minorities -Welfare program changes such as erosion of benefits and tightening of eligibility criteria were the greatest contributors to increases in poverty for single-headed families	Citations: Rollins et al., 2001 References: McChesney, 1990 Shinn, 1992
Steib, S. D., & Wendy, W. B. 2004	Like Musical Chairs? Become a Child Welfare Worker	-Describes ways in which the child welfare system limits opportunities and options for families and children -Multiple systems lead to an increase in the "number of losers" as "options diminish each round"	Citations: none References: none
Zahniser, J. H. 2007	Homelessness and Musical Chairs: Quicken Your Step or Include More Seats?	-Scholars argue that "comprehensive policies and community development approaches, which ensure enough 'chairs' are available to even the most vulnerable 'players,' are crucial" -Affordable housing units directly determine the prevalence of homelessness -Supportive housing supports homelessness prevention agendas	References: Shinn, 2000

Housing Interventions

A rapid, evidence-based solution, and one that is included in the federal housing strategy, is the use of rent supplements for people with lower income to allow them to access market housing. We have found some populations were able to access appropriate housing with even a small housing gift or supplement. In one research project looking at how to best house homeless youth (Forchuk et al., 2013), study participants identified that a difference of as little as $50 a month would allow them to access housing outside of the downtown core of a large urban centre. This would put them further away from high-risk environments such as the drug and sex trades, while also allowing them to build new social supports.

In conducting this research, we were surprised that participants suggested such low amounts as all they required. Why only $50? Respondents indicated that they felt that once securely housed, they would be able to work to make up the $50 difference, but more money than that would be difficult for them to regularly replace. We partnered with the Sisters of St. Joseph (London, Ontario), a local religious organization committed to a mission of helping others in need, who provided this $50 a month gift as their contribution to the research. We found that only a few youth required the supplement for longer than 12 months and that, within the year, approximately 80% of the 187 homeless youth in this project were successfully housed. Thus, it cost $90,000 in total to be able to successfully house 150 previously homeless youth.

In another study, an intervention with a four-site study across Canada (Victoria, Calgary, London, and Toronto) to service homeless veterans was evaluated (Forchuk et al., 2017). The London and Victoria sites included the option of obtaining rent supplements, which averaged $200 a month, to aid in accessing market housing for individuals involved with the project. Single female veterans and/or those with families were best able to be successfully housed with this type of housing option, although male single veterans also accessed this resource. In Victoria, which had two housing options, Calgary, and Toronto, the "chairs" were increased through acquiring dedicated veteran housing.

Another strategy is to reduce the number of people circling the "chairs." Guaranteed basic income and increases to minimum wage are examples of poverty reduction strategies. Employment supports and social enterprises (businesses run by social agencies that provide employment for social "profit" rather than for a financial profit) have been found to be particularly effective in this regard (Chan, 2015; Elson & Hall, 2012). An example of this approach from London, Ontario, is Youth Opportunities Unlimited (YOU). YOU provides vulnerable youth with employment through enterprises such as a café, woodworking, and the production of food preserves. These are real jobs paying real wages. Poverty reduction strategies such as these reduce the people circling the "chairs" in the game of musical chairs.

The music that keeps stopping at unexpected intervals represents the difficult transitions in the lives of the people circling the chairs. Common examples of such transitions include losing a job, family break-ups, aging out of child protection services, transitioning from armed forces to civilian life, and chronic illnesses and conditions, including addiction, that become less manageable. Specific programs can be developed to assist people through some of these difficult transitions. However, if the strategies do not also increase the chairs or reduce the number of people circling them, then the result affects who becomes homeless rather than reducing or actually ending homelessness.

The Need for Supports

Some individuals have circled the chairs for so long, it is like they have dug a ditch so deep they feel they cannot climb out. For people with long histories of homelessness, the chairs are even more difficult to find and to keep. The opposite of homeless is homed. For someone who has been homeless for an extended period, ongoing personal support is required in order to trust that the housing can become a home. Many people with long histories of homelessness take months to more than a year to trust that they really are *home*. During this transition period, many still leave a packed knapsack near the door with their dearest belongings just in case the music stops again. Others limit acquiring new belongings to avoid the pain of losing them all over again. This uncertainty can even delay some sleeping in their beds so that they do not become too comfortable, as they believe and fear that all around them could easily evaporate and be lost again.

Simply housing a person without providing social support to help them through this difficult readjustment period is setting them up for future failure. In our four-city project related to homeless veterans, people had been housed, on average, six times in five years. The most common reason for losing new housing was inadequate ongoing social support during the transition period. When supports were provided as part of the project across the four Canadian communities, only one veteran returned to a state of homelessness.

4. CONCLUSION

If we want to stop people on our streets from unnecessarily freezing to death in a nation as rich as Canada, we need to provide more shelter beds. However, if we want to stop homelessness, we need to create more access to affordable housing, address poverty, and support people during tough life transitions, as well as provide dedicated supports during the shift from homeless to homed. These are not insurmountable goals, especially for those of us who have gotten tired of watching others play musical chairs—though, of course, we do not become as tired as those who are continually forced to play the game.

No more musical chairs! Rather than representing musical chairs, these chairs represent the positive change that can be created by having room for everyone. These empty chairs await participants at the table of the Connect peer support group held weekly at Canadian Mental Health Association offices on Huron Street in London, Ontario.
Source: Photo by Justin Langille

REFERENCES

Apicello, J. (2010). A paradigm shift in housing and homeless services: Applying the population and high-risk framework to preventing homelessness. *The Open Health Services and Policy Journal, 3*(2), 41–52. Retrieved from https://benthamopen.com/contents/pdf/TOHSPJ/TOHSPJ-3-41.pdf

Buckner, J. C. (2014). The why and who of family homelessness. In M. E. Haskett, S. Perlman, & B. A. Cowan (Eds.), *Supporting families experiencing homelessness: Current practices and future directions* (pp. 3–22). New York, NY: Springer.

Camillus, J. C. (2008). Strategy as a wicked problem. *Harvard Business Review.* Retrieved from https://hbr.org/2008/05/strategy-as-a-wicked-problem

Chan, A. N. W. (2015). Social support for improved work integration: Perspectives from Canadian social purpose enterprises. *Social Enterprise Journal, 11*(1), 47–68.

Christensen, H. (2009). How psychologists can help to end homelessness. *InPsych Archive. Australian Psychology Society.* Retrieved from https://www.psychology.org.au/for-members/publications/inpsych/Archive/How-psychologists-can-help-to-end-homelessness

Elson, P. R., & Hall, P. V. (2012). Canadian social enterprises: Taking stock. *Social Enterprise Journal, 8*(3), 216–236.

Forchuk, C., Richardson, J., & Atyeo, H. (2017). A Canadian model for housing and support of veterans experiencing homelessness. Retrieved from http://www.homelessprevention.ca/evaluation-report.html

Forchuk, C., Richardson, J., Laverty, K., Bryant, M., Rudnick, A., Csiernik, R., … Kelly, C. (2013). Service preferences of homeless youth with mental illness: Housing first, treatment first, or both together. In S. Gaetz, B. O'Grady, K. Bucceri, J. Karabanow, & A. Marsolais (Eds.), *Youth homelessness in Canada: Implications for policy and practice* (pp. 95–110). Toronto, ON: Canadian Homelessness Research Network Press.

McChesney, K. Y. (1990). Family homelessness: A systematic problem. *Journal of Social Issues, 46*(4), 191–205.

Rittel, H. W. J., & Webber, M. M. (1973). Dilemmas in a general theory of planning. *Policy Sciences, 4*(2), 155–169.

Rollins, J. H., Saris, R. N., & Johnston-Robledo, I. (2001). Low-income women speak out about housing: A high-stakes game of musical chairs. *Journal of Social Issues, 57*(2), 277–298.

Sclar, E. D. (1990). Homelessness and housing policy: A game of musical chairs. *American Journal of Public Health, 80*(9), 1039–1040.

Shinn, M. (1992). Homelessness: What is a psychologist to do? *American Journal of Community Psychology, 20*(1), 1–24.

Shinn, M. (2000). Homelessness. In J. Rappaport & E. Seidman (Eds.), *Handbook of community psychology* (pp. 976–979). New York, NY: Kluwer Academic/Plenum.

Shinn, M., & Gillespie, C. (1994). The roles of housing and poverty in the origins of homelessness. *American Behavioral Scientist, 37*(4), 505–521.

Zahniser, J. H. (2007). Homelessness and musical chairs: Quicken your step or include more seats? *PsycCRITIQUES, 52*(13).

SECTION II

METHODOLOGICAL ISSUES

Method:

meth·od 'meTHəd

noun: a particular way of studying something in order to discover new information about it or understand it better.

The goal of this book is to examine the relationship between poverty, mental health, and social inclusion, but how? How does one discover the relationship between such pervasive yet inexact concepts? This second section provides insights into some of the research methods employed to examine these ideas in a more ordered, and thus understandable, manner. The section begins with "Doing Participatory Action Research," an examination of the primary approach that was employed in investigating the relationship between poverty, mental health, and social inclusion. Participatory action research (PAR) is a dynamic method that functions to place those with the lived experience of the phenomenon being examined on par with those studying the issue. This is achieved by actively engaging those individuals throughout the entire research process from idea generation to developing and implementing the plan, to drawing conclusions and ultimately in taking action based upon the findings. Chapter 4 outlines the principles and practice of this important method and how it can be used when working with vulnerable, socially excluded groups.

Chapter 5, "The Article Idea Chart," provides an example of how to apply PAR to invite and encourage all of those interested in the issue being studied to become actively involved in the research. The Article Idea Chart became a tool to engage all partners: academics, community agency and government representatives but particularly those with lived experience. The objective was to make everyone feel welcome in contributing to the project's outcomes not only by providing insights into lived experiences but by becoming involved from the very beginning of the process, by helping to shape the questions being asked. The chapter offers insights into how a simple activity, regularly repeated and emphasized, can form the foundation and ground the process in the philosophy and principles of PAR.

In research, the most critical step is developing the actual question to be investigated, but without anyone to ask, this becomes a moot exercise. Chapter 6, "Strategies for Retaining a Sample of Homeless Youth," offers insights into the procedures employed throughout this project in collecting information from a mobile, transient, and thus hard to reach, population. The chapter focuses on the different approaches attempted to follow homeless youth in one community

Crew supervisor Greg throws a strap over the Impact Junk Solutions truck to secure a load to be taken to a recycling facility in February 2014.
Source: Photo by Justin Langille

longitudinally and the relative success of each strategy. The key take-away for the project team arising from the activity was the importance of building relationships with both community agencies and vulnerable individuals themselves in keeping connected throughout the investigative process.

The concluding chapter of the methodological issues section examines the Stigma Scale. A core issue in the intersection of poverty, mental health, and social inclusion is the idea of stigma, which is a devastating psychosocial issue for many individuals with mental health issues. How do we measure abstract constructs such as this? Chapter 7 provides insights into this by detailing a study of 380 individuals with a self-reported mental health diagnosis. Information obtained from the sample living in London, Ontario, is compared to a group from the United Kingdom using a new tool: the Stigma Scale. Data for the Canadian sample is examined and compared with those from the United Kingdom. Not surprisingly, despite the geographic divide, both groups experienced stigma because of their mental illness. However, there were differences in how the two groups perceived this stigma and were affected by it that point to strategies that can address this issue.

CHAPTER 4

Doing Participatory Action Research

Cheryl Forchuk

1. INTRODUCTION

The work of both Community University Research Alliances (CURAs) involved participatory action research (PAR). To understand the work of the CURAs that will be discussed in this book, it is first important to understand what PAR is and how it is both different from and similar to other research approaches. As mentioned in the Introduction, we have built this research initiative on a long-standing, productive partnership that required careful attention to the dynamics of both group structures and group processes.

Traditionally, action research and PAR have been categorized as a part of the critical research paradigm. However, more recently, the term *participatory* has become classified within its own unique paradigm (Lincoln et al., 2018). The focus of PAR is not simply on understanding the phenomena under study but also on creating a process of change. The purpose of the participatory paradigm is not only to understand "what is" but to also reveal the potential of "what could be." PAR is a form of action research that explicitly involves key stakeholders, including people with lived experience of the phenomena being studied, through each stage of the research process, from the point of conceiving the idea to the time of publishing the results. So, when studying complex and emotional social issues such as homelessness or poverty, our goal is about creating strategies for change that address these challenging issues that are grounded in the realities of those impacted by them.

The methodology of PAR can encompass qualitative methods, quantitative methods, or mixed methods. A question we generally ask ourselves as we design a PAR project is, "What kind of information would be needed to create and sustain the changes that we would like to see?" Often, policy- and decision-makers need quantitative data, such as rates of readmissions, cost of services, and improvements in quality of life, to justify their fiscal decisions. However, decision-makers can also be moved by the stories and contextual nuances provided through qualitative data. Since we are often looking at creating effective interventions, we do need to know if the interventions are actually doing what we would like them to do, yet we also need to be realistic in that our solutions will not achieve perfection but rather are part of an unfolding process. We need to discover the areas and strategies that could be improved and the actions that are needed to improve them. In focus groups related to our interventions, we frequently ask key stakeholders what is going well and what needs improvement. When asking focus group members for

Steve helps a co-worker navigate a couch out from a basement in the Blackfriars neighbourhood in London, Ontario, in April 2014. Returning to work has been essential for Steve's successful recovery from mental illness and substance abuse.
Source: Photo by Justin Langille

insights or tips, they typically offer other ideas for programs or areas to implement change, which provide us with practical solutions that we can use to improve the intervention(s) developed and tested in the research study. Table 4.1 summarizes some of the literature to assist in understanding this approach to research.

2. PROCESSES FOR PAR

We are often asked how we actually do this type of work. One of the most important aspects at the beginning of a project or program of research is to identify key stakeholder groups. We often work with partners over several projects. Most of the partners in the second CURA, which is the focus of this book, have worked together with us across two decades. Most often, as the principal investigator, I would reach out personally to new potential partners. However, sometimes linkages were made through existing partners, and sometimes new partners reached out to us.

It is important to include multiple perspectives; thus, partners could be an agency/organization providing services or with an interest in the topic, a program within an agency/organization, individuals with lived experience, or people simply

Table 4.1: Action Research and Participatory Action Research

Definition	Author
Action Research	
Definition and purpose: Action research is "a reciprocal process where participants and professional researchers together define problems to be examined, co-generate relevant knowledge about them, learn and execute social research techniques, take actions and interpret the results of actions based on what they have learned" (p. 167). "Good designers and facilitators define the problems with process participants and teach and use social research techniques (for example, social mapping, focus-group interviews, environmental scanning) to design a process that produces relevant knowledge leading to action" (pp. 167–168). "With the goal of action/social change ... action research aims to increase the ability of the involved community or organization members to control their own destinies more effectively and to keep improving their capacity to do so" (p. 168).	Greenwood & Levin, 2007

Table 4.1: Continued

Definition	**Author**
Process: Action research is a "continuous spiral of planning, acting, observing, reflecting, and planning again, which creates the conditions under which learning communities may be established ... communities of enquirers committed to learning about and understanding the problems and effects of their own strategic action." Participants engage in "large group processes where they experience transformative learning when they are invited to challenge prior beliefs and understandings and reframe what they know. This new knowledge fosters action to bring social reality into alignment with what is understood. Participants improve their capacity to control their own destinies." "Large group process is based on continual reflection and has four general areas: conceptualization of the task (the initial decisions about the goals and the desired outcomes), the framing of the event (who should be included, what ground rules should be followed, what role should process facilitators take), the design of the event itself (how the large group will be engaged and in what specific tasks), and, finally, the plans for follow-through" (p. 170).	Greenwood & Levin, 2007
Participatory Action Research (PAR)	
In participatory action research, knowledge is founded in transformation and experience as demonstrated through shared research inquiry between the researcher and subject(s).	Lincoln et al., 2018
"In participatory action research 'researchers' and 'participants' fully share aspects of the research process to undertake emancipatory projects" (p. 162).	Olesen, 2018
"PAR generates knowledge reflexively through critically analyzing previous actions; this knowledge then informs subsequent actions toward transformative change. This process requires creating shared spaces in which different knowledge systems and skills of all can be valued, exchanged and critiqued within and despite divergences, contradictions and/or conflicts" (p. 46). Knowledge is "situated," that is, there is a recognition that each co-researcher brings "a partial understanding, constrained by his/her social location and open to being reconstructed through dialogue and actions; this relates to rethinking reflection and reflexivity ... that is relationally grounded and co-constructed" (p. 410).	Lykes et al., 2018

interested in the issue area. However, essential to PAR is to involve and engage people who are living or have lived with the situation. For example, in studying poverty, the experiences of people living in poverty are important. However, it is also important, and different, to include people who have lived in poverty but are no longer living in this situation. We also need to understand the perspectives of people who are part of existing support systems as well as those directly impacted by intractable problems. Family members are also vital to include as key stakeholders. We also strove to include people who worked on the front lines and those offering supports and services to people living in poverty and whose roles focused on developing strategies to assist people to exit poverty. In considering stakeholders within front-line services, we found and continue to find it useful to identify agencies in the community that refer service users to social programs. This assists us in understanding the broader system and the interfaces that exist in the community network, as well as where gaps in the systems exist.

This is important for the broader identification and implementation of solutions. While people who are experiencing the issues and the front-line staff who are supporting people can usually see problems within the system, they generally do not have the power to make the changes needed to alter conditions. It is therefore vital to also identify who the policy- and decision-makers are and to include these people as key stakeholders on the project. These can include individuals in administrative and leadership roles within community agencies and support services. The broader political perspective is also critical to include here. We need to engage elected officials at all levels of government, as well as those working in influential government roles, to collaborate and provide their perspective in the process. Of course, since this work is a research activity, key stakeholders also include people with expertise in the research methods that we employ and in the general content area, which in this work was poverty. During the early phase of the work, meetings will often include asking attendees, "Who is not here that needs to be here?" Thus, it is easy to see that very shortly one could have a very large group!

Of course, there are challenges with having a large group. There will be inherent differences of opinion and perspective. There will be challenges in keeping people engaged and ensuring that people have significant roles that are appropriate and are of personal value, rather than one of tokenism. It is always critical to employ strategies that ensure all members have a voice. There needs to be room for people who want a little involvement, as well as room for people who would like to be much more involved. Attention to these issues requires careful consideration of the structures required to support the process of PAR. The structures we used included an overall advisory committee responsible for broader decision-making, along with subcommittees that took on more specific but limited tasks (Table 4.2). Given the potential complexities of a structure like this, it is important to spend time when forming a new group to establish ground rules based on common values. For example: everyone has a voice; respect each other and allow everyone air time. We have often found it helpful to put these on posters or PowerPoints and start the meetings with a reminder of our common practices.

3. CONSIDERATIONS FOR STRUCTURE

Community Engagement

In our experience, the structures to support PAR evolve with the stage of the research process. Sometimes, as a new area is being explored, we have found it easiest to call a large group meeting at the beginning of the project to brainstorm ideas. This can take a couple of hours to complete, depending on experience of the participants and the degree of group rapport. Large group brainstorming sessions can also be helpful when considering ideas for new directions. For example, shortly after our first CURA finished, which examined housing, homelessness, and mental health, we had three monthly meetings in the basement of a community agency, where 60 to 75 people gathered to determine our next research priorities. While discussing what issues of homelessness-related work needed to be addressed in greater depth, we identified that youth and families had become subpopulations of emerging concern. This led us to draft outlines of how we would want to proceed in a PAR approach to generate solutions for issues affecting these two specific groups. A few months later, a call for proposals came out that was relevant to this problem and we were successful in obtaining youth-related project funding (Chapter 20). However, a far lengthier period passed between the time families were identified as a key target and funding opportunities to examine the needs of this group were found, but when the call for proposals was made, we were already in position to respond (Chapter 18). Funding calls often have a very short window of opportunity, so it is important to have ideas and proposals ready. We would not have been able to work through the community-related issues and reach consensus on priorities if we had waited for the call to start this work; there simply would not have been enough time. Thus, it is important to have research teams, ideas, and proposals in place and ready for a funding call.

While we were preparing for the second CURA to begin, we held face-to-face meetings to determine the areas of priority for the research. Since several out-of-town participants were involved with the project, we decided to have regular teleconference meetings to allow them to participate more readily. At this point, we were working on the actual proposal, so the teleconference meetings were useful to share and review the emerging draft. We basically tore apart the proposal and completely reworked it at least three times over the project's developmental year. Not everyone could make every teleconference meeting, but we had roughly 30 people actively involved throughout this process. Admittedly, this entire process would have been more difficult and time-intensive if we did not already have well-established relationships that existed prior to the call for proposals, but it was this level of engagement that helped the second CURA secure funding.

Large group meetings were used in our PAR process to engage the broader community. When we learn that we have been awarded research funding, we plan a formal launch event. Launch events always involve the group that is currently working on the project, but they are also used to create greater awareness among additional decision-makers and the media. In particular, we have always attempted to attract elected officials to these events to ensure they are aware early on about the purpose of the project and to provide them with the opportunity to speak about the importance of this work for the community. One of our intended outcomes in involving decision-makers and politicians is to build support for future change that is sustainable beyond the research funding period.

During multi-year projects, such as the CURAs, we build in community forums on an annual basis. Any research participant involved in the study, as well as the project partners and other stakeholders, can attend these free events. Students from related programs, elected officials, and the media are always invited to attend for free as well. The purpose of these community forums is to provide research updates, discuss interpretations of findings, and identify ideas regarding future directions of the research. Panels representing various key stakeholder groups provide feedback throughout the forum on what they are hearing and learning through their involvement in the research process. Another important role of the annual community forum is to open the invitation to join research committees. Anyone attending the event can sign up using the sheets at the event registration table. As well as there being no cost to participate, those attending are provided lunch as well as refreshment breaks. We regularly hosted over 200 people at these events, with some occasions topping 300 attendees. We generally include an icebreaker at the beginning of the day, such as using a "bingo" type card where attendees need to go around the room and find people with certain characteristics listed in each box, such as the ability to play a musical instrument or disliking sandwiches. While completed bingo cards are entered for door prizes, the real purpose is to get people talking with each other in a non-threatening context.

Forums evolved to include both small and large group activities along with an informal arts-based event the night prior to the event. People with lived experience of poverty and/or mental illness in particular have the opportunity to display and sell artwork and crafts. Musical performances would include researchers and research staff, members of community agencies, and people with lived experience. We would include a few people who typically only performed on the street, busking during the evening. We consistently received positive feedback from attendees that having this type of event the night before the more formal conference was very helpful in changing power dynamics and increasing people's comfort in speaking out during the main event.

At the end of projects, we also held a large public group meeting to share our results. The audience would be similar to those attending annual meetings, but we would invite people from a wider geographic area. For the CURAs' final large meetings, we had attendees from most Canadian provinces as well as a few people from outside the country. These concluding events can include guest speakers and/or have a call for abstracts to encourage presentations related to the multiple substudies within the program of research. For multi-year PARs, such as the CURA that is the focus of this book, the closing event would run two to three days. This concluding event is also considered a celebration of what has been accomplished to date. Smaller PARs can also host a closing event, even if it is merely a cake-cutting and acknowledgement of the successes of the project. These types of closing rituals also help to highlight the relationships built between individuals who might otherwise never have met each other.

In promoting the broader impact of PARs, it is key to have someone available to identify members of the press or elected officials who attend. In our first CURA, we created a dedicated media subcommittee and this task was part of their mandate. A large number of elected provincial and federal officials attended one of the first CURA forums. However, on the morning of the second day, the local newspaper had publicly reported that there had been no municipal elected officials present and questioned why, since local politicians had also been invited. Fortunately, on the second day of the event, there were half a dozen municipal elected officials in attendance who had been recognized by members of the media subcommittee and introduced by the day's moderator.

As PAR is about social action and social change, it is contingent on the research team to ensure ongoing community engagement and to give voice to those who are often excluded from our social discourse. During the annual forums, we intentionally created comfortable spaces and used members from our peer support program to be vigilant for anyone who appeared stressed or overwhelmed by the event in order to offer support. We usually also had agency tables staffed by individuals not only to provide networking opportunities but to provide necessary support if required. Research staff wore identifiable t-shirts and could be approached as a contact to discuss any issues or concerns affecting participants. Given the scope of a free public event with 150–300 attendees, there is a vast range of roles that need to be filled for the event to be successful. We found it helpful to have detailed agendas that included who was responsible for what within our research team. Everyone working at the event has their own specific role, and there were summary sheets provided to team members listing the roles and responsibilities to help make the event run more smoothly.

Creating Committee Structures with Fluidity

Following the principles of PAR, leadership was shared by a Community Director and an Academic Director. The Community Director had a leadership role in a mental health consumer-survivor organization and was a person with lived experience, while the Academic Director held a permanent faculty appointment in nursing and psychiatry. A paid Research Coordinator was an important component of the leadership team and was responsible for a great deal of coordination among the committees.

Table 4.2 provides an overview of the committees that comprised the CURA that the Community Director and Academic Director shared in chairing. However, within the first year, other individuals were invited to chair some of the committees, both to help balance the co-directors' workload and to increase the numbers and responsibilities among interested volunteers. In Table 4.2, the column for members was not who the membership was limited to but rather who tended to volunteer over the five years for each committee. Anyone could volunteer for any committee, other than the executive committee that met weekly to oversee the day-to-day operations of the CURA. People were encouraged to move between committees and often did. Over time, the policy and ethics committee and the media and politics committee began to have overlap in tasks and in membership, which led them to begin to share minutes with each other, while the advisory committee received minutes from all of the committees.

Sharing Information and Encouraging Participation

Our method for managing publications is described in detail in Chapter 5, "The Article Idea Chart." This involved a very transparent process to encourage and facilitate a wide spectrum of individuals to become involved in the development and writing of the numerous research articles that arose from this project. In addition

Table 4.2: CURA2 Committees

Committee	Purpose	Chair	Members
Executive Committee	Manage the day-to-day operations of the CURA (standing weekly meeting)	Research Coordinator	Community Director Academic Director
Advisory Committee	Provide overall direction and vision of CURA All other committees report to this committee	Community Director Academic Director (alternate)	Any member of any subcommittee can join; membership includes people with lived experience, community agencies, researchers, and front-line staff
Research Committee	To oversee all research components: annual surveys, focus groups, individual interviews	Academic Director	Research team members, community members, people with lived experience, and other volunteers
Community Projects Committee	To oversee emerging community issues and strategy development	Community Director	Community agencies, people with lived experience, research team members, and other peers and professional staff from community agencies
Student Curriculum Committee	To oversee students and curriculum issues	Faculty member Volunteer	Faculty, students, Community Director, Academic Director, people with lived experience
Annual Forum Committee	To oversee the planning of community forums	Community Director	Academic Director, Research Coordinator, people with lived experience, media relations specialist, front-line staff, community volunteers
Policy and Ethics Committee	To oversee policy and ethics work	Faculty/ researcher with related expertise	Community and Academic Directors, elected officials, people in government roles, other researchers, people with lived experience
Media and Politics Committee	To oversee knowledge exchange related to general public and politicians	Academic Director	Community Director, media relations expert, elected officials, community agencies, people with lived experience

to academic papers, and again to be congruent with PAR principles, a series of two-page summary documents were also produced. This was to better allow all the research that was appearing in peer-reviewed journals to also be available in a more accessible format for community members, elected officials, and agencies. The two-page summaries were frequently used to inform program changes in response to the emerging evidence that was founded during the study. For example, in our homeless youth study, we found that approximately one-third of the youth were parents, but that youth housing was rarely planned with a second bedroom. As well, in the same study, we learned that health-care access was an issue. By being able to prepare a fact-based summary document, Youth Opportunities Unlimited (YOU), a partnering agency, was able to successfully develop a funding proposal to address both issues that created new programming that is currently operating. When making formal and more informal presentations, whenever possible, community members were involved, including people with lived experience and staff from community agencies, as well as people directly providing services.

Diane assembles parts on the floor of the Goodwill's RMHC Social Enterprise program in St. Thomas, Ontario, in April 2014.
Source: Photo by Justin Langille

Impact Junk Solutions employee Allan is reflected in a mirror attached to a dresser being taken away from the home of an individual who recently passed away in the northwest end of London, Ontario, in March 2014.
Source: Photo by Justin Langille

Arts-based approaches are often used as a qualitative data collection method, with one popular example being Photovoice. We regularly used arts-based approaches as methods for encouraging participation in public events and to promote greater community engagement, rather than data collection. We also used arts-based approaches for knowledge exchange and dissemination activities of study findings. For example, photographs by Justin Langille (several of which can be found throughout this book) were used to generate deeper understandings of the solutions that were proposed by study participants. Justin accompanied people who were involved in social enterprise and peer support programs and spent significant time discussing which photographs were most meaningful to the them. In our final conference, we had a set of these photographs displayed over a week-long community arts exhibit to encourage members of the public to view and discuss issues related to poverty and social inclusion, as well as to inspire discussion of potential solutions. The exhibit was housed at Goodwill Enterprises, a social enterprise, and received extensive media coverage.

Another arts-based method that we used to illustrate some of our qualitative findings was theatre. We produced a play about "the tornado of mental illness," which drew comparisons as to how tornado survivors, who have lost their homes in a natural disaster, and people with mental illness, who have lost their homes from having a medical illness, are treated by society. Most of the dialogue for the play was pulled directly from statements captured in CURA focus groups. The play has been presented many times at conferences and student events, and notably, to a national committee examining homelessness.

In a different study not related to CURA, I had a musically gifted research assistant, Tanya Lysiak-Globe, who put a series of qualitative quotes together as musical lyrics to song. The project was based on the transitional discharge model, which uses a safety net of staff and peer-based relationships to bridge the discharge process between the hospital and the community. When the songs were performed, Tanya and a former client sang a duet, to piano and guitar. This musical method of knowledge dissemination was also applied as photos were transitioning in the background.

The use of art as a knowledge-exchange medium allows the emotions of the situation to be more fully conveyed. No matter how good we considered our findings, I have never seen an audience in tears when presenting a scientific paper. However, I have, on many occasions, seen an audience in tears when more creative formats were used to showcase the personal experience of intractable social problems. Another benefit of arts-based methods is that they are an accessible method by which to convey important understandings to a broad audience.

4. SUMMARY

Participatory action research is an art as well as a science. It involves an inclusive process to engage a broad range of stakeholders throughout the research. Ideally, long-standing research relationships are established beforehand, ones that can sustain numerous activities over time and are able to identify and test solutions to difficult social problems. Fluid and creative structures and processes are required to sustain participation and true partnership. The following chapters are examples of what PAR can uncover and what changes it can produce.

REFERENCES

Greenwood, D. J., & Levin, M. (2007). *Introduction to action research: Social research for social change* (2nd ed.). Thousand Oaks, CA: SAGE Publications.

Lincoln, Y. S., Lynham, S. A., & Guba, E. G. (2018). Paradigmatic controversies, contradictions, and emerging confluences, revisited. In N. K. Denzin & Y. S. Lincoln (Eds.), *The SAGE handbook of qualitative research* (5th ed., pp. 108–150). Thousand Oaks, CA: SAGE Publications.

Lykes, M. B., Lloyd, C. R., & Nicholson, K. M. (2018). Participatory and action research within and beyond the academy: Contesting racism through decolonial praxis and teaching "against the grain." *American Journal of Community Psychology, 62*(3–4), 406–418.

Olesen, V. (2018). Feminist qualitative research in the millennium's first decade: Developments, challenges, prospects. In N. K. Denzin & Y. S. Lincoln (Eds.), *The SAGE handbook of qualitative research* (5th ed., pp. 151–175). Thousand Oaks, CA: SAGE Publications.

CHAPTER 5

The Article Idea Chart: A Participatory Action Research Tool to Aid Involvement in Dissemination

Cheryl Forchuk and Amanda Meier

1. INTRODUCTION

Participatory action research (PAR) is a research approach that has gained prominence in recent years, because of its focus on the contributions of key stakeholders from all constituent groups within the community or organization under study and its goal of creating positive change through the research process. PAR is thought to be particularly well suited to research in the mental health field (Csiernik et al., 2018; Nelson et al., 1998; Speers & Lathlean, 2015). In fact, Ochocka et al. (2002) go so far as to claim that the use of PAR in community mental health research is a "moral imperative" (p. 386). Individuals with a mental health diagnosis, who often refer to themselves as consumer-survivors, have traditionally been left voiceless, both in health-care services and society in general (Leff & Warner, 2006). PAR allows for the "voice of the consumer" to be acknowledged in research (Rogers & Palmer-Erbs, 1994, p. 10) because they are given the opportunity to be actively involved in the research process. As aptly stated by one consumer-survivor researcher within a PAR project, "psychiatric consumer-survivors are both witnesses to the system and the reason for the system's existence" (Ochocka et al., 2002, p. 379). The involvement of consumer-survivors in PAR projects also helps ensure that the topics are of social importance to the population being studied and that the results are shared in accessible ways (White et al., 2001).

In PAR projects, all members are included and participate actively throughout the research process, from initial project design to data collection, to analysis (Whyte, 1991). Multiple perspectives on a topic can increase the quality of data collected, the range of interpretations and conclusions, and recommendations for change. The dissemination of results and recommendations is arguably the most important aspect of PAR projects, as Montoya and Kent (2011) explain: "It is vitally important to communicate results and interpretations with community partners and to present information in a way that is both informative and respectful" (p. 1003).

It is through the appropriate dissemination of findings that positive societal change is enacted. In community mental health research, including consumer-survivors in the dissemination process helps ensure that scientific findings are communicated in not only appropriate ways but also efficient and accessible ones (Montoya & Kent, 2011). If disseminated effectively, PAR results can reach beyond an academic audience to policymakers, social service agencies, health-care services, and consumer-survivors themselves to promote positive action within communities. In this chapter, we describe the deliberate development and use of an Article Idea Chart, an additional tool designed to create even greater involvement by all stakeholders in the dissemination stage of PAR projects.

2. THE CURA PROJECT: ENSURING PARTICIPATION

The Article Idea Chart was implemented as part of the Community University Research Alliance (CURA) that examined the issues of poverty and social inclusion for mental health consumer-survivors. Stakeholders included consumer-survivors, their family members, service providers from mental health and income support agencies, employers, students, policymakers, and academic researchers. In accordance with PAR principles, the CURA team acknowledged the importance of equally engaging stakeholders in all aspects of the research process. The active inclusion of stakeholders began during the proposal-writing phase and continued for the duration of the program by inviting individuals from various stakeholder groups to engage in the program through committee membership. It was vital to involve diverse stakeholders early in the research process so that they could direct the research questions asked and methodologies employed. In addition, investment by stakeholders throughout the research process increased the likelihood of them feeling connected to the program and wanting to contribute to dissemination activities. Once committees were developed to guide the program, the Article Idea Chart was introduced and used to encourage active participation by all stakeholders in dissemination activities.

To effectively manage the various aspects of the CURA, a total of eight committees and subcommittees were developed (see Table 4.2). Seven subcommittees managed the day-to-day program activities, annual forum arrangements, community projects, media and government relations, policy and ethical issues, curriculum development, and research activities. The eighth, an advisory committee, served as the steering committee, receiving reports from all subcommittees and overseeing the overall program. This structure was beneficial as it permitted all members to take part in committees that fit their personal and professional interests. In addition, each committee focused on specific issues and plans, thereby allowing the program to be managed more effectively and efficiently. Each committee was also involved in the important task of writing and presenting program findings relevant to their work.

Individuals became involved in CURA committees in a variety of ways. During the proposal-writing phase, academic researchers from disciplines related to the CURA topic were invited to participate. Mental health and income support agencies throughout London and surrounding areas were contacted to request that one or more service providers from each agency participate as a partner in the program. Can-Voice, a consumer-survivor peer support agency, was invited to be the lead community agency, with multiple members becoming involved in the program, including one individual accepting a community lead role to complement the research lead. Any interested individual from any stakeholder group could also attend or join any committee. Further, invitations to join the CURA were delivered in the quarterly program newsletter distributed to local agencies, during research interviews, and at presentations and annual program forums. These deliberate and frequent invitations were part of the PAR process and represented the ongoing goal of promoting inclusion of stakeholders to provide the program with enriched knowledge and experiences from new members over time.

The committee structure and deliberate effort to include stakeholders positively affected all aspects of the program. Not only did the diverse voices of stakeholders enrich data collection but they also enhanced the ways in which dissemination activities were undertaken. In addition, the Article Idea Chart encouraged all stakeholders to actively participate in writing and dissemination on issues pertinent to them, further embracing the inclusivity PAR projects strive to achieve. The integrated nature of the process also meant that it would not be possible to engage stakeholders in the Article Idea Chart if they were not actively involved in the program through committee membership.

3. THE ARTICLE IDEA CHART

The Article Idea Chart (Table 5.1) was developed during an earlier CURA project examining housing and mental health (Forchuk et al., 2011). The chart was created to engage all committee members from various backgrounds in the writing process and dissemination of PAR results. The Article Idea Chart was a regular agenda item that was distributed to all committee members during each meeting. Any individual member was given the opportunity to propose topics for publication, including written articles for academic journals or non-academic audiences such as community newsletters, websites, or blogs. In addition, any individual from any committee was given the opportunity to join and contribute to existing topic groups. Once a group was formed, with membership typically ranging from three to eight people, they began to meet separately from regular committee meetings to develop the article. Progress and updates on current articles were then shared across all committee meetings. The development and use of this tool was a deliberate means to encourage all stakeholders to become involved in the dissemination process. By allowing all members to propose topics of interest to them and to join existing topic groups, the writing process and authorship becomes more open and transparent. As the Article Idea Chart continued to be reviewed at each committee meeting, there were instances when similar topics were combined and, conversely, times when one topic was split between two separate groups as the data required and permitted. Each topic group was provided the support of a research staff member for literature reviews, data analysis, and assistance in writing. The quality of work was further enhanced by the participation of various stakeholders with differing academic backgrounds. All members who signed up to participate were expected to play an active role in the writing process, including ensuring the material could be understood by the intended audience. The decision on submission location and target audience was decided solely by the working group who created the article.

As illustrated in Table 5.1, the time between "date claimed" and "submission" was typically lengthy, due, in part, to the fact that some committee members claimed topics of interest to them early in the research process before all data was collected and also due to there being dozens of ideas being considered throughout the project. As team members remained actively engaged in the program for several years through committee meetings and events, wait times between claim dates and submission dates rarely became a concern.

The Article Idea Chart was successfully used in the inaugural CURA. In that project, 39 topic ideas were proposed, leading to just over 20 articles being published. Some of the original topics were merged and a few were abandoned if no one joined the group and the proposer did not wish to pursue the topic without others. Of the articles, 18 were originally published in academic journals and were later compiled into an edited book entitled *Homelessness, Housing, and Mental*

Table 5.1: Article Idea Chart for PAR Projects

Topic	Author(s)	Data Source	Audience	Date Claimed	Action/ Progress	Submitted (date)
Fairness and Social Justice	S. Benbow, A. Rudnick, C. Forchuk, B. Edwards	Year 1 Open-Ended Questions	*Disability and Society Journal*	2012 07	submitted	2013 04
CURA Impact	P. Hall, S. Perry, C. Forchuk	Year 1 Partner Interviews	*Action Research Journal*	2012 01	being edited	aim: 2013 09
Stigma Scale	R. Csiernik, C. Forchuk, B. Edwards, A. Meier	Year 1 Stigma Scale data	*Social Work Research*	2012 09	being written	aim: 2013 09

Health (Forchuk et al., 2011). Contributing authors within the book came from a wide variety of backgrounds, bringing varying personal and professional expertise on mental health and housing to the articles. Academic professionals, service providers, consumer-survivors, and students all worked together as authors of articles within the book. Compiling the articles into one source allowed for a broader range of audiences to access the material, as the manuscript was given away and sold at CURA events and forums. In addition to these articles, a program newsletter was created by a group of writers and distributed to all partners and local agencies quarterly. The initial CURA program utilized the Article Idea Chart specifically for written dissemination, though the tool could be easily expanded to include oral presentations and conference proceedings.

The Article Idea Chart functions as a deliberate way to encourage participation in written dissemination. However, engaging stakeholder groups traditionally unfamiliar with research presents ongoing challenges. In the first CURA, consumer-survivors and service providers participated in publication development, but academic team members often outnumbered members of the other stakeholder groups. In addition, academic journals were the most frequent publisher of the research results. Despite this trend towards traditional research audiences, the program nonetheless strove to make the findings as inclusive and accessible as possible, including through distribution of the quarterly newsletter, posting of findings on the program website, presentation of results at community forums, and publishing of articles on community agency websites, when permitted. These challenges reflect the fact that academic members continue to be the most comfortable with research writing and dissemination. However, the use of the Article Idea Chart serves as an explicit invitation to other members to become involved in aspects of research not traditionally open to them and has been successful in engaging diverse authorship.

While CURA programs are five-year, large-scale projects with the potential for several publications and presentations, the Article Idea Chart can be used for smaller studies as well. For example, it was utilized with a shorter, two-year research project entitled "Poverty and Mental Health: Issues, Challenges and Solutions," funded by the Ontario Mental Health Foundation in 2013. While the timeline, scope, and membership of this study was smaller than that of CURA programs, the Article Idea Chart was used and produced 12 distinct topics. Thus, a PAR project need not be large-scale to use this tool. It is simply a deliberate methodology for ensuring all team members, regardless of academic background, are provided the opportunity to participate in publications or presentations on topics of interest to them, further enhancing the goals of PAR.

4. CONCLUSION

The PAR research process is beneficial as it engages all affected stakeholders on a given topic and removes traditional academic researchers from the role of expert. It is especially well suited for mental health research as a means of engaging consumer-survivors in projects concerning the systems in which they participate and, in this way, aiding in contributing to social inclusion. While many authors discuss the importance of PAR and explain ways in which to engage community members in the research team, rarely do publications explicitly discuss tools and methodologies used to ensure the full participation of all team members in one of the most important aspects of PAR research: dissemination of results. The Article Idea Chart is a tool that has been utilized successfully in several PAR projects. It can be revised to suit the needs of other PAR projects and can be expanded to include presentation topics and conference proceedings. The Article Idea Chart removes any confusion from dissemination by making the process transparent and openly available to all team members, regardless of stakeholder group.

REFERENCES

Csiernik, R., O'Regan, T., Forchuk, C., & Rudnick, A. (2018). Nursing student's perceptions of participatory action research. *Journal of Nursing Education, 57*(5), 282–286.

Forchuk, C., Csiernik, R., & Jensen, E. (Eds.). (2011). *Homelessness, housing, and mental health: Finding truths—creating change.* Toronto, ON: Canadian Scholars' Press.

Leff, J., & Warner, R. (2006). *Social inclusion of people with mental illness.* Cambridge, UK: Cambridge University Press.

Montoya, M. E., & Kent, E. E. (2011). Dialogical action: Moving from community-based to community-driven participatory research. *Qualitative Health Research, 21*(7), 1000–1011.

Nelson, G., Ochocka, J., Griffin, K., & Lord, J. (1998). "Nothing about me, without me": Participatory action research with self-help/mutual aid organizations for psychiatric consumer/survivors. *American Journal of Community Psychology, 26*(6), 881–912.

Ochocka, J., Janzen, R., & Nelson, G. (2002). Sharing power and knowledge: Professional and mental health consumer/survivor researchers working together in a participatory action research project. *Psychiatric Rehabilitation Journal, 25*(4), 379–387.

Rogers, E. S., & Palmer-Erbs, V. (1994). Participatory action research: Implications for research and evaluation in psychiatric rehabilitation. *Psychosocial Rehabilitation Journal, 18*(2), 3–12.

Speers, J., & Lathlean, J. (2015). Service user involvement in giving mental health students feedback on placement: A participatory action research study. *Nurse Education Today, 35*(9), e84–e89.

White, G. W., Nary, D. E., & Froehlich, A. K. (2001). Consumers as collaborators in research and action. *Journal of Prevention & Intervention in the Community, 21*(2), 15–34.

Whyte, W. F. (Ed.). (1991). *Participatory action research.* Newbury Park, CA: SAGE Publications.

CHAPTER 6

Strategies for Retaining a Sample of Homeless Youth

Cheryl Forchuk, Tony O'Regan, Momodou Jeng, and Amanda Wright

1. INTRODUCTION

Across Canada, it is estimated that 40,000 to 65,000 youth between the ages of 16 and 24 experience homelessness each year (Evenson, 2009; Gaetz et al., 2016), making up 20% of the homeless population accessing shelters (Segaert et al., 2012). It is estimated that 50 to 70% of persons who are experiencing homelessness have mental health issues, which may include substance use disorders (Drake et al., 1991). Homeless youth have been identified as a highly transient population (Ferguson et al., 2010; Hyde, 2005), with more than 65% self-identifying as nomadic (Sanders et al., 2008), making the tracking of research participants a very challenging task. Further, it is generally recognized that all actual numbers are most likely higher due to underreporting (Padgett et al., 2006).

Frequent address and phone number changes (Ward & Henderson, 2003) and limited conventional social networks (Falci et al., 2011) make maintaining current locator information difficult (Farabee et al., 2011). Nevertheless, it is important to include members of hard-to-reach populations in research to ensure proper representation of the general population and to explore their specific needs. Odierna and Schmidt (2009) found that participant retention rates were lowered from 89% to 71% 12 months after baseline when hard-to-reach populations were included.

2. RETENTION STRATEGIES

Locator information is generally the key to maintaining participants in a longitudinal study (Robinson et al., 2007). Researchers are most successful in tracking participants when all possible location information is obtained, such as full names, aliases, social insurance and driver's licence numbers, current or best mailing addresses, phone numbers, email, phone numbers and email of participants' contacts, places frequented, involvement with social services or judicial systems, and any plans to move (United States Department of Health and Human Services [USDHH], 2006). Collecting collateral contact information, such as contact information of those who might know the participant's whereabouts, is a very successful locating strategy (Hobden et al., 2011). Updating locator forms at each interview (Cottler et al., 1996) and keeping in contact with participants between interviews (Robinson et al., 2007) are also useful strategies to maintain current information. A 24-hour message line can be a useful way for participants to call and update their locator information, schedule interviews, or disclose other needs related to the study (McKenzie et al., 1999).

Email

Email has become an effective means of communication for street youth (Lankenau et al., 2010). In a Canadian study of 20 street youth, approximately 70% of the sample self-assessed their computer abilities on a structured interview as "better than average" and 85% indicated comfort using computer technology (Karabanow & Naylor, 2010). This sample of youth reported "feeling connected" through the Internet and access to computers was identified as primarily being available at drop-in centres or public libraries, where they could check their email. Additional studies have reported that 80% of youth experiencing homelessness accessed the Internet more than once a week, and as many as 25% accessed the Internet for one hour or more daily (Rice & Barman-Adhikari, 2014; Rice et al., 2010). The availability of public Internet access through libraries, smartphone technology, and public WiFi increases accessibility among this population. Importantly, Rice et al. (2011) found that only 22% of homeless youth did not have access to a cellphone. In another study by Eyrich-Garg and Moss (2017), the use of the Internet by homeless participants at public libraries, places of employment, and on their mobile phones improved communication between participants and researchers. These studies highlight the increasing accessibility of the Internet and the importance of collecting email addresses when tracking homeless youth. Street youth are generally able to check their email through a variety of means, although less frequently than a housed population.

Social Service Agencies

Tracking participants through social service agencies can be difficult due to staff turnover and confidentiality and consent issues when using agency information

(Ward & Henderson, 2003). Agency tracking may be more successful when the agency is directly involved in the research process and deriving benefit from this involvement. These considerations motivate the agency's tracking efforts in collaboration with the research team (Pollio et al., 2000; Veldhuizen et al., 2015). Creating and maintaining strong relationships with social service or health-care agencies in the community can be beneficial in locating participants through formal agency databases or other informal means (McKenzie et al., 1999).

System Tracking

Bureaucratic obstacles aside, system tracking, such as accessing judicial records or other public and private service records, can be most useful in tracking the whereabouts of participants. However, accessing such databases often proves difficult, again due to issues surrounding confidentiality and consent (Cottler et al., 1996; USDHH, 2006). Furthermore, these records tend to leave out certain populations in their reports. For instance, criminal records databases may be the easiest type of database to access, but these leave out individuals who have not been convicted of any crimes (Williams & O'Donnell, 2014).

Outreach

When researchers are unsuccessful in locating participants through regular contact methods, fieldwork or outreach should be employed (Cepeda & Valdez, 2010; Cottler et al., 1996; Lankenau et al., 2010; McKenzie et al., 1999; Robinson et al., 2007; Villacorta et al., 2007). Outreach entails researchers visiting known hangout locations, social service agencies, drop-in centres, shelters, and neighbourhoods related to the study population, as well as hand-delivering letters or reminders (McKenzie et al., 1999; Villacorta et al., 2007). Field visits also have the indirect benefit of allowing researchers to maintain a visible presence within the population, building rapport and monitoring participants' locations, even if there are no interviews imminent (Villacorta et al., 2007).

Outreach specialists, carefully selected and specifically trained to the needs of the population, have been successfully utilized in a number of studies (McKenzie et al., 1999). For example, in tracking research on Mexican-American heroin users, Cepeda and Valdez (2010) used culturally appropriate outreach specialists, native to the neighbourhood of participants. The retention success of Villacorta et al.'s (2007) research, involving socially marginalized young Peruvian adults, was attributed to extensive outreach efforts, with researchers developing a vast understanding of the participants' lifestyles before beginning research. "Helper participants" were also employed in this study to spread the word of upcoming interviews at local participant hangouts, and additional visits were scheduled at 4-, 6-, 16-, and 20-month intervals, specifically to locate participants and update their locator information. Furthermore, their field visits allowed for monitoring of participants, while outreach workers also took part in local events to maintain relationships and locate participants. Outreach workers created a network among the participants and the researchers while also helping to locate individuals via the network (Lankenau et al., 2010).

Incentives

Providing incentives to participants has proven to be a beneficial retention strategy (Cepeda & Valdez, 2010; McKenzie et al., 1999; Robinson et al., 2007; Veldhuizen et al., 2015). Incentives can range in amounts and come in cash or gift certificate form. Studies using incentives have had higher retention rates than those without (Cepeda & Valdez, 2010; Lankenau et al., 2010; McKenzie et al., 1999; Robinson et al., 2007). However, immediate cash incentives have proven to be the most effective in retaining contact between the research team and participants (Cepeda & Valdez, 2010). Another tactic that has aided in maintaining retention is to increase the amount paid with each follow-up interview (Lankenau et al., 2010; Veldhuizen et al., 2015). Other incentives such as free counselling services or personalizing interviews to specific participants have also demonstrated increased retention rates (McKenzie et al., 1999). However, these incentive strategies may be perceived as coercive and an infringement of the right to voluntary consent.

Organizing Tracking Information

Documentation of both successful and unsuccessful contact attempts are useful in tracking exactly when and where participants can be found. Researchers have used spreadsheets to organize this information so that participants' past and current locations can be easily referred to (Cepeda & Valdez, 2010; McKenzie et al., 1999). Time frames for re-contacting vary among studies, but it has been useful to begin re-contacting participants at least a month in advance, to provide adequate time to locate individuals and also to determine a day and time for their interview (Ward & Henderson, 2003; Yeterian et al., 2012).

Branding

Sending various items to participants, such as thank-you cards, reminder cards, newsletters, calendars, and birthday cards with gift certificates are worthwhile retention strategies that add a personal touch (Cepeda & Valdez, 2010; McKenzie et al., 1999; USDHH, 2006; Yeterian et al., 2012). Branding the research through the use of specific logos has also been shown to enhance retention as it allows participants to recognize the logo in various locations and contact researchers directly (Villacorta et al., 2007; Walton et al., 1998). Study logos can also be displayed on items that are given to participants in longitudinal studies, such as on pens and grocery bags, which can act as an incentive for continued participation (Holt et al., 2015).

Authentic Relationships

Karabanow et al. (2016) addressed the development of authentic relationships between researchers and subjects in longitudinal studies through an anti-oppression research framework. An anti-oppression framework is one used within a range of disciplines including social work, anthropology, sociology, nursing, and psychology. This framework allows the researcher to acknowledge and understand the power dynamics within the relationship as well as the privilege that is particular to the position of the researcher (Baines & Edward, 2015). Objective research techniques conventionally used do not allow researchers to recognize oppressive privilege within research methods, relationships, and practices (Baines & Edwards, 2015). In developing authentic relationships researchers lower the power differential between themselves and study participants and indicate that there is more to the participant that is valued besides their status within the confines of the study.

Successful Approaches

Cottler et al. (1996) achieved a retention rate of 96.6% in a vulnerable sample by using locator forms, phone tracking, and persistent and extensive outreach. The researchers noted the importance of budgeting to allow for costly extensive outreach efforts. These researchers also used system tracking, meaning they were able to track their participants through various systems, such as the social welfare or criminal justice systems, which contributed to their retention rate. Two "trackers" were employed for the duration of their study, allowing for consistent and involved outreach workers, which proved beneficial for their research.

Researchers cite persistence, creativity, and flexibility as basic but important aspects when tracking transient populations (Cottler et al., 1996; McKenzie et al., 1999). Outreach workers must exhaust all avenues in order to locate the most difficult-to-locate participants. Researchers must also be flexible regarding scheduling and locations of interviews (Cottler et al., 1996). Ease and location of the interview are important to consider when working with homeless youth, as they could influence retention rates (Robinson et al., 2007). In the current study, tracking strategies including social service agency, email, and outreach were utilized. Retention strategies involved documenting tracking information and giving out items branded with the study logo.

3. METHODS

The research team did not set out at the beginning of the study to report tracking and retention strategies as a primary objective. The main objective of Youth Matters in London, a participatory action research (PAR) project, was to investigate and better understand youth participants' choices regarding mental health and addictions treatment and service options over a three-year period. The inclusion requirement for this project was that participants must have a serious or moderate self-reported mental health issue with or without a coexisting substance use disorder. It was not a requirement to have been formally diagnosed with a mental health or an addiction disorder. Participants were given an option to choose help with housing first, treatment first, both together, or something else if preferred, as well as being able to change their initial choice across the study time frame (Forchuk et al., 2013). The overall enrolment for the study was 187 youth from the City of London, Ontario, and surrounding areas. The age requirement for enroling in the study was 16 to 24 years, self-reporting mental health issues and/or addiction issues, and currently homeless or precariously housed. The definitions of "homelessness status" and "precariously housed" were consistent with the At Home/Chez Soi Project: "not having a place to stay for more than seven nights and having little chance of finding a place to stay in the next month" (Mental Health Commission of Canada, 2012).

Procedures

Ethics approval was granted by the Research Ethics Board of Western University before study commencement. Recruitment was facilitated by a community partnership with the Youth Action Centre (YAC), a drop-in centre for homeless youth with street involvement operated by Youth Opportunities Unlimited (YOU). YAC dedicated one worker specifically to address housing and/or treatment needs of homeless youth involved in the study. Although this position was funded directly through the research grant, the incumbent was not part of the research study team and no participant information was shared between the worker and the researchers. The ethics application referred to this additional worker to increase capacity for the project. Word of mouth and snowball sampling were also successful recruitment strategies. Although the study planned to recruit 150 youth, a total of 187 eventually participated in the study.

Analysis of contact approaches was done by referring to research coordinator field notes and contact lists (which modelled Cottler et al.'s [1996] locator forms) provided by participants at each interview. Contact information typically included personal phone number (landline and/or cell), email address, and current "address" (typically shelter or friends). Contact information for family and/or friends included names, relationship, phone numbers, and email addresses. Agencies used by participants were also identified by organization name, phone number, and a contact person or case worker when it was appropriate.

A combination of strategies was used to locate participants. Outreach approaches were used when contact information that had been provided failed to locate participants, again modelling Cottler et al.'s (1996) approach. Outreach, with a goal of being sensitive and respectful to the needs of participants, consisted of designated research assistants visiting areas where homeless youth were known to gather to locate participants for interview. These sites included social service agencies, social assistance offices, and other popular meeting places. No concerns were expressed regarding surveillance by any participant at any time during the study. The use of promotional items, such as bags and lanyards with easily recognizable logos, were used to identify research assistants and participants. These lanyards were suggested by the youth on the advisory group and given to youth at each interview. They included a phone number and Internet site that could be used to access the study, and in at least a few instances the lanyards were actually used by participants.

4. FINDINGS

Demographic information is presented in Table 6.1. The sample was made up of 122 (65%) males and 62 (33%) females, with a mean age of 20 years (SD = 2.4). On average, participants reported experiencing two years (SD = 28.27) of homelessness throughout their lifetime. Substance-use disorders (34.2%) and mood disorders (31.6%) were the top two psychiatric diagnoses reported by participants.

Following initial enrolment, attempts were made to contact each participant for three follow-up interviews, six months apart. Table 6.2 summarizes the overall retention rates for the study. Of the 23 participants lost to follow-up at the first follow-up interview, one person passed away, one person declined to participate in

Table 6.1: Homeless Youth Sample Characteristics

Variable	n (%)
Age (years) [Mean (SD)]	20.9 (2.4)
Gender	
Male	122 (65.2)
Female	62 (33.2)
Not identify male or female	3 (1.6)
Country of Birth	
Canada	175 (93.6)
USA	4 (2.1)
Other	8 (4.3)
Level of Education	
Completed grade school	149 (79.7)
Completed high school	27 (14.4)
Some postsecondary	11 (5.8)
Marital Status	
Single, never married	146 (78.1)
Cohabitating with partner	37 (19.8)
Married	1 (0.5)
Separated	1 (0.5)
Don't know	2 (1.1)
Current Primary Employment Status	
Employed	13 (7.0)
Unemployed	140 (74.9)
Student	31 (16.6)
Volunteer work, unpaid	1 (0.5)
Other	1 (0.5)
Don't know	1 (0.5)
Current Sources of Income	
Welfare/income assistance	95 (50.8)
Personal Needs Allowance	29 (15.5)

Table 6.1: Continued

Variable	n (%)
Other	17 (9.1)
Earnings from casual work	16 (8.6)
Panhandling	13 (7.0)
No income	12 (6.4)
Partner/family support	11 (5.9)
Disability income	9 (4.8)
Earnings from regular work	7 (3.7)
Illegal means	7 (3.7)
Busking	5 (2.7)
Ontario Student Assistance Program (OSAP)	3 (1.6)
HST/income tax rebate/cheque	3 (1.6)
Children's Aid Society support	3 (1.6)
Baby bonus	2 (1.1)
Squeegeeing	2 (1.1)
Pension	1 (0.5)
Total income in the previous month (n = 186) [Mean (SD)]	$970.55 ($2,339.55)
Primary Diagnosis	
Substance-related disorder	64 (34.2)
Mood disorder	59 (31.6)
Disorder of childhood/adolescence	25 (13.4)
Anxiety disorder	22 (11.8)
Mental health diagnosis present, but type unknown	9 (4.8)
Schizophrenia	5 (2.7)
Other	2 (1.1)
Developmental handicap	1 (0.5)
Total amount of time spent being homeless during the lifetime (months) [Mean (SD)]	24.4 (28.3)
Longest single period of homelessness (months) [Mean (SD)]	12.2 (21.3)
Number of undesirable moves in the previous 5 years (n = 179) [Mean (SD)]	9.1 (17.2)

Table 6.2: Retention Rates of the Homeless Youth Sample Following Successive Interviews

Interview No.	N	Lost to Follow-Up	n	%
1 (baseline)	-	-	187	100
2 (6 months)	187	23	164	88
3 (12 months)	164	4	160	86
4 (18 months)	160	6	154	82

further interviews, and the remainder could not be contacted. The project team was therefore successful in retaining 164 youth (88%) for the first follow-up (Interview Two). In subsequent interviews (Three and Four), four and six participants (respectively) were lost to follow-up because they could not be contacted. Out of those that were contacted, all consented to participate in the interviews. The retention rates for Interviews Three and Four were 86% and 82%, respectively. As illustrated in Table 6.2, the biggest drop in participant retention occurred between the first and second interview. In terms of participant retention between interviews, 97% of those participants who completed Interview Two also completed Interview Three, and 96% of those who completed Interview Three also completed Interview Four. These retention rates over time suggest a strong willingness by homeless youth to participate in the research study.

In total, 665 interviews took place. This number includes the initial 187 at enrolment, and 164, 160, and 154 at each successive follow-up interview. Table 6.3 summarizes the different contact strategies/methods that were successful in locating participants for each interview. As indicated in Table 6.3, the most successful method of contacting participants for all follow-up interviews was through the YAC, where 371 (78%) of the follow-up interviews were scheduled. Of the 371 interviews, 20 were contacted through the YAC outreach program (differentiated from YAC's main operating location). Email was the distant second most successful strategy at relocating participants for follow-up interviews, as 26 (5.4%) follow-up interviews were scheduled through this method. Contact methods through phone (own) and outreach work done directly by the project research team were the least successful as 18 (3.8%) and 11 (2.3%) participants were scheduled for Interviews Three and Four, respectively, using these methods. For 41 (8.6%) follow-up interviews, a single contact method could not be determined,

Table 6.3: Successful Contact Strategies for Retaining the Sample of Homeless Youth

Interview No.	Phone (own)	Phone (family or friend)	Email	YAC	Outreach	Jail/ Detention	Unknown	Total
Two	3	3	4	137 (5 Outreach)	1	1	15	164
Three	5	2	6	128 (8 Outreach)	3	2	14	160
Four	10	0	16	106 (7 Outreach)	7	3	12	154
Total	18	5	26	371 (20 Outreach)	11	6	41	478

as multiple methods were utilized. For example, one participant mentioned having received both a message from a sibling and an email, but then came to the YAC to find a member of the research staff. Despite multiple contact methods being used in some cases, the primary contact methods for over 90% cases were identified. The presence of successful contact methods other than the YAC emphasizes the need to keep ongoing, detailed records at each point in time for both the documentation of successful strategies and research purposes.

5. DISCUSSION

A major strength of this project was the participatory action research (PAR) approach involved. In particular, persevering with this study resulted in the inclusion of an otherwise disregarded and vulnerable population and fostered the development of authentic relationships, contributing to social inclusion. Compared with other vulnerable population research, the retention rate in this study was extremely high. The development of rapport and a genuine relationship through ongoing connections has been identified as instrumental in creating "hope" for participants (Hall, 1992; Karabanow et al., 2016; Rodríguez & Brown, 2009), which improved the engagement of research subjects. Participants considered "regulars" at the YAC had formed relationships with the staff, were easiest to locate, and were still accessing the YAC six months after the initial interview. Participants lost to follow-up during the first and second interviews were mostly not considered YAC regulars or did not access the YAC and had been recruited through word of mouth. Also, the issue of aging out is noteworthy; some participants may have been lost because they became too old to access the YAC, although, as stated earlier, other locations were arranged to maintain contact.

Email was the second most effective strategy for connecting with the homeless youth population in the study. The participants themselves identified email as an important piece of tracking information. Although some participants did not check their email often, it was one of the more reliable contact methods, in comparison with phone numbers, which often change. At times, responses would be received several months after attempting to contact participants by email, which demonstrates that when the study has flexible timelines, email increases as a retention method. Email was also useful in maintaining contact with participants who were transient as, in general, they would keep the same email address but frequently changed their phone numbers.

High retention was also made possible by using strategies involving documenting and organizing the tracking/contact information, and by giving out items with the study logo on it. Contacting some participants was a challenge but was successful with time and persistence. Though not considered for this study, the profusion and popularity of social media applications accessible to youth, such as Facebook, Instagram, and WhatsApp, offer other creative methods that could be utilized to further improve retention.

Limitations

As previously discussed, multiple strategies were used to retain participants. However, lapses in field notes made it difficult to discern which retention strategy was responsible for locating some participants. In redoing the study, we would have made our field notes and tracking methods more detailed to better discern tracking methods for every participant at each interview. In many cases, emails asked participants to either respond or to "drop by the Youth Action Centre"; therefore, it was sometimes unclear whether it was the research team's efforts or the YAC's outreach that was the successful method of contact. In the future, detailed accounts of strategies used, as well as asking participants at each interview to specify which method located them, would be helpful to provide a comprehensive explanation of successful strategies.

6. CONCLUSION

Developing and maintaining relationships with social service agencies from the planning stages of the project is important in this type of research. Agencies proved to be most helpful when aware and involved in the project, which again speaks to the value of using a PAR approach. As outlined earlier, consistently using the same staff in outreach efforts helps to build relationships with the agencies, and their staff assists in tracking. Furthermore, due to the research team's involvement in other research projects in the city, positive collaborative relationships with agencies existed prior to this particular project, which also aided the tracking efforts.

Flexibility of research staff working hours and time devoted to outreach, as well as budgeting adequately for this, is important in planning for this type of study to be able to regularly locate participants of this population. It also proved incredibly important to use multiple strategies in locating, as in this study some youth participants preferred contact through a local agency while others preferred alternative methods of communication. Paramount in working with this and related populations in increasing retention rates is patience and perseverance.

REFERENCES

Baines, S., & Edwards, J. (2015). Considering the ways in which anti-oppressive practice principles can inform health research. *The Arts in Psychotherapy, 42*(1), 28–34.

Cepeda, A., & Valdez, A. (2010). Ethnographic strategies in the tracking and retention of street-recruited community-based samples of substance using hidden populations in longitudinal studies. *Substance Use & Misuse, 45*(5), 700–716.

Cottler, L. B., Compton, W. M., Ben-Abdallah, A., Horne, M., & Claverie, D. (1996). Achieving a 96.6 percent follow-up rate in a longitudinal study of drug abusers. *Drug and Alcohol Dependence, 41*(3), 209–217.

Drake, R. E., Osher, F. C., & Wallach, M. A. (1991). Homelessness and dual diagnosis. *American Psychologist, 46*(11), 1149–1158.

Evenson, J. (2009). *Youth homelessness in Canada: The road to solutions.* Raising the Roof. Retrieved from http://www.raisingtheroof.org/

Eyrich-Garg, K. M., & Moss, S. L. (2017). How feasible is multiple time point web-based data collection with individuals experiencing street homelessness? *Journal of Urban Health, 94*(1), 64–74.

Falci, C. D., Whitbeck, L. B., Hoyt, D. R., & Rose, T. (2011). Predictors of change in self-reported social networks among homeless young people. *Journal of Research on Adolescence, 21*(4), 827–841.

Farabee, D., Hawken, A., & Griffith, P. (2011). Tracking and incentivizing substance abusers in longitudinal research: Results of a survey of NIDA-funded investigators. *Journal of Addiction Medicine, 5*(2), 87–91.

Ferguson, K. M., Jun, J., Bender, K., Thompson, S., & Pollio, D. (2010). A comparison of addiction and transience among street youth: Los Angeles, California, Austin, Texas, and St. Louis, Missouri. *Community Mental Health Journal, 46*(3), 296–307.

Forchuk, C., Richardson, J., Laverty, K., Bryant, M., Rudnick, A., Csiernik, R., ... Kelly, C. (2013). Service preferences of homeless youth with mental illness: Housing first, treatment first, or both together. In S. Gaetz, B. O'Grady, K. Buccieri, J. Karabanow, & A. Marsolais (Eds.), *Youth homelessness in Canada: Implications for policy and practice* (pp. 95–112). Toronto, ON: Canadian Homelessness Research Network.

Gaetz, S., O'Grady, B., Kidd, S., & Schwan, K. (2016). *Without a home: The national youth homelessness survey*. Toronto, ON: Canadian Observatory on Homelessness Press.

Hall, B. L. (1992). From margins to center? The development and purpose of participatory research. *The American Sociologist, 23*(4), 15–28.

Hobden, K., Forney, J. C., Durham, K. W., & Toro, P. (2011). Limiting attrition in longitudinal research on homeless adolescents: What works best? *Journal of Community Psychology, 39*(4), 443–451.

Holt, C. L., Le, D., Calvanelli, J., Huang, J., Clark, E. M., Roth, D., ... Schulz, E. (2015). Participant retention in a longitudinal national telephone survey of African American men and women. *Journal of Ethnicity & Disease, 25*(2), 187–192.

Hyde, J. (2005). From home to street: Understanding young people's transitions into homelessness. *Journal of Adolescence, 28*(2), 171–183.

Karabanow, J., Kidd, S., Frederick, T., McLuckie, A., & Quick, J. (2016). Methodological reflections on research with street youth. *Journal of Social Work, 18*(5), 578–597.

Karabanow, J., & Naylor, T. D. (2010). "Being hooked up": Exploring experiences of street youth and information technologies. In E. D. Looker & T. D. Naylor (Eds.), *Digital diversity: Youth, equality, and information technology* (pp. 161–178). Waterloo, ON: Wilfred Laurier University Press.

Lankenau, S. E., Sanders B., Hathazi D., & Jackson-Bloom, J. (2010). Recruiting and retaining mobile young injection drug users in a longitudinal study. *Substance Use & Misuse, 45*(5), 684–699.

McKenzie, M., Peterson Tulsky, J., Long, H. L., Chesney, M., & Moss, A. (1999). Tracking and follow-up of marginalized populations: A review. *Journal of Health Care for the Poor and Undeserved, 10*(4), 409–429.

Mental Health Commission of Canada. (2012). *At Home/Chez Soi interim report.* Retrieved from www.mentalhealthcommission.ca

Odierna, D. H., & Schmidt, L. A. (2009). The effects of failing to include hard-to-reach respondents in longitudinal surveys. *American Journal of Public Health, 99*(8), 1515–1521.

Padgett, D. K., Gulcur, L., & Tsemberis, S. (2006). Housing first services for people who are homeless with co-occurring serious mental illness and substance abuse. *Research on Social Work Practice, 16*(1), 74–83.

Pollio, D. E., Thompson, S. J., & North, C. S. (2000). Agency-based tracking of difficult-to-follow populations: Runaway and homeless youth programs in St. Louis, Missouri. *Community Mental Health Journal, 36*(3), 247–258.

Rice, E., & Barman-Adhikari, A. (2014). Internet and social media use as a resource among homeless youth. *Journal of Computer-Mediated Communication, 19*(2), 232–247.

Rice, E., Lee, A., & Taitt, S. (2011). Cell phone use among homeless youth: Potential for new health interventions and research. *Journal of Urban Health, 88*(6), 1175–1182.

Rice, E., Monro, W., Barman-Adhikari, A., & Young, S. D. (2010). Internet use, social networking, and HIV/AIDS risk for homeless adolescents. *Journal of Adolescent Health, 47*(6), 610–613.

Robinson, K. A., Dennison, C. R., Wayman, D. M., Pronovosta, P. J., & Needham, D. M. (2007). Systematic review identifies number of strategies important for retaining study participants. *Journal of Clinical Epidemiology, 60*(8), 757–765.

Rodríguez, L. F., & Brown, T. M. (2009). From voice to agency: Guiding principles for participatory action research with youth. *New Directions for Youth Development, 2009*(123), 19–34.

Sanders, B., Lankenau, S. E., Jackson-Bloom, J., & Hathazi, S. D. (2008). Multiple drug use and polydrug use amongst homeless traveling youth. *Journal of Ethnicity in Substance Abuse, 7*(1), 23–40.

Segaert, A., Homelessness Partnering Secretariat, & Human Resources and Skills Development Canada. (2012). *The national shelter study: Emergency shelter use in Canada 2005–2009.* Gatineau, QC: Homelessness Partnering Secretariat & Human Resources and Skills Development Canada.

United States Department of Health and Human Services. (2006). Practical strategies for tracking and locating youth. *Proposed National Youth in Transition Database.* Retrieved from https://www.acf.hhs.gov/cb/resource/practical-strategies-nytd

Veldhuizen, S., Adair, C. E., Methot, C., Kopp, B. C., O'Campo, P., Bourque, J., … Goering, P. N. (2015). Patterns and predictors of attrition in a trial of a housing intervention for homeless people with mental illness. *Social Psychiatry and Psychiatric Epidemiology, 50*(2), 195–202.

Villacorta, V., Kegeles, S., Galea, J., Konda, K. A., Cuba, J. P., Cáceres Palacios, C. F., & Coates, T. J. (2007). Innovative approaches to cohort retention in community-based HIV/STI prevention trial for socially marginalized Peruvian young adults. *Clinical Trials, 4*(1), 32–41.

Walton, M. A., Ramanathan, C. S., & Reischl, T. (1998). Tracking substance abusers in longitudinal research: Understanding follow-up contact difficulty. *American Journal of Community Psychology, 26*(2), 233–253.

Ward, J., & Henderson, Z. (2003). Some practical and ethical issues encountered while conducting tracking research with young people leaving the "care" system. *International Journal of Social Research Methodology, 6*(3), 255–259.

Williams, I. L., & O'Donnell, C. R. (2014). Web-based tracking methods in longitudinal studies. *Evaluation and Program Planning, 45*(1), 82–89.

Yeterian, J. D., Dowa, S. J., & Kelly, J. F. (2012). Ensuring retention in longitudinal studies: A practical evaluation of an intensive follow-up protocol and suggested adaptations. *International Journal of Social Research Methodology, 15*(5), 369–383.

CHAPTER 7

The Stigma Scale: A Canadian Perspective

Amanda Meier, Rick Csiernik, Cheryl Forchuk, and Laura Warner

1. INTRODUCTION

It is estimated that 20% of Canadians live with mental illness, with close to 500,000 missing work each week for psychiatric reasons (Mental Health Commission of Canada, 2014a). The Mental Health Commission of Canada (2014a) also reports that 60% of people with mental health issues do not seek help for fear of being labelled. Stigma towards those who are perceived as different has existed for centuries, with mental illness stigma being a particularly prominent and detrimental issue in society today (Arboleda-Flórez & Stuart, 2012). Expanded understanding of stigma and its associated consequences for individuals with mental illness is necessary to counteract its oppressing impact within society.

Mental Illness Stigma

Stigma has been defined as "a feeling of being negatively differentiated owing to a particular condition, group membership or state in life" (Arboleda-Flórez & Stuart, 2012, p. 458). There are two main forms of mental illness stigma discussed in the literature. Public stigma, also referred to as societal stigma, denotes prejudicial attitudes held by the public towards people with mental illness (Arboleda-Flórez & Stuart, 2012; Corrigan et al., 2003). Self-stigma, also known as internalized stigma, refers to personal shame, withdrawal, and loss of self-esteem experienced by some people with mental illness. Self-stigma is often triggered by applying the negative stereotypes held by the public to oneself (Chronister et al., 2013; Corrigan et al., 2003).

There is no single cause of stigma; instead, it has multiple interconnecting sources, though misguided perceptions about mental illness and those who are living with mental health issues are believed to be one of the most prominent sources. Previous research has demonstrated that members of the public lack knowledge of mental illnesses and hold many misinformed beliefs about individuals with mental illnesses. Crisp and colleagues (2000) surveyed 1,737 British adults to determine public opinions regarding individuals with mental illness. They found that approximately 70% of respondents believed people with schizophrenia, alcohol dependency, or drug addiction were dangerous, which has been an ongoing issue with this population (Csiernik et al., 2007). Wang and Lai (2008) surveyed 3,047 adults in Canada to obtain attitudes concerning depression and found that 45% of participants considered people with depression as unpredictable, with over 20% considering them dangerous. Stuart (2003) conducted a review of mental health and violence literature and concluded that the general public exaggerates the strength of relationship between mental illness and violence, as well as exaggerating their own personal risk of being harmed by individuals with mental illness. Some researchers have traced the connection between mental illness and violence to the often-unrealistic portrayals of individuals with mental illness in the media (Blood et al., 2002; Byrne, 2000; Leff & Warner, 2006). Another common misguided belief about individuals with mental illness is that their illnesses are self-inflicted, making them blameworthy for their situation (Corrigan et al., 2003; Corrigan & Watson, 2007; Crisp et al., 2000). Unfortunately, stigmatizing attitudes are not limited to the general public but often occur within individuals' social circles as well. For example, Moses (2010) interviewed adolescents with mental health issues and found that 46% reported stigmatization from their family members and 62% experienced stigmatization from peers. In Crisp et al.'s (2000) study, 50% of respondents reported knowing someone with a mental health issue; however, 70 to 80% of them also reported generalized negative views about individuals with mental illness.

Experiencing stigmatizing attitudes from the public and within social circles can lead to numerous detrimental effects on an individual's wellness. Livingston and Boyd (2010) conducted a systematic review of 45 stigma and mental health articles and found that the social effects of stigmatization include exclusion, diminished social support, low subjective quality of life, and poor self-esteem. Further, self-stigma was found to be positively associated with symptom severity and negatively associated with adherence to treatment (Livingston & Boyd, 2010; Perlick et al., 2001). Wright et al. (2000) surveyed 88 individuals with mental illness recently discharged from hospitals and found that stigmatization was associated with increased stress and a weakened sense of mastery among participants. Common consequences of experiencing stigmatization include shame, secrecy, isolation, social exclusion, and feeling like an outsider within one's family (Byrne, 2000). Yanos et al. (2010) further found that self-stigma is associated with poorer vocational outcomes. In recent years, policymakers have begun to acknowledge the detrimental effects of stigmatization and programs have been developed to counteract misinformation about mental health among the public. However, individuals continue to experience mental illness stigma within their communities and social circles. Stigma has been described as potentially more detrimental than mental health issues themselves and is considered one of the greatest obstacles remaining in the treatment of mental illness (Cechnicki et al., 2011; Chronister et al., 2013).

The Stigma Scale

The Stigma Scale was developed by King et al. (2007) as a standardized measure of the stigma of mental illness. Items for the scale were developed based upon results from an earlier study by Dinos et al. (2004). In the initial study, 46 individuals from community and day mental health services in North London, United Kingdom (UK), participated in qualitative one-on-one interviews concerning their feelings and experiences with mental illness. King et al. (2007) reviewed the results and developed a 42-item scale using participant phrases regarding stigma experiences; the process of item development involved adapting participant phrases to make them more general and applicable to other people's experiences. The scale was pilot-tested with 193 mental health services users, 93 of whom were asked to complete the scale once at baseline and again two weeks later. Items with low test-retest reliability were dropped, resulting in a final scale with 28 items. The final version contains three subscales determined by factor analysis of the pilot results: discrimination, disclosure, and potential positive aspects of mental illness (King et al., 2007).

We conducted an extensive search of literature by reviewing all articles that have cited King et al. (2007) and searching the PsycInfo, CINAHL, and Social Sciences Abstracts databases for the keyword "Stigma Scale." Through this review, we found that the Stigma Scale has been utilized in a small number of studies; however, it has been modified or adapted in most of them. Schwenk et al. (2010) conducted a cross-sectional, Web-based survey study with 769 medical students at the University of Michigan to evaluate their levels of depression, stigma, and suicidal ideation; some statements for the survey were drawn from the Stigma Scale but adapted to reflect the population of medical students and specific depression experiences. Sanders (2012) used a mixed methodology to investigate how women with a psychoactive drug dependency use mutual support to counteract stigma in Maryland. She distributed surveys to women attending Narcotics Anonymous meetings including items adapted from the Stigma Scale to reflect the specific issue of drug addiction. Further, the Stigma Scale has been used in three graduate theses from United States universities: Conrad-Garrisi (2011) administered the full Stigma Scale during a correlation study examining the relationship between a number of variables and mental health recovery with 143 members of psychiatric rehabilitation "clubhouses"; Hall (2012) adapted the Stigma Scale during a vignette-based survey study examining intimate partner violence with 250 male and female undergraduate student participants; and Walston (2012) used the positive aspects of mental illness subscale from the Stigma Scale to investigate illness acceptance as a mediator to schizophrenia recovery in 100 participants diagnosed with schizophrenia receiving outpatient mental health treatment.

The purpose of our study was to examine stigma experiences for individuals living with mental illness in London, Ontario, to provide a direct comparison between a Canadian sample and the King et al. (2007) results.

2. METHOD

Design

This study employed a cross-sectional descriptive comparative research design using data from the first year of the CURA examining poverty, mental health, and social inclusion. Research ethics approval was obtained from the Research Ethics Board at Western University, London, Ontario.

Sample

A total of 380 mental health consumer-survivors from Southwestern Ontario participated in the study. Individuals were recruited if they had been diagnosed with a mental illness for a minimum of one year prior to participation (self-reported), were between the ages of 18 and 75, spoke and understood English, and provided informed consent. Quota sampling was used to ensure equal representation by sex (male and female) and housing status (homeless, residing in a group living setting, unemployed housed, and employed housed). Participants were recruited over a six-month period in the summer and fall of 2011, with interviews taking place at locations chosen by participants.

Instrument

The Stigma Scale contains 28 items rated on a five-point Likert scale ranging from one (strongly disagree) to five (strongly agree). Item wording alternates between positive and negative statements to avoid response set bias, with negative statements undergoing reverse scoring during analysis (King et al., 2007). Thirteen items on the scale pertain to discrimination experiences (i.e., "perceived hostility by others or lost opportunities because of prejudiced attitudes"), ten items evaluate a person's willingness to disclose mental health information to others, and five items concern a person's acknowledgement of the positive aspects of their mental illness (King et al., 2007, p. 250). The scale can be analyzed to yield one total score and three subscale scores.

A total stigma score can be determined by adding all responses; the lowest possible total score is zero and the highest possible total score is 112, with higher scores indicating more mental illness stigma. A discrimination subscale score can be determined by adding responses to the 13 discrimination items; the lowest possible discrimination score is zero and the highest possible discrimination score is 48, with higher scores indicating more discrimination experiences due to mental illness. A disclosure subscale score can be obtained by adding responses to the 10 disclosure items; the lowest possible disclosure score is zero and the highest possible disclosure score is 44, with a higher disclosure score indicating a lower likelihood of disclosing mental illness information. A positive aspects subscale score can be determined by adding responses to the five positive aspects items; the lowest possible positive aspects score is zero and the highest possible positive aspects score is 20, with higher scores indicating a lower likelihood of seeing the positive aspects of mental illness.

Previous analyses have found the Stigma Scale to have good reliability. In the original study by King et al. (2007), the Cronbach's alpha was determined to be 0.87 for the total score, with alphas for the subscales being 0.87 (discrimination), 0.85 (disclosure), and 0.64 (positive aspects). The overall Stigma Scale was also shown to be negatively correlated with the Self-Esteem Scale, demonstrating its concurrent validity (King et al., 2007).

Data Collection

Each of the 380 participants completed one-on-one interviews with trained research assistants. Research assistants read all items of the Stigma Scale out loud to participants, and participants rated their responses verbally or by pointing at the instrument. Responses were recorded using paper-and-pencil methods and entered into electronic databases after the interview. An honorarium of $20 was given at the end of each interview to compensate for time and travel.

Data Analysis

Frequencies and percentages of sample characteristics were calculated. Responses to items in the Stigma Scale were scored according to the guidelines set out by King et al. (2007). These were then used to determine the scores for each of the three subscales and an overall total scale score. Reliability of the Stigma Scale was assessed through a Cronbach's alpha for the final scale and each of the subscales. This was also assessed for the individual items, examining the Cronbach's alpha with each item removed.

Measures of central tendency were calculated for each item and t-tests were used to determine if significant differences existed between the measures calculated for the current sample and those reported by King et al. (2007). Measures of central tendency were also calculated for the subscales and compared to those found in the King et al. (2007) article through t-test analyses. As the original King et al. (2007) article did not contain sample sizes for the subscales, these were estimated by summing the number of missing responses from each of the individual items. Using this conservative method, sample sizes were calculated to be 150 (discrimination subscale), 164 (disclosure subscale), 172 (positive aspects subscale), and 100 (total score). Mean differences for the subscales were then standardized using the pooled standard deviation. All mean differences (individual items and subscales) were calculated so that a positive value indicated higher stigma in the Canadian sample. A Bonferroni correction was applied to account for the multiple testing, lowering the threshold from $p < 0.05$ to $p < 0.0016$.

3. FINDINGS

Description of Sample

Characteristics for both the UK and Canadian samples are presented in Table 7.1. There was little difference in age (UK 42.9 years vs. Canadian 40.7 years), though the UK sample had a slightly greater percentage of males (57.1% vs. 50.0%) and a slightly lower proportion of individuals currently employed (17.0% vs. 24.7%). Ethnicity could not be directly compared due to differences in data collection, though it did appear that the UK sample contained a slightly higher percentage of Caucasians (87.4% vs. 75.5%). Additionally, psychiatric diagnoses were classified in slightly different manners, although in both samples each individual could

Table 7.1: Comparison of Demographics between the UK and Canadian Samples

	UK Sample (n = 193)	**Canadian Sample (n = 380)**
Age (years) [Mean (SD)]	42.9 (12.4)	40.7 (14.0)
Sex/Gender		
Male	109 (57.1%)	190 (50.0%)
Female	82 (42.9%)	190 (50.0%)
Ethnicity		
Caucasian	159 (87.4%)	287 (75.5%)
African-American	11 (6.0%)	4 (1.1%)
Indian/Bangladeshi	18 (9.0%)	N.R.
Native American	N.R.	45 (11.8%)
Other	25 (13.7%)	44 (11.6%)
Currently Employed	34 (17.0%)	94 (24.7%)

report more than one. Both samples reported similar rates of mood and anxiety disorders, while the UK sample reported slightly higher rates of schizophrenia and personality disorders.

Reliability of the Stigma Scale

Table 7.2 highlights the results of the reliability testing in the Canadian sample, as well as the comparison data from King et al. (2007). The Cronbach's alpha for the total scale score in the Canadian sample was 0.86, which was similar to the alpha of 0.87 in the UK sample. When examining how this changed with item deletion, the alphas ranged from 0.86 to 0.87 in the Canadian sample. The alphas for the subscales were all calculated to be lower in the Canadian sample than in the UK sample (discrimination 0.83 vs. 0.87; disclosure: 0.79 vs. 0.85; positive aspects 0.46 vs. 0.64).

Total Stigma Scores

Total stigma scores for the Canadian sample ranged from 9 to 99 (possible range was 0 to 112). In comparison to the UK sample, the Canadian sample scored lower

Table 7.2: Summary of Reliability Analysis Results for the UK and Canadian Samples

	UK Sample	Canadian Sample	
	Cronbach's Alpha	Cronbach's Alpha	Range of Alphas When Items Removed
Disclosure	0.85	0.79	0.76–0.81
Discrimination	0.87	0.83	0.81–0.83
Positive Aspects	0.64	0.46	0.26–0.60
Total	0.87	0.86	0.86–0.87

Table 7.3: Summary of Stigma Scale Scores for Canadian and UK Samples

	UK Sample		Canadian Sample			
Subscales	Response *n*	Mean (SD)	Response *n*	Mean (SD)	Mean Difference	Standardized Difference
Discrimination	150	29.1 (9.5)	371	25.0 (9.0)	-4.1	-0.49*
Disclosure	164	24.7 (8.0)	367	22.9 (7.6)	-1.8	-0.23
Positive Aspect	172	8.8 (2.8)	375	8.0 (3.1)	-0.8	-0.27
Total Score	100	62.6 (15.4)	362	56.0 (15.8)	-6.6	-0.42*

Note: *$p < 0.0016$

on both the total stigma score (56.0 vs. 62.6, $p < 0.0016$) and the discrimination subscale (25.0 vs. 29.1, $p < 0.0016$; Table 7.3). Although this trend was repeated for the disclosure subscale (22.9 vs. 24.7) and positive aspects subscale (8.0 vs. 8.8), neither of these differences were found to be statistically significant. These results indicate the UK sample was experiencing a higher level of discrimination and stigma in general than were those who comprised the Canadian sample.

Table 7.4: Responses to the Stigma Scale Items for the Canadian and UK Samples

Statement		Strongly Agree	Strongly Disagree	UK Sample		Canadian Sample		Mean Difference
				Response *n*	Mean (SD) Median	Response *n*	Mean (SD) Median	
1	I have been discriminated against in education because of my mental health problems (Dc)	4	0	188	1.59 (1.03) 1.5	379	1.91 (1.36) 2.0	0.32
2	Sometimes I feel that I am being talked down to because of my mental health problems (Dc)	4	0	189	2.40 (1.24) 3.0	379	2.42 (1.26) 3.0	0.02
3	Having had mental health problems has made me a more understanding person (P)	0	4	190	1.08 (0.89) 1.0	379	1.22 (1.11) 1.0	0.14
4	I do not feel bad about having had mental health problems (D)	0	4	188	2.32 (1.26) 3.0	378	1.63 (1.27) 1.0	0.69*U
5	I worry about telling people I receive psychological treatment (D)	4	0	189	2.71 (1.18) 3.0	374	2.20 (1.26) 2.0	−0.51*U
6	Some people with mental health problems are dangerous (P)	4	0	190	2.82 (0.95) 3.0	378	2.67 (1.13) 3.0	−0.15
7	People have been understanding of my mental health problems (P)	0	4	185	1.84 (1.06) 2.0	378	1.61 (1.08) 1.0	−0.23

Table 7.4: Continued

Statement		Strongly Agree	Strongly Disagree	UK Sample		Canadian Sample		Mean Difference
				Response *n*	Mean (SD) Median	Response *n*	Mean (SD) Median	
8	I have been discriminated against by police because of my mental health problems (Dc)	4	0	188	1.72 (1.21) 2.0	375	1.79 (1.40) 1.0	0.07
9	I have been discriminated against by employers because of my mental health problems (Dc)	4	0	187	2.08 (1.16) 2.0	378	1.88 (1.34) 2.0	-0.20
10	My mental health problems have made me more accepting of other people (P)	0	4	191	1.19 (1.01) 1.0	378	1.18 (0.99) 1.0	-0.01
11	Very often I feel alone because of my mental health problems (Dc)	4	0	190	2.85 (1.14) 3.0	377	2.32 (1.30) 3.0	-0.53^{*U}
12	I am scared of how other people will react if they find out about my mental health problems (D)	4	0	192	2.65 (1.13) 3.0	378	2.08 (1.30) 2.0	-0.57^{*U}
13	I would have had better chances in life if I had not had mental health problems (Dc)	4	0	191	2.89 (1.15) 3.0	378	2.76 (1.20) 3.0	-0.13
14	I do not mind people in my neighbourhood knowing I have had mental health problems (D)	0	4	192	2.58 (1.34) 3.0	377	2.13 (1.24) 2.0	-0.45^{*U}

Statement		Strongly Agree	Strongly Disagree	UK Sample		Canadian Sample		Mean Difference
				Response *n*	Mean (SD) Median	Response *n*	Mean (SD) Median	
15	I would say I have had mental health problems if I was applying for a job (D)	0	4	189	2.16 (1.31) 2.0	378	2.44 (1.37) 3.0	0.28
16	I worry about telling people that I take medicines/tablets for mental health problems (D)	4	0	191	2.58 (1.18) 3.0	371	1.91 (1.19) 2.0	−0.67*U
17	People's reactions to my mental health problems make me keep myself to myself (Dc)	4	0	188	2.40 (1.19) 3.0	377	2.23 (1.24) 2.0	−0.17
18	I am angry with the way people have reacted to my mental health problems (Dc)	4	0	190	2.23 (1.18) 2.0	377	2.11 (1.26) 2.0	−0.12
19	I have not had any trouble from people because of my mental health problems (Dc)	0	4	192	2.24 (1.14) 2.0	378	2.28 (1.22) 3.0	0.04
20	I have been discriminated against by health professionals because of my mental health problems (Dc)	4	0	189	1.95 (1.28) 2.0	378	1.84 (1.30) 1.0	−0.11
21	People have avoided me because of my mental health problems (Dc)	4	0	189	2.30 (1.18) 3.0	378	2.04 (1.21) 2.0	−0.26

Table 7.4: Continued

Statement		Strongly Agree	Strongly Disagree	UK Sample		Canadian Sample		Mean Difference
				Response *n*	Mean (SD) Median	Response *n*	Mean (SD) Median	
22	People have insulted me because of my mental health problems (Dc)	4	0	192	2.01 (1.20) 2.0	378	2.12 (1.25) 2.0	0.11
23	Having had mental health problems has made me a stronger person (P)	0	4	188	1.78 (1.23) 2.0	375	1.35 (1.14) 1.0	−0.43*U
24	I do not feel embarrassed because of my mental health problems (D)	0	4	190	2.16 (1.22) 2.0	376	1.65 (1.22) 1.0	−0.51*U
25	I avoid telling people about my mental health problems (D)	4	0	191	2.68 (1.10) 3.0	377	2.29 (1.17) 3.0	−0.39*U
26	Having had mental health problems makes me feel that life is unfair (Dc)	4	0	191	2.53 (1.16) 3.0	375	2.06 (1.18) 2.0	−0.47*U
27	I feel the need to hide my mental health problems from my friends (D)	4	0	190	2.12 (1.22) 2.0	376	1.70 (1.18) 1.0	−0.42*U
28	I find it hard telling people I have mental health problems	4	0	191	2.70 (1.16) 3.0	376	2.10 (1.18) 2.0	−0.60*U

Notes: D, disclosure; Dc, discrimination; P, positive aspects; *U, UK sample reported higher mean score ($p < 0.0016$)

Issues in the United Kingdom

UK participants experienced more stigma on 12 items of the Stigma Scale (see Table 7.4). Significantly more UK participants reported feeling bad about having mental health problems (mean difference –0.69, $p < 0.0016$), feeling alone because of their mental health problems (mean difference –0.53, $p < 0.0016$), and feeling embarrassed because of their mental health problems (mean difference –0.51, $p < 0.0016$). UK participants indicated that they worried about telling people they received psychological treatment (mean difference –0.51, $p < 0.0016$) and/or that they took medicine/tablets for mental health problems (mean difference –0.67, $p < 0.0016$) significantly more than Canadian participants.

In terms of disclosure, UK participants indicated that they were significantly more scared of how people would react if they found out about their mental health problems (mean difference –0.57, $p < 0.0016$), avoided telling people about their mental health problems (mean difference –0.39, $p < 0.0016$), minded if people in their neighbourhood knew about their mental health problems (mean difference –0.45, $p < 0.0016$), felt the need to hide their mental health problems from their friends (mean difference –0.42, $p < 0.0016$), and generally found it hard to tell others about their mental health problems (mean difference –0.60, $p < 0.0016$). Finally, significantly fewer UK participants agreed with the notion that having a mental illness made them a stronger person (mean difference –0.43, $p < 0.0016$), and significantly more UK participants felt having mental health problems made them feel life was unfair (mean difference –0.47, $p < 0.0016$). The results demonstrate that individuals in the UK feel more negatively about their mental illnesses and are more hesitant to disclose mental illness information to friends and acquaintances when compared to Canadian participants.

Common Issues

There were 16 items on the Stigma Scale that elicited similar results between Canadian and UK participants. Both Canadian and UK participants reported that they somewhat agreed they had been talked down to because of their mental health problems and that they had some trouble from other people because of their mental health problems. Neither set of participants agreed or disagreed as to whether they had been insulted because of their mental health problems, whether the reactions of others made them keep their mental illness information to themselves, or whether they were angry with the way others have reacted to their mental health problems. In terms of specific discrimination, participants reported similar rates of discrimination from police, employers, the education system, and healthcare providers, with results indicating that participants somewhat disagreed to experiencing discrimination from all sources. Both Canadian and UK participants agreed with the notion that some people with mental health problems are

Joe rests while the Impact Junk Solutions crew begins to deconstruct a table too large to carry out of an assisted living facility near downtown London, Ontario, in March 2014.
Source: Photo by Justin Langille

dangerous. Both sets of participants agreed that having mental health problems made them more understanding people and more accepting of others. However, both sets of participants also agreed with the statement that they would have had better chances in life if they did not have mental health problems. Canadian participants did not report significantly more stigma than UK participants on any of the scale items.

4. DISCUSSION

This study was the first in Canada to use the full Stigma Scale (King et al., 2007) as a measure of mental illness stigma. While other studies throughout North America have used excerpts of the scale or modified it to fit other populations, we have used the scale in its entirety for the population for which it was designed.

As this was the first study to use this scale in Canada, complete results for both the Canadian sample and the original pilot sample from King et al. (2007) were provided. This allows a full description of similarities and differences between the two geographic regions concerning their stigma experiences.

Despite the difference in time between the two samples, there were several similarities. In general, both samples reported experiencing degrees of mental illness stigma, including being talked down to because they had a mental illness and believing they would have had better chances in life if they did not have mental health problems. Neither sample agreed with statements that they had been discriminated against by police, employers, the education system, or health-care providers, groups that have previously been identified as being particularly stigmatizing (Leff & Warner, 2006; Pinfold et al., 2003; Schulze & Angermeyer, 2003). These results are positive and suggest that attitudes towards mental illness may be evolving among various groups of people. Further, both sets of participants agreed with the notions that having mental health problems made them more understanding and accepting people. While the results demonstrate that stigma continues to exist, some specific findings indicate that discrimination within certain social groups may be improving and people with mental illness are better able to acknowledge the positive impact mental illness has had on their acceptance of others, which in turn can have a positive effect upon social inclusion.

There were also several differences between the two samples. UK participants reported significantly more stigma than Canadian participants on close to half of the scale items, including fear of telling others about their mental illness and hesitation to disclose mental illness information. In contrast, Canadian participants did not report significantly more stigma on any scale items, indicating that efforts to reduce stigma in Canada may be particularly effective. There is no established empirical explanation for what has led to differences between Canada and the UK with regards to their distinct experiences with stigma as it pertains to mental health. However, one needs to examine not only policies and educational practices pertaining to mental health and mental illness but the overall economic and ideological differences in policies between the two nations. Those with mental health issues have routinely been oppressed (Forchuk et al., 2011); however, while Canada has followed the UK in neoliberal ideology beginning in the latter half of the 20th century, the economic fallout of the 21st century has not been as harsh and thus there has been less need to further marginalize traditional targets. As well, in Canada there has been an active media campaign regarding issues of mental health, including focusing upon workplace mental health issues, sponsored by the Conference Board of Canada and leading corporations including Bell Canada and the Toronto Dominion Bank (Thorpe & Chénier, 2011). As well, changes to occupational health and safety policy have occurred, which may help to explain the distinction between the nations (Edwards, 2014).

Implications

The current results have provided insight into the stigma experiences of Canadian participants and compared them to UK findings for the purposes of identifying similarities and differences between the distinct geographic regions. The overall results are clear: stigma continues to exist for mental health consumer-survivors. Despite recent campaigns to eradicate stigma, such as the Opening Minds campaign in Canada (Mental Health Commission of Canada, 2014b) and the Time to Change (2014) campaign in the UK, mental health consumer-survivors continue to be a disenfranchised and marginalized group who feel socially excluded and that their opportunities in life have been limited by their mental health issues. There have undoubtedly been some improvements in stigmatizing attitudes and social exclusion in recent years, demonstrated by participants reporting little discrimination from police, employers, the education system, and health-care providers. However, participants within both countries reported both public stigma and internalized stigma in their lives, factors that contribute to social exclusion. Taken together, these results indicate the need for continued, and perhaps varied, anti-stigma methods to continue to enhance the social inclusion of this population. Many anti-stigma programs target specific groups; for example, the Opening Minds campaign has targeted youth, employers, health-care professionals, and the media (Mental Health Commission of Canada, 2014b). Based upon the current findings, the campaign appears to be successful in reaching its target groups. However, other members of the public may be missed within the campaign reach if they are not specifically identified. Varied methods for the general population and other targeted groups may be required to reduce stigma in areas that continue to be problematic for mental health consumer-survivors.

Interestingly, both sets of participants agreed with the notion that individuals with mental illness can be dangerous. Stuart (2003) concluded his review of mental health and violence literature with the following quote: "Members of the public undoubtedly exaggerate both the strength of the relationship between major mental disorders and violence, as well as their own personal risk from the severely mentally ill" (p. 124). Exaggerated beliefs that others with mental illness are dangerous may contribute to personal shame and embarrassment when one has a mental illness. Anti-stigma programs may benefit from working to dispel misguided notions about the connection between mental illness and violence, both for members of the general public and for mental health consumer-survivors who may be misinformed about the connection as well.

Limitations

This study employed only cross-sectional data. While the large-scale program is longitudinal, only data from the first year of the program was collected. It is possible that stigma experiences vary over time and may be impacted by other life circumstances. The current study extracted data from one point in time, so variations in experiences over time and the factors associated with those changes could not be examined. Further, data was collected from one geographic region in Canada through quota sampling. Generalization to other regions in Canada is therefore limited based on the sampling strategy used. While these results provided insight into the stigma experiences of Canadian participants, the findings require replication in other Canadian regions before basing interventions and programs on them.

5. CONCLUSION

The current study provided foundational results of the Stigma Scale in a Canadian context. Not surprisingly, stigma remains an issue for Canadians with mental health issues, contributing to their perceptions of social exclusion. However, when compared to participants from the United Kingdom, Canadian participants reported less stigma across several domains. These findings indicate that Canadian anti-stigma efforts appear to have had some successes in lessening stigma experiences for mental health consumer-survivors, though continued and varied efforts are necessary to truly eliminate stigma in society. As Canadian participants reported fewer stigma experiences, anti-stigma efforts within the UK, and perhaps other jurisdictions as well, may benefit from incorporating some Canadian methods into their anti-stigma programs to create greater social inclusion.

REFERENCES

Arboleda-Flórez, J., & Stuart, H. (2012). From sin to science: Fighting the stigmatization of mental illness. *The Canadian Journal of Psychiatry, 57*(8), 457–463.

Blood, R., Putnis, P., & Pirkis, J. (2002). Mental illness news as violence: A news frame analysis of the reporting and portrayal of mental health and illness in Australian media. *Australian Journal of Communication, 29*(2), 59–82.

Byrne, P. (2000). Stigma of mental illness and ways of diminishing it. *Advances in Psychiatric Treatment, 6*(1), 65–72.

Cechnicki, A., Angermeyer, M. C., & Bienlańska, A. (2011). Anticipated and experienced stigma among people with schizophrenia: Its nature and correlates *Social Psychiatry and Psychiatric Epidemiology, 46*(7), 643–650.

Chronister, J., Chou, C.-C., & Liao, H.-Y. (2013). The role of stigma coping and social support in mediating the effect of societal stigma on internalized stigma, mental health recovery, and quality of life among people with serious mental illness. *Journal of Community Psychology, 41*(5), 582–600.

Conrad-Garrisi, D. (2011). Inter/intrapersonal variables and readiness for change on achieving recovery. *Wayne State University Dissertations*, 232.

Corrigan, P., Markowitz, F. E., Watson, A., Rowan, D., & Kubiak, M. (2003). An attribution model of public discrimination towards persons with mental illness. *Journal of Health and Social Behavior, 44*(2), 162–179.

Corrigan, P. W., & Watson, A. C. (2007). The stigma of psychiatric disorders and the gender, ethnicity, and education of the perceiver. *Community Mental Health Journal, 43*(5), 439–458.

Crisp, A. H., Gelder, M. G., Rix, S., Meltzer, H. I., & Rowlands, O. J. (2000). Stigmatisation of people with mental illnesses. *The British Journal of Psychiatry, 177*(1), 4–7.

Csiernik, R., Forchuk, C., Speechley, M., & Ward-Griffin, C. (2007). De "myth" ifying mental health—findings from a Community University Research Alliance (CURA). *Critical Social Work, 8*(1), 1–15.

Dinos, S., Stevens, S., Serfaty, M., Weich, S., & King, M. (2004). Stigma: The feelings and experiences of 46 people with mental illness: Qualitative study. *The British Journal of Psychiatry, 184*(2), 176–181.

Edwards, C. A. (2014). Ontario WSAIT strikes down mental stress restrictions. *Canadian Occupational Safety*. Retrieved from http://www.cos-mag.com/legal/legal-columns/4119-ontario-wsib-strikes-down-mental-stress-restrictions.html

Forchuk, C., Csiernik, R., & Jensen, E. (Eds.). (2011). *Homelessness, housing and mental health: Finding truths—creating change*. Toronto, ON: Canadian Scholars' Press.

Hall, T. L. (2012). How would you feel? Stigma and self-esteem in student responses to intimate partner violence vignettes. *UMI Dissertations Publishing*, 1512041.

King, M., Dinos, S., Shaw, J., Watson, R., Stevens, S., Passetti, F., … Serfaty, M. (2007). The Stigma Scale: Development of a standardized measure of the stigma of mental illness. *The British Journal of Psychiatry, 190*(2), 248–254.

Leff, J., & Warner, R. (2006). *Social inclusion of people with mental illness*. Cambridge, UK: Cambridge University Press.

Livingston, J. D., & Boyd, J. E. (2010). Correlates and consequences of internalized stigma for people living with mental illness: A systematic review and meta-analysis. *Social Science and Medicine, 71*(12), 2150–2161.

Mental Health Commission of Canada. (2014a). *Stigma and discrimination*. Retrieved from http://www.mentalhealthcommission.ca/English/issues/stigma?terminitial=31

Mental Health Commission of Canada. (2014b). *Initiatives: Opening minds*. Retrieved from https://www.mentalhealthcommission.ca/English/opening-minds

Moses, T. (2010). Being treated differently: Stigma experiences with family, peers, and school staff among adolescents with mental health disorders. *Social Science & Medicine, 70*(7), 985–993.

Perlick, D. A., Rosenheck, R. A., Clarkin, J. F., Sirey, J. A., Salahi, J. Struening, E. L., & Link, B. G. (2001). Stigma as a barrier to recovery: Adverse effects of perceived stigma on social adaptation of persons diagnosed with bipolar affective disorder. *Psychiatric Services, 52*(12), 1627–1632.

Pinfold, V., Huxley, P., Thornicroft, G., Farmer, P., Toulmin, H., & Graham, T. (2003). Reducing psychiatric stigma and discrimination: Evaluating an educational intervention with the police force in England. *Social Psychiatry and Psychiatric Epidemiology, 38*(6), 337–344.

Sanders, J. M. (2012). Use of mutual support to counteract the effects of socially constructed stigma: Gender and drug addiction. *Journal of Groups in Addiction & Recovery, 7*(2–4), 237–252.

Schulze, B., & Angermeyer, M. C. (2003). Subjective experiences of stigma: A focus group study of schizophrenic patients, their relatives and mental health professionals. *Social Science and Medicine, 56*(2), 299–312.

Schwenk, T. L., Davis, L., & Wimsatt, L. A. (2010). Depression, stigma, and suicidal ideation in medical students. *Journal of the American Medical Association, 304*(11), 1181–1190.

Stuart, H. (2003). Violence and mental illness: An overview. *World Psychiatry, 2*(2), 121–124.

Thorpe, K., & Chénier, L. (2011). *Building mentally healthy workplaces: Perspectives of Canadian workers and front-line managers*. Ottawa, ON: Conference Board of Canada.

Time to Change. (2014). About mental health. Retrieved from http://www.time-to-change.org.uk/talk-about-mental-health

Walston, G. A. (2012). Mental health recovery in schizophrenia: Illness acceptance as a mediator for recovery. *ProQuest Information & Learning*, AA13493644.

Wang, J., & Lai, D. (2008). The relationship between mental health literacy, personal contacts and personal stigma against depression. *Journal of Affective Disorders, 110*(1–2), 191–196.

Wright, E. R., Gronfein, W. P., & Owens, T. J. (2000). Deinstitutionalization, social rejection, and the self-esteem of former mental patients. *Journal of Health and Social Behavior, 41*(1), 68–90.

Yanos, P. T., Roe, D., & Lysaker, P. H. (2010). The impact of illness identity on recovery from severe mental illness. *American Journal of Psychiatric Rehabilitation, 13*(2), 73–93.

SECTION III

BECOMING SOCIALLY EXCLUDED

Belongingness is a core human desire. It is discussed in the literature of all helping professions and is a focus of individual, family, group, and community-focused counselling. Section III of the book examines, in depth, implications of not belonging, of becoming socially excluded, and how this affects different mental health consumer-survivor and homeless subgroups.

The opening chapter, "Poverty Trajectories Experienced by Persons with Mental Illness," provides a better understanding of the relationship between mental illness, poverty, and becoming socially excluded, by comparing three groups of individuals with mental illness in Canada: those who see their financial status as improving, worsening, or staying the same. Qualitative data was collected from 34 focus group participants who highlighted facilitators and barriers to financial improvement that moved them towards or further away from participation in the mainstream, and thus to belonging.

In Chapter 9, "Using a Capabilities Approach to Understand Poverty and Social Inclusion of Mental Health Consumer-Survivors," a large mixed-methods longitudinal study was used to explore the capabilities approach and its application to these intersecting issues. Using thematic coding, four key ideas emerged: (1) poverty, "You just try to survive"; (2) stigma, "People treat you like trash"; (3) shared concern and advocacy, "Everyone deserves housing"; and again, not surprisingly, (4) belonging, or the lack thereof, "You feel like you don't belong." The analysis provided offers a deeper understanding of poverty and other social determinants of the experiences of mental health consumer-survivors, including the synergism of poverty and social exclusion.

Chapter 10, "Until You Hit Rock Bottom There's No Support," examines the multidimensional nature of social exclusion in the lives of mothers experiencing homelessness in Southwestern Ontario. The chapter reports findings from one segment of a larger study that critically examined the sociopolitical context, health needs, exclusionary and inclusionary forces, and strategies of resistance demonstrated by mothers experiencing homelessness. Central to the women's experiences of mothering while homeless were their interactions with "the system." The contradictory nature of these systems was categorized into four subthemes: (1) "Until you hit rock bottom there's no support," (2) "It's just not enough": Insufficient support, (3) "Help comes with a price": Support with surveillance, and (4) "Every shelter is so different": Organizational philosophies impacting support. The contradictory nature of the system creates an illusion of support, but in the mothers' lived realities existing systems actually perpetuated experiences of exclusion in spaces ironically designed to enhance inclusion.

The raw emotion of those who offered insights into their lived experience is evidenced in the title of Chapter 11, "Sheltering Indigenous Women with Mental Illness in Ontario: Being 'Kicked' and Nurtured." For individuals living with mental health challenges, the provision of homeless shelters can offer a temporary respite during times of overwhelming life circumstances. There is, however, limited evidence regarding the subjective experience of Indigenous women in Canada who have relied upon shelter services to temporarily avoid homelessness. This chapter helps the reader to develop an understanding of the day-to-day experiences of Indigenous women as they seek and provide safety, comfort, health, and healing in the context of mental illness and insecure housing. Narrative analysis was used to identify common experiences among 11 shelter service users and 10 shelter service providers, all of whom were Indigenous women. Regardless of whether the women received or provided shelter services, they consistently described experiences about being "kicked" and nurtured. Their stories about being "kicked" described experiences associated with compounding losses. Juxtaposed to this reality were accounts about being nurtured or "lifting each other up." Nurturing relations were essential to address the pervasive health and social disparities experienced by the women. Relationships within homeless shelters were directed towards supporting the health and well-being of individual women within their broader community.

Chapters 12 and 13 examine a group of homeless individuals whose social exclusion has only recently become recognized across Canada: veterans. Major Steven D. Pirie, who served at Kandahar Air Base, Afghanistan, speaks of his personal experience, what it is like to be in a war zone, and the impacts it leaves in his contribution, entitled "The Mental Health of Those Who Serve Canada." While historically the physical risk has been known and appreciated among activity duty combatants, it is only recently and slowly that the mental health issues that military service creates have become recognized. Major Pirie asks readers to consider the unique circumstances faced by Canadian veterans and the importance of learning more about this group and the impact military service has upon their mental health and social inclusion when they leave active duty. These ideas are expanded upon in the following chapter, "Addressing Homelessness among Canadian Veterans." The authors discuss the Canadian Model for Housing and Support for Veterans Experiencing Homelessness, which began in 2012 as a project

Moving from Exclusion to Inclusion: Personal. Connect (peer support) founder Michelle takes a breath in front of her home in London, Ontario. Throughout her recovery journey, Michelle has relied on relaxing deep breathing techniques to support her recovery from mental illness.

Source: Photo by Justin Langille

Moving from Exclusion to Inclusion: Community. A Connect (peer support) group member leaves a group session at the Huron Street Canadian Mental Health Association offices. The group offers individuals suffering mental illness a chance to relate to others and avoid the isolation that can result from depression, anxiety, and other mental illnesses.
Source: Photo by Justin Langille

to generate knowledge and to test housing-with-support strategies for addressing homelessness among Canadian veterans in Victoria, Calgary, London, and Toronto. Chapter 13 outlines the project in detail, highlights research findings, and concludes by providing suggestions to strengthen our capacity to respond to the issue of veteran homelessness across Canada.

CHAPTER 8

Poverty Trajectories Experienced by Persons with Mental Illness

Cheryl Forchuk, Phyllis Montgomery, Abraham Rudnick, Pam Lahey, Benita Cohen, Ruth Schofield, Stewart E. Perry, Robin Coatsworth-Puspoky, Betty Edwards, Bethany Butzer, and Amanda Meier

1. INTRODUCTION

Research presented thus far has demonstrated how poverty and mental health issues are linked, and that the alleviation of poverty is a crucial factor in the prevention of and recovery from mental illness (Canadian Mental Health Association [CMHA], 2007; Frankel, 1996; Lightman et al., 2009; Ross et al., 2000; Wilton, 2004a). The goal of this study was to gain insight into the relationship between poverty and mental illness by exploring and describing the financial experiences of individuals living with mental health issues. This inquiry allowed for an in-depth examination of the multifaceted and complex relationship between poverty and mental illness. It also provided insight into targeted interventions for social reintegration in which the economic/financial influences on mental illness and social inclusion are considered.

Definitions of Poverty

In the past decade, literature about the number of people who are poor, how to define and measure poverty, what causes and sustains poverty, and the health implications of poverty at individual, community, and global levels has become more prevalent. In Canada, as elsewhere, definitions of poverty are contested, and there is not a single poverty-line measure. From a monetary perspective, poverty is calculated as 50% of the median income in Ontario (Ministry of Children, Community and Social Services, 2013). Canadian families and unattached individuals had a median after-tax income of $57,000 in 2016 (Statistics Canada, 2018), meaning that having an after-tax income of less than $28,500 would be considered poor. From a physical subsistence perspective, poverty is described as experiencing varying levels of material and social deprivation of basic life necessities relative to a combination of educational, economic, and occupational criteria (Canadian Institute for Health Information, 2008; Williamson & Reutter, 1999).

Regardless of the definition, such conditions impose limitations on the capacity of persons and communities to achieve their full potential (Raphael, 2011). Using Statistics Canada data, the overall poverty rate for all Canadians was 18.7% in the mid-1980s; by 2008, the rate decreased to 13.6% (Raphael, 2011). Although Raphael (2011) attributes the decline to social capital, social relations that have productive benefits, these rates remain high in comparison to other developed nations. Further, these figures suggest poverty's persistence and ongoing threat to the social fibre of Canadian society (Balmer et al., 2010).

Poverty and Mental Illness: Double Jeopardy

The effects of poverty on health have been known since the 19th century (Raphael, 2016). To explain mental health differences between social groups, Canadian and American psychiatric epidemiology studies consistently show that lower social classes have higher rates of mental illness (Frankel, 1996). Using data from Statistics Canada's National Population Health Survey, Ross et al. (2000) found that adults who are low income are 2.4 times more likely to report high mental health distress compared to adults who are high income and 1.8 times more likely than adults who are middle income. The poorest Canadians have 128% more mental and behavioural disorders than their higher-income counterparts (CMHA, 2007; Lightman et al., 2009). In particular to Canadian adults with mental illness, 27% experience poverty compared to 13% of persons who are non-disabled (Wilton, 2004b).

People with mental illness are consistently overrepresented among the homeless population, and psychiatric illness is a common risk factor for homelessness (Eynan et al., 2002; Kuno et al., 2000; Steinhaus et al., 2004; Sullivan et al., 2000). In their examination of the demographic characteristics of homeless shelter users, Goering et al. (2002) found that approximately two-thirds of their sample had been diagnosed with a mental illness at some point in their lives. Data from the Homeless Individuals and Families Information System (HIFIS, 2011) highlight the social and financial costs involved in the complex interplay between poverty and mental illness.

Poverty Trajectories: An Alternative Approach

Prior research suggests that when poverty and mental illness occur together, the individual's experience is often different, and potentially more difficult, than when either situation occurs independently (Cohen, 2000). Researchers also suggest that individuals experience a variety of pathways leading into and out of poverty (McDonough et al., 2005). A few interventions aiming to alleviate poverty for individuals with mental illness have taken place. Ware and Goldfinger (1997) collected ethnographic data from 118 individuals with mental illness living in shelters in Boston, Massachusetts, over an 18-month period. The authors randomly assigned participants to live in subsidized independent apartments or in shared, staffed residences called evolving consumer households (ECHs). Their findings revealed that the two most successful methods to alleviate poverty for the ECH tenants were creating alternative sources of income and pooling resources among residents. Additional research has found that providing peer support and housing assistance upon psychiatric discharge is extremely helpful in preventing homelessness, which is an extreme outcome of poverty (Forchuk, Chan, et al., 1998; Forchuk et al., 2013a, 2013b; Forchuk, Jewell, et al., 1998; Forchuk et al., 2005).

Although some interventions have taken place to identify ways to alleviate poverty, research is still required to further understand the pathways leading into and out of poverty from the perspective of those living with mental illness.

This then leads to two pressing questions:

1. What "brings people up"? In other words, what types of resources, services, and support facilitate financial improvement for people with mental illness?
2. What "brings people down"? In other words, what challenges and barriers do people with mental illness face when trying to improve or maintain their financial situation?

2. METHOD

Design

An ethnographic approach was taken to address these two questions using data from a two-year mixed-method participatory action research (PAR) study. Focused ethnography was undertaken in order to concentrate on the specific issues surrounding economic status voiced by persons with mental illness and investigate the topic in a time-limited manner through focus group sessions with individuals who have experienced mental illness. The focus group sessions allowed for dialogue and interaction among study participants for a fuller exploration of the issues than could be obtained by interviews alone. Ethics approval was obtained from the Western University Research Ethics Board.

Setting

The setting was London, Ontario, Canada, a midsized city with a population of approximately 380,000, surrounded by rural areas. For individuals, the median total income in 2016 was $32,599, and for households, the median total income was $62,011. In London, the prevalence of low income in 2015 based on low-income cut-offs, after tax was 11.6%, representing 43,860 individuals. This was higher than rates for both Ontario (9.8%) and Canada (9.2%; City of London, 2018).

Sample

The research team used quota sampling to provide representation from all types of housing situations. Twenty-five percent of the sample was homeless, 25% resided in a group home, 25% were independently housed and unemployed, and 25% were

A canopy of trees envelops downtown London, Ontario, in August 2017.
Source: Photo by Justin Langille

independently housed and employed. Within each of the groups, 50% were male and 50% were female. To be eligible to participate, individuals were required to be 18 years or older; living with a self-identified mental illness for at least one year prior to data collection, including concurrent psychiatric diagnoses and substance misuse; able to comprehend, speak, and read English; and provide informed consent. Representatives from health and social service organizations including food banks, drop-in services, shelters, and community mental health clinics identified potential participants and invited them to participate in the study. Potential participants also responded to posters that were placed in community locations such as grocery stores and libraries. Research staff then met with potential participants to confirm eligibility and enrol them in the study.

In total, 250 people volunteered to participate in structured interviews. All of these individuals were also invited to participate in single-session focus groups. Interested participants were divided into three categories based on their responses to a financial status question during the quantitative interview: whether they reported their financial status as *getting better*, *staying the same*, or *getting worse* in the previous year. As fewer participants reported their financial status as improving compared to the other categories, all interested participants within the getting better category were invited to attend the appropriate focus group. As there were larger numbers of participants within the staying the same and getting worse groups, a subset of interested participants was randomly selected and invited to the appropriate focus groups. A total of 34 participants, 17 men and 17 women, participated in one of five focus groups. One focus group was held for the getting better category (n = 9), two focus groups were held for the staying the same category (n = 11 total), and two focus groups were held for the getting worse category (n = 14 total). The research team did not intentionally select equal numbers of males and females within the focus group sample; equal representation by males and females occurred by chance. Specific demographic information regarding the 34 focus group participants was not collected, as demographic information was available for the larger sample. Instead, sex and age were estimated by note-takers and integrated into the focus group transcripts.

Data Collection

Data were collected through in-depth focus groups, which met for one to two hours each within a hospital boardroom. The groups were audio-recorded, and these recordings were transcribed verbatim and validated by a second team member. In addition to the group facilitator, two note-takers attended each group and recorded field notes to assist in determining which participants made each comment and to note nonverbal communication. This information was integrated into the transcript such that the final document for each group included the verbal and nonverbal communication.

Data Analysis

Although data on the specific topic of interest was collected through a focused ethnography approach, the verbatim transcripts, with integrated field notes, were analyzed by a subset of the project researchers using Leininger's phases of ethnographic analysis (Leininger, 1985, 1987, 1990). In accordance with this method, the transcripts were coded according to the topics discussed (e.g., importance of helping each other, difficulties with income support programs). This was then further reviewed to identify thematic patterns. The data from each financial status category (getting better, staying the same, getting worse) were first analyzed separately and then compared and contrasted.

3. FINDINGS

Stuck in a Cycle

The qualitative analysis of the data revealed that participants' financial situations often followed a circular pattern, described as a cycle or trap that was difficult to escape:

> I'm not around a whole bunch of people where everybody's working and this guy's got a cottage and a boat and we're going camping next weekend. We're all here, all the time, stuck in a rut, with nothing to do, nowhere to go, nothing to eat and I got no extra money in my pocket to do anything. And when you've fallen into that cycle, it's a hard habit to break.
>
> Like you get stuck. As soon as someone finds out that you have a mental [illness]. Like I'm bipolar. So as soon as I say, "Well I'm bipolar," and the boss finds out, you're gone or, "Oh well I'm not going to hire her because she's unwell." And then you're stuck on disability support. When you're on a fixed income it is extremely hard to get yourself off that fixed income.
>
> We'll take away your house and we'll take away your furniture, put you back in jail, and start all over again and just keep going. And that's all it is a vicious cycle.

Facilitators for Improving One's Financial Situation

In addition to the overarching theme of feeling stuck in a cycle, the focus group discussions also highlighted several facilitators and barriers that the participants experienced when trying to improve their financial situation. Many of the facilitators and barriers were common across all three financial trajectory groups and are presented together. Facilitators and barriers that were specific to one or two financial trajectory groups are presented separately.

Participants in all three financial status categories were asked to identify factors that had helped them improve their financial situation. In other words, even though some participants felt that their overall financial situation was stagnant or worsening, they were asked to discuss factors that have helped them. This highlights the important consideration that financial status is not unidirectional.

Common Facilitators among Financial Trajectory Groups

Supportive Relationships

Participants expressed the importance of having supportive relationships with individuals and agencies. These relationships appeared to improve participants' financial status in a variety of ways. Some examples of supportive relationships included having an understanding landlord when rent is late, having friends and family to "prop you up" emotionally, and having an employer who understands potential difficulties associated with having a mental illness. More specifically, advocates from peer support or government agencies were viewed as being extremely helpful in increasing participants' knowledge of the resources that were available to them:

> I've had people to advocate on my behalf though and that was through counsellors and doctors and that kind of thing. If I hadn't, I probably would not be aware of any of the services available or be able to push through in order to get it.

Part-Time Work

Participants reported that obtaining a part-time job helped them financially: "I was waiting for disability staying at the [shelter]. And my financial situation improved because I got work in the kitchen. So, I make an extra $200 a month."

A desire for full-time work was not expressed by participants. It is unclear whether this reflects an inability of the participants to get full-time work, their

Goodwill RMHC Social Enterprise program employee Donald applies reflective tape to a stack of pylons in March 2014.
Source: Photo by Justin Langille

perception that no one would hire them for a full-time job, or a desire to work only part-time.

Government-Supported Income Increases

Increases in government-funded income helped improve participants' financial situations. Some participants specifically described the financial improvements that occurred when switching from Ontario Works (general welfare) to Ontario Disability Support Program (disability support). In particular, disability support was viewed as providing a more consistent, stable income, whereas general welfare had many rules in which participants could lose income if they were receiving support from other sources: "On welfare you go to school, they dock you. You do everything you do, they dock you. On disability they don't" and "Welfare hounds for every little thing but disability, there's your money every month."

Distinct Facilitators between Financial Trajectory Groups

Overcoming Addiction

Participants in the getting better category discussed that their experiences of poverty were often intertwined with addiction to drugs and alcohol. Becoming sober aided in improving their financial situation by freeing up money to spend on expenses like rent and food:

> I have probably been in poverty ever since childhood and anyone I have ever known has, mostly drugs and I mean, poverty. But I have been clean now for almost a year and since I got out of that, things have just opened right up ... I don't feel that poor inside anymore.
>
> A big part of my poverty was being intertwined with drugs. And a lot of times, those go hand in hand.

Members of the getting worse and staying the same categories did not mention being helped by overcoming addiction. This could be because the individuals in these categories continued to struggle with addiction, that they never had addiction issues, or that those who had an addiction did not mention it in their group session.

Education

Educational programs helped participants in the staying the same category improve their financial situation. By sharing this information, these participants not only informed the results of the present study but also helped make the other participants in their focus group aware of resources that could help them. This type of information exchange revealed how such groups can serve a research and practical purpose. Members of the getting better category also shared that employment courses were helpful in improving their financial situation:

> It's a two-week course called Career Directions. And it's like a personality kind of thing, it finds out where you're going and possible directions where you might want to go. And it's like: Whoa! Opening up the curtains wide where it was all dark for me.

Barriers to Improving One's Financial Situation

Similar to the first research question, participants were asked to identify factors that had contributed negatively to their financial situation. In other words, even though some participants felt that their overall financial situation was getting better, they were still asked to discuss factors that have brought them down. Again, this highlights the fact that financial status is often in flux.

Common Barriers among Financial Trajectory Groups

FEELINGS OF HOPELESSNESS AND POWERLESSNESS

Participants expressed a profound sense of hopelessness and powerlessness, many believing that their futures felt bleak. They had nowhere to go, nothing to do, and no way to change their situations. They felt trapped in a downward spiral and unable to get out. They hoped that their problems would go away, but felt powerless to do anything about it:

> Do you remember when you were a little kid? And you went to mommy and daddy and you needed that extra 10 dollars to go to the movies and they told you no? Well we're asking total strangers for that extra 10 dollars and constantly hearing no.
>
> The light at the end of the tunnel. For a lot of people there isn't one … you get so much on your plate and you're just sagging under the weight.
>
> We're the bottom of the bottom of the bottom … you're completely helpless.
>
> We know what the problems are but we don't know how to fix them … or we don't have the money or the connections obviously to fix anything.

LACK OF AWARENESS OF RESOURCES

Focus group participants stated that information on available services, money, and resources was not readily available to them. A few participants praised workers who gave them good information; however, one participant expressed suspicion about government workers hiding money and resources. In general, the participants found it difficult to navigate available resources and expressed a desire to have someone assist them. It could be the case that the stress of living in poverty makes it difficult for people to cognitively process, work through, and select appropriate resources.

> When you're going through hell, a piece of paper isn't going to help you, is it? You need someone to navigate that piece of paper with you.

STIGMA/DISCRIMINATION

Stigma and discrimination from friends, family, employers, and strangers contributed negatively to participants' financial situation. Participants expressed frustration at the common belief that they were receiving government assistance because they were too lazy to get a job or that they were all addicted to drugs/alcohol. This led some participants to hide their mental illness from others due to fear of being stigmatized. For example, one participant described lying and telling someone that he was receiving disability support for a back injury, not mental illness, because people had discriminated against his mental illness in the past. There was a strong sense that participants wanted others to know that they were not receiving social assistance simply because they wanted to: "Poverty will never change until they realize that we're not here because we want to be" and "A lot of people don't understand that most of us aren't here because we choose to be. You know, we're here because, for whatever reason, we're sick or we lost our job and we ran into issues."

EMPLOYMENT-RELATED DIFFICULTIES

Not surprisingly, work-related difficulties affected participants' financial status in a negative way. These difficulties appeared to take place in two main areas: difficulties at current jobs and difficulties obtaining employment. Difficulties within current jobs centred on a lack of understanding from employers: "The thing is, is that with mental illness ... you don't want to disclose it to your employer because you get judged."

Participants perceived that they had difficulties obtaining employment because of discrimination from potential employers and resume gaps that made it difficult to find employment after disability. Some participants also mentioned a lack of motivation to obtain employment because earnings were deducted from their government income and they would lose privileges such as bus passes.

EDUCATIONAL LIMITATIONS

A lack of financial stability precluded participants from taking advantage of educational opportunities. For example, one participant noted that she could not afford to pay a $50 deposit on textbooks when she was living on $100 per month. Without any opportunities to improve their education, the participants felt that they could not get ahead financially:

> I want to go back to school ... and she [worker] would not allow me to go to school to better myself so I can get off the system. They just said they can't fund that sort of thing ... if they were smart they would, like for people that really want to go get that education they would actually help see them succeed in that so they can get themselves better. Otherwise it's just going to be another, you know, five years I might be on the system.

ISSUES WITH CHILDREN

Financial instability contributed to several issues in caring for children. Specifically, participants experienced difficulties in maintaining custody of children when they were dealing with health and financial issues. Participants also found it difficult to secure adequate funding for their families with children or for children with special needs.

> They should separate families from single people. Because kids are going to grow up, fortunately, and get less expensive. But it's hard as a family.

Distinct Barriers between Financial Trajectory Groups

HOUSING ISSUES

Members of the getting worse category experienced difficulties around the cost of living and wait times for low-income housing. Participants in the staying the same and getting better categories both discussed that living in low-income housing often contributes to addiction through contact with neighbours who have addiction issues. Members of the getting better category also experienced bullying by landlords that contributed negatively to their financial situation.

ISSUES WITH GOVERNMENT ASSISTANCE

Issues with government assistance was a common barrier to financial stability. However, the focus of this issue was different among the categories. Participants in the getting worse category expressed a fear of losing government assistance, as this would also result in losing medical benefits and having to start over financially:

> Welfare automatically gives you medical coverage, dental coverage. I mean it's not the greatest, but I know for me when I go back to work, I still have to start at square one. I'm not going to have benefits for three months.

Members of the staying the same category felt they were not getting a large enough increase in government assistance over time:

> For the longest time disability support did not receive any increase where welfare was getting an increase every year. You get it in November every year, you get a 2% increase, that's it, that's a bag of milk a month.

Participants in the getting better category discussed the lack of incentive to get off of government assistance: "It's like a life sentence and you don't have any incentive to get work and get up off disability." In general, it appears that the members of all three financial status categories encountered issues with government assistance; however, they perceived these issues in distinct ways.

4. DISCUSSION

This research highlighted several important considerations regarding poverty and mental illness. Prior research tended to focus solely on the downward financial drift that can happen when poverty and mental illness co-occur (Hurst, 2007; Jarvis, 2007; Leff & Warner, 2006; Perry, 1996). However, participants in the present study self-identified as belonging to one of three distinct financial status categories: getting worse, staying the same, getting better. This suggests that individuals with mental illness can experience a variety of poverty trajectories. Although some participants did describe feeling stuck in a downward financial cycle, this was not the case for everyone.

The research also revealed that members of all three financial status categories brought up very similar facilitators and barriers to improving their financial situation, suggesting that individuals who experience poverty and mental illness often encounter similar issues (McDonough et al., 2005). It is important to note, however, that subtle differences were found between the groups with regards to certain facilitators and barriers. For example, individuals in the getting better category spoke about the importance of overcoming addiction to facilitate financial and emotional improvement, whereas members of the other categories did not. Previous poverty alleviation interventions have identified a number of ways in which to reduce poverty for individuals with mental illness, including the creation of alternate sources of income, the pooling of resources among co-tenants, and providing peer support to assist with the search for housing (Forchuk et al., 2013a; Forchuk et al., 2005; Ware & Goldfinger, 1997). Participants in the current study provided support for the notion that alternative and additional sources of income are necessary for the alleviation of poverty, including increased government assistance and more educational and subsequent employment opportunities. Peer support in the form of advocacy was viewed as a vital relationship to have when attempting to improve one's financial situation. Although participants in the current study did not specifically discuss the idea of pooling resources, participants agreed with the potential usefulness of other poverty alleviation strategies from earlier interventions.

Implications

The majority of the facilitators and barriers that were raised in the focus group discussions related to broad-level systems and structures such as government assistance, education, employment. These findings are consistent with other research indicating the relationship between poverty and mental illness is a multidimensional systemic social issue (Curtis et al., 2006; Draine et al., 2002; Nelson et al., 2003). Systems-level solutions are therefore necessary to improve the financial status of individuals with mental illness, a finding that is consistent with evidence from other studies regarding the connection between community context, public policy, and social inclusion in community well-being and overall quality of life (Raphael et al., 2000). Participants in this study shared that increases in government assistance, as well as education and employment opportunities, helped them improve their financial situation. However, many participants also expressed frustration over the same factors, noting that in many cases, there was inadequate funding and support allotted to these areas.

Evidence on the link between poverty and mental illness, let alone social inclusion, has been slow to make its way into public policy in Ontario, the rest of Canada, and around the world. Since the 2008 economic downturn, the Ontario government has shifted to an austerity agenda and has been aggressive in its efforts to find cost savings within government, something witnessed with the election of a new Conservative government in 2018. Unfortunately, this is often done at the expense of the most marginalized populations.

Ontario is not the only area facing these issues. As countries around the world continue to struggle with economic uncertainty, funding for social assistance and mental health programs continues to face reductions (Aviram et al., 2012). Thus, the likelihood of improving the income of those with mental illness is currently questionable, despite the current findings that suggest that funding would be highly beneficial not only for improving the lives of individuals with mental illness but also for reducing the financial burden placed on government systems when support is unavailable. Increased awareness of these issues and findings is necessary when new government policies are in development.

It is also important to keep in mind that the participants revealed several non-systems-level facilitators and barriers, such as having supportive relationships or experiencing housing issues. This finding suggests that financial status improvements can also be achieved by focusing on community- and individual-level interventions. Previous interventions and current findings have found that advocacy through peer support and the creation of alternate or additional sources of income can improve financial outcomes for individuals with mental illness and in turn decrease feelings of social exclusion (Forchuk et al., 2013a; Forchuk et al., 2005; Ware & Goldfinger, 1997).

REFERENCES

Aviram, U., Ginath, Y., & Roe, D. (2012). Mental health reforms in Europe: Israel's rehabilitation in the community of persons with mental disabilities law: Challenges and opportunities. *Psychiatric Services, 63*(2), 110–112.

Balmer, B., Dineen, M., & Swift, J. (2010). *Persistent poverty: Voices from the margins.* Toronto, ON: Between the Lines.

Canadian Institute for Health Information. (2008). *Reducing gaps in health: A focus on socio-economic status in urban Canada.* Ottawa, ON: Author.

Canadian Mental Health Association [CMHA]. (2007). *Poverty and mental illness.* Retrieved from https://ontario.cmha.ca/documents/poverty-and-mental-illness/

City of London. (2018). *Poverty and income.* Retrieved from https://www.london.ca/About-London/community-statistics/social-issues/Pages/Poverty.aspx

Cohen, C. I. (2000). Overcoming social amnesia: The role for a social perspective in psychiatric research and practice. *Psychiatric Services, 51*(1), 72–78.

Curtis, S., Copeland, A., Fagg, J., Congdon, P., Almog, M., & Fitzpatrick, J. (2006). The ecological relationship between deprivation, social isolation and rates of hospital admission for acute psychiatric care: A comparison of London and New York City. *Health & Place, 12*(1), 19–37.

Draine, J., Salzer, M., Culhane, D., & Hadley, T. (2002). Poverty, social problems, and serious mental illness. *Psychiatric Services, 53*(7), 899–900.

Eynan, R., Langley, J., Tolomiczenko, G., Rhodes, A. E., Links, P., Wasylenki, D., & Goering, P. (2002). The association between homelessness and suicidal ideation and behaviors: Results of a cross-sectional survey. *Suicide and Life-Threatening Behavior, 32*(4), 418–427.

Forchuk, C., Chan, L., Schofield, R., Martin, M. L., Sircelj, M., Woodcox, V., … Overby, B. (1998). Bridging the discharge process. *Canadian Nurse, 94*(3), 22–26.

Forchuk, C., Godin, M., Hoch, J. S., Kingston-MacClure, S., Jeng, M. S., Puddy, L., … Jensen, E. (2013a). Preventing homelessness after discharge from psychiatric wards: Perspectives of consumers and staff. *Journal of Psychosocial Nursing and Mental Health Services, 51*(3), 24–31.

Forchuk, C., Godin, M., Hoch, J. S., Kingston-MacClure, S., Jeng, M. S., Puddy, L. … Jensen, E. (2013b). Preventing psychiatric discharge to homelessness. *Canadian Journal of Community Mental Health, 32*(3), 17–28.

Forchuk, C., Jewell, J., Schofield, R., Sircelj, M., & Valledor, T. (1998). From hospital to community: Bridging therapeutic relationships. *Journal of Psychiatric and Mental Health Nursing, 5*(3), 197–202.

Forchuk, C., Martin, M.-L., Chan, Y. L., & Jensen, E. (2005). Therapeutic relationships: From psychiatric hospital to community. *Journal of Psychiatric and Mental Health Nursing, 12*(5), 556–564.

Forchuk, C., Ward-Griffin, C., Csiernik, R., & Turner, K. (2011). Surviving the tornado of mental illness. Psychiatric survivors' experiences of getting, losing and keeping housing. In C. Forchuk, R. Csiernik, & E. Jensen (Eds.), *Homelessness, housing and mental health: Finding truths—creating change* (pp. 49–58). Toronto, ON: Canadian Scholars' Press.

Frankel, B. G. (1996). *The sociology of health and health care: A Canadian perspective.* Toronto, ON: Copp Clark Publishing.

Goering, P., Tolomiczenko, G., Sheldon, T., Boydell, K., & Wasylenki, D. (2002). Characteristics of persons who are homeless for the first time. *Psychiatric Services, 53*(11), 1472–1474.

Homeless Individuals and Families Information System [HIFIS]. (2011). *A benchmark for research into the Canadian homeless population.* Retrieved from http://homeless.samhsa.gov/ResourceFiles/67511_EN_w11.pdf

Hurst, C. E. (2007). *Social inequality: Forms, causes, and consequences* (6th ed.). Boston, MA: Pearson Education.

Jarvis, G. E. (2007). The social causes of psychosis in North American psychiatry: A review of a disappearing literature. *The Canadian Journal of Psychiatry, 52*(5), 287–294.

Kuno, E., Rothbard, A. B., Averyt, J., & Culhane, D. (2000). Homelessness among persons with serious mental illness in an enhanced community-based mental health system. *Psychiatric Services, 51*(8), 1012–1016.

Leff, J., & Warner, R. (2006). Poverty and social disadvantage. In J. Leff & R. Warner (Eds.), *Social inclusion of people with mental illness* (pp. 41–52). Cambridge, UK: Cambridge University Press.

Leininger, M. M. (1985). Ethnography and ethnonursing: Models and modes of qualitative data analysis. In M. M. Leininger (Ed.), *Qualitative research methods in nursing* (pp. 33–72). Orlando, FL: Grune and Stratton.

Leininger, M. (1987). Importance and use of ethnomethods: Ethnography and ethnonursing research. In M. Cahoon (Ed.), *Recent advances in nursing* (pp. 12–15). London, UK: Churchill Livingstone of Edinburgh.

Leininger, M. (1990). Ethnomethods: The philosophic and epistemic bases to explicate transcultural nursing knowledge. *Journal of Transcultural Nursing, 1*(2), 40–51.

Lightman, E., Mitchell, A., & Wilson, B. (2009). *Poverty is making us sick: A comprehensive survey of income and health in Canada.* Toronto, ON: Wellesley Institute and Community Social Planning Council of Toronto.

McDonough, P., Sacker, A., & Wiggins, R. D. (2005). Time on my side? Life course trajectories of poverty and health. *Social Science & Medicine, 61*(8), 1795–1808.

Ministry of Children, Community and Social Services. (2013). *Breaking the cycle: The fifth progress report.* Retrieved from http://www.children.gov.on.ca/htdocs/English/documents/breakingthecycle/2013AnnualReport.pdf

Nelson, G., Hall, G. B., & Forchuk, C. (2003). Current and preferred housing of psychiatric consumer/survivors. *Canadian Journal of Community Mental Health, 22*(1), 5–19.

Perry, M. J. (1996). The relationship between social class and mental disorder. *Journal of Primary Prevention, 17*(1), 17–30.

Raphael, D. (2011). *Poverty in Canada: Implications for health and quality of life* (3rd ed.). Toronto, ON: Canadian Scholars' Press.

Raphael, D. (2016). *Social determinants of health: Canadian perspectives* (3rd ed.). Toronto, ON: Canadian Scholars' Press.

Raphael, D., Phillips, S., Renwick, R., & Sehdev, H. (2000). Government policies as a threat to health: Findings from two Toronto community quality of life studies. *Canadian Journal of Public Health, 91*(3), 181–185.

Ross, D. P., Scott, K. J., & Smith, P. J. (2000). *The Canadian fact book of poverty.* Ottawa, ON: Canadian Council of Social Development.

Statistics Canada. (2018). *Canada income survey, 2016.* Retrieved from https://www150.statcan.gc.ca/n1/daily-quotidien/180313/dq180313a-eng.htm

Steinhaus, D. A., Harley, D. A., & Rogers, J. (2004). Homelessness and people with affective disorders and other mental illnesses. *Journal of Applied Rehabilitation Counseling, 35*(1), 36–40.

Sullivan, G., Burnam, A., & Koegel, P. (2000). Pathways to homelessness among the mentally ill. *Social Psychiatry and Psychiatric Epidemiology, 35*(10), 444–450.

Ware, N. C., & Goldfinger, S. M. (1997). Poverty and rehabilitation in severe psychiatric disorders. *Psychiatric Rehabilitation Journal, 21*(1), 3–9.

Williamson, D. L., & Reutter, L. (1999). Defining and measuring poverty: Implications for the health of Canadians. *Health Promotion International, 14*(4), 355–364.

Wilton, R. (2004a). More responsibility, less control: Psychiatric survivors and welfare state restructuring. *Disability & Society, 19*(4), 371–385.

Wilton, R. (2004b). Putting policy into practice? Poverty and people with serious mental illness. *Social Science & Medicine, 58*(1), 25–39.

CHAPTER 9

Using a Capabilities Approach to Understand Poverty and Social Inclusion of Mental Health Consumer-Survivors

Sarah Benbow, Abraham Rudnick, Cheryl Forchuk, and Betty Edwards

1. INTRODUCTION

At the beginning of the century, over one-quarter of Canadian mental health consumer-survivors lived in poverty (Wilton, 2004). Subsequent research conducted globally has consistently found a significant relationship between poverty and mental illness (Lund et al., 2010), including in Canada (Csiernik et al., 2017). Access to basic human resources, such as adequate housing and income, contributes to feelings of positive self-worth, life satisfaction, social network development, and community integration (Arthurson et al., 2007; Hastie, 2010; Levy & Friedman, 2019). However, mental health consumer-survivors are considered one of the most socially excluded and marginalized groups in our society (Montgomery et al., 2019; Morgan et al., 2007; Stuart, 2008). This is evidenced in the stigma and discrimination mental health consumer-survivors experience in the housing market, in seeking employment, in social relationships, in access to resources, in community integration, and in social policies (Benbow et al., 2011; Forchuk et al., 2006; Gordon et al., 2017). Such disadvantage experienced by mental health consumer-survivors often results in social isolation, persistent poverty, decreased feelings of dignity and self-worth, lack of employment, substandard housing, homelessness, limited and insufficient access to resources and social services, and even physical abuse (Overton & Medina, 2008). Given these conditions of disadvantage and inequity, in this chapter, we seek to examine issues of poverty and other social barriers influencing mental health consumer-survivors' everyday life and to better understand their experience of poverty and social exclusion through a social justice lens focusing on the coexistence of, and the relation between, poverty and social exclusion.

Capabilities Approach

The theoretical lens informing this analysis is the Capabilities Approach, a social justice framework that focuses on both basic justice and quality of life. It is grounded in and extends the work of Amartya Sen (1992, 1999a, 1999b) and is influenced by the work of Aristotle and Karl Marx. The Capabilities Approach "is a broad normative framework for the evaluation and assessment of individual well-being and social arrangements, the design of policies, and proposals about social change in society" (Robeyns, 2005, p. 94). The core element of this framework is based on what people are able to do and be while recognizing individual differences and the diversity among people in society, as well as the unique needs that arise from such diversity (Robeyns, 2005). Within the Capabilities Approach there is an emphasis on recognizing that different people have different needs and these needs must be examined and addressed by decreasing barriers to quality of life and the realization of capabilities. With a focus on what people can be and do,

A broom is set aside while the Impact Junk Solutions crew loads the contents of an abandoned apartment into their truck on a cold day in February 2014.
Source: Photo by Justin Langille

resource allocation can be tailored based on individual need (Robeyns, 2005). For example, within this framework, a mental health consumer-survivor who is unable to maintain full-time employment due to illness or long-term disability would have different resource needs than a physically challenged or able-bodied person without a mental health history who is able to maintain full-time employment and thus obtain sufficient income.

In contrast to the Capabilities Approach, Rawls's Justice as Fairness Approach emphasizes distribution of primary social goods based on fairness and equality of opportunity (Ruger, 2004). Sen has critiqued Rawls's approach to social justice by stating that it fails to take into consideration mental and physical challenges, health, racial and social factors, and other inter-individual differences that influence and determine resource need. Rawls's (1999) theory was developed based on a view of "normal cases," which conceptualized people as equal, free, and capable of contributing to society in a meaningful way. Such a conceptualization may exclude individuals who deviate from the "norm" and have unique needs as a result, although Rawls and, even more so, Norman Daniels have argued that justice as fairness can be applied to so-called non-normal situations and have applied Justice as Fairness to health-related issues (Daniels, 1985). Sen further critiques Rawls's approach:

> The primary goods approach seems to take little note of the diversity of human beings.... If people were basically very similar, then an index or primary goods might be quite a good way of judging advantage. But, in fact, people seem to have very different needs varying with health, longevity, climatic conditions, location, work conditions, temperament, and even body size.... So what is being involved is not merely ignoring a few hard cases, but overlooking very widespread and real differences. (Sen, 1980, pp. 215–216).

Another significant attribute of the Capabilities Approach is the focus on agency and an individual's role in creating change at individual, collective, and policy levels (Ruger, 2004). This aspect of the Capabilities Approach stresses the roles of empowerment and action demonstrated by individuals and communities (Nussbaum, 2011; Ruger, 2004).

Nussbaum (2011) identifies the existence of entrenched social injustice and inequality as central to the Capabilities Approach framework, as is the acknowledgement of one's choice and freedom and the role of the government and public policy. A key question within this social justice framework asks: "*What does a life worthy of human dignity require?*" (Nussbaum, 2011, p. 32). Nussbaum (2011) suggests that the answer to this is, at a bare minimum, meeting ten central capabilities, such as bodily health, control over one's environment, and affiliation with others. Admittedly, such a list may not be exhaustive, nor is it necessarily sound to hierarchically order it or related matters, as Sen himself recognizes (Sen, 2006). Hence, we focus here on more generic aspects of the Capabilities Approach.

The Capabilities Approach echoes the World Health Organization's (2001) framework of disability in emphasizing the social and environmental factors impacting disability, which shape experiences of social integration. This social view of disability, philosophically loaded as it may be (Kristiansen et al., 2009), can be particularly helpful in informing research on disadvantaged populations and individuals who are not only deserving of opportunities but also must be considered differentially and with an emphasis on their actual and potential abilities.

In a Canadian study, mental health consumer-survivors indicated that their devastating loss of social support networks and housing were more related to societal responses to their diagnosis rather than to the illness itself (Forchuk et al., 2006). These findings highlight survivors' experiences of social exclusion and inclusion. Social inclusion and exclusion are those societal processes which support or hold back certain groups, such as those living in poverty with mental illness, from meeting their full potential in society (The Canadian Community Economic Development Network, 2008). Social inclusion is not the opposite of social exclusion, and there can be inclusionary experiences within an exclusionary process. When we refer to social exclusion, we are acknowledging the continuum and coexistence of inclusion and exclusion. This population has long been viewed and studied as an exemplar of a socially disadvantaged group and has been identified as one of the most stigmatized and excluded groups in society (Morgan et al., 2007; Stuart, 2008). The purpose of our study was to better understand the experiences of social exclusion and poverty among mental health consumer-survivors through the social justice lens of the Capabilities Approach and, more generally, of the social view of disability, so as to inform policy on better supporting this population.

2. METHODS

Research Design

The research employed participatory action research (PAR) as the study's methodological framework to investigate and better understand the experience of social exclusion and poverty among mental health consumer-survivors in Ontario,

Canada, using specific guidelines for community-based research developed by Israel et al. (1998, 2003, 2005). This included an examination of building on community strengths, facilitating collaborative partnerships, capacity building and co-learning, and development through sustainable community-based collaboration (The Canadian Community Economic Development Network, 2008). Community members, including mental health consumer-survivors, consumer-survivor organizations, and service providers working with mental health consumer-survivors, participated throughout the research process.

Data Collection Methods

Participants (n = 380) were recruited to participate if they had been diagnosed with a mental illness for a minimum of one year, were over the age of 18 and less than 75 years of age, and spoke and understood spoken English to the degree necessary to participate in the study. Four subgroups were recruited: homeless men (n = 55) and women (n = 55), employed housed men (n = 45) and women (n = 45), unemployed housed men (n = 45) and women (n = 45), and men (n = 45) and women (n = 45) residing in group living settings. There were 50 participants recruited from each of the homeless subgroups (men/women), since there were more expected retention challenges in that group during the yearly follow-up interviews over the four years of data collection. Sample sites included homeless shelters, group living settings for mental health consumer-survivors, community and mental health consumer-survivor agencies, public housing, Employee Assistance Programs, and fee-for-service mental health services.

Each of the 380 participants responded to open- and closed-ended questions regarding their perceptions of fairness and ethics pertaining to their life circumstances. This was followed by the completion of 13 quantitative research questionnaires during a face-to-face structured interview. Each interview lasted approximately 1.5 hours. Examples of the open-ended questions included, "What is your experience of poverty?" and "How does poverty relate to your experience of mental illness?" These semi-structured questions were based on study purpose, influenced by the theoretical lens on social justice, existing literature, and input from mental health consumer-survivors involved in the study development. The responses to the qualitative interview questions were written rather than audio-recorded due to pragmatic reasons related to the large sample size and length of the interview inclusive of 13 quantitative surveys. The qualitative component consisted of short-answer questions and was not the main focus of the interview. However, ethical clearance was granted to audio-record interviews.

During each interview, interviewers completed field notes, which included descriptions of the setting and participants, as well as general impressions (Thorpe & Holt, 2008). The purpose of the field notes was to capture any contextual pieces and participant emotion, such as discomfort, which would not otherwise be captured via question responses or transcriptions. Participants were given a $20 Canadian honorarium for their time and travel. Demographic information related to age, income, employment, education, housing history, and mental illness characteristics of participants were collected.

Research Ethics

Research ethics approval was obtained from Western University's Research Ethics Board for Non-Medical Research Involving Human Subjects. Being mindful that mental health consumer-survivor participants may be experiencing numerous stressors, research assistants conducting the interviews were equipped with community resources and were prepared for emergency referral should a participant express the need for crisis resources or support.

Data Analysis

The participant responses to the open-ended interview questions were analyzed based on the research purpose and questions. The analysis was theoretically informed by Nussbaum's Capabilities Approach to social justice (Nussbaum, 2011). Lofland and colleagues' framework for analytical coding (Lofland et al., 2006) also informed data analysis. The process began by reviewing participant responses line by line to identify initial emerging codes and refine and focus them into categories. This was an interactive process of coding and categorizing, then returning to the data until no new codes were identified. This was a cyclical and interactive method of categorizing, sharing findings with the research team, and further refining. Lofland et al.'s (2006) analysis approach requires a "memoing" process occurring during the analysis, whereby the researcher makes notes during and after reviewing participants' responses. Memoing notes are focused primarily on theoretical perspectives, crucial issues, and emerging codes.

3. FINDINGS

Fifty percent of participants were male (n = 190) and 50% female (n = 190). Participants were between the ages of 18 and 72, with mean age of 40.7 years at the time of enrolment. Approximately 67% of participants had experienced homelessness at least once in their life. Mean income for one month prior to enrolment was $1,068. The majority of participants were single, never married (62%; n = 264). Grade school was the highest level of education completed for approximately 47% of participants, with high school being the highest for 30% of participants, and community college/some university being the highest level completed for 22%. Approximately 75% (n = 286) of participants were unemployed at the time of enrolment.

Four themes emerged during the course of the interviews: (1) Poverty: "You just try to survive," (2) Stigma: "People treat you like trash," (3) Belonging: "You feel like you don't belong," and (4) Shared concern and advocacy: "Everyone deserves housing."

Les moves a desk through a garage to the crew's truck in March 2014. Extra income from working with Impact Junk Solutions has given Les choices for better housing, nutrition, and the opportunity to continue working despite retiring.
Source: Photo by Justin Langille

Poverty: "You Just Try to Survive"

Numerous participants shared the sentiment that their mental health well-being and poverty-related experiences were intertwined or, as several participants noted, "they go hand in hand." Participants shared the sequential nature of having a mental illness that often resulted in losing employment or no longer being able to attend school, which led to a loss of housing and not being able to afford food. One participant noted, "I started to live in poverty after (my) mental illness because it affected my ability to work." Another participant shared a similar story when discussing his poverty experience: "Typically the worse depressed I am, the worse my money situation is, cause I'm not going to work and I'm not making money." Participants noted that they often had to make compromising choices between basic life necessities as a result of their extreme poverty. One woman stated, "When you're disabled you balance between paying rent and paying groceries, you can't make ends meet." Another participant stated, "You are stuck between what do I buy: groceries or meds?"

Some participants noted that they received protective support from family members, particularly in terms of offering financial support, but the bottom line was clear: lack of support compromised financial well-being and/or worsened poverty and mental well-being. Participants also discussed the catastrophic impact that poverty had on their mental health, noting that "poverty amplifies everything." The impact was so strong that four participants expressed their past intent of suicide when discussing their experiences with poverty. The participants shared:

> Sometimes because of poverty you feel like you wanna commit suicide.

> The stress is to the point I tried to commit suicide not once, but twice. If this is what the world is I don't want to be a part of it.

> … living cheque to cheque. Sleeping wherever I can, sleeping with whoever I can, prostitution. Feelings of apathy … I've thought of suicide but I'm too much of a coward.

> I had a breakdown to the point that I wanted to commit suicide. I didn't give a shit, I just gave up everything.

Participants shared that due to their poverty they could not take care of themselves and could not access or afford the resources, such as medications, that they needed. One woman noted:

> It's hard. It's a cycle because it's hard to maintain stable mental health while you're in poverty because you don't have a stable environment and it's hard to have a stable environment when you don't have stable mental health.

Many of the participants identified that they grew up in poverty and that their experience was intergenerational. Food insecurity was also prominent in the experiences of poverty. Going without eating, being hungry, and being unable to feed their children were common food insecurity experiences shared by participants. One woman stated her experience of poverty as: "Not having enough to eat. Going without food so my children can have food. Not having enough for bus fare to get to the doctor's. Not having the $2 for prescription. Lost hydro [access to electricity]. Turned to prostitution … became homeless." There was an emphasis on survival and an inability to meet basic needs, further compounding and in some instances contributing to worsened mental health conditions: "Well it's hard enough trying to survive with mental illness. You don't need the extra burden of poverty. You just try to survive." Reiterating this notion, another participant stated, "It [poverty] makes life challenging because your basic needs are not met. So, life becomes about surviving, not living."

Stigma: "People Treat You like Trash"

The experience of stigma was consistently discussed among study participants. Stigma was described as an external force negatively impacting the opportunities, well-being, and health of the participants. For participants, stigma resulted in unequal employment and housing opportunities, as well as a decreased sense of self-worth and social exclusion. The stigma discussed was based on a multitude of factors including societal and individual response to compromised mental well-being, mental health system involvement, addiction, gender, sexual orientation, education level, homelessness, poverty, and/or social status; however, the stigma as it related to mental well-being and poverty was the most prominent. Speaking specifically to his employment experience, one participant shared that "there is stigma to mental illness because people with mental illness do not get hired as much. They do not also get a decent pay." Similarly, participants expressed that there is stigma held by landlords and the general public. One participant expressed that the stigma in his life is enacted by "people saying negative things, like when I apply for something and I get shut down ... or calling the landlords from the phone upstairs and it comes up as the name of the shelter and they automatically think that you are a junkie." Multiple participants shared the stigma of residing in a homeless shelter while applying for housing or job opportunities and the often-overwhelming challenges that accompanied this process as a result of their current location in shelter.

Participants also expressed that they experienced significant stigma from the general public based on their homelessness status and compromised mental well-being. One participant shared the negative perceptions she experienced as a result of her homelessness status: "I must be an addict, must be a thief, must be unreliable or dishonest." In this way, homelessness was not viewed as an unjust circumstance but rather as a flawed individual characteristic or trait. Several participants shared that they are looked down on by people in society and have experienced harassment and name-calling based on their homelessness status, mental health condition, and/or for receiving governmental social and financial assistance, such as that from the Ontario Disability Support Program (ODSP). The enacted stigma made it harder for study participants to make their way and integrate into the community.

At times, the external stigma experienced was so pervasive that participants' concept of self was affected, resulting in internalized stigma. This was evident when participants referred to themselves as "abnormal," "worthless," "hopeless," and "helpless." Some participants expressed that they didn't blame people for judging them and assumed responsibility for their circumstances and internalized negative perception of themselves, by blaming themselves for others' judgement of them. One participant stated, "I am disgusted with myself too." While many participants recognized their mistreatment and labelled it as such, for those who felt they somehow deserved and accepted others' judgement, the deeply entrenched external stigma was internalized to the point of seeming to dominate their view of themselves and thus further excluding them from social inclusion.

Belonging: "You Feel like You Don't Belong"

A sense of wanting to belong was expressed by study participants and described in terms of their experiences of social inclusion and exclusion in society. A number of factors shaped the participants' experiences of belonging or of not belonging. For many, feeling "different" or "less than" as a result of their experienced stigma shaped their experience of belonging or lack thereof. Feeling like an outsider was described as "when you're considered a freak, loser, moron, just because you're different it makes people look down on you twice as much." Many participants shared the feeling of not fitting in with family, community, and society, which resulted in feelings of isolation and rejection. One participant stated, "Family don't want nothing to do with you. You feel like you don't belong." Other participants described their sense of belonging as a direct result of their mental health consumer-survivorship and their addiction itself. One participant stated, "I've pushed people away and people have pushed me away because they can't stand to see me hurt myself. The main reason I use (drugs) is because of my sexual abuse past that's how I deal with it."

Poverty was discussed as a barrier to belonging and participating in community activities that cost a fee. However, study participants expressed a sense of belonging when they engaged with other people who suffered similar stressors, such as poverty. Other inclusionary factors that increased a sense of belonging among study participants were identified as positive family support, being a member of agencies where they felt accepted, welcomed, and "normal," and the existence of peer support networks. When referring to a local organization for homeless youth, one participant stated, "They're basically the only family I got." This statement reflects the importance of such agencies as well as the coexistence and interactive nature of inclusion and exclusion. Participants reported experiencing much belonging and inclusion within certain organizations, but a general feeling of exclusion within society at large.

"Everyone Deserves Housing": Shared Concern and Advocacy

Participants clearly and consistently articulated the need for change, a shared concern for individuals in similar positions, and the need for advocacy. Participants identified several barriers and forms of injustice that they faced in trying to seek support and be included. In doing so, they recognized the need for change and outlined several recommendations for improvement. Most recommendations were at the policy level. Participants identified several social resources that require improvement, such as access to adequate housing, income, transportation, and equitable and fair treatment for mental health consumer-survivors who are living in poverty. As identified in the prior themes, participants expressed not having enough income to meet basic needs such as food and shelter. As well, participants identified that limited or lack of affordable housing and being wait-listed negatively impacted their access to housing.

At the community agency level, participants shared the concern that many social agencies are operating under-staffed and that available treatment is subsequently negatively impacted. Several participants noted the need for increased outreach, one-to-one contact, and non-judgemental workers, advocates, and counsellors. For the most part, participants identified that they were worthy of better and more equitable treatment in the health, economic, housing, and social sectors. Peer support from individuals who have similar experiences was noted as an important method of support and inclusion.

Participants extended their recommendations for change beyond thinking solely of their own situation in their attempts to advocate for improved conditions for all mental health consumer-survivors living in poverty. One participant stated, "There must be a way of helping out homeless people, like shelters or something … I could work at a food bank.… Everyone deserves housing." Another participant noted, "everyone deserves a living wage." While some participants shared their ability to speak and advocate for themselves, others felt that there is a huge need for advocates: "You can't speak for yourself, you need an advocate to speak for you and you have to jump through hoops just to get enough money to survive."

4. DISCUSSION

According to Nussbaum (2006), an urgent and significant contemporary problem is the need to ensure justice for people with physical and mental disabilities. Based on this study's findings, it is clear that social justice is not being met in the lives of mental health consumer-survivors, at least in Canada. At its core, the Capabilities Approach requires that we question if human dignity is being respected (Nussbaum, 2006). Feelings of shame, helplessness, hopelessness, decreased self-worth, and thoughts of suicide experienced by the study participants reflect the implications of societal, and subsequently internalized, stigma for one's dignity and overall quality of life. Further, participants' responses clearly indicate that opportunities for a life with human dignity for mental health consumer-survivors (Nussbaum, 2006) were perpetually denied as a result of societal and systemic discrimination and exclusion. This was perhaps most poignantly captured when one participant, reflecting on his current compromised mental well-being, lack of employment, and housing status, stated, "I am disgusted with myself too." Even those who did not echo these feelings of worthlessness recognized the lack of and need for housing, supports, resources, and societal change for mental health consumer-survivors. This illuminated another form of discrimination and maltreatment at a systemic level in the lack of policies that are supposed to, but do not, ensure equitable access to resources and services.

Benbow (2009) identifies mental health consumer-survivors as a group that is subjected to societal abuse. That is, a result of unjust social structures with mental health consumer-survivors being prevented from reaching their full potential, from meeting their basic human needs, and subsequently being excluded from many aspects of society. If social justice is premised on the notion that human life is deserving of dignity, we question why mental health consumer-survivors have been deemed so "undeserving" of such a life, and how such inequality can be countered (Forchuk, 2008).

Nussbaum (2011) suggests that promoting social justice requires, at a bare minimum, making societal opportunities available for people to meet the aforementioned ten capabilities. While all ten capabilities impact the lives of mental health consumer-survivors, based on our findings some capabilities had more weight than others. Bodily health, including access to adequate shelter and food, was an extremely prevalent capability that was not met, as outlined in each of the four themes. According to the demographic questionnaire, 67% of study participants experienced homelessness at some point in their lives. Yet the United Nations declared access to safe and adequate housing as an international human right (United Nations, 1948). Despite this recognition of the importance of housing, individuals with mental disability are more likely than the general population to experience homelessness and poverty (Kim et al., 2007). Homelessness can further compromise mental well-being and together they can further compound each other. The very existence of homelessness represents inequality in access to housing for mental health consumer-survivors. In 2007, a United Nations special rapporteur condemned Canada for its current state of housing and homelessness, especially for unique subgroups of the homeless population such as those with psychiatric disability living in poverty (United Nations, 2007). The rapporteur urged the Canadian government to adopt a national housing policy as Canada remains one of the only developed countries without such a policy (see Chapter 2).

Further, lack of food security and being forced to choose between basic needs to ensure access to food was a common experience shared by participants. The poverty rate among mental health consumer-survivors is more than double that of the general population (Wilton, 2004). Remedies for these systemic problems must be focused on the macro-level systems issues and reform, such as insufficient social support and financial assistance. However, before such changes can occur, the problem must be viewed as a result of societal processes, rather than as a consequence of flaws of mental health consumer-survivors. Furthermore, Raphael

(2016) notes that poverty and income inequality have been increasing in Canada; this, in addition to the reduction of services and supports, contributes to social exclusion.

Related to this is another form of exclusion of mental health consumer-survivors, which is evidenced in them not being able to seek employment on an equal basis with others. This relates to Nussbaum's (2011) capability of control over one's environment. Stable employment among mental health consumer-survivors has positive impacts on recovery and can enhance quality of life, self-worth, and a sense of belonging (Bush et al., 2009). However, the high unemployment rate among mental health consumer-survivors reflects a complex and multifaceted issue. Seventy-five percent of study participants were unemployed. It has been proposed that high unemployment rates among mental health consumer-survivors are

Working at Goodwill's RMHC Social Enterprise program allows part-time employee Joyce to pay for groceries she would struggle to otherwise on a fixed income, she says.
Source: Photo by Justin Langille

related to stigma and discrimination, disability, non-modified workplace options, insufficient support, mental health crises, and lack of training or education, as well as a myriad of other potential factors, such as the challenges of residing in a shelter while seeking employment or in attempting to maintain employment (Baldwin & Marcus, 2006, 2007).

Krupa et al. (2009) suggest that anti-stigma campaigns targeting employment could systematically improve the potential for paid work, which could in turn positively impact the quality of life and sense of belonging for mental health consumer-survivors. Additionally, with employment would come a subsequent increase in finances, which could positively impact social inclusion. For example, through employment, survivors may have access to more funds that would enable them to better fulfill basic human needs, as well as potentially enhancing their community participation in events with a financial cost. This may, in turn, counter some forms of stigma (Krupa et al., 2009). The Canadian Mental Health Association (2011) has outlined several approaches for employers to better support mental health consumer-survivors in sustaining meaningful employment, such as through individualized employment options, flexibility, and understanding.

Stigma impacts mental and emotional well-being, as well as access to basic resources. According to Nussbaum (2011), the capability of affiliation includes being treated as equal to and as worthy as others, as well as one's ability to recognize and show concerns for others. Feelings of unworthiness and inadequacy were all too common in participant responses. While self-stigma or internalized stigma has been explored in the literature related to mental health consumer-survivors (Corrigan et al., 2006), the potential catastrophic result of such shame expressed in participants' suicidal ideation has not been sufficiently discussed. The fact that four participants expressed past suicidal ideation as a result of their circumstance and the subsequent extreme feelings of worthlessness and hopelessness demonstrate the devastating impact of societal abuse some mental health consumer-survivors face. This, again, cannot be remedied solely in addressing these issues at an individual level, as it is not in the individual where the main problems related to social exclusion lies. Rather, social exclusion lies in societal practices and processes that perpetuate stigma and the condemning of mental health consumer-survivors in our society (Benbow, 2009; Forchuk, 2008; Forchuck et al., 2006).

Despite the experienced stigma, participants also revealed their sense of advocacy and a shared concern for others. In the fourth theme, shared concern and advocacy: "Everyone deserves housing," participants shared their recommendations for an improved future and, in doing so, advocated for others experiencing similar forms of systemic societal stigma. The need for service providers to act as advocates in navigating the system was also expressed. The social welfare system, the housing system, the employment markets, and the health-care system have been identified as very challenging systems for mental health consumer-survivors to navigate without support from service providers or advocates (Benbow et al., 2011; Forchuk et al., 2006). Peer support from consumer-survivor groups has also been identified as an important and inclusionary form of support for mental health consumer-survivors (Schutt & Rogers, 2009).

5. CONCLUSION

Using the Capabilities Approach, the results from this study revealed the socially unjust life circumstances of mental health consumer-survivors in Canada. In answering Nussbaum's question "What does a life worthy of human dignity require?" (Nussbaum, 2011, p. 32), the participants shared the counterpart; that is, they shared what a life deprived of human dignity is comprised of: stigma, discrimination, lack of access to affordable housing, insufficient income, and an overall feeling of exclusion. The Capabilities Approach provides a fitting lens to understand the experiences of social exclusion and poverty in the lives of mental health consumer-survivors, emphasizing justice, uniqueness, fairness, and dignity.

REFERENCES

Arthurson, K., Worland, P., & Cameron, H. (2007). *A place to call my own: Identifying best practice in housing and mental health.* Adelaide, SA: State of Australian Cities Conference. Retrieved from http://www.fbe.unsw.edu.au/cityfutures/SOAC/aplacetocallmyown.pdf

Baldwin, M. L., & Marcus, S. C. (2006). Perceived and measured stigma among workers with serious mental illness. *Psychiatric Services, 57*(3), 388–392.

Baldwin, M. L., & Marcus, S. C. (2007). Labour market outcomes of persons with mental disorders. *Industrial Relations, 46*(3), 481–510.

Benbow, S. (2009). Societal abuse in the lives of individuals with mental illness. *Canadian Nurse, 105*(6), 30–32.

Benbow, S., Forchuk, C., & Ray, S. L. (2011). Mothers with mental illness experiencing homelessness: A critical analysis. *Journal of Psychiatric and Mental Health Nursing, 18*(8), 687–695.

Bush, P. W., Drake, R. E., Xie, H., McHugo, G. J., & Haslett, W. R. (2009). The long-term impact of employment on mental health service use and costs for persons with severe mental illness. *Psychiatric Services, 60*(8), 1024–1031.

Canadian Community Economic Development Network—Ontario. (2008). *A community's agenda for strengthening Ontario's communities.* Retrieved from http://www.ccednet-rcdec.ca/files/ON%20Policy%20Framework%202008.pdf

Canadian Mental Health Association. (2011). *Get informed.* Retrieved from http://www.cmha.bc.ca/get-informed/public-issues/cross-cultural

Corrigan, P. W., Watson, A. C., & Bar, L. (2006). The self-stigma of mental illness: Implications for self-esteem and self-efficacy. *Journal of Social and Clinical Psychology, 25*(8), 875–884.

Csiernik, R., Csiernik, B., & Brideau, M. (2017). A thirty year retrospective on the income adequacy of Canadian provincial social assistance payments to non-institutionalized disabled adults. *Canadian Review of Social Policy/Revue Canadienne de Politique Sociale, 77*(Summer/Fall), 95–119.

Daniels, N. (1985). *Just health care: Studies in philosophy and health policy.* Cambridge, UK: Cambridge University Press.

Forchuk, C. (2008). Some psychiatric survivors can't survive the system. *Canadian Nurse, 104*(8), 44.

Forchuk, C., Nelson, G., & Hall, G. B. (2006). "It's important to be proud of the place you live in": Housing problems and preferences of psychiatric survivors. *Perspectives in Psychiatric Care, 42*(1), 42–52.

Gordon, S., Davey, S., Waa, A., Tiatia, R., & Waaka, T. (2017). *Social inclusion and exclusion, stigma and discrimination, and the experience of mental distress.* Auckland, New Zealand: Mental Health Foundation of New Zealand.

Hastie, B. (2010). Linking cause and solution: Predicting support for poverty alleviation proposals. *Australian Psychologist, 45*(1), 16–28.

Israel, B. A., Eng, E., Schulz, A. J., & Parker, E. A. (2005). Introduction to methods in community-based participatory research for health in Israel. In B. A. Israel, E. Eng, A. J. Schulz, & E. A. Parker (Eds.), *Methods in community-based participatory research for health* (pp. 1–26). San Francisco, CA: Jossey-Bass.

Israel, B. A., Schulz, A. J., Parker, E. A., & Becker, A. B. (1998). Review of community-based research: Assessing partnership approaches to improve public health. *Annual Review of Public Health, 19*, 173–202.

Israel, B. A., Schulz, A. J., Parker, E. A., Becker, A. B., Allen, III, A. J., Guzman, R., & Lichtenstein, R. (2003). Critical issues in developing and following CBPR principles. In N. Wallerstein, B. Duran, J. Oetzel, & M. Minkler (Eds.), *Community-based participatory research for health* (3rd ed., pp. 31–45). San Francisco, CA: Jossey-Bass.

Kim, M. M., Swanson, J. W., Swartz, M. S., Bradford, D. W., Mustillo, S. A., & Elbogen, E. B. (2007). Healthcare barriers among severely mentally ill homeless adults: Evidence from the Five-Site Health and Risk study. *Administration & Policy in Mental Health & Mental Health Services Research, 34*, 363–375.

Kristiansen, K., Vehmas, S., & Shakespeare, T. (Eds). (2009). *Arguing about disability: Philosophical perspectives*. London, UK: Routledge.

Krupa, T., Kirsch, B., Cockburn, L., & Gewurtz, R. (2009). Understanding the stigma of mental illness in employment. *Work, 33*(4), 413–425.

Levy, D., & Friedman, Y. (2019). Postforced eviction communities: The contribution of personal and environmental resources to the sense of belonging to the community. *Journal of Community Psychology, 47*(1), 104–116.

Lofland, J., Snow, D., Anderson, L., & Lofland, L. H. (2006). *Analyzing social settings: A guide to qualitative observation and analysis* (4th ed.). Belmont, CA: Wadsworth Thomson.

Lund, C., Breen, A., Flisher, A. J., Kakuma, R., Corrigall, J., Joska, J. A., … Patel, V. (2010). Poverty and common mental disorders in low and middle income countries: A systematic review. *Social Science & Medicine, 71*(3), 517–528.

Montgomery, P., Wuest, A., Forchuk, C., Smith-Carrier, T., Jeng, M. S., & Rudnick, A. (2019). Social inclusion as freedom for persons living with mental illness. *Canadian Journal of Community Mental Health, 37*(4), 23–35.

Morgan, C., Burns, T., Fitzpatrick, R., Pinfold, V., & Priebe, S. (2007). Social exclusion and mental health: Conceptual and methodological review. *British Journal of Psychiatry, 191*(6), 477–483.

Nussbaum, M. C. (2006). *Frontiers of justice: Disability, nationality, species membership*. Cambridge, MA: Belknap Press.

Nussbaum, M. C. (2011). *Creating capabilities: A human development approach*. Cambridge, MA: Belknap Press.

Overton, S. L., & Medina, S. L. (2008). The stigma of mental illness. *Journal of Counseling & Development, 86*(2), 143–151.

Raphael, D. (2016). *Social determinants of health: Canadian perspective* (3rd ed.). Toronto, ON: Canadian Scholars' Press.

Rawls, J. (1999). *A theory of justice* (Rev. ed.). Cambridge, MA: Harvard University Press.

Robeyns, I. (2005). The capability approach: A theoretical survey. *Journal of Human Development, 6*(1), 93–117.

Ruger, J. P. (2004). Ethics of social determinants of health. *The Lancet, 364*(9439), 1092–1097.

Schutt, R. K., & Rogers, E. S. (2009). Empowerment peer support: Structure and process of self-help in a consumer-run center for individuals with mental illness. *Journal of Community Psychology, 37*(6), 697–710.

Sen, A. (1980). Equality of what? In S. M. McMurrin (Ed.), *The Tanner lecture on human values* (Vol. 1). Cambridge, MA: Cambridge University Press.

Sen, A. (1992). *Inequality reexamined*. New York, NY: Oxford University Press.

Sen, A. (1999a). *Commodities and capabilities*. New York, NY: Oxford University Press.

Sen, A. (1999b). *Development as freedom*. New York, NY: Alfred A. Knopf.

Sen, A. (2006). What do we want from a theory of justice? *Journal of Philosophy, 103*(5), 215–238.

Stuart, H. (2008). Fighting the stigma caused by mental disorders: Past perspectives, present activities, and future directions. *World Psychiatry, 7*(3), 185–188.

Thorpe, R., & Holt, R. (2008). Field notes. *The SAGE dictionary of qualitative management research*. Thousand Oaks, CA: SAGE Publications.

United Nations. (1948). *Universal Declaration of Human Rights*. Retrieved from http://www.un.org/en/documents/udhr/

United Nations. (2007). *United Nations Special Rapporteur on Adequate Housing, Miloon Kothari: Mission to Canada*. Retrieved from http://www.unhchr.ch/huricane/huricane.nsf/0/90995D69CE8153C3C1257387004F40B5?opendocument

Wilton, R. D. (2004). More responsibility, less control: Psychiatric survivors and welfare state restructuring. *Disability & Society, 19*(4), 371–385.

World Health Organization. (2001). *International classification of functioning, disability, and health*. Retrieved from http://www.who.int/classifications/icf/wha-en.pdf

CHAPTER 10

"Until You Hit Rock Bottom There's No Support": Contradictory Sources and Systems of Support for Mothers Experiencing Homelessness in Southwestern Ontario

Sarah Benbow, Cheryl Forchuk, Carolyn Gorlick, Helene Berman, and Catherine Ward-Griffin

1. INTRODUCTION

As this book has already clearly indicated, homelessness is well established as a significant social and health issue in Canada (Hwang et al., 2009; Kelly & Luxford, 2017; Raphael, 2016). Among those experiencing homelessness in Canada, mothers and their families represent a vulnerable and growing segment of the homeless population due to poverty, lack of affordable housing, and intimate partner violence (Bryant & Shapcott, 2016; Chambers et al., 2014; Gaetz et al., 2013). Further, homeless mothers are among those who are most socially excluded from the full economic, social, and, subsequently, health benefits of society (Labonté, 2016).

Social exclusion, defined as "an expression of unequal relations of power among groups in society, which then determine unequal access to economic, social, political, and cultural resources" (Galabuzi, 2016, p. 254), has been identified as an important social determinant of health (Galabuzi, 2016; Labonté, 2016; Raphael, 2016). Historically, researchers examining social exclusion and health have focused primarily on material deprivation and poverty (Stewart et al., 2008; Wilson et al., 2007), with others employing a social determinants of health approach to understand the concept (Chambers et al., 2014; Reid, 2004; Watson, 2012). Stewart et al. (2008) compared experiences of social exclusion between participants with low income and high income living in Toronto and Edmonton. The findings demonstrated that limited financial resources, poor health, and negative societal attitudes impeded community involvement for participants of lower income. Watson (2012) employed a social determinants of health lens to understand the experience of social exclusion and health among hidden homeless individuals in Ontario.

Her findings drew attention to structures of exclusion, including a lack of sufficient housing policies and increasing poverty, while providing an understanding of the health impacts associated with material and social deprivation.

Benbow, Rudnick, Forchuk, and Edwards's work (Chapter 9) yielded four themes regarding poverty, stigma, belonging, and shared concern and advocacy. Similar findings were shared by low-income women in an earlier study by Reid (2004), who used feminist action research to explore social exclusion and poverty in women's health in British Columbia. A social determinants of health lens was employed, leading to the discovery of women's experiences of exclusion at the cultural, institutional, and material levels. Participants experienced social exclusion in the form of stereotypes and labels, not having their needs met by the system, and their lack of access to basic needs.

Overall, individuals experiencing homelessness experience higher rates of nearly all morbidities than the general population and, even more significantly, have increased mortality rates (Canadian Observatory on Homelessness, n.d.; Fazel et al., 2014). For women, unique complexity shapes their homelessness experiences. This includes mothering without a home (Greaves et al., 2006; Milaney et al., 2017), intimate partner violence (Pavao et al., 2007), trauma (Huey et al., 2013; Lewinson et al., 2014; Torchalla et al., 2015; Walsh et al., 2013), increased rates of depression (Bassuk & Beardslee, 2014; Poleshuck et al., 2013; Weinreb et al., 2006), as well as discrimination within health and social sectors (Benbow et al., 2011).

Intimate partner violence is considered one of the leading causes of homelessness among women and mothers (Lewinson et al., 2014). Likewise, trauma, in the form of physical and sexual assaults, is common before and during homelessness (Yeater et al., 2010). Lewinson et al. (2014) conducted a study with 21 women, with and without physical custody of children, who were experiencing unstable housing. The study illuminated narratives of current and childhood trauma, exploitation, physical, emotional, and sexual abuse, increased environmental stressors, and increased exposure to crime. Researchers also noted the protective factors women demonstrated in fleeing unsafe situations to ensure their safety and the safety of their children; however, the very act of becoming homeless increased further risk of trauma (Lee & Schreck, 2005).

Mothers experiencing homelessness are also at increased risk of experiencing mental health issues, commonly including depression (Bassuk & Beardslee, 2014), substance use (Azarmehr et al., 2018), and bipolar, psychotic disorders, and schizophrenia (Hanranhan et al., 2005). Benbow et al. (2011) conducted a qualitative secondary analysis examining health experiences of mothers with mental illness experiencing homelessness from a social justice lens. The cyclical nature of homelessness, abuse, and illness was clearly evident. Mothers were also found to experience human rights violations in discriminatory housing practices related to their mental illness/disability status, racial-ethnic background, and mothering status.

This chapter reports findings from one segment of a larger study (Benbow, 2015) that critically examined the sociopolitical context of social exclusion and health for mothers experiencing homelessness. Two specific research questions are examined: (1) What are the sociopolitical contexts of mothers' experience of social exclusion?; and (2) How do the experiences of social exclusion and social inclusion shape their health?

2. METHODS

The research was conducted within the critical research paradigm. From this perspective, attention is given to the political and structural elements shaping social positioning, life experiences (Carroll, 2004), and ultimately health (Eakin et al., 1996). The criticality of the study ensures that attention to one's individual story is situated and contextualized within a larger nuanced system of inequity (Berman et al., 2009b). Thus, a critical orientation to narrative inquiry was employed, informed by the work of a number of scholars (Chase, 2005, 2011; Labov, 1972; McCormack, 2000a, 2000b, 2004). With narrative inquiry, focus is placed on the story, the art of storytelling, and the co-construction of knowledge between the researcher and participants; emphasis is placed on the meaning and contextual elements of life events shared (Chase, 2005).

Recruitment

Data were collected at various homeless shelters and programs that provide services for women and mothers who are homeless. Participants were sampled purposefully based on self-identified homelessness and motherhood status and were recruited via flyer distribution, meet-and-greet sessions, and word of mouth. Snowball sampling techniques were used once interviews were underway, where women who participated shared research contact information with other mothers they knew who were experiencing homelessness. Women who self-identified as mothers, over the age of 18, able to speak and understand spoken English, and who were experiencing homelessness or who had experienced homelessness in the past year were eligible to participate in this study.

Additionally, at the suggestion of participants, individual interviews and focus groups were held with service provider participants. During the interview process, mothers were asked about rules/policies impacting their health. During this discussion, mothers recommended further discussion and follow-up with service providers. Inclusion criteria required that potential service provider participants had provided care to mothers experiencing homelessness in the past year. The inclusion of service provider perspective, at the request of mother participants, further supported an understanding of the sociopolitical contexts within mothers' lives and was consistent with the research questions and the critical nature of inquiry.

Sampling continued until data reflected the richness and complexity required to meet the study purpose (Patton, 2002). Twenty-six mothers participated in the study, 14 of whom chose to participate in individual interviews, while 12 chose to engage in group interviews. There was a total of three group interviews, each consisting of two to four women. Service provider participants (n = 15) also opted for both individual and group interviews, with a total of six individual interviews and one focus group consisting of nine service provider participants. Data collection took place over a period of seven months; the initial four months were heavily focused on initial interviews with mothers experiencing homelessness, while the follow-up interviews and interviews with service providers primarily occurred in the final months. Ethics approval was obtained from Western University, London, Ontario.

Data Collection

In-depth, semi-structured interviews were carried out with 26 women. Women were able to choose between individual or group interviews and were provided with a $20 honorarium. Interviews lasted approximately 1.5 to 2 hours and were guided using open-ended questions with probes. Consistent with narrative inquiry, follow-up interviews were offered. Twelve women chose to participate in follow-up interviews. During the follow-up interviews, further interpretations and synthesis of data were shared to gain further insight and to ensure co-construction of knowledge and shared understandings were achieved (Chase, 2005; Duffy, 2007). Fifteen service providers participated. A semi-structured interview guide with probes guided the interview and a $10 gift card was provided as honorarium.

Analysis

The analysis of transcripts from initial, follow-up, and focus group interviews was informed by the processes outlined by McCormack (2000a, 2000b, 2004), which involved developing interpretive stories and viewing the stories through multiple lenses. This process has been referred to as the act of "storying stories"

(McCormack, 2004, p. 220). Developing an interpretive story involved identifying and examining the structures of the story; this included reading the transcript line by line and identifying the beginning, middle, and end (Riessman, 1993). This was followed by highlighting the text with a different colour for each narrative lens identified. In viewing the transcript through multiple lenses, special attention was paid to the *moments*, *language*, and *context* in which the stories were produced. These are dimensions in which people construct and reconstruct their stories to give meaning to their lives (McCormack, 2000a). The lens of *moments* refers to epiphanies and significant moments in the narrative. McCormack (2004) suggests viewing the transcript through the lens of *language*, wherein attention is paid to "what is said, how it is said, and what remains unsaid" (p. 225). Further, through the lens of *context*, the sociopolitical, cultural, and structural conditions within the participants' experiences were analyzed.

Consistent with various critical narrative approaches (Caxaj et al., 2014; Caxaj & Gill, 2017; Haldenby et al., 2007), each narrative was given a title based on the interpreted meaning and these titles served as the initial codes. The initial codes were then refined, revised, and collapsed into themes as interviews and analysis continued. During follow-up interviews, the emerging codes were discussed with the participants. Special attention was paid to collective and contradicting meanings of and within stories and across study participants, while understanding how these realities are shaped by social and political systems (Berman et al., 2009a). Consistent with qualitative research, analysis began at the outset of the interview; however, formal "line-by-line" analysis began by analyzing the mothers' transcripts. Once emerging and recurring themes were identified, service provider transcripts were analyzed and integrated to illuminate and support the contextual and systemic factors shaping mothers' experiences of social exclusion.

3. FINDINGS

On average, the 26 women were 27.4 years of age and had 1.6 children, the majority of whom were under the age of 5. Most mothers had physical custody of at least one of their children (n = 19). Nineteen mothers self-identified as having or having had a mental illness, including depression, anxiety, post-traumatic stress disorder, panic disorder, or addiction. Seventeen mothers were born in Canada. While ten mothers identified as Caucasian, mothers with a variety of racial and ethnocultural identities participated in the study. Twenty-one mothers were receiving social assistance in the form of financial support. All service provider participants (n = 15) were women working with mothers who were experiencing homelessness.

Ten service providers were counsellors and two were housing advocates, while three were case managers.

Central to the women's experiences of mothering while homeless were their interactions with "the system." The system, as they discussed it, referred to federal, provincial, and municipal policies that governed their lives, as well as organizational, institutional, and social support services accessed or attempted to be accessed by them. The way in which mothers referred to the system was as an interactive entity, an active participant in shaping their lives. As all mother participants were currently experiencing homelessness, they all expressed interaction with some aspect of the system including shelter, housing, social assistance, child welfare, and health care. The various social safety nets were described by participants as essential for their survival.

Mothers discussed organizations that enhanced their sense of inclusion and facilitated empowerment by offering resources, a sense of community, and increased access to basic needs, such as food and housing. The mothers noted that they would not have survived without certain agencies such as shelters and drop-in centres. However, these same organizations at other times contributed to their exclusion. The contradictory nature of these systems was categorized into four themes: (1)"Until you hit rock bottom": No support; (2) "It's just not enough": Insufficient support; (3) "Help comes with a price": Support with surveillance; and (4) "Every shelter is so different": Organizational philosophies impacting support.

"Until You Hit Rock Bottom": No Support

A predominant concern raised by mothers was the notion that "you are only let in when you're so far out" or that "until you hit rock bottom there's no support." This concern referred to the dire state one had to be in to be able to access necessary support for survival. Many mothers reported that the detrimental impacts of unavailable services resulted in extreme crises that could have been prevented had they been able to access supports sooner. As a mother shared:

> it's unfortunate that it has to get to the point where you have to go to a shelter, instead of having a support system up before that ... I did call a shelter ... "we can't really do much for you unless you come in here" ... If women have a place to go, a safe place to talk to somebody for that hour they would probably make healthy choices before it got to the point where they had to come here [shelter].

The women and service providers alike emphasized the magnitude of extreme crisis needed to access support, rather than the availability of adequate support to avoid crisis. Service providers made special note of the overwhelming demand and need for mental health support and services for women experiencing homelessness. They reported limited support available until a woman is in such extreme need that she requires emergency hospitalization for mental health stabilization and safety. For example, in a focus group, service providers reported that a mother who desperately needed mental health care was unable to acquire the necessary supports until her illness was so severe that she attempted to die by suicide; it was only then that she was able to receive the mental health care she needed and had tried previously to access.

"It's Just Not Enough": Insufficient Supports

Further, service providers often felt helpless to best support women due to broader systems' issues, such as the lack of available general and specialized mental health supports and lack of affordable housing. Service providers reported the challenges in supporting women to access housing. A service provider indicated that the public housing wait list "is pushing the ten-year mark.... So then people are forced to go to slumlords."

Service providers and mothers indicated that the support to get out of crisis was insufficient to help them survive, let alone thrive. While the majority of the women were receiving social assistance, prominent in their stories and those of service providers was that they were receiving insufficient financial support. Service providers noted that the struggles women experienced were worsened due to "the amount of money they are getting from Ontario Works. It's not enough for somebody to live on, so in terms of financially being able to afford to buy their food for the month ... you know it's just not enough money." No matter their current source of income (financial assistance from the government, sex work, and/or other forms of employment), their income was insufficient to meet basic human needs. A participant shared this perspective of Ontario Works:

> Anything is better than nothing and it beats having to sell yourself on the streets, but I need more money for food and shelter ... Ask any mom on OW, food is an issue. We don't have enough money. I have to ask my mom to bring me food, but I'm still left without.

Buying groceries and clothing, paying for electricity and transportation, and accessing safe housing were simply not possible. Further, lack of sufficient supports played out in women's lives from one generation to another:

> I've just witnessed it, I've seen it all over the place ... like a lot of my friends struggling, some of my friends can't even come to school 'cause mom's working two or three jobs to get the bills proper, get the lights back on ... so there you go, she's missing out on her education ... she's gonna end up in the same lifestyle her mom's doing, and it just keeps continuing, continuing, continuing. There's no help ...

This woman emphasized not only the responsibility placed on mothers to care for and provide for their children while living in poverty but also the way in which the cycle of poverty easily perpetuates across generations. When insufficient financial and social support exists, responsibility must be placed on children to contribute to the survival of their families.

Also common among women's stories was food insecurity, past, present, or as a serious concern for the future. Many women shared the common experience of going without meals to ensure their children were fed. Women shared that "food was scarce" and "a really stressful and scary thing." Participants' mothering was at the forefront of conversations about food insecurity. One young woman emphasized that while she and her children were in shelter, she knew they would be fed. She contrasted this with her experiences prior to shelter residence, when she was never certain she would have food for each meal. Service providers and women alike reported the great benefit to being in shelter in terms of access to resources and advocacy. As a service provider noted:

> They do become healthier while they are here ... we have nurses come, a nurse practitioner, and a public health nurse, once a week, so I mean that is good for women, they can access, if they don't have a doctor, it is a way they can get connected, and they don't have to leave the building ... they are safe here, the service comes to them ...

Women reported that while in shelter they had increased access to health-care services, but many noted they only have access while experiencing homelessness. Women discussed their fear of leaving the shelter, because once they leave many shelter supports and resources were no longer available. A woman noted:

> I finally have the help I need here. I can see a counsellor everyday if I need to. My son sees a nurse and counsellor. They saved my life, well me mentally I mean. But when I leave we won't have them, you know. I trust them, you know? It just sucks.

Service providers expressed the increased complexity mothers with mental illness faced in accessing supports:

> If you have children, women downplay their symptoms because they are afraid their children will be taken, or arranging childcare you know, what to go to an appointment or to sit in emerg [the emergency room], like we have had women say, "I will not go to emerg because I don't have anyone to watch my child.

Community workers and women alike recognized the unique need for specialized services for mothers experiencing homelessness at the intersection of many vulnerabilities.

"Help Comes with a Price": Support with Surveillance

Women expressed the existence of a false sense of support within a system that is meant to be supportive. For example, a mother with two children residing in shelter noted, "once you have the support you need, you have to constantly prove you need it." This was common when participants discussed gaining access to social assistance in the form of financial aid, mental health support, and access to housing. In proving that they deserved these services, mothers had to demonstrate their worthiness of some services, despite the fact that these supports were put to place to ensure that all members of society could have their basic human needs met.

The women also reported that often "help comes with a price." For many, the cost was the relinquishing of a private life, with their day-to-day living being placed under scrutiny. They feared the consequences of system interactions, such as child welfare system involvement, increased stigma and discrimination, and surveillance. Women noted that some organizations, which were supposed to offer refuge, protection, and support, did the opposite. Women expressed their experiences with these particular services as repeated "markers of mistakes," "jail-like," controlling, and provoking fear and judgement. The negative aspects added to the fear of system involvement, so much so that women were reluctant to seek much-needed help and support from them:

> A couple of times we were in the shelter and [child protection services] was called and we weren't doing anything ... they come to a person who has like two or three kids ... and they are going to apprehend their kids, and I just think, ... you have no clue what it is like to have to raise a child, and to go through struggles every day ... how dare you look down your nose at me ... from mothers who are so trying.

This woman further discussed how she did not feel supported to maintain custody of her children and spoke about the subsequent trauma of having her children apprehended. Women's interactions with the child welfare system were complex. Distrust in the child welfare system was common to the mothers' experiences of parenting without a home. Women expressed their fear of child welfare system involvement, rather than viewing it as a source of support and as a resource. While a few women noted the positive help, guidance, and support they received from child welfare services for themselves as children and/or for their own children, this was the exception and was not common to most women. Mothers expressed that compounding vulnerabilities, such as young age, living in poverty, experiencing mental health crises, and parenting without a home placed them in precarious and powerless positions when working with child protection services. Another woman reported feeling targeted due to her age and lack of employment:

> [Child protection services (CPS)] picks on mothers, targets younger moms. If you don't have support they target you. I was 18 years old when I had my daughter ... They harassed me for three to six months. Like, I take care of my daughter. There is food for her in my fridge; there isn't a bruise on her. I put my foot down—I said, "You guys have no reason to come here." If I was a woman who was older and had a job they wouldn't have targeted me. They shouldn't target us because we have no family or are in shelter. These moms should not have their kids removed for things beyond their control ... I thought CPS was there to support us? Well then support us!

Sharing this woman's concerns, one service provider challenged the accepted social norms regarding apprehension of children and supporting mothers and reiterated the detrimental impact of support that came too late:

> I think that as a society, we would be much more comfortable with the notion of taking women's children away from them, than providing the background services that would facilitate that woman continuing on in a mothering capacity ... so they're in crisis, so it looks like they're incompatible with parenting but it just has to be the place in which we've intervened is too late because they're that much further off.

"Every Shelter Is So Different": Organizational Philosophies Impacting Support

At a shelter/organizational level, service providers noted that organizational philosophies, values, policies, procedures, and regulations shaped women's interactions with support services. For example, several women working in a shelter for women experiencing interpersonal violence noted their organization's feminist intersectional philosophical underpinnings, and the ongoing examination of current policies and procedures to ensure the needs of women were met and power differentials addressed. These service providers noted their women-centred values and discussed the ways in which the organization was striving to ensure the values, voice, and autonomy of the women they worked with were incorporated into their approaches to care. Other service providers working within agencies not guided by feminist or intersectional philosophies noted that a more explicit women-centred and anti-oppressive approach was needed to better support women. Two service providers felt, at times, that their organization's authoritative approach further inhibited women's power and control and created distrust and less effective care. These service providers desired to work within an anti-oppressive organization where the agency would be required to create and enact policies that challenged current power differentials and valued the inclusion of women's voices in shaping the care provided.

Many mothers noticed a difference in how they were treated within and across various agencies, indicating how the autonomy and treatment of service users varied from agency to agency. The underlying philosophies or intrinsic values of the agencies influenced women's desire to seek support and help, as well as either trust or distrust in the system. For example, a woman shared her fear of disclosing her drug dependency out of worry that she would not be able to remain in shelter and that she would not be able to see her daughter. She discussed the negative interactions she had with multiple counsellors and service providers from a variety of agencies, who made her feel "like shit" about her addiction as a mother. She knew she needed help, but at the same time felt she had to hide her addiction so as not to compromise shelter access. After she overdosed, she was referred to a shelter that was inclusive of women suffering from addiction. Not only did this shelter allow her to stay, despite her addiction, but they were able to support her through her addiction. She emphasized that they treated her "like a person" and did not "talk down" to her. Within this agency she noted that she felt heard, valued, respected, and supported. Service providers echoed the importance of inclusivity in services. They reported the struggle in having turned women away from services, based on policies, due to addictions or sex trade involvement and the subsequent inability for women to meet "curfew," or not being able to locate adequate support for mothers due to the exclusion criteria within other agency policies.

4. DISCUSSION

The study's participants expressed their view that the system played a monumental role in their lives. In this way, the system was an active participant in their lives, thus drawing attention to the structures of exclusion that shaped participants' health experiences. As advocates, helping professionals need to recognize the immense injustice within the system itself and to help shift dominant discourses of blame to instead critique a flawed system. These advocacy efforts need to target change at the macro, mezzo, and micro levels.

At the macro level, poverty and the lack of affordable housing were central in the way in which social exclusion was enacted in mothers' lives. The majority of participants received financial support in the form of social assistance, yet study participants remained in the depths of poverty. Existing poverty reduction strategies within Canada have focused primarily on job readiness and training, in addition to incremental, and insufficient, increases to social assistance (Government of Ontario, 2014) without notable success at actually reducing poverty (Plante, 2019). That is, employment and job readiness does not necessarily eliminate poverty, but may in fact result in added stress and caregiver strain for lone mothers. Instead, poverty reduction advocates and researchers alike have advocated for an evidence-informed approach to poverty reduction that would support access to a Guaranteed Basic Income (Benbow et al., 2016; Hyndman & Simon, 2015; Smith-Carrier & Lawlor, 2016). Such a strategy would ensure that mothers, and others living in poverty, would have sufficient financial security to access basic human needs, such as food and housing, which would ultimately yield positive health and social outcomes (Forget, 2011; Smith-Carrier, 2017).

Further, homelessness has detrimental effects on all other determinants of health and its existence is reflective of extreme social exclusion (Watson, 2012). Helping professionals have a role in advocating for increased access to affordable housing for all, inclusive of special considerations for specific populations, such as mothers experiencing homelessness. Those in health and social services can advocate for evidence-informed solutions to ending homelessness, such as Housing First initiatives. Housing First involves the immediate provision of permanent housing and wraparound supports to individuals experiencing homelessness while encompassing five overarching principles:

- immediate access to housing with no housing readiness conditions;
- consumer choice and self-determination;
- a recovery orientation;
- individualized and person-driven supports; and,
- social and community integration (Geller, 2014).

At the mezzo and micro levels, mothers expressed much gratitude for available social programs and supports. However, participants' expressed feelings of inclusion and support were experienced within the context of exclusion, which underscores the simultaneous nature and non-linear relationship between inclusion and exclusion (Caxaj & Berman, 2010; Pease, 2009; Reid, 2004; Yanicki et al., 2014). However, participants expressed that experiences of inclusion existed within the circumstance of exclusion. In this way, exclusion and inclusion were inextricably linked; however, within the context of this study and in the lives of study participants, social inclusion was predominantly experienced only within spaces of exclusion, as emphasized in the quote "You are only let in when you are so far out." This speaks to the continued need to advocate for upstream health promotion initiatives aimed at promoting the health and well-being of families and communities prior to them being in crisis.

While mothers expressed great praise for some services, they also noted the inadequate, subpar, and discriminatory treatment they received in accessing other services. Such treatment can result in poorer health outcomes for those who need it most (Browne et al., 2015; EQUIP Health Care, 2018). Helping professionals can engage in critical reflection and challenge personal stigma or discriminatory values held or enacted in providing care for marginalized groups, such as mothers experiencing homelessness. It would also be of value for future research to examine changing dynamics of the parental landscape in Canada and the compounding impacts of poverty. This is also important in that, based on the premise of compassion and respect, simple shifts in our approach can make a difference: instead of asking "what's wrong with people?" as advocates we must ask, "what's happened to people?" (Wathen, as cited in Bieman, 2018).

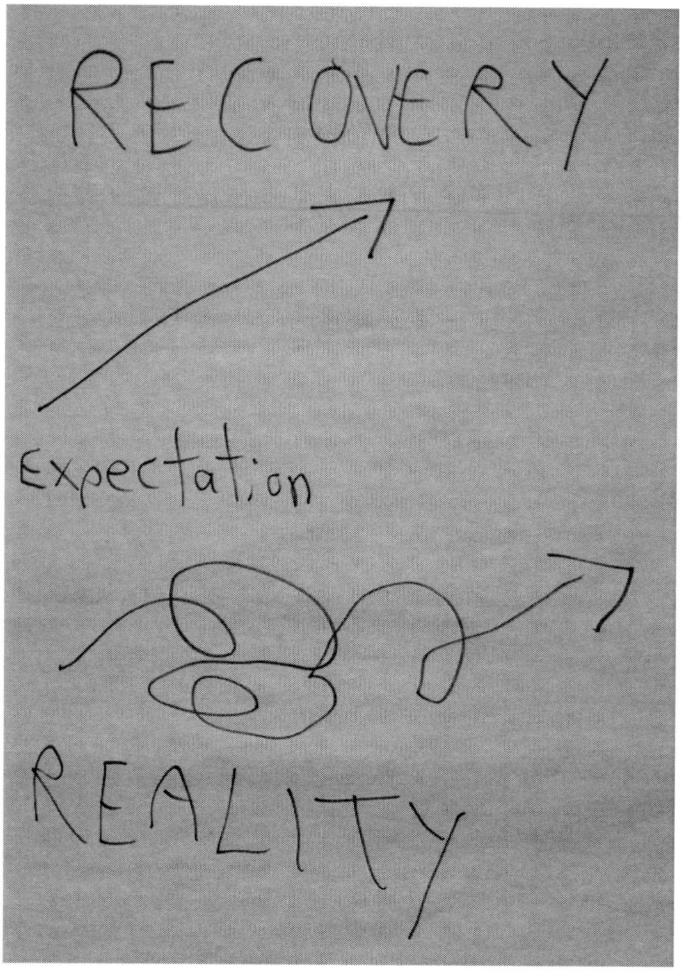

Moving from Exclusion to Inclusion: Representative. A diagram of recovery trajectories drawn on chart paper during one of the first sessions of a Connect (peer support) group. Many members of the group felt their experience in the group could best be represented by images of the activities they engaged in to further their recovery. This diagram also reflects the non-linear journey discussed by women in this study.
Source: Photo by Justin Langille

REFERENCES

Azarmehr, H., Lowry, K., Sherman, A., Smith, C., & Zuniga, J. A. (2018). Nursing practice strategies for prenatal care of homeless pregnant women. *Nursing for Women's Health, 22*(6), 489–498. doi:10.1016/j.nwh.2018.09.005

Bassuk, E. L., & Beardslee, W. R. (2014). Depression in homeless mothers: Addressing an unrecognized public health issue. *American Journal of Orthopsychiatry, 84*(1), 73–81.

Benbow, S. (2015). Mothers experiencing homelessness: Social exclusion, resistance, and health. *Electronic Thesis and Dissertation Repository*, 3407. Retrieved from https://ir.lib.uwo.ca/etd/3407

Benbow, S., Forchuk, C., & Ray, S. (2011). Mothers with mental illness experiencing homelessness: A critical analysis. *Journal of Psychiatric and Mental Health Nursing, 18*(8), 687–695.

Benbow, S., Gorlick, C., Forchuk, C., Ward-Griffin, C., & Berman, H. (2016). Ontario's poverty reduction strategy: A critical discourse analysis. *Canadian Journal of Nursing Research, 48*(3–4), 100–109.

Berman, H., Irías Gíron, E. R., & Marroquín, A. P. (2009a). A narrative study of refugee women who have experienced violence in the context of war. *Canadian Journal of Nursing Research, 41*(1), 144–165.

Berman, H., Mulcahy, G. A., Forchuk, C., Edmunds, K. A., Haldenby, A., & Lopez, R. (2009b). Uprooted and displaced: A critical narrative study of homeless, Aboriginal, and newcomer girls in Canada. *Issues in Mental Health Nursing, 30*(7), 418–430.

Bieman, J. (2018). Cup of kindness from clinicians an elixir for better patient health: Western University study. *The London Free Press.* Retrieved from https://lfpress.com/news/local-news/cup-of-kindness-from-clinicians-an-elixir-for-better-patient-health-western-study-says

Browne, A. J., Varcoe, C., Ford-Gilboe, M., & Wathen, C. N., on behalf of the EQUIP Research Team. (2015). EQUIP Healthcare: An overview of a multi-component intervention to enhance equity-oriented care in primary health care settings. *International Journal of Equity in Health, 14*(1), 152–162.

Bryant, T., & Shapcott, M. (2016). Housing. In D. Raphael (Ed.), *Social determinants of health: Canadian perspectives* (3rd ed., pp. 343–359). Toronto, ON: Canadian Scholars' Press.

Canadian Observatory on Homelessness. (n.d.). *Chronic illness/disesases and mortality.* Retrieved from https://www.homelesshub.ca/about-homelessness/health/chronic-illnessesdiseases-and-mortality

Carroll, W. K. (Ed.). (2004). *Critical strategies for social research.* Toronto, ON: Canadian Scholars' Press.

Caxaj, C. S., & Berman, H. (2010). Belonging among newcomer youths: Intersecting experiences of inclusion and exclusion. *Advances in Nursing Science, 33*(4), E17–E30.

Caxaj, C. S., Berman, H., Varcoe, C., Ray, S. L., & Restoulec, J.-P. (2014). Gold mining on Mayan-Mam territory: Social unravelling, discord and distress in the Western highlands of Guatemala. *Social Science & Medicine, 111*(1), 50–57.

Caxaj, C. S., & Gill, N. K. (2017). Belonging and mental wellbeing among a rural Indian-Canadian diaspora: Navigating tensions in "finding a space of our own." *Qualitative Health Research, 27*(8), 1119–1132.

Chambers, C., Chiu, S., Scott, A. N., Tolomiczenko, G., Redelmeier, D. A., Levinson, W., & Hwang, S. W. (2014). Factors associated with poor mental health status among homeless women with and without dependent children. *Community Mental Health Journal, 50*(5), 553–559.

Chase, S. E. (2005). Narrative inquiry: Multiple lenses, approaches, voices. In N. K. Denzin & Y. S. Lincoln (Eds.), *The SAGE handbook of qualitative research* (3rd ed., pp. 651–679). Thousand Oaks, CA: SAGE Publications.

Chase, S. E. (2011). Narrative inquiry: Still a field in the making. In N. K. Denzin & Y. S. Lincoln (Eds.), *The SAGE handbook of qualitative research* (4th ed., pp. 421–434). Thousand Oaks, CA: SAGE Publications.

Duffy, M. (2007). Narrative inquiry: The method. In P. L. Munhall (Ed.), *Nursing research: A qualitative perspective* (4th ed., pp. 401–421). Sudbury, MA: Jones & Bartlett Publishers.

Eakin, J., Robertson, A., Poland, B., Coburn, D., & Edwards, R. (1996). Towards a critical social science perspective on health promotion research. *Health Promotion International, 11*(2), 157–165.

EQUIP Health Care. (2018). *EQUIP primary health care.* University of British Columbia. Retrieved from https://equiphealthcare.ca/primary-health-care/

Fazel, S., Geddes, J. R., & Kushel, M. (2014). The health of homeless people in high-income countries: Descriptive epidemiology, health consequences, and clinical and policy recommendations. *The Lancet, 384*(9953), 1529–1540.

Forget, E. (2011). The town with no poverty: The health effects of a Canadian Guaranteed Annual Income field experiment. *Canadian Public Policy, 37*(3), 283–305.

Gaetz, S., Donaldson, J., Richter, T., & Gulliver, T. (2013). *The state of homelessness in Canada 2013.* Toronto, ON: Canadian Homelessness Research Network Press.

Galabuzi, G.-E. (2016). Social exclusion. In D. Raphael (Ed.), *Social determinants of health: Canadian perspectives* (3rd ed., pp. 388–418). Toronto, ON: Canadian Scholars' Press.

Geller, L. (2014). Putting housing first. *Canadian Nurse.* Retrieved from https://www.canadian-nurse.com/articles/issues/2014/june-2014/putting-housing-first

Government of Ontario. (2014). *Realizing our potential: Ontario's poverty reduction strategy, 2014–2019.* Retrieved from http://www.ontario.ca/document/realizing-our-potential-poverty-reduction-strategy-2014-2019

Greaves, L., Chabot, C., Jategaonkar, N., Poole, N., & McCullough, L. (2006). Substance use among women in shelters for abused women and children: Programming opportunities. *Canadian Journal of Public Health, 97*(5), 388–392.

Haldenby, A. M., Berman, H., & Forchuk, C. (2007). Homelessness and health in adolescents. *Qualitative Health Research, 17*(9), 1232–1244.

Huey, L., Fthenos, G., & Hryniewicz, D. (2013). "If something happened, I will leave it, let it go and move on": Resiliency and victimized homeless women's attitudes toward mental health counseling. *Journal of Interpersonal Violence, 28*(2), 295–319.

Hwang, S. W., Wilkins, R., Tjepkema, M., O'Campo, P. J., & Dunn, J. R. (2009). Mortality among residents of shelters, rooming houses, and hotels in Canada: 11 year follow-up study. *British Medical Journal, 339*, b4036.

Hyndman, B., & Simon, L., for the Health Equity Workgroup. (2015). *Basic income guarantee backgrounder.* Ontario Public Health Association. Retrieved from http://www.opha.on.ca/getmedia/bf22640d-120c-46db-ac69-315fb9aa3c7c/alPHa-OPHA-HEWG-Basic-Income-Backgrounder-Final-Oct-2015.pdf.aspx?ext=.pdf

Kelly, L., & Luxford, Y. (2017). Come walk with me: Homelessness, nursing and engaged care. *Collegian, 24*(5), 417–420.

Labonté, R. (2016). Social inclusion/exclusion and health: Dancing the dialectic. In D. Raphael (Ed.), *Social determinants of health: Canadian perspectives* (3rd ed., pp. 419–433). Toronto, ON: Canadian Scholars' Press.

Labov, W. (1972). The transformation of experience in narrative syntax. In W. Labov (Ed.), *Language in the inner city: Studies in the Black English Vancouver* (pp. 354–396). Philadelphia, PA: University of Pennsylvania Press.

Lee, B. A., & Schreck, C. J. (2005). Danger on the streets: Marginality and victimization among homeless people. *American Behavioral Scientist, 48*(8), 1055–1081.

Lewinson, T., Thomas, M. L., & White, S. (2014). Traumatic transitions: Homeless women's narratives of abuse, loss, and fear. *Affilia, 29*(2), 192–205.

McCormack, C. (2000a). From interview transcript to interpretive story: Part 1—viewing the transcript through multiple lenses. *Field Methods, 12*(4), 282–297.

McCormack, C. (2000b). From interview transcript to interpretive story: Part 2—developing an interpretive story. *Field Methods, 12*(4), 298–315.

McCormack, C. (2004). Storying stories: A narrative approach to in-depth interview conversations. *International Journal of Social Research Methodology, 73*(3), 219–236.

Milaney, K., Ramage, K., Yang Fang, X., & Louis, M. (2017). *Understanding mothers experiencing homelessness: A gendered approach to finding solutions for family homelessness.* Toronto, ON: Canadian Observatory on Homelessness Press.

Patton, M. Q. (2002). *Qualitative research and evaluation methods* (3rd ed.). Thousand Oaks, CA: SAGE Publications.

Pavao, J., Alvarez, J., Baumrind, N., Induni, M., & Kimerling, R. (2007). Intimate partner violence and housing instability. *American Journal of Preventative Medicine, 32*(2), 143–146.

Pease, B. (2009). The other side of social exclusion: Interrogating the role of the privileged in reproducing inequality. In A. Taket, B. R. Crisp, A. Nevill, G. Lamaro, M. Graham, & S. Barter-Godfrey (Eds.), *Theorising social exclusion* (pp. 37–46). Abingdon, UK: Routledge.

Plante, C. (2019). Policy or window dressing? Exploring the impact of poverty reduction strategies on poverty among the Canadian provinces. *Journal of International and Comparative Social Policy, 35*(1), 112–136.

Poleshuk, E. L., Cerrito, B., Leshoure, N., Finocan-Kaag, G., & Kearney, M. H. (2013). Underserved women in a women's health clinic describe their experiences of depressive symptoms and why they have low uptake of psychotherapy. *Community Mental Health Journal, 49*(1), 50–60.

Raphael, D. (Ed.). (2016). *Social determinants of health: Canadian perspectives* (3rd ed.). Toronto, ON: Canadian Scholars' Press.

Reid, C. (2004). *The wounds of exclusion: Poverty, women's health, and social justice.* Edmonton, AB: Qualitative Institute Press.

Riessman, C. K. (1993). *Narrative analysis.* Newbury Park, CA: SAGE Publications.

Smith-Carrier, T. (2017). Reproducing social conditions of poverty: A critical feminist analysis of social assistance participation in Ontario, Canada. *Journal of Women, Politics, & Policy, 38*(4), 498–521.

Smith-Carrier, T., & Lawlor, A. (2016). Realising our (neoliberal) potential? A critical discourse analysis of Ontario's Poverty Reduction Strategy in Ontario, Canada. *Critical Social Policy, 37*(1), 105–127.

Stewart, M., Reutter, L., Makwarimba, E., Veenstra, G., Love, R., & Raphael, D. (2008). Left out: Perspectives on social exclusion and inclusion across income groups. *Health Sociology Review, 17*(1), 78–94.

Torchalla, I., Linden, I. A., Strehlau, V., Neilson, E. K., & Krausz, M. (2015). "Like a lots happened with my whole childhood": Violence, trauma and addiction in pregnant and postpartum women from Vancouver's Downtown Eastside. *Harm Reduction Journal, 12*(1), 1–10.

Walsh, C., Krieg, B., Rutherford, G., & Bell, M. (2013). Aboriginal women's voices: Breaking the cycle of homelessness and incarceration. *Pimatisiwin: A Journal of Aboriginal and Indigenous Community Health, 11*(3), 377–394.

Watson, J. (2012). Exploring health and social exclusion within hidden homeless. *Electronic Theses and Dissertations*, 5584. Retrieved from https://scholar.uwindsor.ca/etd/5584

Weinreb, L. F., Buckner, J. C., Williams, V., & Nicholson, J. (2006). A comparison of the health and mental health status of homeless mothers in Worcester, Mass: 1993 and 2003. *American Journal of Public Health, 96*(8), 1444–1448.

Wilson, K., Eyles, J., Elliott, S., Keller-Olaman, S., & Devcic, D. (2007). Linking social exclusion and health: Explorations in contrasting neighbourhoods in Hamilton, Ontario. *Canadian Journal of Urban Research, 16*(2), 126–148.

Yanicki, S. M., Kushner, K. E., & Reutter, L. (2014). Social inclusion/exclusion as matters of social (in)justice: A call for nursing action. *Nursing Inquiry, 22*(2), 121–133.

Yeater, E. A., Austin, J. L., Green, M. J., & Smither, J. E. (2010). Coping mediates the relationship between posttraumatic stress disorder (PTSD) symptoms and alcohol use in homeless, ethnically diverse women: A preliminary study. *Psychological Trauma: Theory, Research, Practice, and Policy, 2*(4), 307–310.

CHAPTER 11

Sheltering Indigenous Women with Mental Illness in Ontario: Being "Kicked" and Nurtured

Phyllis Montgomery, Sarah Benbow, Laura Hall, Denise Newton-Mathur, Cheryl Forchuk, and Sharolyn Mossey

1. INTRODUCTION

In Canada, the health and well-being of Indigenous women is particularly compromised in comparison to their non-Indigenous female counterparts. The individual and collective vulnerabilities of Indigenous women are represented by multiple intersecting "realities of everyday life in which Indigenousity, female gender, racism, sexism, and poverty are lived and experienced simultaneously, not sequentially" (Culhane, 2009). It has been well documented that Canadian Indigenous women have a significantly lower life expectancy (Smylie, 2009) and higher prevalence of depression, addictions, and self-injury (Donner et al., 2008; Reading & Wien, 2009). Further, Indigenous women are reported to have higher social surveillance, incarceration rates, incidences of violence, transgenerational trauma, discrimination, and lower income levels, all of which impact health and contribute to social exclusion (Haskell & Randall, 2009; Native Women's Association of Canada, 2004; Reading & Wien, 2009; Scott, 2007; Stout, 2010). As a group, Indigenous women are more often homeless compared to both non-Indigenous women and Indigenous men (Native Women's Association of Canada, 2007), which has further compromised their overall well-being inclusive of mental health.

Impacted by entrenched historical and contemporary health and social inequities (Green, 2010; Native Women's Association of Canada, 2004), Indigenous women often enter homeless shelter services to seek refuge (Richter & Chaw-Kant, 2008; Ruttan et al., 2008). For insecurely housed Canadians, such as Indigenous women, the use of adult shelter services has been fundamental to sustaining day-to-day survival in the midst of entrenched health and social disparities. In this way, homeless services focus predominantly on fulfilling immediate basic needs

(Benbow et al., 2011). Shelters offer services that are intended to transition vulnerable women from homelessness to stable housing through the concurrent provision of necessary health and social services. The coordination and timeliness of appropriate services to break the cyclic nature of homelessness is challenging given the variability and complexity of needs that threaten well-being (Richter & Chaw-Kant, 2008; Young & Moses, 2013).

In general, Canadian women have described their homeless shelter experiences as disempowering, un-dignifying, and regimented (Lyons et al., 2016; Novac, 1996; Scott, 2007). Liebow's (1993) ethnographic study suggested that racial divisiveness is pervasive within shelter life. In particular for women with mental illness who may be subjected to overt and covert hostility associated with racial tensions, self-imposed isolation was a protective strategy that further undermined their mental health. Other authors reported that the need to balance individual and collective security is a complex undertaking for community workers navigating cultural tensions and advocating for broader social justice (Berman et al., 2009; Krausz et al., 2013; Lyon-Callo, 2004; Lyons et al., 2016). Further, social disparities impede exit from the shelter circuit, keeping Indigenous women dependent on services that may not be culturally sensitive (Thurston et al., 2011).

Several authors have identified the need for focused research that explores the well-being of Indigenous women when their capacity to fulfill family and community responsibilities is disrupted (Berman et al., 2009; Ruttan et al., 2010; Stout, 2010). The purpose of this chapter was to develop an understanding of the day-to-day experiences of Indigenous women as they seek safety, comfort, health, and healing in the context of mental illness and insecure housing. As important, this chapter provides the accounts of receiving and providing shelter services as told by Indigenous women. Green (2010) identified that individual and collective experiences of Indigenous women are reflective of social realities that warrant acknowledgement and intervention by psychiatric mental health nurses. The results of this chapter have the potential to sensitize helping professionals to the complexity of Indigenous women's quest to achieve wellness of body, mind, and spirit as described by the First Nations and Inuit Mental Wellness Advisory Committee (2007), an underdeveloped area of health and counselling practice.

2. METHODS

Design

This study's design was a supplementary secondary qualitative approach to examine a data subset not fully addressed in a primary study (Heaton, 2008). The five-year primary study used a mixed methods participatory action approach to examine housing issues and solutions for individuals with mental illness (Forchuk et al., 2011). It generated an extensive repository of data, approved for secondary analyses. The dataset, particular to Indigenous women who used or provided shelter services, was accessed for this supplementary study to elicit a focused description of their knowledge about and experiences of shelter care. This secondary analysis was important to search for new knowledge that is informed by the voices of Indigenous women (Kenny, 2006; Ruttan et al., 2008; Smith, 1999).

To uphold the ethical principle of beneficence, the anonymity and uniqueness of each woman was safeguarded through data extraction, secure storage, and representation in the findings. This was particularly salient given that participant data could reveal their identity to members of their small communities. Cultural sensitivity throughout the research process was guided by the Indigenous research team members.

Sample

The original study recruited individuals from a variety of mental health, housing, and social services in Southern Ontario, all of whom were involved in either service use or service provision (Forchuk et al., 2011). For this study, data was extracted from group interviews specific to 21 English-speaking women who self-identified as Indigenous, including First Nation, Métis, or Inuit. It is acknowledged that each of these three groups of Indigenous Peoples is distinct, with unique heritages, languages, cultural practices, and spiritual beliefs as described by the Government of Canada (2012). Of this sample, 11 self-identified as having a history of mental illness and insecure housing that required use of homeless shelter services. The remaining ten Indigenous women in the dataset were employed in the provision of homeless shelter services.

Data Collection and Analysis

Data particular to the 21 Indigenous women were extracted from the 8 primary study, tape-recorded, verbatim focus group transcripts, which were anonymized. Evident across the transcripts were stories co-constructed during participation in the focus groups. Stories, the unit of analysis in this study, are told to communicate internal understanding of life experiences and situations (Holloway & Freshwater, 2007; Riessman, 2008).

Data analysis involved a structural narrative approach to systematically identify and group stories based on shared structure, meaning, and function (Bailey et al., 2013). The structure refers to how stories are constructed by participants (Labov & Waletzky, 1972). The story meaning represents the participants' intended message

(Agar & Hobbs, 1983). Finally, the function of a story denotes the implications of what is being told to the researcher (Bailey et al., 2013). This approach necessitated the research team members to engage in serial open conversations leading to shared interpretations of the structure, meaning, and function of each story grouping with the intent of honouring the voices of the participants. This interactive and iterative approach was supported by the work of Peat (2002).

To preserve each Indigenous woman's anonymity, entire stories are not presented. Rather, one or two sentences were extracted from the accounts of several women to illustrate story structure, meaning, and function while indicating auditability, analytic logic, and credibility (Riessman, 2008). Within these extractions, textual clarifications were added within square brackets. The use of quotations was to note the precise lexicon of participants not attributable to or tidied by the researchers.

3. FINDINGS

In total, the women told 124 stories, describing daily experiences involving tenacious efforts to secure a "good life" for themselves and others in the context of mental illness and insecure housing. The experiences described by shelter service users and providers were similar. Their stories, reflecting a cohesive account of sheltering while vulnerable, were labelled being "kicked" and being nurtured. To varying degrees, these two groups of contrasting stories occurred in the lives of all participants. Below is a sequential presentation of the structure, meaning, and function of each of the two story groups.

Being "Kicked" Stories

Within this first group of stories, service users and service providers described a legacy of historical oppression with which they live on a day-to-day basis. Largely influenced by negativity, the women shared experiences likened to being perpetually "kicked," and thus the labelling of this group of stories. For some service users, being "kicked" was attributed to not only having a mental illness and insecure housing but also the "colour of my skin." For some service users, being "kicked" was related to generalization of Indigenous women as "untrustworthy."

Structure

The common structural element across all "kicked" stories was that of multiple, diverse, compounding, and often unresolved loss. Service users and providers detailed removal from or denial of resources such as personal possessions, relationships, autonomy, community influence, service, and land often entrenched in racial discrimination. The following excerpts illustrate the element of loss within the "kicked" stories.

> Service user 3: My grandfather makes [a special artefact] and he is 87 years old. He gave me one. I had it in the apartment. I lost the apartment and I lost my treasure. He [landlord] threw everything in the dump.
>
> Service user 5: I'm in a shelter because I lost my boyfriend and I lost our place.
>
> Service user 9: We are actually told we [Indigenous women] are no good for nothing and there is no way around that.
>
> Service provider 2: And out here all we have is our skin.
>
> Service provider 5: Our women have no property rights. When we leave [our reserve] we leave our land our home what we have built our whole life. As an Aboriginal woman I understand our reality, our issues, the Indian Act.
>
> Service provider 6: We know what it is like to deal with people who don't care. We know what it is like to be assumed that you are guilty even before you have a chance to explain. We know what that feeling is as it is also our experience. It is also our sisters' and brothers' experience. It happened to our parents, our cousins, our boyfriends, our girlfriends. It is there and it is bad.

The presence of repeated losses reinforced women's perception of exclusion, objectification, and deprivation, which was characteristic of the experience of being "kicked." Service users who were "kicked" out of places and service providers who were excluded or "kicked" out of processes witnessed the accumulation of their losses. Ultimately, this created an entrenchment of their respective needs as "virtually invisible" and unmet. Being kicked distanced them from where "they want[ed] to be and how they need[ed] to be." From a service user perspective, "always having doors slammed in your face" further threatened mental well-being. Service providers recognized that in the presence of loss and absence of stable mental health and secure housing, shelter users would remain "broken," "out of place," and preoccupied with just trying to "survive day-to-day."

Meaning and Function

The women told "kicked" stories to convey cumulative losses of that which was perceived as essential to health and well-being. Persistent discrimination and social inequities became commonplace in the lives of shelter service users and providers. Both shelter users and providers gave testimony to the contextual aggression and deprivation within their life and work circumstances. The participants acknowledged that an "unsupportive society" heightened suffering and perpetuated their sense of loss. With each repetitive and forceful kick, both shelter users and providers came to live in a sustained state of vulnerability. As described by a service provider, "their [shelter users'] crust starts to form," and "then their mental illness really kicks in." Succinctly stated by one shelter user, her life in disadvantage was "a constant audition" for a more meaningful and healthy existence. Overall, being kicked restricted women's capacities and opportunities for "peace."

These stories function to provide insight into the insidious nature of loss that pervades the life experiences of both shelter service users and providers in this study. Although experienced to varying degrees, each woman was affected, directly or vicariously, by society's ineffectual response to eradicate homelessness and promote mental well-being. Further, this group of stories identifies the need for members of the community mental health network to provide culturally appropriate individualized assessments and cooperative interventions relative to trauma that could be experienced by some Indigenous women using and providing homeless shelter services. A failure to consider the possibility of such trauma risks "further and further and further and further and further" omissions in the comprehensive and coordinated service provision for Indigenous women living with mental illness and insecure housing.

Being Nurtured Stories

Within the second group of stories, service users and providers both described the need for and practices of gently "lifting each other up" in the context of the life circumstances described in the being "kicked" stories. Most nurturing stories described providers' attempts to "contribute good things" through nurturing of self, "our sisters," and "our people as a whole." Nurturing involved a respectful attention to the physical, emotional, social, spiritual, and cultural aspects of one another.

Structure

The common structural element across the being nurtured stories was partnering to address diverse needs. The presence of unmet needs necessitated respectful connections between service users, providers, and external others to fulfill immediate needs. The following excerpts illustrate the impetus for partnering within the nurturing stories.

> Service user 2: When I say I am sick I am really sick. And just like other people I need help from those [individuals who are supposed to help].

> Service user 6: As a single mother with kids I feel I need to hook up with someone because I can't do this alone to make ends meet. I would love to be on my own, but I can't right now.

> Service user 7: At many shelters, there are certain times where we can't eat. We don't even have a place to sit at [name of shelter]. At this shelter they do have good meals and fresh beds. If I don't have a place to sit I now know I can come here.

> Service provider 5: The Indian Act has to be interpreted. It is huge for our people in terms of where we can live, what are our rights, all those things that significantly impact on Indigenous women.

> Service provider 8: We had a woman who was going to be evicted while she was in the hospital. She called us. We went to her house and packed her stuff up for her. Whatever we can do to help we try to do it.

> Service provider 10: We care for some women who are so poor that they can't help their children. Not that they don't want to, not that they are bad people, not that they are not worthy. They simply can't do it alone.

Nurturing involved "providing for and being available to" one another, "one woman at a time." The acts were to foster in the service users a sense of being "cared for" and feeling "cared about." Efforts to counter the described losses in the "kicked" stories and establish a support network required service providers to be "pretty sophisticated in social politics." Their nurturing practices were guided by reasonable actions that addressed a woman's needs rather than rigid compliance with "institutionalized routines." For example, providers recognized the need to "let some women sleep" and "take the time they needed" to initiate restoration of "body, mind, and spirit." Cultural sensitivity was described as a welcome component of nurturing interactions. Simple actions such as speaking "our own languages" and sharing foods that "not only sustained us physically but provided cultural nourishment" were described as means of connecting with and nurturing one another.

Meaning and Function

Participants told being nurtured stories to illustrate the potential of positive and authentic connectedness in overcoming unmet needs both to promote individual "balance" and create a community of healthy Indigenous women. This group of stories portrays optimism for a future in which Indigenous women's identity as "beautiful, strong, caring, and kind" women is unmasked. These stories function to demonstrate that authentic nurturing focused on the individualized fulfillment of needs has the potential to extend "servicing" to "healing" for Indigenous women. Nurturing and healing work that is initiated by service users and providers within homeless shelters complements community mental health practice efforts for optimizing well-being.

4. DISCUSSION

This chapter's findings expand the community mental health body of literature regarding Indigenous women living with mental illness and homelessness. In juxtaposition to being "kicked," being nurtured stories present a simultaneous reality characterized by genuine concern and person-centred actions between and among Indigenous women. As such, findings suggest a turbulence between social exclusion and inclusion. In concert, the two types of stories illustrate the importance of validating the historical and contemporary contextual reality of Indigenous women and their strategic efforts to actualize person dignity, connectedness with valued others. The being "kicked" and nurtured stories depict individual and shared efforts towards balance of body, mind, and spirit; a fragile stability between social exclusion and social inclusion. Although the mandate of homeless shelter services is not mental health, the women's stories demonstrate that nurturing has the potential to promote individual mental well-being. Within spaces that offer safety and comfort, even if time-limited, a woman's journey for physical, emotional, mental, cultural, and spiritual well-being is made possible (Stout, 2010). Supportive friendships among Indigenous women in shelter or on the street can provide a "sense of home, comfort, and protection" (Christensen, 2017, p. 97) in the context of structural, not individual, vulnerabilities rooted in colonialism. Women who receive and provide sheltering services and the organizations in which services are structured are integral to building a community that not only espouses but enacts social justice.

Community building, as conceptualized by Walter and Hyde (2012), necessitates authentic "communityness," beyond the sharing of geographic space. In this process, members are connected by activities that foster a sense of belonging and social inclusion through the fair and equitable distribution of community resources. The nurtured stories within this research suggest the presence of emergent communityness. In contrast, "kicked" stories emphasize the ongoing presence of health and social inequities that continue to pervade the lives of Indigenous women, hallmarks that communityness and social justice have not yet been achieved.

Community building practices involve multidimensional engagements using a range of strategies to acknowledge diverse beliefs, interests, and strengths, with the goal of building capacity in the entire system, and all its participants, to operate as a community. Exploring ways of working together for community building necessitates affirming and acknowledging one another's legitimacy and legal entitlements, embracing diversity, identifying common goals such as health equity, engaging in creative planning, integrating multiple visions and strategies, and accepting responsibility to remain connected (Walter & Hyde, 2012). Shelter service user and provider partnering for fulfillment of immediate needs as represented in the nurturing stories in this study can be supported by mental health practitioners' conscious, inclusionary, and community building practices (Benbow, 2009; Green, 2010; Walter & Hyde, 2012). This chapter's findings suggest an orientation for fostering community development as opposed to a singular best practice to address the disparaging circumstances of individual women involved in shelter life. As argued by Johnstone (2001), mental health practitioners have a responsibility to challenge the status quo and advocate for inclusivity as strategies to subvert the normalized culture of prejudice and discrimination against vulnerable populations.

The loss feature of the being "kicked" stories can be perceived as a manifestation of poverty and exclusion associated with colonialism (Smith, 1999; Stout, 2010). According to de Leeuw et al. (2010), the Canadian legacy of colonialization permeates the mental health of Indigenous people. Thus, mental health practitioners' mindfulness of the impact of historical processes, such as the Indian Act, and the social determinants of health are able to provide a more comprehensive assessment of Indigenous women's mental health (Benbow et al., 2011; Browne et al., 2005; Christensen, 2017; Stout, 2010). Koptie (2010) cautioned that definitions of poverty, underpinned by tenets of assimilation, negate the efforts of Indigenous people to overcome their "trajectory of suffering" in a colonial context.

The being nurtured stories that were shared not only pay tribute to the resilience and strength of Indigenous women in adversity but support the movement away from an account solely focused on abuse and pain to one of strength, hope, and acknowledgement of Indigenous experiential knowledge (Brascoupé & Waters, 2009; McKegney, 2007). Indigenous worldviews generally tend to emphasize responsibility for the whole of the community rather than individual members. Helping professionals' awareness of this orientation may foster a partnering with Indigenous women in their efforts to shift practices from an emphasis on service provision to connectedness and inclusivity with sensitivity to context and culture. This "coming-to- know" (Peat, 2002) requires attention to processes through further dialogue among a range of community stakeholders to understand the circumstances required for Indigenous women to actively engage in their wellness (Kenny, 2006).

Forging authentic relations between mental health and social service providers is imperative to ensure that individual rights and needs are met and, at a much broader level, social inclusion and social action for community building can be achieved for marginalized populations (Berman et al., 2009; Canadian Nurses Association, 2010; Labonté, 2012). To bridge the chasms that continue to exist within health and social services, mental health practitioners can function in a variety of roles such as care advocate, case manager, and consultant. The roles of care manager (Ciccone et al., 2010) and navigator (Wells et al., 2008) to support individuals living with other chronic challenges warrant greater examination for feasibility with this population. In conclusion, future research guided by Indigenous methodologies, such as sharing circles (Lavallée, 2009), is recommended to extend the findings of this work. Such approaches offer the possibility of acquiring further understanding of the complex realities of mental health and housing challenges for Indigenous women in a culturally appropriate manner beyond what was accomplished here.

REFERENCES

Agar, M. H., & Hobbs, J. R. (1983). Natural plans: Using AI planning in the analysis of ethnographic interviews. *Ethos, 11*(1/2), 33–48.

Bailey, P. H., Montgomery, P., & Mossey, S. (2013). Narrative inquiry. In C. T. Beck (Ed.), *Routledge international handbook of qualitative nursing research* (pp. 268–281). London, UK: Routledge.

Benbow, S. (2009). Societal abuse in the lives of individuals with mental illness. *Canadian Nurse, 105*(6), 30–32.

Benbow, S., Forchuk. C., & Ray S. L. (2011). Mothers with mental illness experiencing homelessness: A critical analysis. *Journal of Psychiatric and Mental Health Nursing, 18*(8), 687–695.

Berman, H., Mulcahy, G. A., Forchuk, C., Edmunds, K. A., Haldenby, A., & Lopez, R. (2009). Uprooted and displaced: A critical narrative study of homeless, Aboriginal, and newcomer girls in Canada. *Issues in Mental Health Nursing, 30*(7), 418–430.

Brascoupé, S., & Waters, C. (2009). Cultural safety: Exploring the applicability of the concept of cultural safety to Aboriginal health and community wellness. *Journal of Aboriginal Health, 5*(2), 6–41.

Browne, A. J., Smye, V. L., & Varcoe, C. (2005). The relevance of postcolonial theoretical perspectives to research in Aboriginal health. *Canadian Journal of Nursing Research, 37*(4), 16–37.

Canadian Nurses Association. (2010). *Social justice: A* means *to an end, an end in itself* (2nd ed.). Ottawa, ON: Author.

Christensen, J. (2017). *No home in a homeland: Indigenous Peoples and homelessness in the Canadian North.* Vancouver, BC: UBC Press.

Ciccone, M. M., Aquilino, A., Cortese, F., Scicchitano, P., Sassara, M., Mola, E., … Bux, F. (2010). Feasibility and effectiveness of a disease and care management model in the primary health care system for patients with heart failure and diabetes (Project Leonardo). *Vascular Health and Risk Management, 6*(6), 297–305.

Culhane, D. (2009). Narratives of hope and despair in Downtown Eastside Vancouver. In L. J. Kirmayer & G. G. Valaskakis (Eds.), *Healing traditions: The mental health of Aboriginal Peoples in Canada* (pp. 160–177). Vancouver, BC: UBC Press.

de Leeuw, S., Greenwood, M., & Cameron, E. (2010). Deviant constructions: How governments preserve colonial narratives of addictions and poor mental health to intervene into the lives of Indigenous children and families in Canada. *International Journal of Mental Health and Addictions, 8*(2), 282–295.

Donner, L., Isfeld, H., Haworth-Brockman, M., & Forsey, C. (2008). *A profile of women's health in Manitoba.* Winnipeg, MB: Prairie Women's Health Centre of Excellence.

First Nations and Inuit Mental Wellness Advisory Committee. (2007). *Strategic action plan for First Nations and Inuit mental wellness draft.* Ottawa, ON: Author.

Forchuk, C., Csiernik, R., & Jensen, E. (2011). *Homelessness, housing and mental health: Finding truths—creating change.* Toronto, ON: Canadian Scholars' Press.

Government of Canada. (2012). *Indigenous Affairs and Northern Development Canada: Terminology.* Ottawa, ON: Author. Retrieved from https://www.aadnc-aandc.gc.ca/eng/1358879361384/1358879407462

Green, B. L. (2010). Applying interdisciplinary theory in the care of Aboriginal women's mental health. *Journal of Psychiatric Mental Health Nursing, 17*(9), 797–803.

Haskell, L., & Randall, M. (2009). Disrupted attachments: A social context complex trauma framework and the lives of Aboriginal peoples in Canada. *Journal of Aboriginal Health, 5*(3), 48–99.

Heaton, J. (2008). Secondary analysis of qualitative data. In P. Alasuutari, L. Bickman, & J. Brannen (Eds.), *The SAGE handbook of social research methods* (pp. 506–519). London, UK: SAGE Publications.

Holloway, I., & Freshwater, D. (2007). *Narrative research in nursing.* Oxford, UK: Wiley-Blackwell.

Johnstone, M.-J. (2001). Stigma, social justice and the rights of the mentally ill: Challenging the status quo. *Australian & New Zealand Journal of Mental Health Nursing, 10*(4), 200–209.

Kenny, C. (2006). When the women heal: Aboriginal women speak about policies to improve the quality of life. *American Behavioral Scientist, 50*(4), 550–561.

Koptie, S. W. (2010). Inferiorizing Indigenous communities and intentional colonial poverty. *First Peoples Child and Family Review, 5*(2), 96–106.

Krausz, R. M., Clarkson, A. F., Strehlau, V., Torchalla, I., Li, K., & Schuetz, C. G. (2013). Mental disorder, service use, and barriers to care among 500 homeless people in 3 different urban settings. *Social Psychiatry and Psychiatric Epidemiology, 48*(8), 1235–1243.

Labonté, R. (2012). Community, community development, and the forming of authentic partnerships: Some critical reflections. In M. Minkler (Ed.), *Community organizing and community building for health and welfare* (3rd ed., pp. 95–109). New Brunswick, NJ: Rutgers University Press.

Labov, W., & Waletzky, J. (1972). Narrative analysis: Oral versions of personal experience. In J. Helms (Ed.), *Essays on the verbal and visual arts: Proceedings of the 1966 annual spring meeting of the American Ethnological Society* (pp. 12–44). Seattle, WA: University of Washington Press.

Lavallée, L. F. (2009). Practical application of an Indigenous research framework and two qualitative indigenous research methods: Sharing circles and Anishnaabe symbol-based reflection. *International Journal for Qualitative Methodology, 8*(1), 21–40.

Liebow, E. (1993). *Tell them who I am: The lives of homeless women.* New York, NY: The Free Press.

Lyon-Callo, V. (2004). *Inequality, poverty, and neoliberal governance: Activist ethnography in the homeless sheltering industry.* Peterborough, ON: Broadview Press.

Lyons, T., Krüsi, A., Pierre, L., Smith, A., Small, W., & Shannon, K. (2016). Experiences of trans women and two-spirit persons accessing women-specific health and housing services in a downtown neighborhood of Vancouver, Canada. *LGBT Health, 3*(5), 373–378.

McKegney, S. (2007). We have been silent too long: Linguistic play in Anthony Apakark Thrasher's prison writings. In *Magic weapons: Aboriginal writers remaking community after residential school* (pp. 59–99). Winnipeg, MB: University of Manitoba Press.

Native Women's Association of Canada. (2004). *Aboriginal women and housing: For the Canada-Aboriginal Peoples roundtable sectoral follow-up session on housing.* Ottawa, ON: Author.

Native Women's Association of Canada. (2007). *Aboriginal women and homelessness: An issue paper.* Corner Brook, NL: Author.

Novac, S. (1996). *A place to call one's own: New voices of dislocation and dispossession.* Ottawa, ON: Status of Women Canada.

Peat, F. D. (2002). *Blackfoot physics: A journey into the Native American universe.* Grand Rapids, MI: Phanes Press.

Reading, C., & Wien, F. (2009). *Health inequalities and social determinants of Aboriginal Peoples' health.* Prince George, BC: National Collaborating Centre for Aboriginal Health.

Richter, M. S., & Chaw-Kant, J. (2008). A case study: Retrospective analysis of homeless women in a Canadian city. *Women's Health & Urban Life, 7*(1), 7–19.

Riessman, C. K. (2008). *Narrative methods for the human sciences.* Los Angeles, CA: SAGE Publications.

Ruttan, L., LaBoucane-Benson, P., & Munro, B. (2008). "A story I never heard before": Aboriginal young women, homelessness, and restoring connections. *Pimatsiwin: A Journal of Aboriginal and Indigenous Community Health, 6*(1), 31–54.

Ruttan, L., LaBoucane-Benson, P., & Munro, B. (2010). "Home and Native Land": Aboriginal young women and homelessness in the city. *First Peoples Child & Family Review, 5*(1), 67–77.

Scott, S. (2007). *All our sisters: Stories of homeless women in Canada.* Peterborough, ON: Broadview Press.

Smith, L. T. (1999). *Decolonizing methodologies: Research and Indigenous Peoples.* New York, NY: Zed Books.

Smylie, J. (2009). The health of Aboriginal Peoples. In D. Raphael (Ed.), *Social determinants of health: Canadian perspectives* (2nd ed., pp. 280–301). Toronto, ON: Canadian Scholars' Press.

Stout, R. (2010). *Urban Aboriginal women and mental health.* Project #215. Winnipeg, MB: Prairie Women's Health Centre of Excellence.

Thurston, W. E., Oelke, N. D., Turner, D., & Bird, C. (2011). *Final report: Improving housing outcomes for Aboriginal people in Western Canada: National, regional, community and individual perspectives on changing the future of homelessness.* Calgary, AB: Department of Community Health Services.

Walter, C. L., & Hyde, C. A. (2012). Community building practice: An expanded conceptual framework. In M. Minkler (Ed.), *Community organizing and community building for health and welfare* (3rd ed., pp. 78–94). New Brunswick, NJ: Rutgers University Press.

Wells, K. J., Battaglia, T. A., Dudley, D. J., Garcia. R., Greene, A., Calhoun, E., … The Patient Navigation Research Program. (2008). Patient navigation: State of the art or is it science? *Cancer, 113*(8), 1999–2010.

Young, M. G., & Moses, J. M. (2013). Neo-liberalism and homelessness in the Western Canadian arctic. *Canadian Journal of Nonprofit and Social Economy Research, 4*(2), 7–22.

CHAPTER 12

The Mental Health of Those Who Serve Canada: A Reflection

Major Steven D. Pirie

"Life is pleasant. Death is peaceful. It's the transition that's troublesome." This statement by the prolific author Isaac Asimov highlights the thought process of every military person who has ever been deployed overseas in the service of their country. It is especially true because physical trauma is one of the inevitable occupational health hazards of war. It is a reality that military personnel accept when they enrol, and it is part of the concept of unlimited liability that forms the profession of arms. As strange as it may seem, during my multiple military deployments, the possibility of death was never a concern. I had, however, more than occasional thoughts about the horrors associated with being dismembered. These thoughts were intensified with each of the frequent rocket attacks on Kandahar Airfield during my deployment in Afghanistan. When outside Kandahar Airfield, one could not help but think of dismemberment as a result of being blown up by a roadside bomb or caught inside a burning armoured vehicle only to survive with disfigurement.

When a soldier steps on a landmine, the physiological consequences of blast pressure, heat, shrapnel, and being thrown about are profound. If the soldier survives the initial ballistic insult to their body, they are programmed, through repetitive and realistic training, to enact a self-preservation drill known as "self-aid." Soldiers will, if able to, seek cover, apply tourniquets, place field dressings on themselves, and signal the fact that they need aid from their platoon mates. Regardless of the extent of physical pain they may experience, they know that as soon as a field medical technician reaches them, they will be offered some relief in the form of an injectable or transmucosal opioid analgesic. This battlefield pain relief has been a mainstay of pre-hospital combat medicine since at least the American Civil War (Vassallo, 2004), and we have come to count on it.

I must admit that, while the possibility of physical injury and dismemberment was a serious concern at the time of my deployment, the threat of mental trauma never crossed my mind, at least not until one of my closest friends brought it up prior to my deployment to Afghanistan. Over dinner one evening, he asked, "Do you think you'll get post-traumatic stress disorder (PTSD) while serving in Afghanistan?" It was a casual question that challenged my sense of mental immunity. I had never even contemplated the possibility of becoming mentally ill from military service, and this self-conceptualization was very irksome. I was suddenly faced with the unique challenges associated with mental as opposed to physical trauma. If I were to be struck by a rocket or blown up by a roadside bomb, I knew what to do. I had the self-aid drill etched into my frontal lobe and knew that a morphine injection or a fentanyl lollipop would soon be offered to ease my suffering. However, I was never prepared for, nor did I think about the possibility of sustaining, an operational stress injury and living with a mental illness such as PTSD. There are no magic lollipops or injections to take away the pain or reduce the suffering from an operational stress injury. This fact was seared into my health-care consciousness in 2009 when I was begged by a young, battle-hardened corporal in the field hospital at Kandahar Airfield to kill him in order to stop his nightmares: here I am, supposed to provide health care to a comrade and alleviate his suffering, and he is asking me to end his suffering by taking his life away! There was no painkiller I could administer to resolve this problem, and it was an unsettling experience that reshaped my view of wartime trauma. This situation opened my eyes to the challenges associated with mental trauma and the fact that these could sometimes be greater than the challenges associated with physical dismemberment.

From a population health point of view, the Canadian Armed Forces is a subset of the Canadian society that it represents. Occupational health screening measures are routinely taken at the time of recruitment to exclude those with a serious pre-existing mental illness incompatible with military service. Hence our mental health is reflective of the mental health of the Canadian public, except for two conditions: depression and stress. It is well documented that the prevalence of depression and the incidence of stress are high among military personnel, likely due to the dangerous and stressful environments in which we often operate. It is estimated that one in five Canadians will develop a mental illness in their lifetime, and the challenges to society represented by this population outside the military are as notable as those within.

Macroscopically, it is the number of operational stress injuries that sets us apart from the civilian population we serve. In the Canadian Armed Forces, mental conditions most commonly manifest as generalized anxiety, major depression, and PTSD, and they cause notable human, organizational, and population health challenges for the military. For instance, the 2011 Canadian Forces Health Services Group Operational Stress Injury Cumulative Incidence Study found that 13% of the personnel deployed on the Canadian mission to Afghanistan up to 2008 were clinically diagnosed with a deployment-related mental injury (National Defence and the Canadian Armed Forces, 2013). While 13% may not sound alarming, it is not an inconsequential proportion in a relatively small military like Canada's, consisting of approximately 68,000 full-time and 32,000 part-time members, and it seems that everyone who has served or is actively serving in the Canadian Armed Forces has a colleague who has suffered or is suffering from a mental injury related to military service.

It is important to point out that the presentation and impact of mental illness among military personnel are markedly variable. There are those who have been mentally ill and have returned to work, only to function at a higher level than before their illness. There are also those who return to work and continue to struggle and those who suffer in silence. The most affected, however, are those who experience severe forms of mental illness that render them unable to meet the universality of service requirements, leading to their release from Her Majesty's service, and those who take the dramatic step of killing themselves as a way out of their mental illness. There are a variety of outcomes and anyone who is serving in the Canadian military today has a story about a colleague. The one commonality among these different scenarios is that they all genuinely require short-term and long-term levels of care and support. Even though the Canadian Armed Forces has completed operations in Afghanistan, there is no reason to believe that the issue of long-lasting mental illness will cease to exist. In addition, proper long-term management and planning are needed so that such experiences are handled based on lessons learned in future operations or wars. Operational stress injuries are now recognized as one of the occupational health hazards of deployed military service. They are becoming a fact of life and, like physical trauma, part of the concept of unlimited liability that forms the profession of arms. It is important that military personnel be well prepared to cope with these situations through rigorous training and a well-resourced mental health service.

As mental injury has increasingly become part of the backdrop of the profession of arms, the Canadian Forces Health Services Group has, along with its civilian partners, gone to great lengths to address the problem through health surveillance, mental health research, and the education of both clinicians and members of the service. The military and its partners have also invested in clinical programs for those afflicted by mental illness. Every person who joins the Canadian Armed Forces, be it as a cook or as a fighter pilot, is placed on the Road to Mental Readiness during basic training. This comprehensive program offers a wide range of services. These include educating members of the Canadian Armed Forces in the continuum of mental health: assisting with stress management, recognizing and managing mental illness, providing mental care for a colleague, accessing professional care resources if required. The program is revisited in greater depth as one is placed in successive leadership roles and/or is deployed in harm's way. It goes beyond simple education to provide an overall strategy of mental resilience training to prevent operational stress injuries and minimize the severity of such injuries should they occur. It also encourages those who sustain mental injuries to seek out timely and proper care when appropriate.

Everyone who encounters a stressful situation should, ideally, not only survive the experience but come out stronger as a result of having survived adversity. This can set a powerful cyclical process in motion if one encounters repeated stressful situations over the lifespan. Members of the Canadian Armed Forces now have a self-aid drill to execute should they suffer or see someone else suffer the effects of a mental injury; it is akin to the drill they follow if they step on a landmine and suffer physical trauma.

While Canada's operations in Afghanistan have been concluded, we still have a long way to go before we discover the "morphine for mental illness." There is still much to be done in terms of understanding and treating mental health issues. The Canadian Armed Forces is losing the service of good men and women as a result of operational stress injuries, and it will require a significant investment in research to stem the flow. The past is not behind us. This is not an academic issue that we can put in a banker's box on a shelf and then move forward. That would be a travesty and a disservice to military personnel. War has been a constant in human history, and it is highly probable, if not certain, that members of the Canadian Armed Forces will find themselves in sizeable operations in the future. We need to learn from the past, study and manage the present reality, and prepare for the future.

Mental health researchers have a moral responsibility to assist in the development of evidence-based strategies to address this challenge. The Canadian Armed Forces knows more about the mental health of its workforce than any other large employer in Canada (National Defence and the Canadian Armed Forces, 2013). Without the help and interest of civilian researchers, however, this body of knowledge will struggle to move forward. I encourage all stakeholders, and especially mental health researchers, to invest in the conduct of research in line with the

Surgeon General's Health Research Program and to become involved in academic endeavours such as those undertaken by the Canadian Institute for Military and Veteran Health Research (https://cimvhr.ca/).

While it might be true that we have made great strides in addressing the mental health of our service men and women, it is also true that more can be done to help those who put their lives on the line for Canada. Research attention is still needed on such topics as the impact of leadership on the mental health of subordinates, the overall impact of mental health on Canadian Armed Forces workplace productivity, the impact of military screening programs, and the effectiveness of various population-centric mental health treatments. I strongly believe that this last topic deserves special attention. If we can find better treatments for mental illness by investing in mental health research, then we can heal and therefore retain more military personnel who suffer from mental health issues. Mental illness is one of the occupational health hazards of war, and we owe it to our men and women in uniform to do more to understand the problem, provide education, build resilience, and deliver care to those affected. Surely, we can all agree that no one who has developed or may develop a mental illness while serving their country should have to beg for death as a treatment for their pain.

REFERENCES

National Defence and the Canadian Armed Forces. (2013). Surgeon General's mental health strategy: Canadian Forces Health Services Group—an evolution of excellence. Ottawa, ON: Government of Canada. Retrieved from http://www.forces.gc.ca/en/about-reports-pubs-health/surg-genmental-health-strategy-toc.page

Vassallo, S. A. (2004). Lewis H. Wright Memorial Lecture. *American Society of Anesthesiologists Newsletter, 68*(7), 9–10.

CHAPTER 13

Addressing Homelessness among Canadian Veterans

Cheryl Forchuk, Jan Richardson, and Heather Atyeo

1. INTRODUCTION

The range of experiences and differing needs among specific homeless subgroups is not well understood. This is especially true for Canadian veterans, a subpopulation gaining increasing recognition among homeless communities across Canada. While it is clear that the needs of Canadian veterans who are homeless differ from the general homeless population, there is little research within the Canadian context to guide housing interventions and related support for this group. Furthermore, individuals may not self-identify as veterans for a variety of reasons and, thus, innovative approaches are necessary to reach this target population.

The Canadian Model for Housing and Support for Veterans Experiencing Homelessness was a two-year evaluation project (2012–2014) funded through the federal Homelessness Partnering Strategy, with in-kind support from Veterans Affairs Canada (VAC) and the City of London and housing through support agencies across four Canadian cities (Table 13.1). This participatory action research (PAR) project developed and evaluated a model of housing and individualized programming to best meet the unique needs of Canadian veterans experiencing homelessness. The project used principles identified previously by veterans who were homeless (Milroy, 2009; Ray & Forchuk, 2011), such as peer support from someone with experience in the military and support for alcohol abuse and related issues. Local community partners experienced in working within the homeless-serving sector collaborated with federal partners; veteran-specific organizations including the Royal Canadian Legion, Operational Stress Injury Clinic (OSIC), and Operational Stress Injury Support Services (OSISS); and other

Table 13.1: Overview of Four Housing First Providers

Location	Capacity	Staffing	Housing Model	Housing & Supports	Peer Support
Toronto	20	Weekday support plus 24/7 on call	Two-bedroom units in one building owned and operated by site	Combined landlord and programs	Mental health peer support
London	10	Seven-day daily support plus 24/7 on call	Scattered sites: private sector apartments	Private landlord and supports by program	OSISS
Calgary	15	On-site 24/7	One-bedroom units in one building owned and operated by site	Combined landlord and programs	Informal
Victoria	11	Weekday volunteer support, no paid staff	Shared accommodations and some private sector	Combined landlord and programs	Veteran volunteers; OSISS

community-based services to provide 56 units of housing with support to veterans who were experiencing homelessness. Each site adhered to similar principles with emphasis on providing veteran-specific support and worked to enable pathways that support long-term housing-with-support solutions. Housing models differed across sites and included varying levels of on-site case management, clinical support, and peer mentorship, allowing for examination of the strengths and limitations of each approach and an opportunity to compare unique adaptations that evolved within each community.

2. THE HOUSING MODEL AND HOUSING-SPECIFIC SUPPORTS

Of the four sites, at the time of the study, one offered transitional housing while allowing flexibility as to the length of stay, whereas the remaining three sites provided permanent housing. Tenants were able to come and go freely at three of the four sites, while one site maintained a controlled entry model where tenants/guests checked in with staff as they entered or left the building. Staffing levels varied by site from daily with or without after-hours on-call support to a 24/7 staffing presence. Across sites, housing staff served as the primary case manager while working closely in partnership with a locally appointed Veterans Affairs Canada case manager, OSIC clinician, and peer support counsellor(s) to ensure that each veteran's housing, social, cultural, and health-related needs were seamlessly addressed. The exception to this was Victoria, where the overall approach was similar; however, supports were overseen and delivered by peer veteran volunteers. Support was individualized such that veteran-identified needs, both social and health, were considered a priority. Each of the sites has evolved and generally increased capacity since the study.

Key Principles

Seven principles based on the work of Milroy (2009) and Ray and Forchuk (2011) formed the basis of the evaluation project. Each project site was consistent in applying these principles while creating strategies to match local conditions and variability:

- Providing housing with support
- Peer support by veterans for veterans
- Provision of services separate from the general shelter/homeless population
- Emphasis on promoting self-respect
- Providing structure through the day
- Addressing co-occurring mental illness, addiction, and trauma-related issues
- Providing a transition process to housing

Veteran-Specific Supports

Once enroled in veteran-specific housing, veterans were assigned a local Veterans Affairs Canada (VAC) case manager for assistance and support regarding service-related benefits. An OSIC clinician addressed care for mental health, addiction, and/or medical concerns arising as a result of military service. Following assessment by VAC/OSIC, veterans dealing with health or social issues that did not relate to military service were formally referred by way of a warm transfer process to appropriate community-based services and supports within public and non-profit sectors. The VAC case manager and OSIC clinician collaborated with housing staff to ensure that recommendations regarding social and health-related needs aligned with housing-specific goals, and housing support staff then provided ongoing support that allowed veterans to initiate and maintain a connection to community-based treatment programs.

Peer Support

Efforts to link veterans with peer support services were made at all sites. In some cases, this involved formal peer support through veteran-affiliated organizations such as OSISS or the Royal Canadian Legion. Community volunteers who had served in the military offered informal peer support at one site; these individuals were not affiliated with any specific agency and had not received formal training yet shared an interest in supporting this population. One site employed a mental health peer support worker as staff.

Housing First and Harm Reduction

A Housing First approach served as the cornerstone of this project, along with provisions to support attainment of permanent housing, with veterans being offered intensive case planning and support aimed at improving health, independent living, living skills, well-being, and social interests. This was based on the foundational principle that individuals experiencing homelessness are better able to address addiction, mental health, trauma, and other health issues from the stability of their own home (Mead, 2003).

Harm reduction practices were observed and combined with assessment and safety planning. Frequent in-home visits by qualified staff and peers were integrated within the housing support model across sites. In-home visits are a key element of a Housing First approach and, in this context, offered a more accurate assessment of housing stability and an opportunity to negotiate in-the-moment solutions to issues that arose. As well, staff and peers were better able to engage with veterans on a more personal level, to advocate, when and where necessary. They were also able to provide a wraparound service to mitigate system navigation issues, as well as to support veterans in working towards their individualized goals as they made the transition from street life to home life. Veterans were not required to observe abstinence rules within their own housing unit at three sites; however, substance use was prohibited in communal areas including the shared patio, hallways, and lounge, in order to respect fellow residents who were in different stages of recovery. In Victoria, veterans were discouraged from using substances on site; this was largely due to the absence of paid staff or after-hours support. Housing tenure for veterans struggling with addiction at this site frequently relied on active involvement with addiction counselling and/or rehabilitation.

3. FINDINGS

Evaluation of this project included a mixed-methods approach. Quantitative analysis was derived from a standardized set of valid, reliable questionnaires administered to veterans at baseline, 3, 9, and 15 months. Questionnaires included demographic and housing histories, Quality of Life Enjoyment and Satisfaction Short Form (Endicott et al., 1993), and the Health, Social, Justice Service Use form. Qualitative analysis was based on three cycles of focus group interviews conducted with veterans, staff, and stakeholders at each site from 2012 to 2014.

Analysis revealed a pattern of chronic homelessness with tremendous physical and mental health consequences occurring many years following release from active military service. The majority of participants were white English Canadian (79%) and male (92.1%) with an average age of 52.8 years. Only 9.7% were Aboriginal or Métis. While 66% of the sample reported having children, the pilot study housed only one single-parent family. The average total time spent homeless for veterans in this study was 5.8 years, with a range of 0–30 years. At enrolment, 69.8% of participants reported situations of absolute homelessness while the remainder were at imminent risk of homelessness. The average number of years served in the Canadian Forces was 8.1 years, with 39.7% having served in overseas deployments. Participants reported an average of 28.4 years since release from military service. The total time-lapse since their first episode of homelessness averaged 9.7 years prior to enrolment, with a range of 0–47 years. This suggested that, for many veterans, homelessness followed a period of prolonged destabilization.

Veterans consistently voiced a desire to re-engage with military culture. Peer support services afforded many veterans an opportunity to reconnect with the camaraderie and sense of pride they once felt while serving their country. However, not all participants regarded their military experiences in a positive light and, therefore, the majority's preference was to access veteran peer support on their own terms and at their own pace. The level of street entrenchment and ongoing substance use among participants proved challenging for veteran peer supporters at one site. Sites where peer support staff and/or volunteers had more experience in working with homeless populations were better able to integrate peer support as a consistent and ongoing aspect of housing with support.

Shifting Needs Once Housed

The sample size of this pilot project was insufficient to support formal analysis of service-use patterns over time. A general trend towards increased community-based care, both social service and health, was observed, along with decreased hospital and emergency-room visits (Figure 13.1).

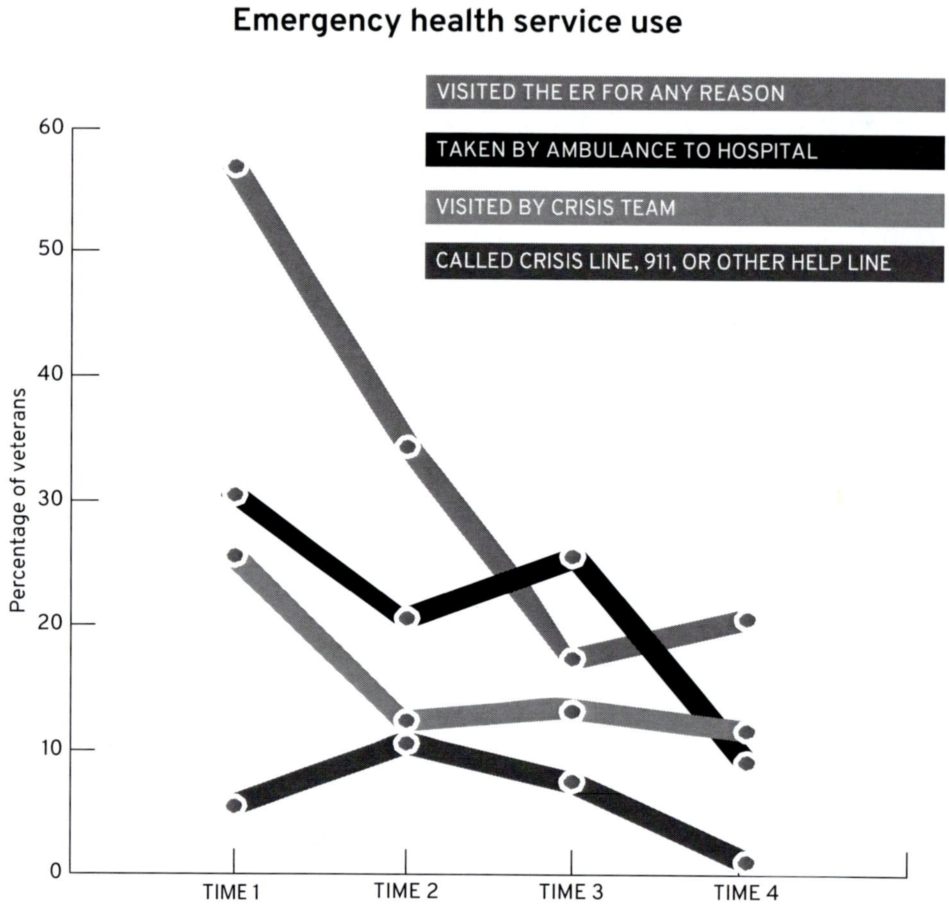

Figure 13.1: Service Utilization across Data Collection Points (0, 3, 9, and 15 months)

These service-use trends resulted in cost savings to the system and suggest a shift in the manner in which the veterans were able to respond to challenges from a crisis and emergency response towards more preventative supports. The provision of permanent stable housing and support contributed to cost savings of up to $536,600 in the first year following enrolment into veteran-specific housing. This figure is based primarily on reduced reliance on emergency shelter and drop-in centre services. The immediate costs of emergency housing and related services far exceed the costs of permanent supportive housing (Calgary Homeless Foundation, 2008; Gaetz, 2012; Pomeroy, 2005). Continued cost savings are therefore anticipated over time in light of the chronicity of homelessness observed among veterans involved in this study sample. Comprehensive tracking and accounting processes are integral to supporting meaningful cost-benefit analyses that illustrate how increased expenditures in one sector—in this case, a housing intervention with support—translates into significant cost savings in other sectors. Such processes should therefore be integrated as a component of program evaluation for evolving interventions that seek to address the issue of homelessness, particularly those targeted at specific subpopulations of the homeless, as this will enhance overall understanding of the true impact of targeted intervention across various systems and sectors.

Local System Collaboration Networking

Collaboration at the local level between a range of sectors and service providers allowed for insight into site-specific strengths and challenges as veterans transitioned from a state of homelessness to being housed. All sites agreed that a concerted effort to establish regular meetings and case conferences to support individual veteran needs was important and provided a forum to address ongoing issues or conflicts. The success of outreach efforts to identify participants often depended upon the knowledge of street-level/homeless-serving programs and other community-based mental health or addiction programs. Once established within the housing program, veteran services and other community support services were instrumental in supporting continued success. The local Housing First agency served as the primary case manager responsible for coordinating services as these agencies were familiar with the housing/homeless-serving sector and were well established in their relationships with community services, mental health, and addiction treatment programs, thus enhancing access to community-based resources if/when these were deemed a necessary component of veteran-specific care. Regular teleconference meetings between housing supports, VAC, OSIC, and peer supports provided an opportunity to consider site-specific obstacles, identify common challenges, and develop shared problem-solving strategies. Sharing of information and ideas improved consistency across sites, thus improving timely access to housing and service delivery generally.

4. DISCUSSION

By providing veteran-specific housing and support to homeless veterans, this project created an opportunity for veterans, many of whom had spent years on the streets or on the verge of homelessness, to achieve new stability in their lives, including some sense of social inclusion. This required coordinated and intensive efforts on the part of participating organizations within housing/homelessness- and veteran-serving sectors. This encompassed development of formal service agreements between agencies and a clear understanding of organizational mandates that govern service delivery. At times, this also required a shift in care delivery to conform to the primary housing agency's core philosophy or approach, particularly in adopting a harm reduction approach to adequately support a Housing First mandate. The initial key principles for addressing homelessness among Canadian veterans remained relevant and were supported throughout the study. However, the depth and scope pertaining to the understanding of these principles increased in complexity over time. The major exception from the original list of principles is that permanent, rather than transitional, housing is needed.

For the veterans who were housed as part of this study, this integrated approach improved access to much-needed resources including income supports, medical, mental health, and addiction treatment, as well as providing an opportunity for psychosocial healing and reconnection to military culture and family supports. Ensuring pathways for open and clear communication between partner organizations serving the homeless veteran population was critical to the success of the program. Mutual problem-solving required all parties to keep an open mind in the face of conflict or tension and be prepared to listen, explain, and/or compromise to ensure the ultimate goals of providing safe, affordable, and stable housing in accordance with the core philosophies.

5. CONCLUSION

The key points arising from this study to consider when providing housing with support for Canadian veterans were:

- Veterans have unique needs when compared with the broader homeless population;
- Structure and routine, including leisure, are important;
- Peer support requires an understanding of both military service and homelessness-related issues;
- Collaboration requires an integrated and shared response between homeless-serving and veteran-serving organizations;
- Permanent, long-term housing solutions with support are preferred over transitional housing models;
- Housing First and harm reduction philosophies and interventions must drive programming;

Homeward Bound: This image illustrates an entrance to an urban campsite by the Thames River in London, Ontario. Many of our homeless veterans lived in the rough prior to entering the program and study.
Source: Photo by Justin Langille

- Choice in housing and living arrangements is important. In particular, the needs of women and families are unlikely to be met by single-site housing models; and
- Programs need to be outcome-focused with housing stability a primary goal. Secondary goals include diversion from emergency services such as shelters, police, and emergency departments.

REFERENCES

Calgary Homeless Foundation. (2008). Report on the cost of homelessness in the city of Calgary. Calgary, AB: Calgary Homeless Foundation.

Endicott, J., Nee, J., Harrison, W., & Blumenthal, R. (1993). Quality of life enjoyment and satisfaction questionnaire: A new measure. *Psychopharmacology Bulletin, 29*(2), 321–326.

Gaetz, S. (2012). The real cost of homelessness: Can we save money by doing the right thing? Toronto, ON: Canadian Homelessness Research Network Press.

Mead, S. (2003). *International peer support.* Retrieved from http://www.intentionalpeersupport.org/wp-content/uploads/2014/12/IPS-An-Alternative-Approach-2014-First-Chapter.pdf

Milroy, H. (2009). From welfare to well-being: Turning things around among homeless veterans. In J. A. Mancini & K. A. Roberto (Eds.), *Pathways of human development: Explorations of change* (pp. 327–346). Lanham, MD: Lexington Books.

Pomeroy, S. (2005). *The cost of homelessness: Analysis of alternate responses in four Canadian cities.* Ottawa, ON: National Secretariat on Homelessness. Retrieved from http://www.homelesshub.ca/ResourceFiles/Cost_of_Homelessness_Pomeroy_English.pdf

Ray, S. L., & Forchuk, C. (2011). The experience of homelessness among Canadian forces and allied forces veterans. Homeless Hub. Retrieved from http://www.homelesshub.ca/sites/default/files/Homelesss%20Vets%20Article.pdf

SECTION IV

CREATING SOCIAL INCLUSION

Section IV offers seven distinct responses to how to create social inclusion for individuals with intersecting issues of poverty and mental health. The first example, most appropriately, given the intent of participatory action research (PAR) to fully engage those with lived experience, was quite independent of the research team's actions. Chapter 14 recounts the unanticipated outcome of "Peer Support as a Direct Benefit of Focus Group Research." Peer support among individuals living with mental health issues can occur in formal or informal settings and result in the exchange of knowledge and acceptance. This chapter recounts the peer support dynamics that spontaneously emerged within focus groups with mental health consumer-survivors who volunteered to participate in the research. The 34 individuals who participated in various focus groups spontaneously engaged in peer support in several ways, including the exchange of practical information, evaluation of information and services, provision of empathy and affirmation, and development of friendships. Participants noted the value of gaining information from and supporting one another with similar life experiences.

Chapter 15, "Seeking and Securing Work: Individual-Level Predictors of Employment of Mental Health Consumer-Survivors," provides a very different perspective on addressing social inclusion but one of equal importance. For individuals with mental health issues who have experienced being part of the psychiatric system, seeking and securing employment involves personal, social, and environmental factors. In Canada, mental health consumer-survivors are under-represented in the workforce. The question is, what services can help address this issue? The chapter discusses how health service utilization, living circumstances, homelessness, substance use, social integration, ethnicity, having children under

18, and being a student are all significant predictors of seeking and securing work. Two other commonly accepted human capital indicators, education and age, were not predictive of employment search behaviour and outcomes with this population. Thus, individual characteristics that predict employment search and success outcomes for mental health consumer-survivors include aspects related to treatment and living circumstances, which stands in contrast to predictors of employment for the general population. This suggests that employment support services need to be tailored more specifically to this population to assist them in becoming more socially included in Canadian society.

What is it like not to officially or bureaucratically exist? For anyone who has lost their identification, driver's licence, credit card, social insurance number, and/or passport, proving who you are can be a daunting task. Without a health card, obtaining access to health-care services is precarious, despite Canada's universal health-care system. Unfortunately, being homeless makes one far more vulnerable to losing one's identification and makes it much more difficult to replace. Chapter 16, "Iris Scanning: A Solution to the Lost Identification Problem Encountered by People Experiencing Homelessness?", discusses a viable response to this, which would further contribute to providing a sense of social inclusion at a time when people are even more vulnerable, when they are in need of medical care and attention. The chapter recounts the outcome of a study that assessed the functionality of iris scanning technology in a community setting, evaluating its acceptability to shelter clients. The research team documented the number of people who agreed to be scanned, the number of people who declined, and the number of successful scans completed in one community shelter. Two hundred scans were collected over the course of three visits. Second iris scans were requested of 50 individuals to allow the research team to assess whether the technology accurately identifies someone over a period of time. The results indicate that most of the study's participants found the technology acceptable and that the number identifier was consistent over repeated scans, making iris scanning a practical tool in properly identifying individuals to expedite their use of health-care services.

Chapter 17, "The Effectiveness of a Shelter Diversion Intervention for Families Who Experience Homelessness," perhaps provides the most hope for those working in this field of practice. While the majority of homelessness research and initiatives in Canada has focused on single individuals, homelessness among families is an increasing reality. Chapter 17 discusses the findings of a small study that found that a straightforward, easy-to-implement intervention can assist families from becoming homeless while maintaining their quality of life. Further, a cost analysis was included as part of the study indicating that, on top of the benefits to family members including experiencing greater levels of social inclusion, there was a six-fold cost savings associated with the program.

Chapter 18, "Preventing Mental Illness Discharge to Homelessness," provides insights into how changing social policy is a critical component in the process of enhancing social inclusion among those with mental health issues. The chapter reviews the findings of a study that assessed the effects of an intervention that was designed to provide on-site, pre-discharge housing assistance for mental health consumer-survivors as they prepared to leave hospital. Participants included service users from acute (n = 219) and tertiary (n = 32) care hospital sites. Data were collected from hospital and shelter databases. Results revealed that, in the majority

Recovery and Social Inclusion: Caring for Another. Connect (peer support) group facilitator Katherine's pet rabbit pauses on its way through a toy tunnel at her home in London, Ontario. Having a pet encourages her to take care of herself so that she is able to have the responsibility of taking care of another living being, she says.
Source: Photo by Justin Langille

Recovery and Social Inclusion: Valuing Daily Routines. Connect member Tammy makes breakfast at home in her kitchen. If there is one thing she can do habitually to set herself up for success in her mental health recovery, Tammy says it's having a good breakfast.
Source: Photo by Justin Langille

of cases, the intervention, discussed in detail in the chapter, reduced the number of individuals discharged to homelessness or to no fixed address. In addition, the costs of implementing and maintaining the intervention were less than the increased medical costs associated with homelessness and housing individuals in shelters. The chapter demonstrates that to address social inclusion among this population, we need to consider not only direct action and counselling but also direct action at the social policy level.

Chapter 19, "An Evaluation of the London Community Addiction Response Strategy: London CAReS," describes the evaluation of a municipal strategy that focused on the housing needs and health outcomes of individuals experiencing addiction, poor mental health, and poverty. The chapter recounts how the initiative evolved, its initial and continuing challenges, and how the program aided in creating social inclusion among its service users, offering a model for other initiatives to emulate.

Section IV's concluding chapter, "Service Preferences of Homeless Youth with Mental Illness: Housing First, Treatment First, or Both Together," continues to reflect the goals of PAR. It discusses the importance of engaging in simple processes, like actually asking service users what they want. Service users have multiple needs, and community-based practitioners, agency administrators, and policy developers actively work to provide what is best, but, as Chapter 20 indicates, what is best depends on the situation and circumstances of each individual person.

CHAPTER 14

Peer Support as a Direct Benefit of Focus Group Research

Cheryl Forchuk, Amanda Meier, Phyllis Montgomery, and Abraham Rudnick

1. INTRODUCTION

Peer support is characterized as a mutual exchange of emotional, social, and instrumental support among mental health consumer-survivors or individuals living with mental illness. Peer support has further been described as "a system of giving and receiving help founded on principles of respect, shared responsibility, and mutual agreement of what is helpful" (Mead et al., 2001, p. 135). There are a number of psychosocial processes involved in peer support, including the provision of social support, the exchange of experiential knowledge, the involvement of an understanding role model, and the enhancement of interpersonal competence through the helping of others (Solomon, 2004). Faulkner and Basset (2012) found that mental health consumer-survivors can benefit from peer support relationships by developing a shared identity, feeling less need to hide their mental health problems, increasing confidence, and being able to put "difficult life experiences to good use" by helping others (p. 43).

There are various levels of peer support relationships ranging from informal to formal peer support. The Mental Health Commission of Canada (Sunderland et al., 2013) describes informal peer support as occurring when "acquaintances notice the similarity of their lived experience with mental health challenges and therefore listen to and support each other" (p. 17). Informal peer support relationships tend to be mutually beneficial, with both individuals striving to find a path towards wellness. Formal peer support involves "program[s] where peer support workers make a connection with individual patients based on similarity of lived experience, and offer the opportunity for a supportive, empowering relationship" and can take place within hospitals, community organizations, workplace-based programs, and consumer-run peer support services (Sunderland et al., 2013, p. 17). Formal peer support is often combined with professional support in mental health settings. Pallaveshi et al. (2013) conducted a study comparing peer-led and professional-led group interventions for individuals with mental illness and addiction issues and found that participants were more comfortable with peer-led interventions but acquired more skills from professional-led interventions, suggesting that a combination of services may be most beneficial. Models of mental health services, such as the Transitional Discharge Model (TDM), include formal peer support as a key component and have been effective in outcomes such as reduced length of hospital stay (Forchuk et al., 2005).

In the context of research, data collection via focus group methodology offers the possibility for the spontaneous development of informal peer support. The implementation of focus groups is strategic in that researchers plan for an open, non-threatening conversational space to facilitate the exchange of participants' perceptions concerning the topic of inquiry and can be a very effective way of exploring or elaborating on issues important to participants (Ivanoff & Hultberg, 2006). Focus groups have been found to have several benefits, such as encouraging the participation of individuals who are reluctant to be interviewed one-on-one or who may feel they have little information to contribute and providing researchers with opportunities to understand the way people view their reality (Ivanoff & Hultberg, 2006; Owen, 2001). In a study examining housing issues for mental health consumer-survivors, Forchuk et al. (2006) explained that the use of focus groups allowed the "actual voices of psychiatric survivors" to be expressed and, consequently, provided more depth and texture to understand their experiences (p. 49). To this end, Koppelman and Bourjolly (2001) outlined the importance of strategic methodological focus group planning for women living with serious mental illness. The women's engagement in open and comfortable discourse about their shared realities was empowering. Other authors have also found that focus group participants enjoyed their discussions together and found the sessions cathartic (Barbour, 2007; Krueger, 1994).

Focus groups may promote peer support because they are intended to "capitalize on the interaction within a group" through using open-ended questions and encouragement from the facilitator for participants to speak to one another about similar issues (Asbury, 1995, p. 414). However, there seems to be little evidence addressing the nature of these interactions or providing illustrations of peer support within current literature (Kitzinger, 1994; Webb & Kevern, 2001). Only one article that specifically focused on interactions between mental health consumer-survivors within focus groups could be located. Owen (2001) used focus group methodology to explore the perspectives of women with serious mental illness. Her findings indicated that interaction did not occur between participants but rather ideas were directed to the facilitator with participants demonstrating reluctance to discuss ideas among themselves. Additional research examining interactions and peer support within mental health consumer-survivor focus groups is necessary to expand knowledge on this important, but not often discussed, aspect of focus group research.

These findings led to the current study, the intent of which is to describe peer support dynamics in focus groups with mental health consumer-survivors addressing poverty and mental health. While observation of participant interactions and peer support dynamics was not the primary purpose of the research project, numerous instances of peer support emerged, leading to a secondary analysis of peer support within a research setting.

2. METHODS

Design

The current study constitutes a secondary supplementary analysis of focus group data. While the primary purpose of the focus groups was to explore the relationship between poverty and mental health from mental health consumer-survivors' perspectives, what was also routinely observed and recorded were peer support dynamics. Following the primary analysis, the authors returned to the data to conduct a supplementary analysis on peer interactions. Quantitative interviews were held with mental health consumer-survivors on the topics of health, income, quality of life, and social support. Subsequent focus group sessions were held with a subset of the quantitative sample. Questions included "What are some of the challenges and obstacles specific to your financial situation?" and "What are some of the resources that have helped you?" (Chapter 8). Ethics approval was obtained from the Research Ethics Board at Western University, London, Canada.

The current supplementary analysis derived from the focus group data with mental health consumer-survivors. All focus group sessions were audio-recorded and transcribed verbatim by trained research staff. Two note-takers were present during each focus group session to record field notes. The field notes included coding the participants to preserve anonymity, recording which coded participant was speaking in each interaction to assist in accurate transcribing, and noting any nonverbal communication that occurred during interactions, such as nodding, touching, and handing out tissues. Two of the authors (Forchuk and Meier) were also present during some of the focus groups and were able to directly observe the verbal and nonverbal interactions between participants, enhancing the accuracy of interpretations that derived from the data analysis.

Sample

The same sample discussed in Chapter 8 was the source for this study.

Data Analysis

The combined transcripts were analyzed using conventional content analysis, which is used when researchers immerse themselves in, and allow insights to emerge from, the data while avoiding preconceived categories (Hsieh & Shannon, 2005; Kondracki et al., 2002). Peer support dynamics were observed when conducting the primary analysis of focus group data. Following the primary analysis, the authors returned to the transcripts and highlighted instances of participant interactions with one another. The interactions were extracted from the transcripts and the authors made notes of their initial impressions of the data. Impressions were discussed in group meetings with all authors. Following discussions of initial impressions, the interactions were grouped together based on similarities in content and tone. The authors attempted to directly reflect participant words and sentiments when labelling the groupings and regularly discussed their labels to ensure that there was agreement in interpretation.

When quotations presented in the findings involve interactions between multiple participants, participants are identified using "Participant 1," "Participant 2," to provide clarity to the reader. To preserve the anonymity of participants, "Participant 1" within one interaction is not necessarily the same individual as "Participant 1" in another interaction. Participants are renumbered within each interaction so as not to identify any specific individual throughout the findings section.

3. FINDINGS

Information about Resources

During the focus group discussions, a facilitator asked participants about the resources that have helped them financially. Instead of directing their responses to the facilitator, participants spoke to one another about the resources they accessed. By describing resources to one another, participants demonstrated expertise in their personal knowledge and eagerness to share their knowledge of resources with other participants. Information was shared about community services, health-care services, financial assistance, employment support, education, and food.

A participant pauses for a moment during a Connect group sharing session in October 2014. Connect facilitates peer sessions where individuals experiencing mental illness can learn and share strategies to help their recovery.
Source: Photo by Justin Langille

Community Services

Participants accessed several community services to obtain peer support, tangible resources, and information. Throughout the focus group discussions, information regarding community services was shared. For example, two participants discussed a drop-in centre for women:

> *Participant 1:* "It's [a program] just for women ... like any ages. You know a lot of young women go there too and their kids too."
> *Participant 2:* "Don't you have to be homeless?"
> *Participant 1:* "No ... you don't have to be. And there's workers there that will talk to you."

When another participant described a different women's program, others joined the conversation and elaborated on the resource, demonstrating their awareness of the same service:

Participant 1: "[Agency] is a transition home for women that are post-psychiatric or homeless and they offer free lunches."
Participant 2: "You can do your laundry there, you can access the computers there."
Participant 3: "You can have a shower there."

Participants provided information to one another on resources that they found beneficial and suggestions for others to consider.

Health-Care Services

As all of the focus group participants had a mental health issue, health-care services were commonly accessed. Participants described some of the difficulties they faced when managing their mental illnesses and others informed them of useful health-care services and resources. Examples include:

Participant 1: "[It's] one of the best books I ever got."
Participant 2: "Oh cool, what's this?"
Participant 1: "It was [name]. If you have any form of depression, I'm telling you man get that book and do it."

and

Participant 1: "There's a place actually here at [hospital] called the [psychiatric care] team."
Participant 2: "Oh yeah?"
Participant 1: "and ... you can refer yourself, or you can go through the ER or you can get your family doctor ... and it's free ... I have the phone number if you want it."
Participant 2: "Okay."

Participants were well informed of health-care services and resources and were able to provide one another with specific details, including workbook titles and program phone numbers.

Financial Assistance

Many focus group participants in the current study were unemployed and accessing or hoping to access finances from Ontario Works (OW) or Ontario Disability Support Program (ODSP). When participants discussed the difficulties they faced or frustrations they had with the programs, others provided suggestions and information about their rights as service users. As stated by one participant,

> There's things that welfare don't even tell you that you're eligible to have ... like they'll buy you a cell phone, they'll pay for your cell phone, there's a travel allowance.

Other participants conversed about the expectation to report all sources of received income:

> *Participant 1:* "They won't deduct birthday gifts but they want you to claim it."
> *Participant 2:* "You have to claim it."
> *Participant 3:* "Legally they can't deduct it but some of them will try."

Employment Support

While most focus group participants were unemployed and accessing financial assistance, many expressed interest in employment. Participants expressed a number of issues when trying to access jobs, including potential OW or ODSP deductions, lack of professional clothing, and gaps in resumes. Despite these issues, participants shared information about employment services and supports they could access in their community. For example,

> There's another facility I know of ... will help people get back into the workplace with a full seminar on preparing yourself for a job, what you should do, the things you should know, the things you should prepare.

Education

Furthering education in the hopes of obtaining future employment was another topic of discussion for participants. As they explained the barriers they faced in terms of education, others provided information on educational supports:

> I went on Ontario Works and they let me go (to school) for the whole day ... and they support me ... if I wasn't on there I would have to do it on my own and it would cost you. If you're on the system they don't charge you for that.

After describing this program, other participants inquired about the organization that ran it. Participants were well informed of various education services and enthusiastic about helping others discover them as well.

Food

Access to healthy and affordable food was a central issue of discussion among focus group participants. They shared information regarding where to access free food while upholding food bank policies: "Every month I write down what food bank I can go to." Further, the following example illustrates a participant's suggestion to secure adequate food on a limited budget:

> *Participant 1:* "A lot of people I know will try to buy their food all at once for the month and that's really hard to do sometimes."
> *Participant 2:* "That's why you need a gift card."
> *Participant 1:* "Yes I thought of doing that."

Some expressed that purchasing healthy foods on a limited budget was possible if they "buy whatever fruits and vegetables are in season ... they tend to be cheapest ... like cabbage ... cabbage has a lot of nutrition, it's very cheap."

Food preparation was also discussed. For example, a participant shared how to make yogurt:

> *Participant 1:* "You can make your own yogurt ... you take a quarter of a cup of yogurt and add water and dried milk powder which you can get from the food bank ... you put it in a casserole dish. You put it in the oven and you turn the oven off and the heat from the oven makes the yogurt grow."
> *Participant 2:* "Really?"
> *Participant 1:* "Yeah and it tastes just like it."

Importance of Information

In addition to directly providing information on resources, participants evaluated the information they gave and received, and acknowledged that they had difficulties accessing the same information when speaking to service providers.

Evaluating Information

During the focus group discussions, there were instances when participants described resources and concluded by evaluating the resource for the benefit of others. Some examples include:

> It's run by consumers of the mental health services system.

> It's not right for everybody. You have to find your own place in the outside world. But it's a good place.

> They have free art supplies to a limited extent … to get out some of those demons inside and to help for things you can't quite describe with words … it's really good at getting some of those difficult things out.

and

> Something that helped me when I first got started with this merry-go-round … every few years I go back to the same counseling agency … I'll go there and talk with the same counselor and I usually learn something new and I feel better than I did before.

Participants not only provided information about resources to one another but also gave insight into the quality of the services by stating whether they were good or bad, helpful or unhelpful.

In addition to evaluating a number of resources, a few participants specifically stated which resources they valued above others and which resources they would recommend to others. One participant explained the importance of overcoming addiction:

> When I got clean, I realized that that's a resource, getting clean. Opens up a whole world for me … I'm a member of society today. I'm capable of making better decisions … if I had one thing to tell everybody that would be it.

Another participant gained insight through a specific personality course he took in the community:

> It's a two week course … finds out where you're going and possible directions you might want to go. And it's like whoa! Opening up the curtains wide where it was all dark for me … I recommend it for everyone here in the room.

It is clear that participants had opinions about which resources they valued and provided important information to one another by stating which resources were helpful and which they valued most.

Lack of Information about Services from Providers

At times, participants expressed their surprise that others were unaware of various pieces of information prior to entering the focus group session. While describing a peer support agency, one participant stated, "Everybody doesn't know about [agency]. It's weird. I don't understand." There were numerous instances of participants stating that they did not know or had never heard of resources. More specifically, participants expressed frustration that no one had previously told them about resources, despite being engaged as service users in the health-care and/or social services sectors. One example involved two participants discussing a peer support agency:

Participant 1: "I've run across peer support in a lot of different ways, I mean I work at [agency]."
Participant 2: "What is [agency]?"
Participant 1: "It's about what you're talking about."
Participant 2: "How come ain't no one said this to me before? Cause I'm really frigged up and need someone."

A number of participants specifically stated that service providers do not provide necessary information and subsequently the primary way they receive information is by speaking to other service users. Examples include:

> Well if you don't know it's there how you gonna get it, if they don't tell you it's there? Most of the information that I've found is from other people that are on the system.

and

Participant 1: "It's not publicized ... all the different people here, how many people knew about all of the different things that were available to different individuals? It's not publicized right."
Participant 2: "You find out about programs that people have gone through."

Support While Exchanging Information

Information exchange and evaluation were two primary ways in which participants demonstrated peer support. A third way in which peer support emerged was through the provision of empathy, affirmation, and the building of friendships.

Affirmation during Information Exchange

Participants were observed as showing empathy and affirming one another during the focus groups. During one exchange, a participant explained her financial and relationship struggles while two other participants took turns patting her back, holding her hand, and handing her tissues when she cried. In another situation, a male participant discussed losing custody of his son with two others expressing compassion for him:

> *Participant 1:* "As soon as I signed over my parental rights I became person non grata, they don't tell me what they're doing with him, where he is, nothing like that."
> *Participant 2:* "I'm sorry to hear that."
> *Participant 1:* "Oh thank you."
> *Participant 3:* "I'm sorry you had to go through that."

Participants also encouraged one another throughout the discussions. Examples include:

> *Participant 1:* "I'm isolating myself … I'm making money but I'm not out there."
> *Participant 2:* "At least you're trying to do it."
> *Participant 1:* "Yeah."
> *Participant 2:* "That's the first step."

and

> *Participant 1:* "For us that are on low income I wouldn't want to live in their shoes because it takes a survivor, and a strength and strong person to be where we are and to go where we're going."
> *Participant 2:* "Exactly, I agree with you."
> *Participants 3 and 4:* (nods)
> *Participant 1:* "Not anybody could walk in our shoes but strong people do."

Empathy and affirmation were observed in several ways, including touch, such as patting another on the back or offering a hug; the provision of information; and verbal encouragement or expressions of understanding. Participants also affirmed the facilitator in the usefulness and benefits they received from the focus groups:

> *Participant 1:* "Right now we're kind of relating to each other like what we have in common is we're having a hard time so we feel a little bit of a connection over that or we've had similar experience there."
> *Participant 2:* "It's a good thing to bring people together."

Building Future Connections

As a final indicator of peer support, some participants made an effort to develop relationships to carry through after the focus groups ended. One particularly pertinent example occurred between three women:

Participant 1: "Would you guys be interested in coming together in a group and then maybe doing like an outing?"
Participant 2: "Yeah."
Participant 1: "'Cause you guys seem like really interesting people."
Participant 3: "… Could you give me your number? That would be awesome."

Other participants expressed more general support by stating that they would be available to others if they were going through difficult situations:

Participant 1: "What about all the lost souls that don't know where to go because they've had so many doors shut in their face?"
Participant 2: "Well honey, you can always come to my house."
Participant 1: "Your door's always open?"
Participant 2: "Sure."

These exchanges indicate that participants valued the connections they built during the focus groups and saw the other participants as potential friends and peers to exchange assistance and companionship with in the future.

4. DISCUSSION

The findings discussed in this chapter illustrated the informal peer support that occurred spontaneously within a research setting. Participants attended a focus group session for the purpose of discussing poverty and mental health but also engaged in peer support through the practical exchange of information and through expressions of support and understanding. Not only did participants share valuable information with the research team, they demonstrated the importance of sharing their experiential knowledge with one another. As a number of participants stated, they tend to discover new information based on the knowledge of others who are in similar situations. This process is an example of the creation of social inclusion.

The information and support exchanged between participants indicates that mental health consumer-survivors benefited from their participation in the focus groups. As stated by one participant, "It's a good thing to bring people together." The potential interpersonal benefits of participating in focus group research are not often acknowledged within Research Ethics Boards (REBs). Within the Canadian Tri-Council Policy Statement (Canadian Institutes of Health Research et al., 2010) discussing REB guidelines, the description of potential research benefits is described as such:

> Research involving humans may produce benefits that positively affect the welfare of society as a whole through the advancement of knowledge for future generations, for participants themselves or for other individuals. However, much research offers little or no direct benefit to participants. In most research, the primary benefits produced are for society and for the advancement of knowledge. (p. 22)

However, as the current study is a secondary analysis, the focus group data was not collected for the purposes of investigating peer support dynamics. There are a number of potential limitations inherent to secondary analyses, including exaggerated researcher bias and insufficient secondary data (Thorne, 1998). Further, researchers must ensure the voices of participants are depicted accurately despite the supplementary nature of the analysis (Thorne, 1998). As two of the authors were directly involved in data collection, all authors discussed and validated each other's interpretations, and attention was paid to including participant quotes and sentiments directly and in context, the authors worked to rectify any potential secondary analysis issues that may have emerged.

Nonetheless, the findings from this study demonstrated that focus group research also promotes direct benefits for participants such as the provision of informal peer support and creation of social inclusion. While the risks associated with such research must still be considered, it appears that focus group methodology may enhance the benefits of research participation beyond the traditional advancement of knowledge for society.

REFERENCES

Asbury, J. (1995). Overview of focus group research. *Qualitative Health Research, 5*(4), 414–420.

Barbour, R. (2007). Ethics and engagement. In R. Barbour, *Qualitative research kit: Doing focus groups* (pp. 93–101). London, UK: SAGE Publications.

Canadian Institutes of Health Research, Natural Sciences and Engineering Research Council of Canada, and Social Sciences and Humanities Research Council of Canada. (2010). *Tri-Council policy statement: Ethical conduct for research involving humans (TCPS2).* Retrieved from http://www.pre.ethics.gc.ca/pdf/eng/tcps2/TCPS_2_FINAL_Web.pdf

Faulkner, A., & Basset, T. (2012). A helping hand: Taking peer support to the 21st century. *Mental Health and Social Inclusion, 16*(1), 41–47.

Forchuk, C., Martin, M.-L., Chan, Y. L., & Jensen, E. (2005). Therapeutic relationships: From psychiatric hospital to community. *Journal of Psychiatric and Mental Health Nursing, 12*(5), 556–564.

Forchuk, C., Nelson, G., & Hall, G. B. (2006). "It's important to be proud of the place you live": Housing problems and preferences of psychiatric survivors. *Perspectives in Psychiatric Care, 42*(1), 42–52.

Hsieh, H.-F., & Shannon, S. E. (2005). Three approaches to qualitative content analysis. *Qualitative Health Research, 15*(9), 1277–1288.

Ivanoff, S. D., & Hultberg, J. (2006). Understanding the multiple realities of everyday life: Basic assumptions in focus-group methodology. *Scandinavian Journal of Occupational Therapy, 13*(2), 125–132.

Kitzinger, J. (1994). The methodology of focus groups: The importance of interactions between research participants. *Sociology of Health and Illness, 16*(1), 103–121.

Kondracki, N. L., Wellman, N. S., & Amundson, D. R. (2002). Content analysis: Review of methods and their applications in nutrition education. *Journal of Nutrition Education and Behavior, 34*(4), 224–230.

Koppelman, N. F., & Bourjolly, J. N. (2001). Conducting focus groups with women with severe psychiatric disabilities: A methodological overview. *Psychiatric Rehabilitation Journal, 25*(2), 142–151.

Krueger, R. A. (1994). *Focus groups: A practical guide for applied research* (2nd ed.). Thousand Oaks, CA: SAGE Publications.

Mead, S., Hilton, D., & Curtis, L. (2001). Peer support: A theoretical perspective. *Psychiatric Rehabilitation Journal, 25*(2), 134–141.

Owen, S. (2001). The practical, methodological and ethical dilemmas of conducting focus groups with vulnerable clients. *Journal of Advanced Nursing, 36*(5), 652–658.

Pallaveshi, L., Balachandra, K., Subramanian, P., & Rudnick, A. (2013). Peer-led and professional-led group interventions for people with co-occurring disorders: A qualitative study. *Community Mental Health Journal, 50*(4), 388–394.

Solomon, P. (2004). Peer support/peer provided services underlying processes, benefits, and critical ingredients. *Psychiatric Rehabilitation Journal, 27*(4), 392–401.

Sunderland, K., Mishkin, W., Peer Leadership Group, & Mental Health Commission of Canada (MHCC). (2013). Guidelines for the practice and training of peer support. Retrieved from https://www.mentalhealthcommission.ca/sites/default/files/peer_support_guidelines.pdf

Thorne, S. (1998). Ethical and representational issues in qualitative secondary analysis. *Qualitative Health Research, 8*(4), 547–555.

Webb, C., & Kevern, J. (2001). Focus groups as a research method: A critique of some aspects of their use in nursing research. *Journal of Advanced Nursing, 33*(6), 798–805.

CHAPTER 15

Seeking and Securing Work: Individual-Level Predictors of Employment of Mental Health Consumer-Survivors

Peter V. Hall, Phyllis Montgomery, Samantha Davie, Kevin Dickens, Cheryl Forchuk, Momodou Jeng, Melissa Kersey, Amanda Meier, Pam Lahey, Abraham Rudnick, Michelle Solomon, and Laura Warner

1. INTRODUCTION

At an individual and system level, enduring mental illness is associated with unemployment and financial burden. Employment is highly valued in contemporary society; not only is employment a way to increase inclusion and earn additional income, it can also be a way that mental health consumer-survivors access social services (Mental Health Commission of Canada [MHCC], 2012, 2013). What accounts for the employment outcomes of mental health consumer-survivors? Recognizing that structural and systemic factors are important, this chapter summarizes a study of individual socio-demographic and health predictors of seeking and securing employment among mental health consumer-survivors residing in an urban region of Southwestern Ontario, Canada.

The estimated annual cost to the Canadian economy to support individuals with mental illness over 20 years of age a decade ago was $51 billion (Lim et al., 2008). Approximately 35% of this total expenditure related to the loss of short- and long-term employment. When they are excluded from the labour market, mental health consumer-survivors, defined as adult persons diagnosed with mental illness of at least one year's duration, depend on social assistance (Drake et al., 2012; Waghorn et al., 2012). One in three persons receiving provincial social assistance from the Ontario Disability Support Program (ODSP) had a mental illness (Lahey, 2007). In 2018, the maximum ODSP monthly payment was $1,169 per single person compared to $733 for "employable" mental health consumer-survivors receiving Ontario Works (OW; Income Security Advocacy Centre, 2018). Being solely dependent on ODSP or OW, however, is often insufficient to

During a February 2014 job, Allan organizes a truckload of quality furniture the crew will take back their warehouse. Working all over the city in a variety of situations enables employees to develop communication and time management skills over time.
Source: Photo by Justin Langille

meet basic needs (see Chapter 2). Hence mental health consumer-survivors receiving financial assistance remain at heightened risk for insecure housing, chronic poverty, poor health, food insecurity, and social exclusion (Csiernik, et al., 2017; Wilton, 2004).

In the past decade, researchers have conceptualized employment as a social determinant of personal well-being (MHCC, 2013). Employment is associated with positive outcomes such as economic security, purposeful use of time through a daily routine, social inclusion and community integration, and self-efficacy (Becker et al., 2007; Bond et al., 2007; Kneebone & Grynishak, 2011; Koletsi et al., 2009; Larson et al., 2007; Pulkki-Råback et al., 2012; Solar, 2011). Further, there is evidence that employment is related to non-vocational personal health outcomes inclusive of cognitive functioning, symptom management, life satisfaction, and recovery (Bell et al., 1993; Bond et al., 2001; Larson et al., 2007; McHugo et al., 2012; Mueser et al., 2004) and contributes to wellness (Csiernik, 2014). In contrast, there is evidence identifying a negative association between employment and personal risk in subgroups of mental health consumer-survivors. Koletsi et al. (2009) reported that employment may lead to stress, interpersonal conflicts, distraction from other obligations, and feelings of decreased control. However, the researchers point out that the positive impacts of employment substantively outweigh the drawbacks.

Despite the positive personal benefits associated with employment, mental health consumer-survivors are less likely to be employed and more likely to be underemployed, compared to individuals living with other types of disabilities (Bond et al., 2007; Drake et al., 2012). The estimated proportion of mental health consumer-survivors in employment is 20% (Corbière et al., 2010). In a sample of persons diagnosed with schizophrenia, over two-thirds of respondents stated they wished to work (Mueser et al., 2001). Mental health consumer-survivors' desire for meaningful work is supported by extensive research (Bond et al., 2007; Koletsi et al., 2009; McGurk et al., 2005; Solar, 2011).

Related to seeking employment, mental health consumer-survivors also experience personal and structural barriers. In a meta-synthesis of 20 international studies examining employment-related views of this population, Fossey and Harvey (2010) reported that two attributes, motivation and perseverance, were essential in response to potential employers' request for disclosure about their mental health and disrupted employment history. In a Canadian study, Corbière et al. (2011) found that mental health consumer-survivors' characteristics of preparation and motivation in job searching predicted 26% of work-seeking behaviours and 8% of work outcomes. There are fairly consistent American reports demonstrating that combinations of mental health consumer-survivors' vulnerabilities, such as poor symptom management; altered cognitive and functional capacity; lack of employment history; education, training, and expertise; and lack of social support, interfered with their employment-seeking practices (Alverson et al., 2006; McGurk & Mueser, 2003).

Such vulnerability, combined with wider structural issues such as inadequacies in the social assistance and benefits system, lack of access to supportive social and employment programs, and discrimination, substantially decreases the likelihood of employability and economic well-being for this group (Bejerholm & Björkman, 2011; Bond & Drake, 2008; Catty et al., 2008; Graham et al., 2012; Laudet, 2012; Tsang et al., 2010; Waghorn et al., 2012). In order for health and employment development professionals, advocacy organizations, and the broader community to work with mental health consumer-survivors seeking employment, there is a need to increase access to funding and educational supports for career development, as well as to educate the public about their abilities (Fossey & Harvey, 2010; MHCC, 2013). In Canada, there is recent recognition of the importance of the provision of a safety net during mental health consumer-survivors' transition from social assistance to financial self-security (MHCC 2012, 2013; Stapleton et al., 2011). At the same time, models and approaches to work-related rehabilitation continue to evolve away from train-and-place models towards models that emphasize work before, or with, training, such as the supported employment, placement and support, and integrated support employment models.

What remains controversial in the literature is the association between individual mental health consumer-survivors' socio-demographic, health, and social characteristics and their practices of seeking and securing employment (Becker et al., 2007; Biegel et al., 2010; Bond & Drake, 2008; Tsang et al., 2010; Twamley et al., 2012; Waghorn et al., 2012). In human capital theory, employment outcomes are assumed to reflect the productivity of the individual. Education, experience, and related indicators of skill and workplace performance have been shown to be correlated with earnings and the likelihood of employment. However, human capital analyses have also shown that many other variables also influence labour market outcomes, from individual factors with at best an indirect relationship to productivity (sex) to institutional (labour unions) and structural factors (differences between economic sectors; Crocker, 2006). Furthermore, it is not clear which individual factors influence the productivity of mental health consumer-survivors nor whether mental health consumer-survivors' work is rewarded in the labour market in the same way as other work-seekers and employees (Gao et al., 2010). For instance, employers may not be aware of the clinical diagnosis of an applicant or employee, and even if they are, it is not clear whether diagnoses accurately predict productivity. Razzano et al. (2005) suggest that it may not be the clinical diagnosis itself that is associated with employment status; rather, the particular experience of the illness by individual survivors may be a better predictor. In their study, hospitalization, cognitive disabilities, and co-occurring health conditions were found to be better predictors of employment than the actual clinical diagnosis.

In summary, much of the reviewed research addressing correlates and consequences of employment involved clinical non-Canadian samples of survivors grouped by their mental illness diagnosis (Bond & Drake, 2008; Catty et al., 2008; McGurk et al., 2005; McHugo et al., 2012; Mueser et al., 2001; Solar, 2011; Tsang et al., 2010; Twamley et al., 2012). To expand this knowledge base, it is worthwhile to investigate employment from the perspective of community-dwelling mental health consumer-survivors. Increased understanding of individual-level correlates of seeking and securing employment for those living in the community can inform mental health care reform in Canada (MHCC, 2012) and elsewhere and advocacy for work-related rehabilitation programs and employment support services. The examination of individual-level factors is not intended to detract from the multi-faceted dynamic of mental health consumer-survivors' employability (Corbière & Lecomte, 2009; Corrigan, 2001). Rather, as suggested by Waghorn et al. (2014), an exploration focused on individual-level characteristics and employment outcomes, inclusive of seeking and securing work, has the potential to reveal mental health consumer-survivors' particular assistance needs and thereby enhance planning and delivery of mental health employment programs. Within ever-tightening health and social budget constraints, the need to acknowledge the intersectionality of multiple factors that can impact working and understand "how different supports may or may not be helpful depending on the characteristics of one's personal situation" seems all that more urgent (MHCC, 2013, p. 106).

This chapter discusses a research initiative that explored four objectives:

1. to describe the profile of mental health consumer-survivors who seek employment;
2. to describe the profile of mental health consumer-survivors who successfully secure work;
3. to describe the profile of the subset of mental health consumer-survivors who secure work among those seeking work; and
4. to examine the profile of those securing part-time work.

2. METHODS

Sample

Individuals were recruited with the assistance of local community agencies. To be enroled in the study, individuals were required to be at least 18 years of age, have at least a one-year history of mental illness, live outside a hospital setting, and be able to provide informed consent. In total, 380 individuals were enroled in the study at baseline.

Measures

A demographics form provided descriptive information about each participant's age, sex, marital status, children under 18, contact with family, living arrangement, education, mental health medication use, substance use, chronic physical illness, head injury, homelessness, and psychiatric hospitalization. Information specific to health variables including general health and social, emotional, and physical functioning were obtained from the SF-36 (2013). The current study utilized one item from the National Population Health Survey to estimate the number of close friends and relatives. The Housing History Survey was used to estimate the number of moves within the past two years. The Health, Social, Justice Service Use questionnaire was used to ascertain whether individuals had utilized health or social services, aside from psychiatric hospitalizations, in the previous month. The Consumer Housing Preference Survey provided information about ethnicity. The Personal Resource Questionnaire measured the total level of support individuals have available. Finally, the Community Integration Questionnaire measured community, home, and social integration, as well as information on an individual's volunteering, student status, and employment status. To assess participants' work situation in the past month, participants were asked to select one of the following responses: a) full-time, working more than 20 hours per week; b) part-time, working less than or equal to 20 hours per week; c) not working, but actively looking for work; d) not working, not looking for work; or e) retired due to age.

Data Analysis

Multivariable logistic regression was used to determine relationships between the predictor variables—sex; age; marital status; children under 18; contact with family; living arrangement; education; current practices of mental health medication; tobacco, caffeine, marijuana, substance, and alcohol use; history of substance use; coexistence of a chronic physical condition; past head injury; past homelessness; ethnicity; recent volunteering; student status; service use inclusive of recent inpatient psychiatric and community services; community, home, and social integration; personal resources; general health; social, emotional, and physical functioning; number of close friends and relatives; and number of moves—and seeking and securing employment.

Four separate logistic regression models were created, one for each study objective. Who seeks work was assessed by comparing those working full-time, part-time, or not working, but actively looking for work (n = 178) to those not working and not looking for work (n = 185). Who secures work in a broad sense was assessed by comparing those working full-time or part-time (n = 94) to those not working, regardless of whether they were looking for work (n = 269). Who secures work in a narrow sense, relative to those looking, was assessed by comparing those

Impact Junk Solutions employee Les in his kitchen in the Old East Village neighbourhood of London, Ontario, in July 2014. A former security guard in his 60s, working for Impact allows Les to work at his own pace and gives him purpose that helps him maintain his recovery.
Source: Photo by Justin Langille

working full-time or part-time (n = 94) to those not working, but actively looking for work (n = 84). Finally, who gets part-time work was assessed by comparing those working part-time (n = 64) to those not working, but actively looking for work (n = 84). Sample size limitations precluded an analysis of the determinants of full-time employment.

Categorical independent variables are presented in Table 15.1 while continuous independent variables are presented in Table 15.2. In the event of a cell count of less than five, the independent variable categories were collapsed, if possible, or the independent variable was not considered in the model. The same set of independent variables was considered for each model. All independent variables were entered into a forward stepwise selection procedure, with a statistical significance of p = 0.10 for entry and p = 0.20 for removal from the model. All

Table 15.1: Characteristics of Different Employment Outcome Groups. Count (Valid Column %)

Independent Variables		Not Working, Not Looking	Looking for Work	Working Full-Time or Part-Time	Working Part-Time	Total Sample
Sex	Male	87 (47)	44 (52)	49 (52)	33 (52)	180 (50)
	Female	98 (53)	40 (48)	45 (48)	31 (48)	183 (50)
Marital status	Single/never married/ separated/ divorced/widowed	162 (88)	75 (89)	76 (81)	55 (86)	313 (86)
	Married/common-law/in a relationship	23 (12)	9 (11)	18 (19)	9 (14)	50 (14)
Children under 18	Yes	57 (31)	36 (43)	16 (17)	9 (14)	109 (30)
Contact with family (missing = 7)	Yes	148 (82)	69 (82)	85 (92)	56 (89)	302 (85)
Current living arrangement	Alone	27 (15)	16 (19)	32 (34)	24 (37)	75 (21)
	With parent(s)/spouse/ partner/relative	30 (16)	19 (23)	27 (29)	14 (22)	76 (21)
	With unrelated person/ homeless	128 (69)	49 (58)	35 (37)	26 (41)	212 (58)
Highest level of education	Grade school or less	101 (55)	48 (57)	24 (26)	22 (34)	173 (48)
	High school	50 (27)	23 (27)	36 (38)	27 (42)	109 (30)
	Community college/university	34 (18)	13 (16)	34 (36)	15 (23)	81 (22)
Currently on mental health medication	Yes	136 (74)	35 (42)	64 (68)	49 (77)	235 (65)
Current substance use issue	Yes	159 (86)	67 (80)	54 (57)	38 (59)	280 (77)

Independent Variables		Not Working, Not Looking	Looking for Work	Working Full-Time or Part-Time	Working Part-Time	Total Sample
Current alcohol use issue	Yes	42 (23)	24 (29)	11 (12)	8 (13)	77 (21)
Current tobacco use issue	Yes	138 (75)	59 (70)	45 (48)	31 (48)	242 (67)
Current caffeine use issue	Yes	65 (35)	25 (30)	22 (47)	13 (20)	112 (31)
Current marijuana use issue	Yes	59 (32)	31 (37)	17 (18)	9 (14)	107 (30)
Past substance use issue but no current substance use issue	Yes	11 (6)	7 (8)	17 (18)	11 (17)	35 (10)
Chronic physical illness	Yes	124 (67)	47 (56)	51 (54)	41 (64)	222 (61)
Past head injury	Yes	93 (50)	47 (56)	39 (42)	22 (34)	179 (49)
Past homelessness	Yes	132 (71)	70 (83)	43 (56)	30 (47)	245 (68)
Ethnicity	Caucasian	133 (72)	64 (76)	78 (83)	51 (80)	275 (76)
	Not Caucasian	52 (28)	20 (24)	16 (17)	13 (20)	88 (24)
Volunteering in past month	Yes	40 (22)	30 (36)	29 (31)	20 (31)	99 (27)
School/training in past month	Yes	10 (5)	14 (17)	9 (10)	5 (8)	33 (9)
Most recent psychiatric hospitalization	Never	72 (39)	41 (49)	35 (38)	21 (34)	148 (41)
	Over one year ago	87 (47)	30 (36)	48 (52)	35 (57)	165 (46)
	Within past year	25 (14)	12 (15)	9 (10)	6 (10)	46 (13)
Used health or social service in past month	Yes	146 (79)	64 (76)	70 (75)	53 (83)	280 (77)

Table 15.2: Descriptive Statistics for Continuous Independent Variables by Employment Outcome Group. Mean (Standard Deviation)

Independent Variable	Not Working, Not Looking	Looking for Work	Working Full-Time or Part-Time	Working Part-Time	Total Sample
Age	42.31 (12.776)	31.99 (12.395)	41.77 (13.846)	44.77 (13.145)	39.78 (13.632)
Community integration score	15.31 (5.672)	16.02 (5.874)	16.82 (5.231)	17.17 (4.854)	15.86 (5.629)
Home integration score	5.15 (3.253)	5.25 (3.430)	5.93 (3.394)	5.96 (3.446)	5.37 (3.338)
Social integration score	6.47 (2.596)	7.52 (2.257)	7.88 (2.453)	7.39 (2.567)	7.08 (2.558)
Personal resource questionnaire score	118.00 (21.904)	118.62 (24.356)	128.99 (22.226)	126.02 (21.691)	120.96 (23.000)
General health score	45.11 (25.540)	49.35 (25.112)	60.53 (24.135)	57.81 (25.101)	50.08 (25.826)
Social functioning score	60.50 (28.335)	58.38 (29.535)	67.11 (27.766)	66.22 (28.842)	61.72 (28.585)
Emotional well-being score	56.587 (22.645)	56.19 (21.110)	64.17 (20.813)	62.63 (21.048)	58.46 (22.034)
Physical functioning score	74.38 (25.399)	82.92 (20.597)	82.29 (21.297)	78.59 (22.528)	78.41 (23.629)
Number of close friends and relatives	8.17 (60.322)	6.65 (22.469)	5.82 (9.901)	3.98 (4.411)	7.21 (44.530)
Number of moves in past 2 years	1.72 (2.199)	2.55 (2.430)	1.18 (1.685)	1.16 (1.683)	1.77 (2.185)

analyses were performed using IBM SPSS 20. Two interaction terms were tested: health or social service use in the past month by most recent hospitalization and health or social service use in the past month by current mental health medication use. These interaction terms were found not to be significant in the presence of their respective lower-order terms, so main effects were estimated with interaction terms removed from the model.

3. FINDINGS

The Sample

The median annual income of participants at the time of the study was $9,760, with a range between $0.00 and $138,000. More than 41.6% of the sample was

Joe prepares to go out after a day of relaxing at home on a day off in April 2014. During a time when he isn't getting out to socialize often, working for Impact allows Joe to develop social connections with co-workers and remain active in gaming.

Source: Photo by Justin Langille

receiving public financial benefits in the form of ODSP or OW. Tables 15.1 and 15.2 present descriptive statistics for the four major groups included in this analysis: not working or looking for work (n = 185), looking for work (n = 84), working full-time or part-time (n = 94), and working part-time (n = 64), along with the total sample (n = 363). Seventeen individuals were retired due to age and hence excluded from this analysis.

The four groups did not differ greatly on sex; marital status; contact with family; ethnicity; health or social services utilization; community, home, or social integration; personal resources; social, emotional, or physical function; or housing tenure. The groups differed on having children under 18, current living arrangement, education, mental health medication use, substance use issues, past substance use issues, chronic physical illness, past head injuries, past homelessness, volunteering, being in school, and most recent psychiatric hospitalization, age, general health, and the number of close friends and relatives.

Those looking for work were more likely to have children under 18, a grade school or lower level of education, a current alcohol or marijuana use issue, a past head injury, past homelessness, be volunteering or attending school, and have never had a psychiatric hospitalization. Those looking for work also tended to be younger than the other three groups. Part-time workers were less likely to have children under 18; a current alcohol, tobacco, caffeine, or marijuana use issue; a past head injury; or past homelessness, although they were more likely to live alone, have a high school education, take mental health medication, or have had a psychiatric hospitalization over one year ago. Part-time workers also had fewer close friends or relatives.

Those working part-time or full-time were less likely to live with an unrelated person or be currently homeless, have a current alcohol or tobacco use issue, have a chronic physical illness, or have a psychiatric hospitalization within the past year, and were more likely to live with a parent/relative/spouse/partner, have a community college/university education, have a current caffeine use issue, and have a past substance use issue. Those working part-time or full-time also tended to have a higher general health score than the other three groups.

Finally, those not working and not looking for work were more likely to live with an unrelated person or be currently homeless, have a current substance use issue of any kind, have a current tobacco use issue, and have a chronic physical illness, although they were less likely to live alone, have a past substance use issue, or volunteer or attend school. Those not working or looking for work also tended to have lower general health but more close friends or close relatives.

Who Seeks Work

In Table 15.3, we compared those active in the labour force with those who were not, regardless of their success in finding work. Specifically, we compared those working full-time, part-time, or looking for work with those not working and not seeking work. Those who were living with unrelated persons, typically in a shelter, group home, or with roommates not related to them, were significantly less likely to be in the labour force (OR 0.326; 95% CI 0.165, 0.645). Living with family, a spouse, related person, or parent also appeared to reduce the chances of being in the labour force, but this was not statistically significantly (OR 0.622; 95% CI

Table 15.3: Logistic Regression Model Comparing Those Working Full-Time, Part-Time, or Not Working, but Actively Looking for Work to Those Not Working and Not Looking for Work (n = 326)

Independent Variable	Odds Ratio	95% Confidence Interval	p-value
Current living arrangement			0.003
Current living arrangement (Lives with spouse/relative/parents)	0.622	(0.277, 1.396)	0.250
Current living arrangement (Lives with unrelated person/homeless)	0.326	(0.165, 0.645)	0.001
Currently on mental health medication	0.308	(0.174, 0.546)	<0.001
Current substance use issue	0.314	(0.166, 0.596)	<0.001
Ethnic background	0.523	(0.291, 0.938)	0.030
Social integration score	1.168	(1.043, 1.308)	0.007
Volunteering once or more in past month	1.636	(0.911, 2.940)	0.099
General health score	1.020	(1.009, 1.030)	<0.001
Hospitalization			0.029
Hospitalization (prior to one year ago)	1.194	(0.672, 2.123)	0.545
Hospitalization (one year ago or more recent)	3.153	(1.329, 7.480)	0.009

0.277, 1.396). Health and social conditions were also important, but not always in the expected ways. Unsurprisingly, those who had a higher general health score (OR 1.020; 95% CI 1.009, 1.030) and social integration score (OR 1.168; 95% CI 1.043, 1.308) were more likely to be in the labour force, while those with current substance use issues (OR 0.314; 95% CI 0.166, 0.596) and those who were not of Caucasian ethnicity (OR 0.523; 95% CI 0.291, 0.938) were less likely to be in the labour force.

Perhaps more surprisingly, those currently on mental health medication were less likely to be in the labour force (OR 0.308; 95% CI 0.174, 0.546), which suggests some relationship between medication and not entering the labour force, a point we return to below. However, those who had a psychiatric hospitalization within the past year were more likely to be in the labour force (OR 3.153; 95% CI 1.329, 7.480). Volunteering was also positively associated with being in the labour force, although this relationship was not statistically significant (OR 1.636; 95% CI 0.911, 2.940). Nonetheless, since volunteering had some relationship with job

Table 15.4: Logistic Regression Model Comparing Those Working Full-Time or Part-Time to Those Not Working, Regardless of Whether They Are Looking for Work (n = 326)

Independent Variable	Odds Ratio	95% Confidence Interval	p-value
Current living arrangement			<0.001
Current living arrangement (Lives with spouse/relative/parents)	0.909	(0.395, 2.093)	0.823
Current living arrangement (Lives with unrelated person/homeless)	0.232	(0.110, 0.492)	<0.001
Current substance use issue	0.404	(0.203, 0.803)	0.010
Ever homeless	0.425	(0.230, 0.786)	0.006
Social integration score	1.217	(1.065, 1.390)	0.004
School or training in past month	0.346	(0.121, 0.990)	0.048
General health score	1.022	(1.010, 1.035)	<0.001
Children under 18	0.280	(0.130, 0.604)	0.001

search behaviour, but no relationship with actually having work (i.e., volunteering is absent from Tables 15.4–15.6), we conclude that this plays a small part of the job search process. Several variables that are typically regarded as explanatory labour supply-side factors were not found to be significant in this study, including education, the presence of dependent children, sex, and marital status.

Who Secures Work in a Broad Sense

The model presented in Table 15.4 attempts to differentiate the characteristics associated with finding employment (full- or part-time) compared to not working (whether looking for work or not). Again, those living with unrelated persons were significantly less likely to be working (OR 0.232; 95% CI 0.110, 0.492), as were those with a current substance use issue (OR 0.404; 95% CI 0.203, 0.803), those who have been homeless (OR 0.425; 95% CI 0.230, 0.786), and those who were in a school or training program (OR 0.346; 95% CI 0.121, 0.990). Those with children under 18 were less likely to be working full- or part-time, as shown

Table 15.5: Logistic Regression Model Comparing Those Working Full-Time or Part-Time to Those Not Working, but Actively Looking for Work (n = 160)

Independent Variable	Odds Ratio	95% Confidence Interval	p-value
Current living arrangement			0.014
Current living arrangement (Lives with spouse/relative/parents)	1.066	(0.360, 3.152)	0.909
Current living arrangement (Lives with unrelated person/homeless)	0.301	(0.116, 0.778)	0.013
Currently on mental health medication	1.935	(0.888, 4.214)	0.097
Current alcohol use issue	0.465	(0.182, 1.189)	0.110
Ever homeless	0.232	(0.100, 0.540)	0.001
In school or training program in past month	0.250	(0.077, 0.814)	0.021
General health score	1.019	(1.003, 1.035)	0.022
Children under 18	0.232	(0.094, 0.574)	0.002

Table 15.6: Logistic Regression Model Comparing Those Working Part-Time to Those Not Working, but Actively Looking for Work (n = 132)

Independent Variable	Odds Ratio	95% Confidence Interval	p-value
Currently on mental health medication	3.846	(1.670, 8.856)	0.002
Ever homeless	0.212	(0.091, 0.494)	<0.001
Children under 18	0.282	(0.109, 0.734)	0.010

in Table 15.4 (OR 0.280; 95% CI 0.130, 0.604), but having children seemed not to affect job search behaviour, since having children was not statistically significantly associated with being in the labour force (i.e., the having children variable is absent from Table 15.3). General health (OR 1.022; 95% CI 1.010, 1.035) and social integration (OR 1.217; 95% CI 1.065, 1.390) were again positively related to having work. However, the lack of correlation of age, sex, marital status, and especially education is noteworthy.

Who Secures Work in a Narrow Sense

The model presented in Table 15.5 represents the standard employment-unemployment binary; those with full- or part-time work are compared to those who are looking for work. Those who had work were more likely to have higher general health (OR 1.019; 95% CI 1.003, 1.035) and be on mental health medication (OR 1.935; 95% CI 0.888, 4.214). The latter finding, although not statistically significant, when contrasted with the model presented in Table 15.3, suggests that those taking mental health medication are less likely to enter the labour force. However, among those who do seek work, those on medication may be more likely to find work. Of course, these two groups, work non-seekers and work finders, could be very different in some unobserved characteristic, so we draw no further conclusions.

Again, those living with unrelated people (OR 0.301; 95% CI 0.116, 0.778), those who have been homeless (OR 0.232; 95% CI 0.100, 0.540), were in school or a training program (OR 0.250; 95% CI 0.077, 0.814), or had children under 18 (OR 0.232; 95% CI 0.094, 0.574) were less likely to have found work. Those who had a current alcohol use issue (OR 0.465; 95% CI 0.182, 1.189) may be less likely to have found work, but this finding was not statistically significant.

Who Secures Part-Time Work

We tried to model success in securing full-time work but the relatively small sample size did not permit us to report these results. The model presented in Table 15.6 compared those working part-time to those seeking work. Ever having been homeless exerted a significantly negative impact on having part-time work (OR 0.212; 95% CI 0.091, 0.494), as did having children under 18 (OR 0.282; 95% CI 0.109, 0.734). The strength and consistency of both homelessness and having children suggest that they exert a major negative influence on securing any type of work.

In contrast, taking mental health medication appeared to be strongly positively related to part-time employment (OR 3.846; 95% CI 1.670, 8.856). Again, education and other traditional human capital variables were not significantly associated with employment outcomes.

5. DISCUSSION

This study focused on exploring individual-level determinants of seeking and securing employment among a community sample of mental health consumer-survivors in Ontario, Canada. Seeking work was positively associated with a high general health score, psychiatric hospitalization within the past year, high social integration score, and volunteerism in past month. Collectively, these indicators of health and social well-being positively influence survivors' search for employment. While unemployed, survivors attribute access into the workforce as a desirable means to strengthen their sense of self-efficacy and community connections (Fossey & Harvey, 2010), as well as increasing feelings of social inclusion. Stapleton et al. (2011) suggested that unemployed mental health consumer-survivors receiving public financial assistance conceptualized work as a short-term strategy to supplement their monthly income. Over time, sustained employment offers the possibility of accumulating sufficient tangible and intangible resources to escape poverty. In this way, the presence of general well-being and the quest to improve one's life circumstances are reflected in an individual's efforts to engage in work-seeking activities.

The mental health consumer-survivors in this study that were less likely to seek employment had been treated with psychiatric medication, were using substances, were living with unrelated others such as in a shelter or group home, and belonged to an ethnic minority. This result suggests that a complex interplay of both individual and social conditions may inhibit work-seeking practices and lower levels of social inclusion. Similarly, researchers have reported that self-perceived disability, comorbidities, and social exclusion are barriers to entering the workforce (Biegel et al., 2010; Bond & Drake, 2008; Razzano et al., 2005). A synergistic coexistence of multiple person-specific and socially constructed disadvantages may keep survivors out of the labour force, and hence by definition, in unemployment.

Interventions to support work-seeking practices warrant expansion beyond an individualist ideology of neoliberalism to include systemic considerations that are not amenable to individual control (Graham et al., 2012). In doing so, survivors are positioned for self-actualization and well-being through appropriate employment supports. It has been reported that job acquisition can be facilitated through an integration of comprehensive assessment of each individual's life circumstances, choices, goals, and work readiness within the context of supported employment services adapted to the broader political, social, economic, and cultural milieu within which they reside (Corbière & Lecomte, 2009; Corrigan, 2001).

In comparison to unemployed survivors in this study, those individuals who successfully secured employment had higher social integration scores, higher general health scores, and indicators of illness management such as prescribed psychiatric medication and acute service access within the past year. Such findings are similar to those of other researchers who report the positive relationship between health and employment for those with mental health issues (Fossey & Harvey, 2010). The conceptualization of work as an allegory to health does not preclude the presence of illness symptoms but rather enables individuals to improve their well-being while employed. The benefits of employment, beyond nominal financial compensation, include opportunities for expanded social contact, a sense of purpose, self-efficacy, and greater feelings of social inclusion (Koletsi et al, 2009; Stapleton et al., 2011; Wilton, 2004).

In this study, no relationship was found between age, education, and employment outcomes. This challenges the traditional understanding of "human capital." As described by Gao and colleagues (2010), human capital is an individual's employability and earning capacity based on abilities and skills developed through education and training. The findings of the current study support a unique understanding of human capital specific to community-dwelling employed mental health consumer-survivors as constituted by social integration, progressive improvement in well-being, and symptom management. Employability is compromised when social integration is threatened, illness symptoms escalate, psychoactive substances are abused, housing is insecure, and responsibility for dependent children is paramount. Development of human capital for this vulnerable population is therefore not limited to an individual's education and training. Rather, human

Steve loads the Impact Junk Solutions truck with goods for recycling in April 2015. Recently returned to work after dealing with a medical condition, Steve credits his job with the crew as key to his success in recovery from mental illness and addiction.
Source: Photo by Justin Langille

capital requires a diverse and tailored network of coordinated housing, financial, childcare, leisure, education, and health services to enable social integration and well-being for individual employment.

Limitations

While the findings presented here are suggestive, this work is not without limitations. First, it is difficult to determine the impact that episodic conditions may have on employment; as episodic conditions fluctuate, so too may employment status fluctuate. This notion may be reflected in the finding that a psychiatric hospitalization within the past year increases the likelihood of being in the labour force. Second, the potential predictor variables are not always static in nature.

Contrary to some static predictors, such as sex or having children aged less than 18, some are quite dynamic and may change over time, including living arrangements, the use of mental health medication, psychiatric hospitalization, and substance use issues. In particular, substance use issues are ever-changing, and the possibility for relapse and/or recovery may have a particularly strong impact on employment outcome. Finally, the research presented here is cross-sectional in nature. From this baseline employment research, all that can be concluded is that there is an association between the statistically significant variables in Tables 15.3 through 15.6 and employment outcomes.

This study has focused on individual characteristics using cross-sectional data from a convenience sample of mental health consumer-survivors. This allowed

Social Enterprise: Another Working Day. Impact Junk is an example of a social enterprise hiring only those with experience of mental illness. The company truck is guided to the edge of a dumping site at one of London's biggest recycling centres to offload refuse.

Source: Photo by Justin Langille

the research team to focus on the characteristics that differentiate employment outcomes among the population, but the study's findings and generalizability are limited by non-random selection of respondents. Over time, this limitation may be corrected by subsequent waves of the survey.

6. CONCLUSION

For mental health consumer-survivors, it seems that individual characteristics are associated with employment outcomes, although in somewhat surprising ways. Variables such as current living arrangements, ethnicity, social integration, general health, volunteering, substance use issues, homelessness, school or training status, and having children under 18 are related to employment outcomes. Similarly,

The 3 Rs: Reduce, Reuse, and Recycle. The Goodwill Social Enterprise program includes a successful toy-recycling component that bags and resells used toys at a low cost for low-income families.

Source: Photo by Justin Langille

health service-related variables such as currently using mental health medication, and psychiatric hospitalization are also related to employment outcomes for mental health consumer-survivors. However, some conventional human capital variables are notably absent from this list of predictors. For example, education, age, sex, and marital status were not found to be associated with employment outcomes among mental health consumer-survivors.

While the research literature emphasizing individual characteristics as predictors of employment is growing, so too does concern that research of this nature may be used to limit access to services. Rather, individual characteristics that predict employment should be used to personalize and enhance service delivery, which, in turn, will have a positive effect on social inclusion (Bond & Drake, 2008).

The 4 Rs: Reduce, Reuse, Recycle, and Renew. Average household items like cutlery are often saved by Impact Junk Solutions employees and taken to their warehouse for storage. The company has open house days during which individuals in need can pick up unwanted items for their new homes.
Source: Photo by Justin Langille

REFERENCES

Alverson, H., Carpenter, E., & Drake, R. E. (2006). An ethnographic study of job seeking among people with severe mental illness. *Psychiatric Rehabilitation Journal, 30*(1), 15–22.

Becker, D., Whitley, R., Bailey, E. L., & Drake, R. E. (2007). Long-term employment trajectories among participants with severe mental illness in supported employment. *Psychiatric Services, 58*(7), 922–928.

Bejerholm, U., & Björkman, T. (2011). Empowerment in supported employment research and practice: Is it relevant? *International Journal of Social Psychiatry, 57*(6), 588–595.

Bell, M. D., Milstein, R. M., & Lysaker, P. H. (1993). Pay as an incentive in work participation by patients with severe mental illness. *Hospital and Community Psychiatry, 44*(7), 684–686.

Biegel, D. E., Stevenson, L. D., Beimers, D., Ronis, R. J., & Boyle, P. (2010). Predictors of competitive employment among consumers with co-occurring mental and substance use disorders. *Research on Social Work Practice, 20*(2), 191–201.

Bond, G. R., & Drake, R. E. (2008). Predictors of competitive employment among patients with schizophrenia. *Current Opinion in Psychiatry, 21*(4), 362–369.

Bond, G. R., Resnick, S. G., Drake, R. E., Xie, H., McHugo, G. J., & Bebout, R. R. (2001). Does competitive employment improve nonvocational outcomes for people with severe mental illness? *Journal of Consulting Clinical Psychology, 69*(3), 489–501.

Bond, G. R., Xie, H., & Drake, R. E. (2007). Can SSDI and SSI beneficiaries with mental illness benefit from evidence-based supported employment? *Psychiatric Services, 58*(11), 1412–1420.

Catty, J., Lissouba, P., White, S., Becker, T., Drake, R. E., Fioritti, A., ... EQOLISE Group. (2008). Predictors of employment for people with severe mental illness: Results of an international six-centre randomised controlled trial. *British Journal of Psychiatry, 192*(3), 224–231.

Corbière, M., Lanctot, N., Lecomte, T., Latimer, E., Goering, P., Kirsh, B., ... Kamagiannis, T. (2010). A pan-Canadian evaluation of supported employment programs dedicated to people with severe mental disorders. *Community Mental Health Journal, 46*(1), 44–55.

Corbière, M., & Lecomte, T. (2009). Vocational services offered to people with severe mental illness. *Journal of Mental Health, 18*(1), 38–50.

Corbière, M., Zaniboni, S., Lecomte, T., Bond, G., Gilles, P.-Y., Lesage, A., & Goldner, E. (2011). Job acquisition for people with severe mental illness enrolled in supported employment programs: A theoretically grounded empirical study. *Journal of Occupational Rehabilitation, 21*(3), 342–354.

Corrigan, P. W. (2001). Place-then-train: An alternative service paradigm for persons with psychiatric disabilities. *Clinical Psychology: Science and Practice, 8*(3), 334–349.

Crocker, R. K. (2006). *Human capital development and education*. Ottawa, ON: Canadian Policy Research Networks.

Csiernik, R. (2014). *Workplace wellness; Issues and responses*. Toronto, ON: Canadian Scholars' Press.

Csiernik, R., Csiernik, B., & Brideau, M. (2017). A thirty year retrospective on the income adequacy of Canadian provincial social assistance payments to non-institutionalized disabled adults. *Canadian Review of Social Policy/Revue Canadienne de Politique Sociale, 77*(Summer/Fall), 95–119.

Drake, R. E., Bond, G. R., Thornicroft, G., Knapp, M., & Goldman H. H. (2012). Mental health disability: An international perspective. *Journal of Disability Policy Studies, 23*(2), 110–120.

Fossey, E. M., & Harvey, C. A. (2010). Finding and sustaining employment: A qualitative meta-synthesis of mental health consumer views. *Canadian Journal of Occupational Therapy, 77*(5), 303–314.

Gao, N., Gill, K., Schmidt, L. T., & Pratt C. W. (2010). The application of human capital theory in vocational rehabilitation for individuals with mental illness. *Journal of Vocational Rehabilitation, 32*(1), 25–33.

Graham, J. R., Gray, E., Jones, M. E., & Shier, M. L. (2012). Individualism: Perceptions of people experiencing difficulties integrating into labour markets. *Canadian Review of Social Policy/Revue Canadienne de Politique Sociale, 62*(Spring), 360–367.

Income Security Advocacy Centre. (2018). *OW and ODSP rates and the OCB (2018)*. Toronto, ON: Author.

Kneebone, R., & Grynishak, O. (2011). Income support for persons with disabilities. *The School of Public Policy Research Papers, 4*(11), 1–19.

Koletsi, M., Niersman, A., van Busschbach, J., Catty, J., Becker, T., Burns, T., ... EQOLISE Group. (2009). Working with mental health problems: Clients' experiences of IPS, vocational rehabilitation and employment. *Social Psychiatry and Psychiatric Epidemiology, 44*(11), 961–970.

Lahey, P. (2007). *Redesigning the ODSP maze*. Canadian Mental Health Association. Retrieved from http://ontario.cmha.ca/network/redesigning-the-odsp-maze/

Larson, J. E., Barr, L. K., Kuwabara, S. A., Boyle, M., & Glenn, T. L. (2007). Process and outcome analysis of a supported employment program for people with psychiatric disabilities. *American Journal of Psychiatric Rehabilitation, 10*(4), 339–353.

Laudet, A. B. (2012). Rate and predictors of employment among formerly polysubstance dependent urban individuals in recovery. *Journal of Addictive Diseases, 31*(3), 288–302.

Lim, K.-L., Jacobs, P., Ohinmaa, A., Schopflocher, D., & Dewa, C. S. (2008). A new population-based measure of the economic burden of mental illness in Canada. *Chronic Diseases in Canada, 28*(3), 92–98.

McGurk, S. R., & Mueser, K. T. (2003). Cognitive functioning and employment in severe mental illness. *The Journal of Nervous Mental Disease, 191*(12), 789–798.

McGurk, S. R., Mueser, K. T., & Pascaris, A. (2005). Cognitive training and supported employment for persons with severe mental illness: One-year results from a randomized controlled trial. *Schizophrenia Bulletin, 31*(4), 898–909.

McHugo, G. J., Drake, R. E., Xie, H., & Bond, G. R. (2012). A 10-year study of steady employment and non-vocational outcomes among people with serious mental illness and co-occurring substance use disorders. *Schizophrenia Research, 138*(2–3), 233–239.

Mental Health Commission of Canada [MHCC]. (2012). *Changing directions, changing lives: The mental health strategy for Canada.* Calgary, AB: Author.

Mental Health Commission of Canada [MHCC]. (2013). *The aspiring workforce: Employment and income for people with serious mental illness.* Ottawa, ON: Author.

Mueser, K. T., Clark, R. E., Haines, M., Drake, R. E., McHugo, G. J., Bond, G. R., … Swain, K. (2004). The Hartford study of supported employment for persons with severe mental illness. *Journal of Consulting and Clinical Psychology, 72*(3), 479–490.

Mueser, K. T., Salyers, M. P., & Mueser, P. R. (2001). A prospective analysis of work in schizophrenia. *Schizophrenia Bulletin, 27*(2), 281–296.

Pulkki-Råback, L., Ahola, K., Elovainio, M., Kivimäki, M., Hintsanen, M., Isometsä, E., … Virtanen, M. (2012). Socio-economic position and mental disorders in a working-age Finnish population: The health 2000 study. *European Journal of Public Health, 22*(3), 327–332.

Razzano, L. A., Cook, J. A., Burke-Miller, J. K., Mueser, K. T., Pickett-Schenk, S. A., Grey, D. D., … Carey, M. A. (2005). Clinical factors associated with employment among people with severe mental illness: Findings from the employment intervention demonstration program. *The Journal of Nervous and Mental Disease, 193*(11), 705–713.

SF-36. (2013). *A community for measuring health outcomes using SF tools.* Retrieved from http://www.sf-36.org/

Solar, A. (2011). Supported employment can reduce social exclusion and improve schizophrenia. *Australasian Psychiatry, 19*(1), 78–80.

Stapleton, J., Procyk, S., & Kochen, L. (2011). *What stops us from working? New ways to make work pay, by fixing the treatment of earnings under the Ontario Disability Support Program.* Centre for Addiction and Mental Health. Retrieved from http://www.camh.net/Public_policy/Public_policy_papers/ODSP%20Report%20final.pdf

Tsang, H. W. H., Leung, A. Y., Chung, R. C. K., Bell, M., & Cheung, W.-M. (2010). Review on vocational predictors: A systematic review of predictors of vocational outcomes among individuals with schizophrenia: An update since 1998. *Australian and New Zealand Journal of Psychiatry, 44*(6), 495–504.

Twamley, E. W., Vella, L., Burton, C. Z., Becker, D. R., Bell, M. D., & Jeste, D. V. (2012). The efficacy of supported employment for middle-aged and older people with schizophrenia. *Schizophrenia Research, 135*(1–3), 100–104.

Waghorn, G., Saha, S., Harvey, C., Morgan, V. A., Waterreus, A., Bush, R., … McGrath, J. J. (2012). "Earning and learning" in those with psychotic disorders: The second Australian national survey of psychosis. *Australian and New Zealand Journal of Psychiatry, 46*(8), 774–785.

Waghorn, G., Saha, S., & McGrath J. J. (2014). Correlates of competitive versus noncompetitive employment among adults with psychotic disorders. *Psychiatric Services, 65*(4), 476–482.

Wilton, R. (2004). Putting policy into practice? Poverty and people with serious mental illness. *Social Science & Medicine, 58*(1), 25–39.

CHAPTER 16

Iris Scanning: A Solution to the Lost Identification Problem Encountered by People Experiencing Homelessness?

Cheryl Forchuk, Lorie Donelle, Miriam Capretz, Fatima Bukair, and John Kok

1. INTRODUCTION

On any given night, there are approximately 35,000 Canadians experiencing homelessness. A conservative estimate of nearly 235,000 Canadians access emergency shelters or sleep on the streets every year (Gaetz et al., 2016). The transient and unstable nature of homelessness makes maintaining belongings challenging. Thus, it is common for individuals who are homeless and/or have mental illnesses to lose pieces of identification, birth certificates, and health and social insurance cards. Loss of identification can leave individuals stranded without any access to continued non-urgent care or services such as rehabilitation facilities. Without access to these services, individuals rely on emergency services, increasing the strain on health-care dollars. Loss of identification is a barrier that has long been faced by homeless people that impairs their access to health care (Stark, 1992). Although Canada has universal health care, the majority of homeless people do not possess proof of coverage due to stolen or lost identification (Hwang et al., 2000). This loss of identification impedes equitable access to health-care services and can result, at times, in denial of care, further excluding this group from mainstream society. One early survey conducted in Toronto stated that 7% of homeless individuals reported having been refused health-care services at least once due to loss of their health card (Crowe & Hardill, 1993).

This chapter explores one solution to this issue, iris scanning, in hopes of finding an identification strategy that is independent of an individual's ability to recall from memory or need to carry identification, and thus improving their access to care. The research questions that guided the exploratory research were:

1. What are the implementation issues related to deploying iris scanners in a homeless shelter?
2. What are the staff perceptions related to acceptability of the technology?
3. What are the service users' perceptions related to acceptability of the technology?
4. What ethical issues are identified related to the use of iris scanning?
5. What policy issues are identified related to the use of iris scanning?

2. METHODS

Description of the Setting

Staff at a homeless shelter coordinated with research staff to strategically set up a table and a few chairs in the open foyer of the shelter to allow for visibility of the research staff. Signs asking for volunteers to participate in this project were placed at both door entrances of the shelter. In addition, volunteers spoke to potential participants and directed them to the main table. The foyer was the best location for research staff to recruit individuals, as it was used as the common socialization area within the facility. This allowed curious participants to more easily approach the table and ask questions about the project.

Recruitment

The research team was at the site from 8:00 a.m. until 6:00 p.m. for three consecutive days. This allowed the research team to approach individuals staying at or coming in to the shelter at breakfast, lunch, and dinner. Individuals at the shelter were either staying there for the month or accessing its services such as the food bank. Individuals entering and exiting the building were approached and informed about the study; 200 participants were recruited by research staff upon full disclosure of the project's objective over three days. Verbal consent was obtained to participate in the study. Of the total participants, 191 agreed to be scanned and interviewed once, while 9 participants agreed to only be interviewed.

Instruments

A researcher-developed questionnaire was generated that inquired about participants' sex, previous use or non-use of the scan, their perception of iris scanning, and whether they preferred an iris scan or a formal identification (ID) card to access health-care service delivery. Iris scanning over the three-day study period was performed using Seek Avenger equipment developed by Crossmatch Technologies.

Data Analysis

SPSS Statistics Software was used to generate descriptive statistics, while qualitative analyses employed thematic grouping of responses, identifying recurrent themes and opinions expressed by participants.

3. FINDINGS

Of the 200 participants who were successfully recruited, 146 (73.0%) identified as male and 54 as (27.0%) female. Of these, 191 agreed to be scanned and

Table 16.1: Iris Scanning—Descriptive Statistics (n = 200)

	Frequency (%)
Gender	
Male	146 (73.0%)
Female	54 (27.0%)
Previously Used Iris Scanner	
Yes	2 (1.0%)
No	198 (99.0%)
Agreed to Scan	
Yes	191 (95.5%)
No	9 (4.5%)
Had Second Scan (n = 187)	
Yes	50 (26.7%)
No	137 (73.3%)
Iris Scan Worked (n = 188)	
Yes	182 (96.8%)
No	6 (3.2%)

interviewed, with 9 opting only to be interviewed (Table 16.1). Fifty of the 191 who agreed to an initial iris scan also agreed to complete a second scan. Reasons for agreeing to scanning included pursuit of safe, reliable identification; curiosity/inclination for new technology; their support of research or belief that the study was for a good cause; or merely because they were directly asked to participate by a research assistant. Those not scanned but interviewed provided two primary reasons: not having enough information to decide and being suspicious and untrusting of the capacity of the system to safeguard and manage the information being collected (Table 16.2).

Table 16.2: Acceptability and Functionality of Iris Scanning ID Method

Question	Answer	#	%
1. Did you use the iris scanner just now?	Yes	191	95.5
	No	9	4.5
2. Reason for agreeing to scanning	Curiosity	50	26.2
	Told to do it/Just because/Don't know	40	20.9
	Free coffee card	38	19.9
	Research/Want to help	18	9.4
	Heard about it/Wanted to do it	16	8.4
	Identification/Security	15	7.9
	Eye problems	7	3.7
	Other	7	3.7
3. Would you prefer an iris scan or an ID card like a health card for service?	Iris scan	146	87.4
	ID card	21	12.6
	Missing	33	
4. Why would you prefer an iris scan?	ID cards get lost/Don't need to carry ID card around	25	32.1
	Fast and easy	22	28.2
	Interesting/Cool	12	15.4
	Better security	8	10.3
	Don't know	1	1.3
	Other	10	12.8
	Missing	68	

Overall, there was broad acceptance of the iris technology as a primary form of identification. Of the 167 individuals who were scanned and provided a response, 146 (87.4%) indicated that an iris scan would be their preferred form of identification, while 21 (12.6%) indicated that they still favoured having a traditional identification card (Table 16.2). Fifty individuals agreed to enrol for a second scan, the purpose of which was to authenticate the first scan. Those that agreed to do so indicated they signed up for the second scan for the same reasons as for the first. Forty-nine of the 50 (98.0%) first and second scans matched, with the only non-match arising due to the participant's eye becoming watery. Field notes indicated that when the participant's eyes became teary during the second the scan, the scanner was not able to generate the same code as during the initial scan. This was remedied by requesting that the one participant blink between scans to allow for a better authentication.

4. DISCUSSION

The high percentage of participants preferring iris scanning as a primary form of identification (87.4%) aligns with issues arising from their status as homeless. Participants wanted to have a reliable way of identification to enhance their access to services including health care, shelter, and utilities, as well as creating a sense of societal belonging. The 12.6% that objected to iris scanning did so due to either fear of being tracked by government agencies (police or security), the information falling into criminal hands for misuse, or simply due to a lack of system capacity to manage the data. These concerns are not unique to those participating in this pilot study but have also been reflected in other similar international studies (Martin & Donovan, 2015; Moody, 2004).

A 98% accuracy rate for second scan authentication of the participants' identity points to the evidence echoed in the literature indicating that iris scanning is a reliable method of biometric identification. The results of this study were almost identical to one conducted by Latman and Herb (2013). In that research, an iris recognition system was evaluated in a sample of 277 participants in the United States for accuracy and reliability. The system was able to enrol, match 1:1, and verify individuals often within three seconds in the first round. The demographic characteristics, room lighting conditions, and eye conditions did not modify the results. While eye condition was not a factor in previous studies, it was noted in this study that teary eyes did influence the code generated by the scanner for one participant. To confirm that teary eyes were the reason behind the mismatched code, the participant was asked and agreed to blink a few times and to undergo a third iris scan. The third code matched the first code, leading on-site researchers to recommend to subsequent participants to blink a few times between scans.

The implication of this research is that if a reliable and sustainable identification system were to be implemented for this population, iris scanning could be a viable and potentially successful option. In addition, implementation of iris scanning could be cost effective with this population, given the frequency of identification card loss, at a rate of 10% a year, and the running of weekly identification clinics held within many larger communities. Of course, public fears and perception of surveillance and safety and security of information must be addressed before implementation. According to Jain et al. (2004), "by using biometrics, it is possible to confirm or establish an individual's identity based on 'who she is,' rather than by 'what she possesses' (e.g., an identification card) or 'what she remembers' (e.g., a password)" (p. 4). In addition, not only does biometric identification have to meet four requirements (universal, distinctive, invariant with time, and be measured quantitatively), it must also be acceptable to the service user, be fast and accurate, and cannot succumb to fraudulent means.

Challenges

Martin and Donovan (2015) reported that when the government of the United Kingdom attempted to implement a nationwide National Identification Scheme based on biometric technology, including iris scanning, finger printing, and face recognition, they assumed that the public would accept the proposal because the technology was straightforward. However, it was quickly discovered that there was not unanimity among the public, with some groups of intended users very accepting of biometrics while others who were knowledgeable of the proposed technology vocally opposed. The key factor that led to the plan's failure was the charged political environment in which the discourse took place, as the technology would appear to pervade the government's relationship with the public, in addition to opposition from a knowledgeable research team at the London School of Economics and a pressure group known as No2ID (Martin & Donovan, 2015). Further, the authors note that the discourses in enacting public acceptability were problematic due to intertwined issues such as rights, autonomy, and citizenship, and that biometric technology was confusing to many, which limited the ability to discuss the proposal in depth.

Moody (2004) attempted to shed light on public perception and acceptance of biometric identification by first comparing the types that are currently in use by many organizations for different purposes. Fingerprint scanning is either performed by silicone or ultrasound scanners; however, results can be affected by skin dryness or dirt and grime build-up on the reader. Nevertheless, it was the most accepted by respondents as a form of identification to access an automated teller machine (ATM), for computer log-on, and for office access (Jain et al., 2004). On the other hand, Moody (2004) reported that iris scanning technology, while more accurate, was the least understood and least accepted. The public feared greater invasion of privacy and identity theft with iris scanning than other biometric options. Moody concluded by recommending that, regardless of the use, the public should be actively involved in the decision-making process to employ biometrics through education and information dissemination about the technology.

A prominent and recurring theme in the literature, as well as in this study's findings, is the perception that biometric technology could be used for unintended purposes. Study participants feared being watched by security or police, information falling into the wrong hands, and the lack of technological capacity for data management and integrity.

5. CONCLUSION

Based on current qualitative and descriptive statistics, as well as the existing literature, it is evident that iris scanning is a safe and reliable form of identification that is minimally invasive and can withstand fraudulent activity among a group of community-based participants accessing homeless shelters. It was deemed an acceptable practice by most of the study's participants. In addition, its implementation offers cost-effective savings within the homeless population given the frequency of identification card replacement and the lack of access to non-emergency health-care services, the latter of which leads to an increase in emergency department usage and cost. In providing a quality-assured iris recognition program, individuals experiencing homelessness can gain access to services that they may not have been able to access previously. Full acceptability of biometrics technology within health care could support quality of care and act on public health matters. This can happen by combining enforceable legislation with public awareness to allay fears of their personally identifiable data falling into criminal hands while assuring the public that third parties will not have access to their information and the system is capable of managing electronic medical records.

REFERENCES

Crowe, C., & Hardill, K. (1993). Nursing research and political change: The street health report. *Canadian Nurse, 89*(1), 21–24.

Gaetz, S., Dej, E., Richter, T., & Redman, M. (2016). *The state of homelessness in Canada 2016.* Toronto, ON: Canadian Observatory on Homelessness Press.

Hwang, S. W., Windrim, P. W., Svoboda, T. J., & Sullivan, W. F. (2000). Physician payment for the care of homeless people. *Canadian Medical Association Journal, 163*(2), 170–171.

Jain, A. K., Ross, A., & Prabhakar, S. (2004). An introduction to biometric recognition. *IEEE Transactions on Circuits and Systems for Video Technology, 14*(1), 4–20.

Latman, N. S., & Herb, E. (2013). A field study of the accuracy and reliability of a biometric iris recognition system. *Science and Justice, 53*(2), 98–102.

Martin, A. K., & Donovan, K. P. (2015). New surveillance technologies and their publics: A case of biometrics. *Public Understanding of Science, 24*(7), 842–857.

Moody, J. (2004). Public perceptions of biometric devices: The effect of misinformation on acceptance and use. *Issues in Informing Science and Information Technology, 1*(4), 753–761.

Stark, L. (1992). Barriers to health care for homeless people. In R. I. Jahiel (Ed.), *Homelessness: A prevention-oriented approach* (pp. 151–164). Baltimore, MD: Johns Hopkins University Press.

CHAPTER 17

The Effectiveness of a Shelter Diversion Intervention for Families Who Experience Homelessness

Cheryl Forchuk, Jan Richardson, Gordon Russell, Chantelle Perreault, Bryanna Lucyk, and Annie Yang

1. INTRODUCTION

Background on Families Experiencing Homelessness

The occupancy rate of family shelters in 2014 had increased by 19% from 2005 (Segaert, 2017). A lack of sufficient income and unaffordable, inadequate, and overcrowded housing are common factors related to families entering homelessness (Gaetz, 2010; Paradis et al., 2014). A survey of 1,500 low-income families in Toronto showed that nine out of ten families were at risk for homelessness (Paradis et al., 2014). Family shelters across Canada have been operating at 90% occupancy rates since 2008, based on current epidemiological data (Gaetz et al., 2016). However, this increased strain on family shelters can be reduced by incorporating early intervention programs that divert at-risk families from ever entering the shelter system.

Consequences of Family Homelessness

Individual interviews, administrative shelter data, and health outcomes all indicate a decline in the quality of life of those experiencing homelessness (Bassuk et al., 1996; Metraux et al., 2011; Sylvestre et al., 2018). Families experiencing homelessness often report negative experiences associated with shelter use, such as overcrowding, lack of privacy, poor hygiene, loss of routine, and disruption of parenting practices (Gültekin et al., 2014; Mayberry et al., 2014; Sylvestre et al., 2018; Tischler et al., 2004). American shelter data from 1990 to 2002 reported that those who had multiple shelter stays in their lifetime had a reduced life expectancy (Metraux et al., 2011). Mothers who had experienced homelessness in their lifetime reported a higher rate of mental health issues and prevalence of chronic health conditions such as asthma, anemia, and ulcers (Bassuk et al., 1996; Vostanis et al., 1998; Weinreb et al., 2006). Higher rates of substance misuse and mental health issues, such as major depressive disorder and post-traumatic stress disorder (PTSD), are commonly found within this population (Bassuk et al., 1996; Weinreb et al., 2006).

Families experiencing homelessness, compared to low-income housed families, are more dependent on emergency and public services to meet their health-care needs (Wood & Valdez, 1991). The annual cost of health-care service utilization, including inpatient hospitalizations, office-based physician visits, and emergency department visits, among individuals experiencing homelessness in Toronto was approximated to be over $7,000 per person per year a decade ago, meaning this cost has since risen substantively (Hwang & Henderson, 2010). Further, health-care utilization costs among families that experience homelessness was three times greater compared to low-income housed groups (Hwang & Henderson, 2010). Duchon et al. (1999) explored the relationship between residential instability and medical care utilization among mothers living in emergency shelters. This group depended on public health clinics and emergency department services as their primary source of health care. The use of behavioural health services was also significantly higher among heads of families with a history of shelter use, compared to low-income housed families (Park et al., 2010). Factors such as residential instability, frequent moves, and the lack of a primary physician are contributing factors for the frequent use of public health-care services among this population (Wood & Valdez, 1991). Clark et al. (2018) found that health-care expenditures rose steadily during the period prior to a family's entry into homelessness. Hence, interventions that help families obtain needed health-care and social service supports at this critical period may reduce the overall reliance on emergency services and decrease the economic impact of prolonged public service utilization (Clark et al., 2018).

Early Interventions for Housing Stability

The use of intervention programs to reduce shelter use for at-risk families has been successful in the United States (Levitt et al., 2013; Shinn et al., 1998). Levitt and colleagues (2013) evaluated the Home to Stay pilot program in New York City that offered intensive housing placements and services for families experiencing homelessness. Relative to a comparison group of families who were using standardized shelter services, families in the Home to Stay program spent less time in shelter, exited the shelter system faster, and had reduced rates of returning to shelter once housed. Similarly, Shinn and colleagues (1998) found that individuals placed in subsidized housing were 20.6 times more likely to maintain stable housing in the future relative to those that were placed in a shelter. These programs indicate that shelter diversion interventions are effective in reducing the risk of families entering the shelter system and the negative trajectories associated with homelessness.

The majority of research in Canada has been on interventions for individuals who are homeless rather than families (Falvo, 2009; Goering et al., 2011). However, positive outcomes for individuals who received housing intervention services have been found. The At Home—Chez Soi project is the largest nationwide research project, conducted across five Canadian cities (Hwang et al., 2012). Results from this study indicated that providing housing-first intervention to individuals living in shelters resulted in more people exiting the shelter system and better housing stability compared to those that received treatment as usual care. However, there is a need to examine whether housing interventions are just as effective for families experiencing homelessness. Additionally, most homelessness prevention programs provide intervention to individuals already living in the shelter system. There is limited research on early intervention efforts that target at-risk families from entering the shelter system prior to an episode of homelessness. To bridge these gaps in the literature, the present study evaluated the utility of a shelter diversion program at preventing vulnerable families from entering the shelter system prior to an episode of homelessness.

2. INTERVENTION

Rotholme Women's and Families' Shelter, part of Mission Services of London (Ontario), received funding to pilot a shelter diversion program to address the influx of families experiencing homelessness and seeking refuge in emergency shelters. This program used early intervention to divert families at risk of homelessness from entering the shelter system by providing them housing, financial, health, and social service supports. At-risk families often call shelters prior to losing their housing. Hence, Rotholme's diversion program took advantage of this critical point of contact by referring families at imminent risk of homelessness to a housing crisis worker, who helped them explore and obtain alternative housing arrangements, services, and supports. The housing crisis worker met families to assess their risk and the level of intervention they required. Services offered by the housing crisis worker included assistance with housing searches, setting up appointments, obtaining up-to-date identification, filing for urgent housing on

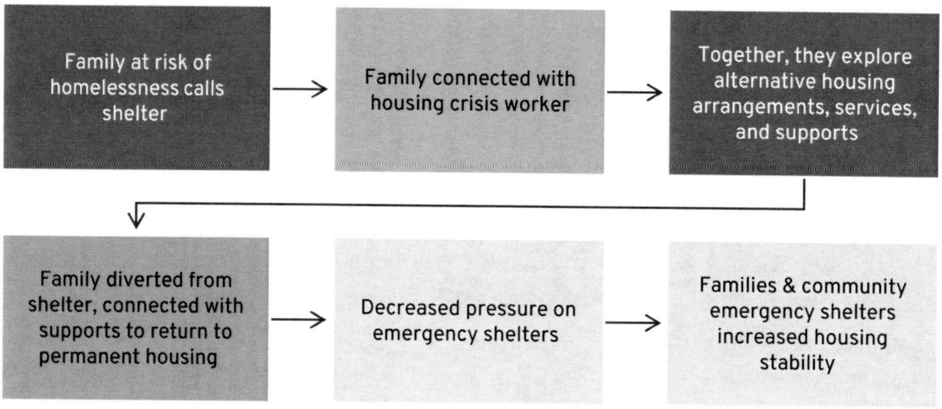

Figure 17.1: Components of the Rotholme Shelter Diversion Pilot Program

behalf of clients, mediating disputes between families and landlords, and preventing eviction. Families were connected to long-term supports such as financial aid, employment services, or mental health services to help maintain permanent housing and mitigate future homelessness episodes (see Figure 17.1).

The evaluation aimed both to determine the degree to which an early prevention program is successful in preventing families from entering shelter and obtaining housing stability and also to explore the degree to which the program was successful in mitigating the risks associated with families experiencing homelessness.

3. METHODS

Procedure

The study employed a mixed-methods longitudinal design over an 18-month period. Data was collected from administrative data, semi-structured interviews, and focus groups. Administrative shelter data was collected on all families accessing the program, between April 2016 and December 2017. It was anticipated that families at risk of homelessness would call local emergency family shelters for support prior to losing housing. Staff and workers at the shelter used this point of contact to recruit families to participate in research interviews. Individual interviews were conducted with parents of families that agreed to participate at four timepoints: baseline, as well as 6, 12, and 18 months post-baseline. Baseline interviews occurred shortly after families called to access emergency shelter services. Focus groups were conducted 6 and 18 months after the baseline interviews with shelter staff and individuals not involved in the shelter diversion program but accessing

Rotholme's emergency shelters during that time. Interviews took approximately one hour to complete. Participants received a $20 honorarium for each interview completed to compensate for their time. Ethics approval for the study was obtained from the Western University Research Ethics Board.

Participants

Administrative shelter data was collected on 406 individuals from 117 families that accessed the diversion program. Shelter staff recruited the families that accessed the Rotholme shelter diversion program for individual interviews. Twenty families consisting of 29 adults and 46 dependents agreed to participate in the study and completed the baseline interview. Dependents included children under the age of 18 and any individual living under the care of the adults in the study, such as persons with ability issues. Fourteen families completed all four interviews, while six families were lost through the follow-up period, leaving the final sample to consist of 14 families comprised of 20 parents and 30 dependents.

Measures

Administrative data

Administrative shelter data from the family shelter was collected on all families that accessed the shelter diversion program. This data provided information on the housing outcome of families, including whether they were able to remain housed at their current residence, had to be rehoused elsewhere, were in the process of moving, ended up in shelter, or if their housing status at termination of the shelter diversion service was unknown. Information on the cost to run the program over 18 months was also obtained.

Demographics

A demographics form collected information on parents of the families that participated in the semi-structured interviews. This included information on age, sex, marital status, number and age of children, country of origin, years of residency in Canada, ethnicity, mental health issues, and reported disability.

Housing History Survey

Measures of housing stability were obtained from the Housing History Survey (HHS; Forchuk et al., 2011) across the four interview time points. This instrument was developed by a Community-University Research Alliance team and has been used in previous studies involving individuals experiencing homelessness (Forchuk et al., 2011; Forchuk et al., 2015). The HHS is used to retrospectively track housing history; types of residences participants have resided in, such as a private house or apartment, social housing, or a shelter; the duration of stay at each residence; and the participant's satisfaction with the housing situation. Housing stability was determined by comparing the number of moves prior to enrolment in the shelter diversion program with the number after the shelter diversion intervention.

Service Use

The Health, Social, Justice Service Use inventory (HSJSU) was developed to access service use among individuals who experience homelessness for the At Home/Chez Soi study in Canada (Goering et al., 2011). The HSJSU was used in the present study to assess service use across the four time points for families who completed a semi-structured interview. The HSJSU includes 24 yes-or-no questions to determine whether participants have used health (nurse, doctor), social (housing worker, social worker), or justice services (probation officers, mental health court) within the past six months. The type, frequency, and reason for services used were also recorded.

Lehman's Quality of Life

The Lehman's Quality of Life—Brief Version (QoL; Lehman, 1983, 1996) is an assessment used to measure subjective and objective components of life quality. This instrument includes a general subjective rating of life quality on a 7-point Likert scale, with scores ranging from 1 (terrible) to 7 (delighted). The QoL also has subjective and objective subscales in life domains that include health, safety, daily activities, family relationships, social relationships, employment, finances, and living situation.

Family Service Prioritization Decision Assistance Tool

The Family Service Prioritization Decision Assistance Tool (F-SPDAT; OrgCode Consulting Inc., 2015) is an instrument designed to assess the level of need and inform service prioritization for social service providers working with families experiencing homelessness. This tool was completed by one parent from each family that participated in the semi-structured interviews across all four time-points. The F-SPDAT contains 20 subscales, including mental health, wellness, and cognitive functioning; physical health and wellness; managing tenancy. The scores from the subscales are combined to produce a total score that indicates level of housing need. Scores range between 0 and 80, with a higher score indicating need for greater intervention. A total score between 54 and 80 indicates the need for a

Housing First intervention, while a score between 27 and 53 indicated need for rapid rehousing. Subscales in the F-SPDAT were combined to produce composite scores in five domains: wellness, risks, family unit, socialization and daily functions, and history of housing.

Data Analyses

Descriptive summaries of administrative shelter data collected on all families that accessed the shelter diversion program at two time-points from April 2016 to March 2017 and April 2017 to December 2017 are presented in Table 17.1. Analyses on this data were completed using IBM SPSS software. Descriptive statistics were completed on demographic variables for all participants that completed the baseline interview. Only participants that completed all four interviews are included in the subsequent longitudinal analyses

4. RESULTS

Administrative Data

Rotholme's Shelter Diversion Program

Administrative data was obtained on all families that accessed Rotholme's diversion program. The percentage of families that accessed shelters decreased over time from 8%, between April 2016 and March 2017, to 3%, between April 2017 and December 2017 (Table 17.1). The cost to employ a housing crisis worker to work with 117 families between April 2016 to December 2017 was $75,514.40, or approximately $645.42 per family (Mission Services correspondence).

Table 17.1: Administrative Shelter Data for All Families That Accessed Rotholme's Diversion Program

Time Period	April 2016–March 2017	April 2017–December 2017
Outcome	**% of Families**	**% of Families**
Stayed in current housing	10.1	24.7
Moved to new housing	35.4	30.1
In process of moving	35.4	34.4
Lost to follow-up	11.4	7.5
Shelter	7.6	3.2

Note: n = 117 families

Families Interviewed

Although only 14 of the 20 families completed all 4 research interviews, administrative shelter data on the housing status for 18 out of the 20 families interviewed was available. At the final interview, the remaining 90% of families who participated in interviews were housed, while the housing status of the other 10% was unknown due to loss of contact.

Interview Data

Descriptive Data and Participant Characteristics

The sample interviewed at baseline included 29 parents (66% female) in 20 families, between 18 and 59 years of age (M = 30.1, SD = 9.08; Table 17.2). Sixty-two percent of individuals were married or in a common-law relationship, 24% were single, and 14% were separated or divorced. Number of dependents in each family ranged from one to four (M = 2.3, SD = 1.08). The ages of dependents ranged from newborn to 25 years (M = 6.5, SD = 8.13). The majority of parents (86%) were from Canada and two-thirds (76%) were Caucasian. Twenty-two parents (79%) reported at least one disability, and ten parents (35%) reported having multiple disabilities. Learning disabilities were the most common (38%), followed by psychiatric (31%) and physical disabilities (31%).

Housing Stability

A Wilcoxon signed-rank test was conducted to determine whether housing stability differed between time-point one and time-point four. Time-point one captured the number of moves participants made in the year preceding enrolment in the study, while time-point four captured the number of moves participants made during the year after receiving the shelter diversion services. There was a significant difference between the number of moves at time-point one (M = 1.30, SD = 1.69) and time-point four (M = 0.40, SD = 0.94; Z = 2.00, p = .046). The frequency of moves decreased from the start of the program to the end of the study period, approximately two years after the start date, indicating improved housing stability.

Service Use

The Wilcoxon signed-rank test was conducted to assess whether the frequency of community, health care, and emergency service use during the one- and six-month interval prior to the first and final interview differed among parents (Table 17.3). There was a significant decrease in the frequency of phone consultations with a

Table 17.2: Demographics of Participants at Baseline

Variable		**n (%)**	***M (SD)***	**Range**
Age			30.1 (9.1)	18–59
Sex	Female	19 (66)		
	Male	10 (35)		
Marital Status	Single	7 (24)		
	Separated/Divorced	4 (14)		
	Married/ Common-law	18 (62)		
Number of Dependents	1 dependent	7 (25)	2.3 (1.1)	1–4
	2 dependents	11 (40)		
	3 dependents	5 (15)		
	4 dependents	6 (20)		
Age of Dependent(s)	>1 year	4 (9)	6.5 (8.1)	0–25
	1–4 years	18 (39)		
	5–9 years	11 (24)		
	10–14 years	9 (2)		
	15–19 years	1 (2)		
	< 20 years	3 (7)		
Country of Origin	Canada	22 (86)		
	Nicaragua	1 (3)		
	Spain	1 (3)		
	Guyana	1 (3)		
	Missing	1 (3)		
Ethnicity/Race	White	22 (76)		
	Black	1 (3)		
	Multiracial	2 (7)		
	Multicultural	2 (7)		
	Missing	2 (7)		
Reported Disability	Visual	3 (10)		
	Physical	9 (31)		
	Learning	11 (38)		
	Psychiatric	9 (31)		
	Hearing	1 (3)		
	Other	4 (14)		

Note: n = 29

Table 17.3: Comparison of Health and Social Service Use Across Time

	Time-Point One		Time-Point Four		
	[a]n (%)	[b]*M (SD)*	[a]n (%)	[b]*M (SD)*	*Z*
Past Month Use of Services					
Visits to service provider	14 (70)	2.05 (2.19)	16 (80)	2.25 (2.36)	0.03
Phone consultations	12 (60)	4.78 (5.75)	5 (25)	2.22 (5.28)	*2.04
Home visits	8 (40)	0.95 (1.47)	4 (20)	0.60 (1.19)	0.21
Past Six Months Use of Emergency and Health Services					
Emergency room visits	9 (45)	0.55 (0.69)	9 (45)	1.50 (3.43)	0.98
Hospital day programs	None	-	6 (30)	1.61 (4.41)	*2.26
Ambulance	1 (5)	0.05 (0.22)	None	-	1.00
Crisis line	3 (15)	0.39 (1.04)	5 (25)	0.22 (0.43)	0.41
Crisis team	3 (15)	0.39 (1.04)	None	-	1.60
Past Six Months Use of Community Services					
Drop-in centres	3 (15)	1.00 (3.06)	2 (10)	0.42 (1.26)	0.54
Food bank	16 (80)	3.40 (4.59)	16 (80)	2.70 (2.00)	0.26

Notes: n = 20; a The number of participants that received the service; b The mean number of service visits across all participants; * $p < .05$

health or social service provider in the past month, between time-point one ($M = 4.53$, $SD = 5.69$) and time-point four ($M = 1.00$, $SD = 2.62$; $Z = 2.04$, $p = .042$). A significant increase was found between baseline ($M = 0.00$, $SD = 0.00$) and the final interview ($M = 1.61$, $SD = 4.41$) for frequency of hospital day program visits ($Z = 2.26$, $p = .024$). No significant differences were found between baseline and the final interview for use of all other community, health-care, and emergency services.

Quality of Life

The Wilcoxon signed-rank test was conducted on LQoL responses to determine whether there were differences in participants' quality of life over time. No significant differences were found on general life satisfaction between the baseline

(*M* = 4.5, *SD* = 1.7) and final interview (*M* = 4.7, *SD* = 1.4; *Z* = .87, *ns*). However, there was a significant increase in the money for self-measure under the LQoL finances domain, the amount of monthly income remaining after deduction from rent and money for food, between time-point one (*M* = 76.7, *SD* = 252.7) and time-point four (*M* = 227.0, *SD* = 376.5; *Z* = 2.41, *p* = .01). No significant differences were found across time for any of the other LQoL domains. This indicates participants' overall quality of life was consistent across the duration of the study.

F-SPDAT

Results from the Wilcoxon signed-rank test suggested no significant differences in total F-SPDAT scores between time-point one (*M* = 29.9, *SD* = 10.8) and time-point four (*M* = 27.5, *SD* = 15.7; *Z* = 0.46, *ns*). This indicates that the level of service need remained consistent across time for participating families.

4. DISCUSSION

Results from the evaluation found that Rotholme's pilot shelter diversion program was successful in helping at-risk families avoid shelter and establish housing stability. The early intervention program connected families with a housing support worker and other necessary resources at a critical period, prior to the family losing housing. This reduced overall shelter use and allowed for the majority of families to avoid entering shelter altogether, thereby decreasing the burden on the shelter system. This is consistent with previous studies that have found shelter diversion programs to be effective in helping families obtain stable housing (Levitt et al., 2013; Shinn et al., 1998). A reduction in the number of moves families made over the duration of the study was also found. This could be an indicator that participants established greater housing stability after accessing program services and were less likely to move around or be rehoused.

The shelter diversion program was also able to reduce the overall cost associated with admitting families into shelter. The cost to employ a housing stability worker to provide services to 117 families over a 1.5-year period was $75,514.40, or approximately $650 per family. In comparison, the average cost of housing a family in shelter is $4,300. Thus, the intervention reduced shelter costs by six-fold.

Additionally, families maintained their baseline levels of quality of life, service use, and service needs over the course of the study. In comparison, previous research has demonstrated that families who are homeless often have poor quality of life, greater reliance on emergency services, and greater physical and mental health needs, all indicators of social exclusion (Caton et al., 2007). Families who accessed the shelter diversion program were able to avoid these negative consequences since the majority of families were able to avoid shelter use and entering into homelessness. Hence, early intervention efforts can effectively mitigate the negative sequela associated with homelessness, enhancing social inclusion.

However, findings must be interpreted with consideration of the study's limitations. Firstly, there was a low number of families who were interviewed, resulting in a small sample size for the study. Thus, longitudinal comparisons of interview data across time were likely underpowered. Secondly, the assumption of symmetry for the Wilcoxon signed-rank test was not met and results from comparative analyses must be interpreted with caution.

Despite these limitations, results from the evaluation of this pilot program demonstrate that early intervention is effective at reducing the burden of family homelessness on the shelter system, health-care system, and economic resources. Furthermore, shelter diversion programs can help prevent families from entering into an episode of homelessness. These findings reinforce the necessity of continued research into program development and implementation of interventions for at-risk families. The growing number of families who are experiencing homelessness highlights a need for further systemic interventions to address the needs of this group.

REFERENCES

Bassuk, E. L., Weinreb, L. F., Buckner, J. C., Browne, A., Salomon, A., & Bassuk, S. S. (1996). The characteristics and needs of sheltered homeless and low-income housed mothers. *Journal of the American Medical Association, 276*(8), 640–646.

Caton, C. L. M., Wilkins, C., & Anderson, J. (2007, September). *People who experience long-term homelessness: Characteristics and interventions.* Paper presented at Toward Understanding Homelessness: The 2007 National Symposium on Homelessness Research. Washington, DC: United States Department of Health and Human Services and United States Department of Housing and Urban Development.

Clark, R. E., Weinreb, L., Flahive, J. M., & Seifert, R. W. (2018). Health care utilization and expenditures of homeless family members before and after emergency housing. *American Journal of Public Health, 108*(6), 808–814.

Duchon, L. M., Weitzman, B. C., & Shinn, M. (1999). The relationship of residential instability to medical care utilization among poor mothers in New York City. *Medical Care, 37*(12), 1282–1293.

Falvo, N. (2009). *Homelessness, program responses, and an assessment of Toronto's Streets to Homes program: CRPN research report.* Canadian Policy Research Networks Inc. and

Social Housing Services Corporation. Retrieved from http://cprn3.library.carleton.ca/documents/50981_EN.pdf

Forchuk, C., Csiernik R., & Jensen, E. (2011). *Homelessness, housing, and mental health: Finding truths—creating change.* Toronto, ON: Canadian Scholars' Press.

Forchuk, C., Reiss, J. P., Mitchell, B., Ewen, S., & Meier, A. (2015). Homelessness and housing crises among individuals accessing services within a Canadian emergency department. *Journal of Psychiatric and Mental Health Nursing, 22*(6), 354–359.

Gaetz, S. (2010). The struggle to end homelessness in Canada: How we created the crisis, and how we can end it. *The Open Health Services and Policy Journal, 3*(21), 21–26.

Gaetz, S., O'Grady, B., Kidd, S., & Schwan, K. (2016). *Without a home: The national youth homelessness survey.* Toronto, ON: Canadian Observatory on Homelessness Press.

Goering, P. N., Streiner, D. L., Adair, C., Aubry, T., Barker, J., Distasio, J., … Zabkiewicz, D. (2011). The At Home/Chez Soi trial protocol: A pragmatic, multi-site, randomised controlled trial of a Housing First intervention for homeless individuals with mental illness in five Canadian cities. *BMJ Open, 1*(2), e000323.

Gültekin, L., Brush, B. L., Baiardi, J. M., Kirk, K., & VanMaldeghem, K. (2014). Voices from the street: Exploring the realities of family homelessness. *Journal of Family Nursing, 20*(4), 390–414.

Hwang, S. W., & Henderson, M. J. (2010). Health care utilization in homeless people: Translating research into policy and practice. *Agency for Healthcare Research and Quality Working Paper,* No. 10002.

Hwang, S. W., Stergiopoulos, V., O'Campo, P., & Gozdzik, A. (2012). Ending homelessness among people with mental illness: The At Home/Chez Soi randomized trial of a Housing First intervention in Toronto. *BMC Public Health, 12*(1), 787.

Lehman, A. F. (1983). The well-being of chronic mental patients: Assessing their quality of life. *Archives of General Psychiatry, 40*(4), 369–373.

Lehman, A. F. (1996). Measures of quality of life among persons with severe and persistent mental disorders. *Social Psychiatry and Psychiatric Epidemiology, 31*(2), 78–88.

Levitt, A. J., Mitchell, K., Pareti, L., DeGenova, J., Heller, A., Hannigan, A., & Gholston, J. (2013). Randomized trial of intensive housing placement and community transition services for episodic and recidivist homeless families. *American Journal of Public Health, 103*(S2), S348–S354.

Mayberry, L. S., Shinn, M., Benton, J. G., & Wise, J. (2014). Families experiencing housing instability: The effects of housing programs on family routines and rituals. *American Journal of Orthopsychiatry, 84*(1), 95–109.

Metraux, S., Eng, N., Bainbridge, J., & Culhane, D. P. (2011). The impact of shelter use and housing placement on mortality hazard for unaccompanied adults and adults in family households entering New York City shelters: 1990–2002. *Journal of Urban Health, 88*(6), 1091–1104.

OrgCode Consulting Inc. (2015). *Family Service Prioritization Decision Assistance Tool (F-SPDAT): Assessment tool for families.* Retrieved from https://d3n8a8pro7vhmx.cloudfront.net/orgcode/pages/313/attachments/original/1479850993/F-SPDAT-v2.01-Family-Fillable.pdf?1479850993

Paradis, E., Wilson, R. M., & Logan, J. (2014). *Nowhere else to go: Inadequate housing and risk of homelessness among families in Toronto's aging rental buildings.* Toronto, ON: University of Toronto Press.

Park, J. M., Metraux, S., & Culhane, D. P. (2010). Behavioral health services use among heads of homeless and housed poor families. *Journal of Health Care for the Poor and Underserved, 21*(2), 582–590.

Segaert, A. A. (2017). *The National Shelter Study 2005–2014: Emergency shelter use in Canada.* Ottawa, ON: Employment and Social Development Canada. Retrieved from https://ighhub.org/sites/default/files/National%20Shelter%20Study%202005-2014.pdf

Shinn, M., Weitzman, B. C., Stojanovic, D., Knickman, J. R., Jiménez, L., Duchon, L., ... Krantz, D. H. (1998). Predictors of homelessness among families in New York City: From shelter request to housing stability. *American Journal of Public Health, 88*(11), 1651–1657.

Sylvestre, J., Kerman, N., Polillo, A., Lee, C. M., Aubry, T., & Czechowski, K. (2018). A qualitative study of the pathways into and impacts of family homelessness. *Journal of Family Issues, 39*(8), 2265–2285.

Tischler, V., Karim, K., Rustall, S., Gregory, P., & Vostanis, P. (2004). A family support service for homeless children and parents: Users' perspectives and characteristics. *Health & Social Care in the Community, 12*(4), 327–335.

Vostanis, P., Grattan, E., & Cumella, S. (1998). Mental health problems of homeless children and families: Longitudinal study. *BMJ, 316*(7135), 899–902.

Weinreb, L. F., Buckner, J. C., Williams, V., & Nicholson, J. (2006). A comparison of the health and mental health status of homeless mothers in Worcester, Mass: 1993 and 2003. *American Journal of Public Health, 96*(8), 1444–1448.

Wood, D., & Valdez, R. B. (1991). Barriers to medical care for homeless families compared with housed poor families. *American Journal of Diseases of Children, 145*(10), 1109–1115.

CHAPTER 18

Preventing Mental Illness Discharge to Homelessness

Cheryl Forchuk, Mike Godin, Jeffry Hoch, Shani Kingston-MacClure, Momodou Jeng, Liz Puddy, Rebecca Vann, and Elsabeth Jensen

1. INTRODUCTION

People with mental illness are consistently overrepresented among the homeless population, and mental illness is a common risk factor for homelessness (Bonin et al., 2009; Eynan et al., 2002; Kuno et al., 2000; Morrell-Bellai et al., 2000; Steinhaus et al., 2004; Sullivan et al., 2000). In a Canadian sample of 300 adult users of homeless shelters, Goering and colleagues (2002) found that 67% of their participants had received a diagnosis of mental illness at some point in their lives. Similarly, Mojtabai (2005) found that 56% of a national sample of 2,974 homeless individuals in the United States met the National Survey of Homeless Assistance Providers and Clients (NSHAPC) broad criteria for mental illness.

The difficulties involved with not having access to stable housing have many unfortunate consequences for people who have a mental health diagnosis. As has been documented thus far, homelessness is related to personal, physical, and psychological issues such as depression, aggressiveness, antisocial problems, criminal activity, legal problems, violence/danger to others, family problems, and substance misuse (Fischer et al., 2008; Forchuk, Brown, et al., 2008; Lauber et al., 2006). Homelessness is also linked to physical health issues such as an increased risk for infection, musculoskeletal disorders, HIV, flu, diabetes, and asthma (Forchuk, Brown, et al., 2008; O'Connell, 2004). When appropriate supports are not in place, homeless individuals can also place an unnecessary burden on health-care systems through their increased use of hospital and emergency room services (Bharel, 2016; Stenius-Ayoade et al., 2017; Thakarar et al., 2015). In their examination of 439 people in Montreal and Quebec City who met DSM-IV criteria for an affective or psychotic disorder, Bonin et al. (2007) found that even in the absence of economic barriers to health care, individuals who live in poverty still experience significant barriers to obtaining proper mental health care. In fact, research suggests that for people who have had a mental illness, getting, losing, and keeping housing is as difficult to experience as it is for someone who has lost their home to a tornado and must then attempt to put their lives back together (Forchuk, Ward-Griffin, et al., 2006).

The issue of homelessness among individuals with mental illness becomes especially disconcerting when the time comes for hospital discharge. Research consistently shows that effective discharge planning is crucial in preventing homelessness (Backer et al., 2007; Tomita & Herman, 2015). Following psychiatric treatment and discharge, however, individuals with mental illness often perceive their housing needs as being left unmet (Drury, 2008). Research has also demonstrated that the first days and weeks following discharge are particularly high-risk periods, with 43% of psychiatric client suicides occurring within the first month post-discharge (Hunt et al., 2009). In addition, it is now commonly believed that the obstacles to securing stable housing are most likely not due to the effects of mental illness on the capacity for daily life but rather the effects of prejudice, poverty, and a lack of affordable housing upon discharge (Draine et al., 2002; Drake & Wallach, 1999; Forchuk et al., 2007; Forchuk, MacClure, et al., 2008).

In both Canadian and American studies, people who have been diagnosed with mental illness consistently indicate that they prefer independent living (Forchuk, Nelson, et al., 2006; Piat et al., 2008; Tsai et al., 2010). For example, in their interviews with 12 individuals with a history of homelessness and mental illness from Hamilton, Ontario, Kirkpatrick and Byrne (2009) found that permanent housing allowed participants to move on from homelessness, reconnect with their social networks, and plan for the future. Indeed, providing stable housing for mental health consumer-survivors post-discharge is consistently associated with beneficial results such as reduced instances of substance misuse, lower rates of hospital use, and higher quality of life (Forchuk, MacClure, et al., 2008; Kertesz & Weiner, 2009; Kirkpatrick & Byrne, 2009; Kyle & Dunn, 2008; Nelson et al., 2007).

A variety of studies have also indicated that reliable housing support encourages stable housing and prevents homelessness and readmission to mental health institutions (Shern et al., 1997; Goldfinger et al., 1999). For example, Lennon et al. (2005) found that an intervention consisting of strengthening people's ties to services, family, and friends and providing them with practical and emotional support was effective in contributing to fewer periods of homelessness. In addition, Nelson et al. (2005) interviewed 20 formerly homeless individuals in Toronto and

Hamilton, Ontario, who had experience with mental illness, and found that these individuals reported more stability in their lives and relationships after entering supportive housing.

Research also suggests that offering Housing First programs, which provide permanent housing upon discharge that is not dependent on treatment compliance, results in lower rates of substance misuse and higher rates of retention in mental health programs than standard care, treatment-first programs (Padgett et al., 2006; Padgett et al., 2011; Pearson et al., 2009). Despite the obvious benefits of providing housing to mental health service users, this population faces many obstacles when it comes to obtaining stable housing, particularly post-discharge (Hegedüs et al., 2018; Keogh et al., 2015; Tsemberis & Eisenberg, 2000).

The Pilot Project

Prior work by Forchuk, Russell, et al. (2006) revealed that in London, Ontario, approximately 200 people annually are discharged directly from psychiatric wards to shelters or the streets. Based on this data, Forchuk, MacClure, et al. (2008) designed a pilot study to address this issue. The initiative consisted of an intervention that involved changing standard policies related to housing and start-up fees for a select group of income support recipients from both the general income support program, Ontario Works (OW), and Ontario Disability Support Program (ODSP). Individuals on the psychiatric ward who were psychiatrically stable, had lost their housing within the month of admission or during the hospitalization, and were about to be discharged without housing were eligible to participate in the study. Eligible participants were randomized into either an intervention group or a usual care group. In the intervention group, a manager at OW or ODSP, depending upon the source of income, was contacted to fast track the community start-up so that first and last months' rent could be paid; this meant that a cheque was generally available within the day. In addition, a housing advocate would see the participant within the day to assist in finding housing.

This intervention was a resounding success, with 100% of the seven participants who received the intervention still housed three and six months later, compared to six of the seven control participants who were still homeless six months later. The seventh escaped homelessness by being recruited into the sex trade. Despite the small sample, the differences between groups were statistically significant ($p < 0.01$). Forchuk, MacClure, et al. (2008) concluded that if psychologically stable service users could not avoid homelessness without the intervention, then more vulnerable individuals would certainly be unable to do so.

Present Study

We believe that the intervention introduced by Forchuk, MacClure, et al. (2008) may be a new best-practice model that could potentially prevent homelessness for all persons discharged from psychiatric care, not just those in London, Ontario. The pilot study's results were promising; however, careful evaluation using a larger sample is required to encourage more widespread implementation. This study examined two specific hypotheses:

1. The intervention will reduce homelessness for individuals discharged from hospital, and service users accessing the service will acquire housing. (H1)
2. The costs of implementing and maintaining the intervention will be less than the increased medical costs associated with homelessness and housing individuals in shelters. (H2)

2. METHODS

Participants

All London, Ontario, psychiatric service users at risk of being discharged to shelters or no fixed address (NFA) were eligible to participate. In total, 112 men and 107 women accessed the intervention from the acute care hospital, the majority of whom (76%) were between the ages of 25 and 54. Those accessing the intervention from the tertiary care hospital included 16 men and 16 women, the majority of whom (81%) were between the ages of 25 and 54. Participants were either inpatient or outpatient service users at either hospital, and they could simply "drop in" to the service without a referral or appointment. A poster was available on the office door noting the times that staff was available. This information was also included on brochures that were available on the wards in several prominent locations, including bulletin boards and common rooms. Some participants were also verbally encouraged by staff members to attend if housing was identified as an issue. Letters of information regarding the study were distributed to service users accessing the service.

Data Collection and Analysis

To determine whether the intervention was successful at reducing discharges to homelessness, administrative data gathered from hospitals and shelters were used to compare the rate of discharge to shelters or NFA in 2008 to the 2002 baseline data collected by Forchuk, Russell, et al. (2006). For the hospitals, existing discharge data regarding addresses were used. For shelters, intake forms were used to determine how many service users came directly from hospital. Both methods likely underestimated the incidence of discharge to NFA but did provide a conservative estimate of the numbers of people coming directly from psychiatric wards into homelessness. Administrative data on the service users who accessed the intervention in 2008 were also used to understand who was utilizing the service as well as the cost of the intervention.

The Intervention

The intervention consisted of two sources of support: assistance from an Ontario Works worker on site at the hospitals with direct computer access to the OW database and assistance in finding housing from a housing advocate with access to all available housing in the city on a database.

Ontario Works Support

A system was needed that could fast track the community start-up by providing money that could pay for the first and last months' rent required by landlords, as well as other minor related expenses. With the usual system of support, this could take a few weeks to process, but with the computer access on the ward this could be provided almost instantly. OW provided a staff person who was present three days per week at the acute care psychiatric ward and tertiary care hospital. This staff person provided assistance to any OW applicants and recipients on the ward in need of income and housing support. There was a direct computer link from the ward to the OW database, which meant appropriate action, including community start-up funding or paying rent or utilities that were in arrears to prevent eviction, could occur immediately. Rather than phoning the senior staff at the income supports office to speed up delivery of funds, this study employed an electronic means to provide nearly immediate service. The computer access was similar to having Internet banking available at the hospital, in that the OW staff could directly pay landlords or for utilities, and the transaction occurred immediately though the Internet. ODSP participated by identifying a key person for the project who could be contacted by phone. People who were inpatients or community service users at the hospitals could drop in without prior appointment or referral during the three scheduled times at each hospital. If assistance was required at other times, hospital staff could call the OW or ODSP staff.

Housing Advocate Support

A Canadian Mental Health Association (CMHA) housing advocate assisted service users in selecting and finalizing housing arrangements. The CMHA worker had access to community housing resources, referral applications for individual support including group homes, and a computer database listing and describing current available rental housing in London. Individuals on the ward could see the properties on a map, view the surrounding areas, and sometimes even have internal views of the dwelling. The housing advocate assisted service users with several types of tasks, including supporting them to call the landlord and at times visiting the potential housing with them. The housing advocate would also assist in setting up payments to landlords if the service user wished this, reviewing lease arrangements, and helping to arrange utility payments if needed. Assistance in finding economical sources of furnishings and supplies was also sometimes required. The housing advocate support tended to be more office-based for the acute care service users and had more of an emphasis on accompanying service users to potential housing sites at the tertiary care sites.

Ethics

The study was approved by the research ethics board at Western University, London, Ontario, and by the hospital research boards at the participating hospitals.

3. FINDINGS

(H1): The intervention will reduce homelessness for individuals discharged from hospital, and service users accessing the service will require housing.

Data from Shelters

In 2002, the shelters reported 194 instances of referrals from psychiatric wards. This was not divided into acute care and tertiary care. Referrals from emergency and medical wards were not collected in 2002. In 2008, data from the shelters showed a total of 11 direct referrals to shelter from the acute care hospital and four instances of discharge from tertiary care psychiatric hospital to shelters. The instances of referrals to shelters from psychiatric wards significantly reduced from 194 to 15 according to shelter data (Table 18.1).

Hospital Data

There were concerns that the 2002 hospital data only revealed 167 cases of discharge to homelessness while the shelters revealed 194 cases (Table 18.1). Fortunately, the method for tracking these discharges was improved after 2002. In particular,

Table 18.1: Number of Service Users Discharged to Shelters or NFA in 2002 and 2008

Data Source	Year	
	2002	2008
Tertiary Care	74	9
Acute Care	93	123
Shelters	194	15

the process of entering the admission address as the default address on the discharge form and thus underestimating the problem in the acute care site was corrected. Also, "risk of homelessness" was included on the standard assessment form (Resident Assessment Inventory, RAI) used for all service users in 2008.

However, one confounding variable was that a withdrawal management centre moved to one of the homeless shelters between the two data collection points. Consequently, discharges to a shelter address were not really to homelessness but rather to an appropriate detoxification service. It was not possible to separate the withdrawal management service users from the shelter service users on the database. One must therefore be cautious in noting changes in trends, as the 2008 data were less likely to miss as many cases and includes some referred to withdrawal management. Accuracy is still dependent upon service users identifying that they had a housing problem, meaning some examples are likely missing from both periods.

Acute Care

Data from the acute care ward showed that a total of 123 individuals were discharged from the acute care ward to shelters or NFA in 2008 out of a total of 1,740 discharges. Of these, seven were discharged to the shelter that also housed the withdrawal management centre in 2008. This compares to the 2002 data with 93 discharges to homelessness out of a total of 1,588 discharges. Based on the total number of discharges from the acute care hospital, there was a 1% increase in discharge from the hospital to the shelters, from approximately 6% to 7% if both datasets were accurate. It appears that there was still a group of people at risk from the acute care site who were not reached by the service. There were only three individuals who accessed the intervention service who became homeless after discharge; these three people were homeless at the time of admission.

Tertiary Care

Administrative data from the tertiary care hospital indicates that nine individuals were discharged from the hospital to NFA in 2008. This includes two individuals who were discharged against medical advice. These particular service users were documented as NFA since the address was unknown but may not necessarily have been homeless. Only two of the individuals discharged to NFA were homeless at the time of admission. These numbers reflect a significant reduction in the instances of discharge to NFA from 74 instances in 2002 down to 9 instances in 2008. Based on the total number of discharges from the psychiatric hospital, there was a significant reduction in discharge numbers from the hospital to the shelters, from 7% of all discharges to 1%.

Housing Advocate Data

A total of 251 unique individuals accessed the service in 2008–2009. Results show that 92.5% of individuals who were at imminent risk of homelessness were attached to affordable permanent or temporary accommodation. In addition, 100% of individuals at risk of homelessness who accessed the service were provided personal support services. In total, 7 individuals relocated to another area and 17 individuals dropped out of the intervention from both hospital sites. Therefore, H1 was supported as those who accessed the service were attached to affordable, stable, transitional, or permanent accommodation. When considering the housing advocate data, aside from the acute care data, it appears that if service users accessed the service, they avoided homelessness. However, not all individuals at risk accessed the service.

(H2): The costs of implementing and maintaining the intervention will be less than the increased medical costs associated with homelessness and housing individuals in shelters.

To address this hypothesis, administrative data regarding the cost of the housing advocate and social service worker available to the wards was used. The cost of shelter support was also compared to the increase in health service use reported in the literature for the homeless population. According to figures calculated for the present study based on costs from the local agencies involved in the intervention, it cost approximately $47,000 per year to implement and run the intervention on a hospital ward for three days per week. The $3,917 spent per month is less than the monthly cost associated with four people who become homeless: $5,200 (London Ontario Community and Protective Services Committee Meeting, 2008).

In the present study, there were 225 people in imminent danger of homelessness who did not become homeless. According to our earlier study (Forchuk, MacClure, et al., 2008), these people would have been homeless for at least six months. Thus, it would have cost at least $292,500 per month if these people had ended up in the shelter system, an individual cost of $1,300 per month, multiplied by the 225 people who did not become homeless. However, this figure does not take into consideration the added cost of dependents who would have also been homeless. We also know that individuals who are homeless have increased health costs as reported by Forchuk, MacClure, et al. (2008). In addition, increased medical costs often occur in the form of maintaining individuals in a psychiatric hospital beyond their period of recovery at a per diem rate of $681 when housing is unavailable (Jacobs et al., 2010). Thus, H2 was also supported.

4. DISCUSSION

The hypotheses of this study were largely supported. According to shelter data, the intervention reduced the number of individuals discharged to homelessness or NFA from 194 to 15. The number of persons discharged from tertiary care to homelessness or NFA also dropped from 74 to 9. The only instance in which the rate of discharge to homelessness increased was for the acute care setting, where the number of service users increased from 93 to 123. It is important to note that this only represents a 1% increase based on the total number of individuals discharged from acute care. As well, due to our ongoing work in this area, staff became more accurate when completing discharge data. In 2002, the default address was the same as the admission address. In 2008, staff had to directly enter the address or lack of it. Future research should examine specific strategies for homelessness prevention that are effective in acute care settings.

The majority of service users accessing the intervention also acquired housing, with 92.5% of those who accessed the service and who were at imminent risk of homelessness being attached to affordable permanent or temporary accommodation. This high success rate is particularly relevant since those requesting the service were primarily individuals with a lower socioeconomic status. Most importantly, the costs of implementing and maintaining the intervention were less than the increased medical costs associated with homelessness and housing individuals in shelters. Specifically, the total cost to implement the intervention on a hospital ward for three days per week ($3,917 per month) was less than the monthly cost of four individuals who become homeless ($5,200).

This study demonstrated the benefit of linking together housing support and income support within a hospital setting. In Chapter 2, we argued that the large number of people with mental health problems who become homeless was related to the disconnection between housing policies, income support policies, and mental health policies, which also contributes to social exclusion. This disconnection is often invisible to the service workers who only see their own sector and may misinterpret the problem as being at the individual service user level. This study demonstrated that reconnecting these different service areas can reduce homelessness. The present findings are also consistent with prior work suggesting that one of the main obstacles to securing stable housing is the societal response to mental illness, not the psychiatric illness (Draine et al., 2002; Drake & Wallach, 1999; Forchuk, Ward-Griffin, et al., 2006).

This study also raised questions around the morality of discharging individuals with a psychiatric illness to shelters or no fixed address. Canada stands alone in its lack of a national housing program. In fact, individuals with mental illness could be argued to experience a form of societal abuse, in which societal structures prevent these individuals from reaching their full potential or even their basic needs, let alone being socially included in society (Benbow, 2009; Forchuk, 2008). Ongoing research needs to further examine the ethical issues surrounding mental illness, hospital discharge, and homelessness.

There were some limitations in this study, particularly concerning the administrative data. As existing databases were used, there were some potential inaccuracies in the data; this included the withdrawal management centre being listed and categorized as a shelter. Many issues were corrected after the pilot project; however, some issues remained that made complete accuracy difficult. A further limitation was that not all individuals at risk accessed the service. While there was great success for individuals who accessed the service, total numbers of those discharged to homelessness were still higher than hoped because some chose not to access the intervention. Finally, the current study is based on 2008 protocols and data. Thus, it is possible that system changes may have occurred since 2008, as well as between the baseline and final study, that could have influenced the changes noted.

The issue of discharge to homelessness for mental health consumer-survivors is a common problem that occurs not only in London, Ontario, but also around the world (Chilvers et al., 2006; Kyle & Dunn, 2008; Padgett et al., 2006; Padgett et al., 2011; Pearson et al., 2009; Tsemberis & Eisenberg, 2000). This is not a simple matter of inadequate discharge planning but relates to the disconnection between mental health, housing, and income support policies (Forchuk, Nelson, & Hall, 2006). Since the problems related to mental health and housing are linked to this disconnection, the solutions also need to cross sectors. This study has demonstrated that homelessness can be reduced by connecting housing support, income support, and psychiatric care. This project was aided by computer linkages and people making connections with one another to make the service possible. The results support the concept that it is a systems issue rather than an individual issue that puts individuals with mental illness at risk of homelessness, thus supporting the idea that these systems issues need systems solutions.

REFERENCES

Backer, T. E., Howard, E. A., & Moran, G. E. (2007). The role of effective discharge planning in preventing homelessness. *The Journal of Primary Prevention, 28*(3–4), 229–243.

Benbow, S. (2009). Societal abuse in the lives of individuals with mental illness. *Canadian Nurse, 105*(6), 30–32.

Bharel, M. (2016). Emergency care for homeless patients: A window into the health needs of vulnerable populations. *American Journal of Public Health, 106*(5), 784–785.

Bonin, J.-P., Fournier, L., & Blais, R. (2007). Predictors of mental health service utilization by people using resources for homeless people in Canada. *Psychiatric Services, 58*(7), 936–941.

Bonin, J.-P., Fournier, L., & Blais, R. (2009). A typology of mentally disordered users of resources for homeless people: Towards better planning of mental health services. *Administration and Policy in Mental Health and Mental Health Services Research, 36*(4), 223–235.

Chilvers, R., Macdonald, G. M., & Hayes, A. A. (2006). Supported housing for people with severe mental disorders. *The Cochrane Database of Systematic Reviews, 2006*(4), CD000453. doi:10.1002/14651858.CD000453.pub2

Draine, J., Salzer, M. S., Culhane, D. P., & Hadley, T. R. (2002). Role of social disadvantage in crime, joblessness and homelessness among persons with serious mental illness. *Psychiatric Services, 53*(5), 565–573.

Drake, R., & Wallach, M. (1999). Homelessness and mental illness: A story of failure. *Psychiatric Services, 50*(5), 589.

Drury, L. J. (2008). From homeless to housed: Caring for people in transition. *Journal of Community Health Nursing, 25*(2), 91–105.

Eynan, R., Langley, J., Tolomiczenko, G., Rhodes, A. E., Links, P., Wasylenki, D., & Goering, P. (2002). The association between homelessness and suicidal ideation and behaviors: Results of a cross-sectional survey. *Suicide and Life-Threatening Behavior, 32*(4), 418–427.

Fischer, S., Shinn, M., Shrout, P., & Tsemberis, S. (2008). Homelessness, mental illness, and criminal activity: Examining patterns over time. *American Journal of Community Psychology, 42*(3–4), 251–265.

Forchuk, C. (2008). Some psychiatric survivors can't survive the system. *Canadian Nurse, 104*(8), 44.

Forchuk, C., Brown, S. A., Schofield, R., & Jensen, E. (2008). Perceptions of health and health service utilization among homeless and housed psychiatric consumer/survivors. *Journal of Psychiatric & Mental Health Nursing, 15*(5), 399–407.

Forchuk, C., Joplin, L., Schofield, R., Csiernik, R., Gorlick, C., & Turner, K. (2007). Housing, income support and mental health: Points of disconnection. *Health Research Policy and Systems, 5*(1), 14.

Forchuk, C., MacClure, S. K., Van Beers, M., Smith, C., Csiernik, R., Hoch, J., & Jensen, E. (2008). Developing and testing an intervention to prevent homelessness among individuals discharged from psychiatric wards to shelters and "no fixed address." *Journal of Psychiatric and Mental Health Nursing, 15*(7), 569–575.

Forchuk, C., Nelson, G., & Hall, G. B. (2006). "It's important to be proud of the place you live in": Housing problems and preferences of psychiatric survivors. *Perspectives in Psychiatric Care, 42*(1), 42–52.

Forchuk, C., Russell, G., Kingston-MacClure, S., Turner, K., & Dill, S. (2006). From psychiatric ward to the streets and shelters. *Journal of Psychiatric and Mental Health Nursing, 13*(3), 301–308.

Forchuk, C., Ward-Griffin, C., Csiernik, R., & Turner, K. (2006). Surviving the tornado of mental illness: Psychiatric survivors' experiences of getting, losing and keeping housing. *Psychiatric Services, 57*(4), 558–562.

Goering, P., Tolomiczenko, G., Sheldon, T., Boydell, K., & Wasylenki, D. (2002). Characteristics of persons who are homeless for the first time. *Psychiatric Services, 53*(11), 1472–1474.

Goldfinger, S. M., Schutt, R. K., Tolomiczenko, G. S., Seidman, L., Penk, W. E., Turner, W., & Caplan, B. (1999). Housing placement and subsequent days homeless among formerly homeless adults with mental illness. *Psychiatric Services, 50*(5), 674–679.

Hegedüs, A., Kozel, B., Fankhauser, N., Needham, I., & Behrens, J. (2018). Outcomes and feasibility of the short transitional intervention in psychiatry in improving the transition from inpatient treatment to the community: A pilot study. *International Journal of Mental Health Nursing, 27*(2), 571–580.

Hunt, I. M., Kapur, N., Webb, R., Robinson, J., Burns, J., Shaw, J., & Appleby, L. (2009). Suicide in recently discharged psychiatric patients: A case-control study. *Psychological Medicine, 39*(3), 443–449.

Jacobs, P., Dewa, C., Lesage, A., Vasiladis, H.-M., Escober, C., Mulvale, G., & Yim, R. (2010). *The cost of mental health and substance abuse services in Canada:*

A report to the Mental Health Commission of Canada. Institute of Health Economics. Retrieved from http://www.ihe.ca/publications/library/2010/the-cost-of-mental-health-and-substance-abuse-services-in-canada/

Keogh, B., Callaghan, P., & Higgins, A. (2015). Managing preconceived expectations: Mental health service users experiences of going home from hospital: A grounded theory study. *Journal of Psychiatric and Mental Health Nursing, 22*(9), 715–723.

Kertesz, S. G., & Weiner, S. J. (2009). Housing the chronically homeless: High hopes, complex realities. *Journal of the American Medical Association, 301*(17), 1822–1824.

Kirkpatrick, H., & Byrne, C. (2009). A narrative inquiry: Moving on from homelessness for individuals with a major mental illness. *Journal of Psychiatric and Mental Health Nursing, 16*(1), 68–75.

Kuno, E., Rothbard, A. B., Averyt, J., & Culhane, D. (2000). Homelessness among persons with serious mental illness in an enhanced community-based mental health system. *Psychiatric Services, 51*(8), 1012–1016.

Kyle, T., & Dunn, J. R. (2008). Effects of housing circumstances on health, quality of life and healthcare use for people with severe mental illness: A review. *Health and Social Care in the Community, 16*(1), 1–15.

Lauber, C., Lay, B., & Rössler, W. (2006). Homeless people at disadvantage in mental health services. *European Archives of Psychiatry and Clinical Neuroscience, 256*(3), 138–145.

Lennon, M. C., McAllister, W., Kuang, L., & Herman, D. B. (2005). Capturing intervention effects over time: Reanalysis of a critical time intervention for homeless mentally ill men. *American Journal of Public Health, 95*(10), 1760–1766.

London Ontario Community and Protective Services Committee Meeting. (2008). *Provincial increase to maximum per diem rate for emergency shelters*. Retrieved from http://council.london.ca/meetings/Archives/Agendas/Community%20and%20Protective%20Services%20Agendas/CPSC%20Agendas%202008/2008-11-10%20Agenda/Item%207.pdf

Mojtabai, R. (2005). Perceived reasons for loss of housing and continued homelessness among homeless persons with mental illness. *Psychiatric Services, 56*(2), 172–178.

Morrell-Bellai, T., Goering, P. N., & Boydell, K. M. (2000). Becoming and remaining homeless: A qualitative investigation. *Issues in Mental Health Nursing, 21*(6), 581–604.

Nelson, G., Aubry, T., & LaFrance, A. (2007). A review of the literature on the effectiveness of housing and support, assertive community treatment, and intensive case management interventions for persons with mental illness who have been homeless. *American Journal of Orthopsychiatry, 77*(3), 350–361.

Nelson, G., Clarke, J., Febbraro, A., & Hatzipantelis, M. (2005). A narrative approach to the evaluation of supportive housing: Stories of homeless people who have experienced serious mental illness. *Psychiatric Rehabilitation Journal, 29*(2), 98–104.

O'Connell, J. J. (2004). Dying in the shadows: The challenge of providing health care for homeless people. *Canadian Medical Association Journal, 170*(8), 1251–1252.

Padgett, D. K., Gulcur, L., & Tsemberis, S. (2006). Housing First services for people who are homeless with co-occurring serious mental illness and substance abuse. *Research on Social Work Practice, 16*(1), 74–83.

Padgett, D. K., Stanhope, V., Henwood, B. F., & Stefancic, A. (2011). Substance use outcomes among homeless clients with serious mental illness: Comparing Housing First with Treatment First programs. *Community Mental Health Journal, 47*(2), 227–232.

Pearson, C., Montgomery, A. E., & Locke, G. (2009). Housing stability among homeless individuals with serious mental illness participating in Housing First programs. *Journal of Community Psychology, 37*(3), 404–417.

Piat, M., Lesage, A., Boyer, R., Dorvil, H., Couture, A., Grenier, G., & Bloom, D. (2008). Housing for persons with serious mental illness: Consumer and service provider preferences. *Psychiatric Services, 59*(9), 1011–1017.

Shern, D. L., Felton, C. J., Hough, R. L., Lehman, A. F., Goldfinger, S., Valencia, E., … Wood, P. A. (1997). Housing outcomes for homeless adults with mental illness: Results from the second-round McKinney program. *Psychiatric Services, 48*(2), 239–241.

Steinhaus, D. A., Harley, D. A., & Rogers, J. (2004). Homelessness and people with affective disorders and other mental illnesses. *Journal of Applied Rehabilitation Counseling, 35*(1), 36–40.

Stenius-Ayoade, A., Haaramo, P., Erkkilä, E., Marola, N., Nousiainen, K., Wahlbeck, K., & Eriksson, J. G. (2017). Mental disorders and the use of primary health care services among homeless shelter users in the Helsinki metropolitan area, Finland. *BMC Health Services Research, 17*(1), 428. doi:10.1186/s12913-017-2372-3

Sullivan, G., Burnam, A., & Koegel, P. (2000). Pathways to homelessness among the mentally ill. *Social Psychiatry and Psychiatric Epidemiology, 35*(10), 444–450.

Thakarar, K., Morgan, J. R., Gaeta, J. M., Hohl, C., & Drainoni, M.-L. (2015). Predictors of frequent emergency room visits among a homeless population. *PLOS ONE, 10*(4), e0124552. doi:10.1371/journal.pone.0124552

Tomita, A., & Herman, D. B. (2015). The role of a critical time intervention on the experience of continuity of care among persons with severe mental illness following hospital discharge. *The Journal of Nervous and Mental Disease, 203*(1), 65–70.

Tsai, J., Bond, G. R., Salyers, M. P., Godfrey, J. L., & Davis, K. E. (2010). Housing preferences and choices among adults with mental illness and substance use disorders: A qualitative study. *Community Mental Health Journal, 46*(4), 381–388.

Tsemberis, S., & Eisenberg, R. F. (2000). Pathways to housing: Supported housing for street dwelling homeless individuals with psychiatric disabilities. *Psychiatric Services, 51*(4), 487–493.

CHAPTER 19

An Evaluation of the London Community Addiction Response Strategy: London CAReS

Cheryl Forchuk, Rick Csiernik, Grant Martin, Laura Warner, Abe Oudshoorn, Wafa'a Ta'an, and Jan Richardson

1. INTRODUCTION

Homelessness in Canada has been on the rise since the 1980s. In 2006, the United Nations Committee on Economic, Social and Cultural Rights made a number of recommendations for the federal, provincial, and territorial governments of Canada to address homelessness and inadequate housing as a national emergency. Research has repeatedly found that individuals with addiction and mental illnesses are overrepresented among those experiencing homelessness (Argintaru et al., 2013; Bharel et al., 2013; Draine et al., 2002; Forchuk et al., 2011; Goering et al., 2002; Hwang et al., 2013; Khandor et al., 2011), with approximately two-thirds to three-quarters of the homeless population experiencing mental health challenges. This chapter describes the evaluation of a municipal strategy that focused on the housing needs and health outcomes of individuals experiencing addiction, poor mental health, and poverty.

Priority populations identified in London's Community Plan on Homelessness (OrgCode Consulting Inc., 2010) and Homeless Prevention System (Neighbourhood, Children and Fire Services, 2013) include those who are experiencing persistent or chronic homelessness or at immediate risk of becoming homeless as a result of having to live on the street for the first time as well as youth, street-involved sex workers, and Indigenous populations. An objective of London CAReS is increasing community integration while decreasing the costs to and demands on emergency, health, social, and justice systems.

London CAReS is a highly flexible service collaboration established to address the needs of individuals experiencing persistent and chronic homelessness. The efforts to assist these persons exist within a context of considerable systemic barriers to long-term housing stability. London CAReS participants are offered access to private market and subsidized scattered-site independent housing, along with intensive in-home and community-based supports necessary to achieve housing stability. Their choice of neighbourhood and community is a primary determinant when selecting their housing.

Similar to other Housing First initiatives, London CAReS is a recovery-oriented model driven by participant choice and strengths. Specifically, London CAReS participants are supported with interventions and other support including health, community services, and justice remedies along with social, recreational, educational, occupational, and vocational activities. Interventions and supports are voluntary, culturally appropriate, individualized, and, most importantly, participant driven. The program is based on respect and social inclusion and encourages social and community integration through employment, vocational, and recreational activities (Gaetz et al., 2013; Tsemberis et al., 2003).

London CAReS applies a Housing First approach, which was developed through Pathways to Housing in New York in the early 1990s. This approach considers housing as a basic human right and provides access to permanent immediate housing of varying types to individuals experiencing homelessness, based on their unique circumstances and with appropriate and dedicated in-home support. Gaetz et al. (2013) reviewed Housing First approaches and outlined common core principles in order to clearly articulate this approach. These principles include:

1. Immediate access to permanent housing with no housing readiness requirement;
2. Consumer choice and self-determination;
3. Recovery orientation;
4. Individualized and service user–driven supports; and
5. Social and community integration.

The Housing First approach is considered a best practice to ending homelessness and has been proven to address homelessness by supporting individuals in obtaining and maintaining homes without increasing poor mental health symptoms or substance use (City of Toronto, 2007; Collins et al., 2012; Goering et al., 2014; Kirst et al., 2015; Metraux et al., 2003; Padgett et al., 2006; Palepu et al., 2013; Toronto Shelter, Support & Housing Administration, 2009; Tsemberis & Eisenberg, 2000; Tsemberis et al., 2003; Tsemberis et al., 2004; Tsemberis et al., 2012). In contrast to the traditional treatment-first approach that believes individuals experiencing homelessness must address their addictions and mental health issues prior to being deemed suitable candidates for housing (Padgett et al., 2006), Housing First does not believe independent housing should be based on sobriety or acceptance of treatment. Housing First programs promote harm reduction strategies and support respectful environments and interventions that meet individuals "where they are at" with their current substance use and treatment goals (Tsemberis & Eisenberg, 2000).

2. LONDON CARES

London CAReS began as an innovative City of London (Ontario) council-approved strategy focused on a community-based systems approach to improving the health and housing outcomes of individuals experiencing homelessness and who live with the complex and co-occurring challenges associated with addictions, poor mental health, and poverty. The first five years of the integrated strategy commenced in 2008 and focused on individuals with these complex and often co-occurring challenges residing in or relying on the downtown and core neighbourhoods for shelter. This first stage of London CAReS was designed and delivered through a range of street-level services aimed at engaging individuals and families experiencing homelessness while liaising with neighbourhood residents, businesses, and other community organizations. In 2011, based on experiences and the findings of an evaluation that took place between 2008 and 2010, along with the approval of the London Community Plan on Homelessness, London CAReS refocused its objectives to build on community integration and housing outcomes for the targeted populations. These recommendations were further supported through the development of London's Homeless Prevention System, which focused attention on prioritized action plans associated with homelessness services. London CAReS shifted its focus to align with Housing First principles and strengthen service collaboration. The restructured London CAReS model of service was based on the cooperation of community services, business and neighbourhood associations, the London Police Service, individuals, and all levels of government with specific leadership by the City of London. The following components form the comprehensive service collaboration:

1. System governance, accountability, and managing director;
2. Street outreach;
3. Housing selection;
4. Housing stability;
5. Syringe recovery; and,
6. Administrative space (Figure 19.1).

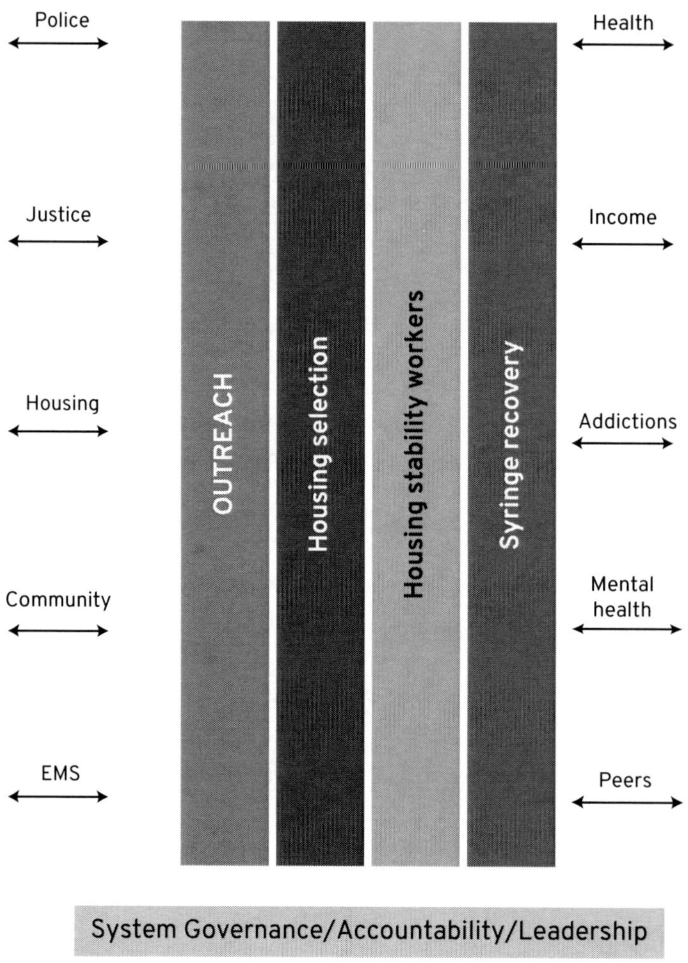

Figure 19.1: London CAReS Model of Collaboration

Component 1: London CAReS Coordinator, System Governance, Accountability, and Leadership

London CAReS is a voluntary service collaboration. It is comprised of three funded organizations: Addiction Services of Thames Valley, Regional HIV/AIDS Connection, and Unity Project for Relief of Homelessness. The three funded agencies, through the participation of their executive directors, along with the London CAReS managing director and the City of London designate, act as the administration committee for the London CAReS strategy.

The administration committee oversees the conduct, outcome, objectives, and evaluation of the London CAReS strategy. The London CAReS managing director administers and oversees all the program components, including street outreach, housing stability, housing selection, and syringe recovery, to ensure a focused, integrated, and collaborative response to priority groups. The London CAReS managing director is employed by one of the funded agencies and is accountable to the London CAReS administration committee. On a quarterly basis, the London CAReS managing director and administration committee report on the program activities and outcomes to representatives of management from key community stakeholder groups and organizations directly or indirectly serving individuals experiencing homelessness.

Component 2: London CAReS Street Outreach

The London CAReS Street Outreach Team establishes and maintains relationships with individuals at risk of persistent homelessness and individuals at imminent risk of homelessness as a result of their first-time street presence. Provision of services on a 24-hour-per-day, seven-day-per-week basis supports active contact with street-involved individuals. This allows street outreach staff to monitor circumstances and emerging concerns. These issues could include individuals and families who might be new to living on the street residing outdoors unsheltered, situations requiring crisis response and diversion, assistance with warm transfers, or creating community linkages with other services or at-risk situations due to use of contaminated street drugs. The team supports individuals "in the moment" in an effort to initiate a rapid exit from the street and into a sustainable housing plan. All Street Outreach Team services are focused on creating opportunities for the individuals or families to transition off the streets or out of emergency shelters and into a home and neighbourhood of their choice.

The Street Outreach Team assists individuals and families to connect with services and resources through warm transfers. Depending on participant needs, services can include more immediate basic needs such as a meal, survival gear, harm reduction supplies, or an emergency shelter bed. However, when individuals indicate readiness to move to housing, immediate opportunities are offered, such as quickly making housing available. The team also provides crisis response, meeting participants where they are in an effort to support diversion from emergency services when these services are not necessary. Housing options can be offered rapidly or at times immediately to a participant due to available housing stock secured through London CAReS housing selection services.

Component 3: Housing Selection

The housing selection component assists London CAReS to provide housing stability by finding private sector and subsidized housing units scattered throughout the city; recruiting landlords; and developing relationships and effective working partnerships with landlords, property owners, and/or property management, and the City of London's Housing Division. Housing Selection staff have an understanding of the needs of housing providers, as well as the ability to provide analysis of housing market trends to assist with housing stock search and acquisition. The primary role of housing selection services is to support the landlord. A 24-hour crisis response is available to landlords and tenants to prevent eviction and build positive tenancy.

Component 4: Housing Stability Team

The Housing Stability Team provides a participant-driven approach aimed at supporting participants as they transition to housing stability. Housing stability workers establish and maintain a relationship with individuals and families who have experienced persistent and chronic homelessness and focus their efforts on supporting housing stability and prevention of homelessness. Housing stability workers offer intensive in-home and community-based ongoing support, as directed by the needs and interests of the participant, connecting the participant to other services and assisting participants to transition into their housing and communities. London CAReS participants that are housed and supported by a housing stability worker have access to a 24-hour crisis support service. The crisis and after-hours support is provided by street outreach and housing stability workers on a scheduled on-call basis.

Component 5: Syringe Recovery

The London CAReS Street Outreach Team provides syringe and drug paraphernalia recovery within the geographical boundaries of London CAReS. They assist with responding to calls received by the London CAReS telephone service, record messages from this service, and assist with all relevant data collection. Data collected assists with identifying and mapping hot spots. Identifying hot spots creates more efficient responses to recovery, allowing for safer public space and reduces the risk of biohazardous material being found in public spaces. Stationary needle collection bins, located in strategic locations, are maintained by the Street Outreach Team as part of a community service to reduce the amount of discarded drug-using equipment on the streets and assist in overall community safety.

Component 6: London CAReS Administrative Space

London CAReS maintains its own secure space used solely for administrative purposes by London CAReS staff and the administration committee. The London

CAReS managing director works on-site and manages the office space in cooperation with the funded agency. The office space is not meant for face-to-face meetings with participants. Participants are supported in the community, be it on the street, in coffee shops, libraries, drop-in centres, their homes, hospitals, community agencies, or police stations.

London CAReS applies the highly successful Four Pillar Approach (City of Vancouver, 2015), which incorporates treatment, prevention, justice response, and harm reduction, to respond to addiction. To this, London CAReS has added a fifth pillar of collaboration and integration. This unifying pillar engages individuals with lived experience, businesses, and residents in the design and delivery of London CAReS.

3. EVALUATION

Objectives

The objective of the research was to evaluate a unique Five Pillar Community Addiction Response Strategy that uses a Housing First approach to improve the housing and health outcomes of individuals experiencing homelessness and the challenges associated with addictions, poor mental health, and poverty. The evaluation addressed two levels of inquiry: individual, the impact of the service on consumers, and community, an exploration of London CAReS implementation and service/agency collaboration. This chapter focuses primarily on the individual-level outcomes across time to compare the year prior to entering the program to the year after. The evaluation explored health and housing outcomes, as well as health-care utilization and emergency shelter use by London CAReS participants before and after enrolment in London CAReS.

Research Questions

Three specific research questions were asked:

Question One: What changes in health, including housing stability, are reported by individuals accessing London CAReS?

Question Two: What is the difference in the use of emergency health services, emergency response, and emergency community services when comparing the year after enrolment in the London CAReS program to the year prior?

Question Three: Is there an increase in the use of addiction and poor mental health prevention and treatment services in comparing the year after London CAReS enrolment to the year prior?

4. METHODS

The research team received ethics approval from Western University in March 2013. The study utilized a mixed-method approach, employing interviews, focus groups, and service databases. Qualitative data was obtained by incorporating open-ended questions into the interviews and by conducting focus groups. Open-ended interview questions explored specific housing, health, and health-care needs of the individual service users and how these changed before and after enrolment in London CAReS. Focus group questions sought to explore common experiences of service users during their involvement with London CAReS and challenges faced in terms of maintaining their housing on a broader policy level by discussing rules that helped or hindered. London CAReS service providers and other stakeholder focus groups examined the positive aspects and challenges of implementing the London CAReS model and experiences of collaboration between London CAReS and other involved agencies. Opportunities for improving the London CAReS service were also discussed.

Qualitative data were obtained from focus groups with 18 London CAReS staff and 28 other key community stakeholders at baseline and 10 months post-baseline. To incorporate as many key stakeholders' views as possible, arrangements were made to meet separately with those key stakeholders unable to make the established focus group times. Key community stakeholders included individuals from a wide range of programs and agencies who interact with London CAReS or London CAReS participants. As such, these key stakeholders provide direct or indirect services to individuals experiencing homelessness. Information elicited through the focus groups included: benefits and breakthroughs of implementing London CAReS; collaboration of London CAReS with other community services; changes in health and housing of individuals accessing services through London CAReS; and challenges and areas of improvement for the London CAReS initiative, which all relate to varying degrees to the creation of social inclusion of London CAReS service users.

Enrolment of service user participants focused on those individuals receiving intensive housing stability support from a housing stability worker, along with some individuals identified through street outreach. The London CAReS participant sample was obtained by London CAReS staff mentioning the study to individuals accessing London CAReS services through the housing stability and street outreach programs. If individuals expressed interest, a member of the research team met with them to explain the study and obtain their informed consent to participate. The sample consisted of 65 London CAReS participants, 40 (61.5%)

of whom enroled from the housing stability program and 25 (38.5%) from the street outreach program.

London CAReS staff also aided in the retention of participants for follow-up as their consistent contact with many of the participants allowed researchers to connect with individuals at baseline and at two follow-up time points, five and ten months post-baseline for both interviews and focus group sessions. Numerous alternative contacts were also obtained, such as family, friends, and service providers at other agencies, who also assisted with finding study participants for follow-up. As compensation for their time, all participants were given $20 in cash at the end of each interview and focus group. All three interviews were completed with 56 (86.2%) of the 65 participants enroled. Of the nine individuals who did not complete all interviews, four were lost to follow-up, one withdrew from the study, one no longer met inclusion criteria, and three passed away. There were 33 participants in the focus groups; 20 of these also participated in individual interviews.

For qualitative analysis of both the interview open-ended question responses and focus group data, the research team used a matrix method (Leininger, 2002; Miles & Huberman, 1994). Focus group discussions were audio-taped and later transcribed and validated. For the focus groups, the matrix consisted of three columns for participant groups—London CAReS participants, frontline London CAReS staff, and other key stakeholders—and rows across for emergent themes. Groups were first analyzed separately using the phases of qualitative data analysis described by Leininger (2002). Research team members developed and validated a coding structure for emerging data to reveal patterns across and between groups and determine any similarities or differences in meanings. The matrix design allowed this direct comparison. Recurrent findings were then synthesized into unique concepts/themes. The data were analyzed until saturation occurred (Leininger, 2002). The advantage of the matrix approach was that it provided a visual overview that captured all the major issues and allowed for connections to be made across datasets (Miles & Huberman, 1994).

Quantitative data used in this study came from several sources: records from four emergency shelters within the City of London; provincial records of participants' health service utilization prior to and after involvement with London CAReS, obtained through an analysis at the Institute for Clinical Evaluative Sciences (ICES) where provincial health data is held; and a final set of quantitative data obtained during the research interviews conducted with London CAReS participants.

During the individual interviews, a selection of previously used and/or validated quantitative research instruments were used to gather data of relevance to the demographic, health, housing, and social integration characteristics of participants (Table 19.1). To address the research questions, the analyses focused on three of the tested instruments described in Table 19.1: The Demographics Form; the Health, Social, Justice Service Use questionnaire; and the Housing History Survey. Individual outcomes were evaluated across time as appropriate for the individual data sources utilized (i.e., interview data versus provincial health data). For individual interviews, data collected at the start of the evaluation (baseline) was compared to that collected at five and ten months into the evaluation using a repeated measures ANOVA analysis. For provincial health-care utilization data, data from six months pre-enrolment was compared to that of six months post-enrolment using paired t-tests for normally distributed data and Wilcoxon signed-rank test for non-normally distributed data. Following this, data from 12 months pre-enrolment was compared to that of 12 months post-enrolment, where data was available, using the paired t-tests and Wilcoxon signed-rank test as described above.

Table 19.1: Research Instruments and Resources

Research Instrument	Purpose	Source
Access	Questionnaire assesses whether participant has a regular doctor, a regular place they go when they're sick (e.g., walk-in clinic, community health centre), and whether there has been a time they needed health care recently but could not access it.	MHCC
Community Integration Questionnaire (CIQ)	Uses 13 questions (summing to 2 scores) to assess the level of physical integration (community presence/participation) and psychological integration (sense of belonging).	Dijkers, 2000
Consumer Housing Preference Survey (Modified Short Version)	Identifies current housing, preferred housing, preferred living companions, and the supports needed.	Tanzman, 1990
Demographics Form	Collects basic demographic information including age, sex, marital status, education, current employment, and presence of any psychiatric diagnoses.	Forchuk et al., 2011

Table 19.1: Continued

Research Instrument	Purpose	Source
Global Assessment of Individual Needs Substance Problems Scale (GAIN-SPS)	Modified from the GAIN Short Screener (GAIN-SS); evaluates the probability an individual is currently experiencing or has previously experienced a substance issue.	Conrad et al., 2008
Health, Social Justice, Service Use	Information collected includes the types and frequency of health care and social service utilization in the recent six months. Includes visits to service providers, visits to the ER, and contact with community authorities (e.g., security, arrests, and detentions by police).	Goering et al., 2011
Housing History Survey	Identifies types of residences lived in over the previous two years, length occupied, reasons for moving, and housing satisfaction.	Forchuk et al., 2011
Lehman Quality of Life: Brief Version	Used to evaluate service users in a number of areas including life in general, health, social relationships, family relationships, safety, finances, and employment. Measurements include both the subjective (service user's perceptions) and the objective (number of activities).	Lehman et al., 1995
Migration Form	Assesses the migration of individuals (recentness) and the reasons for it. Also includes an assessment of the situation under which the individual became homeless.	Kauppi et al., 2009
Perceived Housing Quality	Examines the quality of current housing (e.g., safety, privacy, friendliness) as well as affordability and length of time in the current housing.	Tsemberis et al., 2003
SF-36 Health Survey	A 36-item self-report checklist of the general physical and emotional health of the participant.	Ware, Jr., & Sherbourne, 1992
Working Alliance Participant Version	Identifies the strength of relationship between the participant and main health-care provider (e.g., London CAReS worker).	Horvath & Greenberg, 1989

5. FINDINGS

Sample Characteristics

Table 19.2 displays the demographic characteristics of the sample. The average age of participants was 41.3 years and almost two-thirds were male (66.2%) and had never been married (64.6%). Most individuals self-identified as being Caucasian (75.4%). Just over a quarter of the sample (27.7%) stated having at least one child under 18 years of age.

The most prevalent self-reported mental health diagnosis in the sample was a substance/addiction issue (55.4%), followed by mood disorders (47.7%) and anxiety disorders (33.8%). Furthermore, over one half of the sample had previously had a psychiatric admission (58.1%). Although 55.4% identified having a diagnosed substance-related disorder, 79.7% reported having a current substance/addiction issue. The most prevalent self-reported substance/addiction issues within the sample included tobacco (56.9%), alcohol (27.7%), and marijuana (24.6%). Almost the entire sample identified with having been homeless sometime in their lifetime (96.9%). On average, homelessness had occurred approximately 4.5 times during their lifetime, with the average age for first-time homelessness being 27.7 years.

Question One: What changes in health, including housing stability, are reported by individuals accessing London CAReS?

Interview Findings

While many (n = 29, 50.8%) participants stated their needs were being met prior to engagement with London CAReS ("perfect," "not bad," and "pretty good), just as many (n = 28, 49.1%) indicated their health-care needs were not being met prior to engagement. Some attributed this to not having a family doctor (n = 2), being homeless (n = 4), due to their psychoactive substance use (n = 2), not being on medication (n = 2), and not eating or having access to enough nutritious food (n = 2). Barriers to accessing health care included lack of transportation, difficulty obtaining a family doctor, and "struggling with being able to get a health card."

Poor health was often associated with being homeless, "struggling" to live on the streets or "going from shelter to shelter," and difficulty finding "somewhere to rest." One individual stated, "I have high blood pressure because of the lifestyle ... [and I] don't sleep good." Others (n = 2) associated poor health with their addiction/substance use. One participant reported "not using clean needles" and another was skipping scheduled appointments due to the person's drug use. Not visiting health-care professionals was a common theme in the open-ended questions and

Table 19.2: Characteristics of the Sample (n = 65)

Characteristic	n (%)
Age (Years) [Mean (SD)]	**41.3 (14.40)**
Gender	
Male	43 (66.2)
Female	22 (33.8)
Ethnic Group	
European origins (i.e., Caucasian)	49 (75.4)
Aboriginal	11 (16.9)
Visible minority/mixed ethnicity	5 (7.7)
Level of Education	
Grade school	26 (40.0)
High school	27 (41.5)
Community college/university	12 (18.5)
Marital Status	
Single, never married	42 (64.6)
Separated/divorced	17 (26.2)
Married/common-law	3 (4.6)
Widowed	3 (4.6)
Has children	38 (58.5)
Number of Children under 18 Years of Age (n = 38)	
0 children	20 (52.6)
1 child	10 (26.3)
2 or more children	8 (21.0)
Has custody of children (n = 18)	1 (5.6)
Currently Employed	**5 (7.7)**
Mental Health Diagnoses	
Substance/addiction Issues	36 (55.4)
Mood disorder	31 (47.7)
Anxiety disorder	22 (33.8)

Table 19.2: Continued

Characteristic	**n (%)**
Disorder of childhood/adolescence	16 (24.6)
Schizophrenia	11 (16.9)
Post-traumatic stress disorder	9 (13.8)
Personality disorder	6 (9.2)
Other	1 (1.5)
Mental health diagnosis present but type unknown	1 (1.5)
Developmental handicap	0 (0)
Organic disorder	0 (0)
Has had a psychiatric admission (n = 62)	36 (58.1)
Number of Psychiatric Admissions in Previous Year (n = 35) [Mean (SD)]	**0.7 (1.37)**
Total Number of Psychiatric Admissions in Lifetime (n = 30) [Mean (SD)]	**5.5 (7.62)**
Currently Has a Substance/Addiction Issue (n = 64)	**51 (79.7)**
Current Substance/Addiction Issues	
Tobacco	37 (56.9)
Alcohol	18 (27.7)
Marijuana	16 (24.6)
Prescription drugs	13 (20.0)
Caffeine	12 (18.5)
Other	11 (16.9)
Cocaine/Crack	5 (7.7)
Heroin	3 (4.6)
Hallucinogens	2 (3.1)
Has been homeless in lifetime	63 (96.9)
Age When First Homeless (Years) (n = 61) [Mean (SD)]	**27.7 (13.43)**
Number of Times Homeless (n = 49) [Mean (SD)]	**4.5 (5.72)**

often related to the effect of addictions on mental health: "I was a drug addict, I wasn't seeking help at all"; "I rarely went to the doctor"; "I was addicted to drugs a lot, I didn't care about myself." The stigma associated with addiction was also mentioned; one person found it "embarrassing" going to the hospital because they were labelled an "addict."

Three respondents indicated their health had not changed since being involved with London CAReS, and a few mentioned that their health has generally gotten worse (n = 7). Those who elaborated further stated this was due to substance use or mental health issues: "some family things went down, and I started using again … right now I'm just trying to get my stability back"; "my health has gotten worse. Not because of London CAReS though."

Overall, after involvement with London CAReS the majority of participants indicated their health had improved (n = 48). For some (n = 8), this was directly an outcome of obtaining housing; "after I met them, it improved. They got me a place. I slept on the streets for 10 years." For others, better health was associated with reduced substance use, being "clean" or "no longer suffering from major addictions." Participants also spoke about eating better and having access to food. Responses also indicated London CAReS was aiding individuals in accessing health care (n = 17) by directly connecting them to services, providing transportation to appointments, and advocating when working with health-care professionals. For example, "London CAReS has advocated for me in situations … I've been in because of my addiction and people in health care actually listen now." Participants viewed London CAReS staff as a support system, offering encouragement for them to visit a health-care professional and being seen as approachable and always being "there" to talk to, specifically in relation to having an "urge" to use substances. One participant mentioned their mental health has been "stabilized" and another noted "I have a place. The depression is less now. My lifestyle is better."

The majority (n = 51, 78.5%) of interview responses indicated housing needs were not being met before involvement with London CAReS; participants described themselves as being "homeless"; "living off shelters"; "on the street"; or "couch surfing." Some (n = 5) respondents described themselves as being in and out of homelessness or being homeless for long periods of time; as one participant noted, "I was homeless for a decade." Participants described their housing needs as being met "poorly," "bad," or "barely at all."

A few respondents expanded upon their difficulties in finding and/or maintaining housing. Only a small number of participants (n = 2) indicated their housing needs were being met before involvement with London CAReS. Participants explained that London CAReS helped them to find or access housing and, in some cases, homes they would not have been able to obtain on their own. Specifically, London CAReS' role in providing assistance with rent and advocating with landlords was discussed. For those who elaborated, this included rent subsidy, paying first and last months' rent, and setting them up with direct payment methods to help secure and maintain homes, as well as helping in making the housing affordable.

Practical assistance, such as arrangements with moving, was also mentioned, including renting a moving truck and actually physically helping the participant move their belongings. Participant responses indicated housing was good quality, of their choice, and met the needs/wants of individuals, such as "they worked with me to find a place based on what I needed"; "they really rally to find you appropriate housing, and not the bottom of the barrel. They're nice apartments with good landlords." A couple of participants described how London CAReS ensured they had housing set up before they were discharged/released from jail or the hospital, mitigating their risks of re-experiencing homelessness and ensuring there isn't a return to the streets or emergency shelter during this transition.

Participants also commented how once they were housed, London CAReS staff worked with them to support their ongoing stability. One individual stated, "they keep in contact with you to keep you stable." Responses indicated they assisted with basic needs, such as support accessing food banks or ensuring food was in the apartment, providing assistance applying for ODSP, and assistance with furniture and homewares.

Most study participants (n = 51) indicated their housing needs were being met and supported by London CAReS. Some participants (n = 4) indicated that, after their involvement with London CAReS, they had yet to receive support in finding housing. A couple of respondents indicated that, although they had received housing support, their housing situation had not improved due to poor quality or conflicting views with their London CAReS staff.

Focus Group Findings

Issues related to substance use and other mental health concerns were major themes of discussion related to changes in health during focus group meetings. In general, London CAReS was viewed as providing support for individuals to reduce or abstain from substance use or ensuring they were using substances safely through harm reduction approaches. Many participants reported not using substances anymore: "I had a seven-year addiction and because of London CAReS I've made it a year straight." Feeling comfortable with their assigned London CAReS staff member and having a positive, supportive relationship meant participants could work on their goals related to their substance use: "I'm also (an) addict and alcoholic so they're helping me stay clean and good. Helping me with triggers and that," and "they don't put us down for our drug use, they bring us needles when we need them at bad times. We can't see anybody else bringing us needles."

Participants also described an improvement in their general health, in particular regarding better access to food. Focus group participants described how London CAReS helped them get groceries by taking them to a store or food bank or by bringing groceries if they were unable to get them themselves. It was reported that, if necessary, Meals on Wheels would be arranged so meals were delivered regularly. One participant mentioned constantly having food now at home and no longer needing to access church or organization meal programs. Another participant commented on having gained weight as "before I was so thin." This was mentioned in the context of a supportive relationship with London CAReS and a decrease in substance use. Lastly, participants in the focus groups also described how London CAReS assisted them to access health care, especially by providing transportation to appointments and picking up prescription medication.

In discussing changes related to housing stability, generally focus group participants reported that London CAReS helped them in accessing housing and "getting off the streets." Assistance with maintaining housing was viewed as highly important in remaining stable: "I would have slipped, I would have gone right back to the streets ... but she [London CAReS staff member] was there for me," and "I bounced around place to place, foster homes, group homes, whatever. This is the longest time in my entire life I have ever stayed in one place."

The barriers participants continued to encounter regarding housing support primarily related to those with special needs and waiting lists. Gaining housing was commented upon as "slow," particularly for wheelchair access and for those with a criminal record. Location of housing was also an issue for some as "the only places they've shown me were remote." There were also concerns expressed due to the lack of transportation and bus passes. Challenges experienced after being housed by London CAReS included lack of furniture and being overcharged by a landlord who "said I damaged the place."

Participants regularly described how addressing housing and substance use helped improve their quality of life. They described how London CAReS has helped them or others gain control of their lives: "you get that little push, they can get you to where you couldn't get yourself" and now they [participants] "take care" of themselves. As one participant described, he "wouldn't be alive right now if it wasn't for London CAReS." Another said, "It's been about 15 months now I think with London CAReS. Before that I was a hopeless junkie on the streets and they saved my life."

Question Two: What is the difference in the use of emergency health services, emergency response, and emergency community services when comparing the year after enrolment in the London CAReS program to the year prior?

Provincial-Level Data

Provincial-level data showed no difference in the number of psychiatric-related emergency room (ER) visits for the sample group at six months post–London CAReS involvement (1.8 vs. 2.5, $p = 0.889$) but did show a reduction in psychiatric-related ER visits at 12 months post–London CAReS involvement (6.4 vs. 4.9 visits, $p = 0.038$), suggesting a longer-term positive impact. There were no significant changes in the number of all cause ER visits in the six-month comparison (3.9 vs. 5.1, $p = 0.783$) or the 12-month comparison (12.4 vs. 10.2, $p = 0.171$).

Focus Group Data

Focus group responses were more positive regarding reduction in emergency services than what was reflected in the provincial dataset. Comments from London CAReS staff focus groups reflected that ER visits would have been far greater if London CAReS was not engaging in crisis response, and that both the police and ER services were appreciative of the diversion and that some London CAReS participants known to be ER frequent users were now housed. Some of the highest users were unfortunately not in the sample group. The difference between the qualitative and quantitative data on ER use may reflect the changes that occurred with a few key individuals who were frequent ER service users. London CAReS key stakeholder participants commented that reduced ER visits were noticed from those that were now stably housed. The highest frequent visitor to the ER was reported as having had 276 ER visits during the previous five years, while the next greatest had 260 ER visits; the second individual had recorded 0 ER visits since being housed through London CAReS.

There was also a drastic reduction in emergency department visits among eight of ten high-needs service users who were specifically tracked. Savings among this group were substantive, as it costs $840 "just to register" and another $250 "if coming by ambulance" and "something like 74% of frequent flyers come to the hospital using ambulance services." Participants also equated fewer ambulance responses with less police involvement. London CAReS staff facilitating home visits with primary care physicians also avoided ER visits. Key stakeholders observed London CAReS participants now attend the ER for more "medically appropriate reasons." The reduction in a few key individuals' use of the ER would create a reduction in health-care costs, even if this small group was not statistically significant when added to the entire cohort.

Monthly Emergency Shelter Bed Data

Monthly emergency shelter bed data revealed a decrease in the average number of days spent in an emergency shelter after first contact with London CAReS (Figure 19.2). A noticeable drop in shelter night use by London CAReS participants was also observed by the key stakeholder focus group participants, though they were not sure how much this might actually be due to being housed, as even when housed some individuals access crash beds because of issues such as loneliness or abuse.

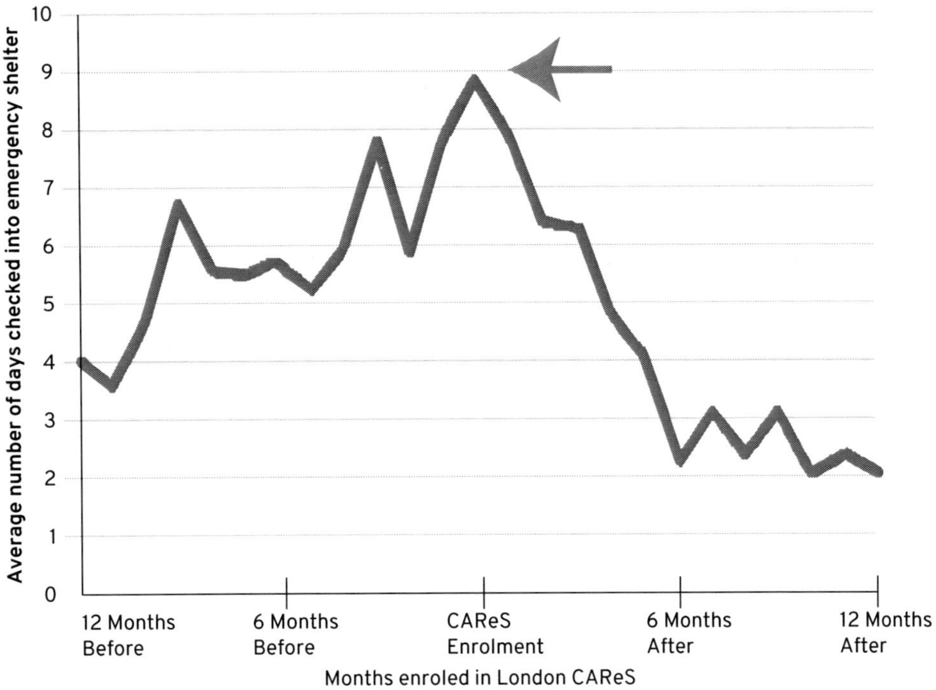

Figure 19.2: Average Number of Days Spent in Emergency Shelter Before and After Enrolment in London CAReS

Question Three: Is there an increase in the use of addiction and poor mental health prevention and treatment services in comparing the year after London CAReS enrolment to the year prior?

ICES Data

Initially, data from ICES was to be used to examine prevention and treatment services for addiction and mental illness. However, as treatment services for addiction are often community based and thus not attached to a person's Ontario Health Insurance Plan card, data on this aspect was not available through ICES. Consequently, the analysis focused on prevention and treatment for mental illness as defined by physician visits for psychiatric or any other reason.

Interview Findings

Interviewed participants indicated that prior to involvement with London CAReS, they accessed a variety of services to meet their health needs, including visiting a physician (n = 6), going to a drop-in centre or health-care centre (n = 8), or going to the hospital (n = 5). Provincial agencies, such as Ontario Disability Support Program (ODSP) and Ontario Works (OW), were mentioned as services helping individuals meet their needs.

There were no significant changes in physician visits between the six months before and after enrolment with London CAReS for either the average number of psychiatric-related visits (8.0 vs. 8.4, $p = 0.889$) or visits for all causes (9.8 vs. 10.6, $p = 0.476$). This observation remained true when comparing the numbers of physician visits both 12 months before and 12 months after enrolment with London CAReS for both the number of psychiatric-related visits (17.5 vs. 16.4, $p = 0.560$) and visits for all causes (22.3 vs. 19.7, $p = 0.325$).

6. DISCUSSION

London CAReS has led to a reduction in homelessness in London, Ontario, through engaging in a collaborative community-based Housing First strategy. Through the support of London CAReS, participants who once experienced chronic and persistent homelessness are now obtaining and maintaining quality homes and developing more established social connections. Consistent with Canadian homelessness literature, London CAReS participants experience high rates of health challenges including physical, mental, and addiction issues (Bharel et al., 2013; Forchuk et al., 2011; Goering et al., 2002; Hwang et al., 2013; Khandor & Mason, 2007). Self-reports of improved health, better access to food, use of harm reduction strategies, and, in some cases, reduced substance use clearly outline the difference London CAReS has made in addressing health-care challenges. All of this works to enhance the social inclusion of London CAReS service users.

The decrease in psychiatric-related ER visits at 12 months after London CAReS involvement, though not at 6 months, suggests London CAReS' facilitation of service integration and community collaboration is effective at diverting individuals from psychiatric ER visits when introduced as a longer-term strategy. This does not occur immediately but rather takes time to become established, which is why continued contact is essential to creating stability in this population's lives. This diversion also suggests that participants are having their mental health concerns adequately addressed in the community, which is dramatically decreasing unnecessary ER visits. The trend of increased physician visits at 6 months and decrease at 12 months post–London CAReS involvement may suggest participants' health-care needs are being addressed early on.

Findings from emergency shelter data indicate that with the focus on housing stability, London CAReS is supporting participants in obtaining and maintaining quality homes and decreasing time spent in emergency shelters. For example, one key stakeholder observed a direct link "between housing stability and London CAReS." Diversion from the London Police Service was also an important change as London CAReS often responds to participants in crisis. This is beneficial to the London Police Service, as their resources are freed up to focus on other matters. The prevention of an unnecessary police contact benefits the participant by allowing for a higher number of supportive responses from London CAReS, which typically are more appropriate than an enforcement response.

A key component of the Housing First success is community integration (Gaetz et al., 2013). While participants did report increased stabilization and community involvement once housed, stigma was experienced by some, and some still reported experiencing difficulty "fitting in" and feeling socially excluded. This continued to act as a barrier to greater community integration and sense of neighbourhood belonging and social inclusion for some study participants. Confronting stigma related to poverty, mental illness, addiction, and homelessness continues to be an item to address. Increased community awareness and collaboration with agencies, neighbourhood associations, and local businesses is helping to alleviate this but needs to be continued.

An additional effort taken by London CAReS was the inclusion of a full-time recreation and leisure support worker to work with participants in engaging in meaningful, neighbourhood-based activities and ultimately promote greater connection to their new surroundings. As well, London CAReS has employed a recreational therapist to work with participants in engaging in meaningful activities to promote community integration. Another challenge has been the need to address a broad range of mental health issues in addition to substance-related concerns. This generally requires access to specialized services, which continues to be an issue for a number of participants and staff to navigate and gain access.

Limitations

Analyses conducted for this report were subject to several limitations. Firstly, the sample size meant that several of the quantitative analyses were underpowered. Secondly, the information on emergency shelter bed usage was collected from a manual search through invoices received by the City of London. Thus, results are based only on individuals whose stay was paid for by the City and not those who were paying some room/board or staying at no charge, such as crash beds and at the withdrawal management centre. Additionally, this analysis was based on the names and dates of birth of study participants, which may not be completely accurate due to individuals sometimes checking into emergency shelters with different personal information or "borrowed" identification. Therefore, it is possible the number of days spent in emergency shelter is a conservative estimate for some individuals who may have checked in under a different name.

With respect to interview data, information collected was based on self-reporting, which may have led to underestimation of certain characteristics. For example, participants may not have accurately reported information pertaining to sensitive topics such as substance use, mental and physical diagnoses, and contacts with the justice system. This underestimation may also have occurred as a result of an inability to recall specific events, as some questions asked the participant to think back in time. The open-ended items on interviews were transcribed by the interview in situ and tended to be short answers.

Finally, as data at ICES often runs a year behind, only a six-month comparison of data could be completed on all participants. Thus, the six months following enrolment in London CAReS was compared to the same period of time prior to enrolment. Although a 12-month window was completed where available, the sample size for this sub-analysis was severely reduced and subsequently the analyses were underpowered.

7. CONCLUSION

The results from this evaluation further support the growing literature that Housing First approaches reduce community homelessness and support individuals in maintaining their homes, contributing to social inclusion. Improved housing and self-reported improved health outcomes were achieved through the support of London CAReS. Diversion from psychiatric-related ER visits suggests participants are experiencing fewer mental health crises, leading them to fewer emergency services and instead increasing contact with community-based supports. This decreases the strain on the health-care system while supporting individuals in the community by preventing hospital visits. The decrease in visits 12 months after receiving support from London CAReS, but not at 6 months, suggests Housing First approaches are successful when implemented as a long-term strategy and that it takes time and continued support to change behaviour. This is consistent with other Housing First research demonstrating that when working with individuals identified as persistently homeless with complex and co-occurring challenges, results require long-term supports to be in place in order to see indicators of stabilization, social inclusion, and decreased experiences of crisis.

Findings from this evaluation demonstrate that Housing First strategies can be successfully implemented in midsized Canadian cities. To the knowledge of the authors, there is no other Housing First four-pillar approach that has incorporated the additional fifth pillar of community collaboration. Addressing homelessness requires a community collaborative response due to the complex challenges facing individuals and families experiencing chronic and/or persistent homelessness. The London CAReS approach outlines the need and success of facilitating a coordinated, unified strategy engaging various service providers, businesses, residents, and individuals with lived experience in delivering the strategy.

REFERENCES

Argintaru, N., Chambers, C., Gogosis, E., Farrell, S., Palepu, A., Klodawsky, F., & Hwang, S. W. (2013). A cross-sectional observational study of unmet health needs among homeless and vulnerably housed adults in three Canadian cities. *BMC Public Health, 13*, 577.

Bharel, M., Lin, W.-C., Zhang, J., O'Connell, E., Taube, R., & Clark, R. E. (2013). Health care utilization patterns of homeless individuals in Boston: Preparing for Medicaid expansion under the Affordable Care Act. *American Journal of Public Health, 103*(Suppl2), S311–S317.

City of Toronto. (2007). *What housing first means for people: Results of streets to homes: 2007 post- occupancy research*. Toronto Shelter, Support & Housing Administration. Retrieved from http://www1.toronto.ca/City%20Of%20Toronto/Shelter%20Support%20&%20Housing%20Administration/Files/pdf/W/whathousingfirstmeans.pdf

City of Vancouver. (2015). *Four pillars drug strategy*. Retrieved from http://vancouver.ca/people-programs/four-pillars-drug-strategy.aspx

Collins, S. K., Malone, D. K., Clifasefi, S. L., Ginzler, J. A., Garner, M. D., Burlingham, B., … Larimer, M. E. (2012). Project-based Housing First for chronically homeless individuals with alcohol problems: Within-subjects analyses of 2-year alcohol trajectories. *American Journal of Public Health, 102*(3), 511–519.

Conrad, K. J., Conrad, K. M., Dennis, M. L., & Riley, B. B. (2008). *GAIN working papers: Rasch analysis of the Substance Problem Scale.* Chestnut Health Systems. Retrieved from http://www.chestnut.org/li/gain/psychometric_reports/gain_working_papers_rasch_analysis_of_the_substance_problem_scale.pdf

Dijkers, M. (2000). *The community integration questionnaire.* The Center for Outcome Measurement in Brain Injury. Retrieved from http://www.tbims.org/combi/ciq

Draine J., Salzer, M. S., Culhane, D. P., & Hadley, T. R. (2002). Role of social disadvantage in crime, joblessness, and homelessness among persons with serious mental illness. *Psychiatric Services, 53*(5), 565–573.

Forchuk, C., Csiernik, R., & Jensen, E. (Eds.). (2011). *Homelessness, housing and mental health: Finding truths—creating change.* Toronto, ON: Canadian Scholars' Press.

Gaetz, S., Scott, F., & Gulliver, T. (Eds.). (2013). *Housing First in Canada: Supporting communities to end homelessness.* Toronto, ON: Canadian Homelessness Research Network Press.

Goering, P. N., Streiner, D. L., Adair, C., Aubry, T., Barker, J., Distasio, J., … Zabkiewicz, D. M. (2011). The At Home/Chez Soi trial protocol: A pragmatic, multi-site, randomised controlled trial of a Housing First intervention for homeless individuals with mental illness in five Canadian cities. *BMJ Open, 1*(2).

Goering, P., Tolomiczenko, G., Sheldon, T., Boydell, K., & Wasylenki, D. (2002). Characteristics of persons who are homeless for the first time. *Psychiatric Services, 53*(11), 1472–1474.

Goering, P., Veldhuizen, S., Watson, A., Adair, C., Kopp, B., Latimer, E., … Powell, G. (2014). *National final report: Cross-site At Home/Chez Soi final project.* Mental Health Commission of Canada. Retrieved from http://www.mentalhealthcommission.ca/English/system/files/private/document/mhcc_at_home_report_national_cross-site_eng_2.pdf

Horvath, A. O., & Greenberg, L. S. (1989). Development and validation of the Working Alliance Inventory. *Journal of Counseling Psychology,* 36(2), 223–233.

Hwang, S. W., Chambers, C., Chiu, S., Katic, M., Kiss, A., Redelmeier, D. A., & Levinson, W. (2013). A comprehensive assessment of health care utilization among homeless adults under a system of universal health insurance. *American Journal of Public Health, 103*(Suppl2), S294–S301.

Kauppi, C., Gasparini, G., Pallard, H., Garg, R., Montgomery, P., & Webster, S. (2009). *Migratory and transient homelessness in Northern Ontario: A study of the pathways to becoming homeless in Sudbury and its related impacts.* Report to the Homeless Partnering Secretariat, Human Resources and Skills Development, and Ministry of Community and Social Services. Retrieved from https://www.nosda.net/Shared%20Documents/Homelessness%20Reports/City%20of%20Greater%20Sudbury/MigratoryandTransientHomelessnessinNorthernOntario.pdf

Khandor, E., & Mason, K. (2007). *The street health report 2007.* Toronto, ON: Street Health in partnership with the Wellesley Institute. Retrieved from http://www.streethealth.ca/downloads/the-street-health-report-2007.pdf

Khandor, E., Mason, K., Chambers, C., Rossiter, K., Cowan, L., & Hwang, S. W. (2011). Access to primary health care among homeless adults in Toronto, Canada: Results from the Street Health survey. *Open Medicine, 5*(2), e94–e103.

Kirst, M., Zerger, S., Misir, V., Hwang, S., & Stergiopoulos, V. (2015). The impact of a Housing First randomized controlled trial on substance use problems among homeless individuals with mental illness. *Drug and Alcohol Dependence, 146*(1), 24–29.

Lehman, A., Kernan, E., & Postrado, L. (1995). *Toolkit for evaluating quality of life for persons with severe mental illness.* Cambridge, MA: The Evaluation Center@HSRI.

Leininger, M. (2002). The theory of culture care and the ethnonursing research method. In M. Leininger & M. R. McFarland (Eds.), *Transcultural nursing: Concepts, theories, research, and practice* (3rd ed., pp. 71–98). New York, NY: McGraw-Hill.

Metraux, S., Marcus, S. C., & Culhane, D. P. (2003). The New York-New York housing initiative and use of public shelters by persons with severe mental illness. *Psychiatric Services, 54*(1), 67–71.

Miles, M. B., & Huberman, A. M. (1994). *Qualitative data analysis: An expanded sourcebook* (2nd ed.). Thousand Oaks, CA: SAGE Publications.

Neighbourhood, Children and Fire Services. (2013). *A homeless prevention system for London, Ontario: A three year implementation plan.* City of London. Retrieved from https://www.london.ca/residents/neighbourhoods/Documents/London's%20Homeless%20Prevention%20System.pdf

OrgCode Consulting Inc. (2010). *London community plan on homelessness.* City of London. Retrieved from http://londonhomeless.ca/wp-content/uploads/2012/12/LondonCommunityPlanonHomelessness.pdf

Padgett, D. K., Gulcur, L., & Tsemberis, S. (2006). Housing First services for people who are homeless with co-occurring serious mental illness and substance abuse. *Research on Social Work Practice, 16*(1), 74–83.

Palepu, A., Patterson, M. L., Moniruzzaman, A., Frankish, C. J., & Somers, J. (2013). Housing First improves residential stability in homeless adults with concurrent substance dependence and mental disorders. *American Journal of Public Health, 103*(Suppl2), S30–S36.

Tanzman, B. (1990). *Researching the preferences of people with psychiatric disabilities for housing and supports: A practical guide.* Burlington, VT: University of Vermont, Centre for Community Change Through Housing and Supports.

Toronto Shelter, Support & Housing Administration. (2009). *Street needs assessment results.* Retrieved from http://www.toronto.ca/legdocs/mmis/2010/cd/bgrd/backgroundfile-29123.pdf

Tsemberis, S., & Eisenberg, R. F. (2000). Pathways to housing: Supported housing for street-dwelling homeless individuals with psychiatric disabilities. *Psychiatric Services, 51*(4), 487–493.

Tsemberis, S., Gulcur, L., & Nakae, M. (2004). Housing First, consumer choice, and harm reduction for homeless individuals with a dual diagnosis. *American Journal of Public Health, 94*(4), 651–656.

Tsemberis, S., Kent, D., & Respress, C. (2012). Housing stability and recovery among chronically homeless persons with co-occurring disorders in Washington, DC. *American Journal of Public Health, 102*(1), 13–16.

Tsemberis, S. J., Moran, L., Shinn, M., Asmussen, S. M., & Shern, D. L. (2003). Consumer preference programs for individuals who are homeless and have psychiatric disabilities: A drop-in center and a supported housing program. *American Journal of Community Psychology, 32*(3–4), 305–317.

United Nations Committee on Economic, Social and Cultural Rights [CESCR]. (2006, May 19). Consideration of reports submitted by states parties under Articles 16 and 17 of the Covenant, Concluding observations of the Committee on Economic, Social and Cultural Rights: Canada. *United Nations Committee on Economic, Social and Cultural Rights, Thirty-sixth session.*

Ware, J. E., Jr., & Sherbourne, C. D. (1992). The MOS 36-item short-form health survey (SF-36): I. Conceptual framework and item selection. *Medical Care, 30*(6), 473–483.

CHAPTER 20

Service Preferences of Homeless Youth with Mental Health Issues: Housing First, Treatment First, or Both Together

Cheryl Forchuk, Rick Csiernik, Jan Richardson, Karen Laverty, Mirella Bryant, Abraham Rudnick, Betty Edwards, Sandra Fisman, Beth Mitchell, Martha Connoy, Mark Dolson, and Chandell Kelly

1. INTRODUCTION

As this book has illustrated, there continues to be a struggle about how to best address issues related to homelessness, mental health, addiction, and social inclusion. However, there has been little discussion pertaining to youth, who make up anywhere from 7.6 to 44% of the homeless population depending upon the North American community (Cauce et al., 2000; Community and Neighbourhood Services Policy and Planning, 2006; Cutuli, 2018; Edmonton Homelessness Count Committee, 2002; Morton et al., 2017). Despite the demonstrated fact that the needs of homeless youth are distinct from those of older homeless individuals (Haldenby et al., 2007; Kidd et al., 2019; Reid et al., 2005), few Canadian studies have examined different housing and treatment options for youth.

Homeless youth experience extremely high levels of trauma, depression, stress, and emotional distress. Mental illness may either be a major cause of homelessness or a response to the stress of life on the streets for this population, including exposure to violence and the peer-related pressures to participate in the sex/drug trade (McCay et al., 2006; Narendorf et al., 2017; Wong et al., 2016). Over time, three distinct options have emerged to address mental health and addiction treatment for homeless and street-involved youth.

Treatment First

Treatment first initiatives seek to provide mental health supports and addiction treatment solutions to the individual. This approach puts an emphasis upon recovery, and the individual's choice is at the centre of treatment and support options.

It operates on the principle that the symptoms and mental health/addiction concerns of the individual need to be addressed immediately.

Housing First

Housing First initiatives focus on moving individuals to appropriate and available housing before any type of intervention is offered and then providing the ongoing supports necessary to keep individuals housed. Housing First creates a recovery-oriented culture that puts the individual's choice at the centre of all its considerations with respect to the provision of housing and support services. It operates on the principle that individuals experiencing homelessness living with addiction and/or mental illness should be provided the opportunity to live in permanent housing of varying types that is otherwise available to people without mental health or addiction issues (Polvere et al., 2014).

The Housing First model is based on the belief that housing is a basic right, and that people receiving mental health services have a right to make their own life decisions. The model is dissimilar from the general service delivery model, the Continuum of Care approach, in that it that assumes that individuals with mental illness cannot maintain independent housing before their mental illness is under control (Tsemberis et al., 2004). Research has demonstrated that the Housing First approach is an effective service option for homeless adults and adults living with mental illness and substance misuse/addiction (Padgett et al., 2006; Tsemberis et al., 2004).

Attention to Both Housing and Treatment Together

Providing housing and treatment together creates a recovery-oriented culture; one that is aimed at fostering hope, healing, and individual empowerment, as well as using the individual's experience of care to inform improvements to services. This approach places the individual's choice at the centre by offering simultaneous housing, mental health, addiction, and support services. It operates on the principle that mental health/addiction concerns and the need for housing both need to be addressed immediately. Housing First and treatment first approaches are offered at the same time.

2. METHODS

Project Design

The main objective of the project was to investigate and obtain a better understanding of youth participants' choices regarding treatment and service options. The study provided participants with a choice between the three treatment and service options described above: (1) mental health and addiction treatment first, (2) Housing First, or (3) both housing and mental health and addiction treatment together. Participants were individually interviewed with a focus on their choices and experiences as youth.

Sample and Inclusion Criteria

The Youth Matters in London project worked with individuals aged 16–25. This range was employed as it is the cut-off used by most youth services in London, Ontario. The project enroled 187 youth who were told that there was no guarantee that they would receive the housing or treatment option they chose. It was explained that each participant would, however, work closely with a service provider towards their treatment/housing preference to find acceptable and affordable housing and/or referral to treatment.

The At Home/Chez Soi definition of homeless was also used for this study (Goering et al., 2014). This definition conceptualizes absolute homeless as having no fixed place to stay for more than seven nights and little likelihood of finding accommodation in the next month or leaving an institution, prison, jail, or hospital with no fixed address. Being precariously housed was defined as those whose main residence is a single-room occupancy (SRO) or a single room rented within a building, rooming house, or hotel/motel, or who in the past year have twice been absolutely homeless, as defined above (Tolomiczenko & Goering, 2001).

Study participants must have been experiencing a mental disorder, as defined by the *Diagnostic and Statistical Manual IV* (DSM-IV-TR), with or without also having a substance misuse issue, though formal diagnosis at the time of entry into the project was not required. The focus was on those youth who were not formally participating in existing mental health treatment services or programs related to finding housing. The study also included homeless youth staying in shelters and those who were using alternatives, such as couch surfing. As homeless and street-oriented youth are particularly difficult to engage in treatment and service programs, especially as many place a low priority on health-related concerns, a clearer understanding of their preferences and choices was essential for establishing appropriate services.

Instrument

From a larger interview schedule, youths' response to the following two questions were used for this study:

1. Which service model did you choose (treatment first, Housing First, both together, or none of these options)?

2. Tell me why you chose that particular service model. (What did you like best about it? What were your concerns about other choices?)

Data Analysis

Participants' responses were sorted by sex and then grouped according to treatment/service option preference. Participants' statements were analyzed by two separate members of the research team, who read and re-read the responses to establish broad themes related to youths' preferences. Coding was open at first to identify, name, and categorize recurring themes from the answers to the two open-ended questions. A selective coding approach was then used to refine themes by either eliminating previous themes or combining themes. Through selective coding, one category was chosen to be the key theme; other categories were then related to this core theme. Youths' responses to each of the open-ended questions were recorded verbatim. Once themes specific to each treatment/service preference were established, responses were then re-read and coded according to these themes.

Research Issue

The naming/listing of identities led to debate among the research team. The terms *male* and *female*, though scientifically accurate, were troublesome for some participants who, due to their age, did not yet identify as s a "man" or a "woman." Rather, they self-identified as "kids," "children," or simply "youth." One youth also identified as transgender, while two identified as "other," reflecting a discomfort with the listed identities.

3. FINDINGS

Demographics

Of the 187 participants, 122 (65.2%) identified as male while 62 (33.2%) identified as female, with two others (1.1%) and one transgender (0.5%). The most common option selected by both males and females was Housing First (40.1%; males = 40.1%; females = 37.1%). Treatment first was the second preference of males (32.0%) followed by housing and treatment combined (14.8%). Female participants were almost evenly split between treatment first (29.0%) and housing and treatment combined (30.6%). Seventeen (9.1%) individuals in the study opted not to engage in any type of intervention, with far more males (12.3%) than females (3.2%) selecting to receive no assistance (Table 20.1).

Table 20.1: Youth Matters in London: Participants Choosing Each Treatment and Service Option

	Male	Female	Other	Transgender	TOTAL	%
Housing first	50	23	2		75	40.1
Treatment first	39	18			57	30.5
Housing and treatment combined	18	19		1	38	20.3
No selection/Other	15	2			17	9.1
TOTAL	122	62	2	1	187	100.0

Qualitative Responses

In the qualitative analysis, responses were sufficiently distinct between self-identified female and male respondents that a gendered presentation of the themes was warranted.

Treatment First: Females

For female participants who chose treatment first, two related themes emerged: I need treatment, and I need treatment, but I already have housing. These themes indicated an urgency to deal with issues relating to addiction and mental health before seeking stable housing, especially in those cases where participants did not have permanent or stable housing.

> Well, I have a place I'm living in right now, and OW [Ontario Works] says it's better for me to not be on my own. I'm in addiction counselling but I still want someone to talk to.

> Because I've had psychological problems before, but they were never diagnosed. I've had depression but I've never seeked help before.

> Because, like, the other day I woke up at 6:00 in the morning puking all over some girl, and I'm getting pill sick.

Treatment First: Males

The situation was similar for male participants in that many who chose the treatment first option already had housing. A key issue for choosing treatment first for male respondents were issues they perceived that stable housing would bring.

> I have a drug addiction. It would be more fair to get treatment first. It makes more sense to me. I'd rather be more comfortable physically before I have my own place. I'm just tired of being an addict.

> I just think people need to help themselves. You gotta be clean before you can be housed. Because if you can't take care of yourself, how are you supposed to take care of the things around you?

> Because I'm a drug addict. Cause I know it's not realistic to have housing and treatment for me, because I will turn my house into a chop-house.

> At the moment, I have semi-stable housing, and I find it's hard to keep housing when you're not mentally/emotionally stable.

Housing First: Females

Two major themes emerged among female respondents who indicated Housing First was the approach they wished to pursue:

1. getting away from negative influences; and
2. providing a stable environment for children.

Typical responses included under the first theme described a desire to remove oneself from negative environments, often associated with alcohol or drugs.

> Cuz that's my basic need. I'm in a bad environment that I can't be in.

> I don't know, it just made sense in order to get away from the alcohol and drugs. I need to get out of the shelters and away from the streets to remove myself from the temptations.

> Because I can't live with my parents, they show me a bad example all the time, they're hypocritical. They tell me if I want to do what I want I have to get my own house and pay my own rent. So that's what I want to do.

A second distinct theme also arose, which centred on the practical and moral pressure for pregnant youth to get off the streets and into their own accommodation. Having a place of one's own was also understood as a condition for keeping or regaining custody of one's children, as well as being necessary to provide basic shelter for a child.

> Because I have a baby on the way and I'm on the streets.

> Mainly my child, I need to take care of her first, then myself. Plus, CAS [Children's Aid Society] is involved and it will look good if I actually have a house.

> I've been trying to fight for my son, between me and my mom. The only way I can get him is if I have my own place. The place where I'm at is not good—I can't even go there.

Housing First: Males

Much like the female participants' responses, males who chose Housing First as their desired outcome expressed an urgent need for a more stable living environment; however, a key difference was the underlying reason for wanting stability. For male participants, the need for stability was a strategy of resilience: stable housing removed the stress of survival on the streets and made it possible to focus on other problems. They believed that the harmful effects of both addiction and mental illness, as revealed by youths' repeated mention of their harmful and negative effects, could be avoided through obtaining stable housing. They stated that they felt that housing would provide them a stable base from which to get their lives in order. Lack of housing was also described as a cause of mental health issues and substance misuse, which served as a form of coping with the stress of life on the streets.

> Basically, with lack of housing I became really depressed and then I started drinking to deal. But if I had a place it probably wouldn't have worked out that way.

> I feel like that my drug addiction is because I don't have a house. I feel like if you don't have a stable environment, you're bound to try to occupy your mind with something else.

> Because, when you're on the streets your mental health problems can affect you more. Because you're more under more stress because you're homeless.

Both Housing and Treatment: Females

For the housing and treatment together preference, the main themes for female participants were:

1. both are easier when done at the same time; and
2. both are top priorities.

For those participants with mental health and substance misuse problems, and who were also homeless or unstably housed, making both options a top priority was logical.

> Cause I don't have a place to live and I'm addicted to oxys; and I want to get off of them. They are both really important things.

> Because they're both top priorities. I've had a huge problem with addictions, I've been on pills since 15 and needles, a lot of health problems. And my daughter, I want to prove to her that I want to do more than what my mom did for me. And housing, oh God, I've just been bouncin' around, and my boyfriend is out in 44 days, so I need a place for me and him, and I'm banned from St. Thomas.

> I don't know, because it made it easier to do both together. I guess the people I surround myself with—those are the two most important topics. They are equal.

Both Housing and Treatment: Males

As with the female participants, the following exemplars indicate why both treatment and housing were a top priority for them.

> Both, 'cause right now I'm living in the [homeless shelter] and I have drug problems. It's easier to take out two birds with one stone.

> Because if you do treatment first, then if they're homeless the treatment is pointless. If you give them Housing First it sets up to give them all that they need to do drugs. If you do both it isolates them so they can start treatment from there.

> I want to figure out how to get an apartment. How to budget the treatment, I want to become a better person, to fix myself.

Neither Housing nor Treatment

A small number of participants were grouped under the "other" category regarding treatment/service preference. This category was used for responses that either indicated a perceived inability to participate in the treatment/service options offered or an inability to receive the treatment/service options offered through the project. This included:

> I chose employment.
>
> I'm not on any drugs right now, and I'm living with my boyfriend.
>
> Right now, I'm court-ordered to live with my mom, so when that's over I'll need help with housing.

4. DISCUSSION

Responses from the two open-ended questions suggest that participants' choice of treatment/service option depended upon whether they had an addiction, together with an understanding that their drug use was a problem, plus their desire to engage in addiction treatment. If that was the case, participants most likely choose the treatment first option. Interestingly, part of the decision-making process driving this choice was that stable housing represented a potentially negative consequence: a regular, safe place to use drugs.

The Housing First option was the most preferred option for both females and males, though a greater proportion of males than females made this their first choice. Unsurprisingly, this preference indicated that housing was a vital concern for these study participants. From the perspective of homeless youth, without the stability of permanent housing one is more vulnerable to stress and anxiety due to environmental (poor weather) and psychosocial stressors, such as peer pressure, to use drugs or engage in criminal activities. It follows that lack of housing or unstable housing can, according to project participants, ultimately trigger or exacerbate a mental health issue such as depression or lead to substance misuse to cope with the stress of homelessness.

According to Tsemberis et al. (2004) and Padgett et al. (2006), individuals who are homeless and suffering from mental illness and addiction see housing as an immediate need; however, access to housing, under the Continuum of Care model, is only provided once individuals complete mental health and/or addiction treatment. The treatment first model is, according to Tsemberis et al. (2004), incompatible with these individuals' priorities. This model also excludes those individuals who are unable or unwilling to follow treatment programs. The results of these studies support the view that the Housing First approach is effective in keeping individuals with a history of homelessness, mental illness, and addiction housed. In the Tsemberis and Padgett studies, approximately 80% of individuals given the Housing First option remained housed. This is similar to the Canadian At Home/Chez Soi project, where 72% of participants remained housed throughout the initiative (Goering et al., 2014). Participants' responses show that those who were given Housing First had a greater sense of choice and independence than those who were given the treatment first approach.

Although the results from the studies mentioned above indicate that most participants prefer Housing First, as did 40% of participants in our study, the picture is complicated by the fact that, due to mental health and addiction issues, not all participants were comfortable with the choice and independence that the Housing First model provides. Considering the diversity of responses and needs of youth in our study, it is clear that a "one-size-fits-all" approach to treatment and service provision is simply not enough. While Housing First is a vital program, it alone is inadequate.

The social, cultural, financial, and existential situations of the study's participants were quite different. The homeless population is not homogenous and thus neither can our responses be. For instance, at one moment, a youth may be precariously housed by staying at friends' places, while taking advantage of the benefits of the social support network provided by friends, such as having access to a group in which to discuss difficult situations; having people to share stories and similar experiences with; and, ultimately, having access to a group that can provide emotional support. Here there is a sense of social inclusion. However, the next moment, often due to circumstances beyond their control, those same youth may find themselves at a homeless shelter, an urban camp, or on the streets with no place to stay and suddenly facing greater social exclusion. They may not know where to seek help or fear the stigma of seeking care in the event of a mental health or addiction crisis. To this end, homeless or street-oriented youth with addiction and mental health problems are anything but a single group with identical needs and preferences. The life-context of each youth is unique, and as such, a "one-size-fits-all" approach cannot address and treat youths' many complex and constantly evolving issues. A variety of housing, mental health and addiction treatment, and service options are needed.

5. CONCLUSION

The purpose of this closing chapter was to report on youths' initial preference of service options for the Youth Matters in London study. We have shown how this choice is complicated by the fact that, due to mental health and addiction issues, not all participants are comfortable with the independence the Housing First model provides. Some youth indicated in the open-ended answers that they found living in an apartment alone isolating and contributing to social exclusion. Since many youths see their peer group as an extended family and support network, the thought of living alone may be quite painful for some, hence the potential discomfort with the independence the Housing First model provides.

The diversity of responses and needs of participants in this study reinforces that a "one-size-fits-all" approach to providing treatment and services is inadequate to capture the full spectrum of needs of street-involved youth. These needs include social and financial difficulties; issues related to teen pregnancy; and the demands of parenting on street youth with children. Many Housing First options assume that youth do not have children of their own and therefore provide accommodation only designed for individuals. However, families need to be taken into consideration when designing Housing First options for this population so that those youth with children can also be rapidly and safely housed. As well, it is assumed that youth, like adults, have the experience and necessary skills for independent living and household management. However, many youths have limited independent living experience, or perhaps none at all, and would be more likely to succeed if Housing First models included a life and living skills development component such as those provided through transitional housing approaches.

Another consideration is the reality that many youths prefer to focus on one goal at a time, especially with respect to life-altering treatment or service initiatives. In many instances, the decision-making abilities of an individual can be influenced by the greater social and cultural context they belong to. This may also affect whether individuals will opt for Housing First if they perceive that the choice will remove them from their established social groups. Also, many youths seem to have difficulty prioritizing health concerns owing to the competing demands of street survival, such as what to eat and when, where to sleep, and avoiding confrontations and "drama" of the street.

With respect to youth experiencing ongoing addiction issues, access to treatment needs to be immediate and may also need to occur before providing housing, since housing may actually serve as a triggering environment for continued drug use. A related issue is that since the major goal in Housing First approaches is to remove individuals from the negative influences of street life, such as the sex and drug trade, we need to find affordable housing in neighbourhoods located outside the downtown core of cities to truly make a difference in providing better, safer options for youth.

REFERENCES

Ayrest, S. L. (1998). Depression and stress in street youth. *Adolescence, 34*(135), 567–575.

Cauce, A. M., Paradise, M., Ginzler, J. A., Embry, L., Morgan, C. J., Lohr, Y., & Theofelis, J. (2000). The characteristics and mental health of homeless adolescents: Age and gender differences. *Journal of Emotional and Behavioral Disorders, 8*(4), 230–239.

Community and Neighbourhood Services Policy and Planning. (2006). *Count of homeless persons in Calgary: Executive summary.* Retrieved from https://homelesshub.ca/sites/default/files/attachments/yu4av1lo.pdf

Cutuli, J. J. (2018). Homelessness in high school: Population-representative rates of self-reported homelessness, resilience, and risk in Philadelphia. *Social Work Research, 42*(3), 159–168.

Edmonton Homelessness Count Committee. (2002). A count of homeless persons in Edmonton. Edmonton, AB: Edmonton Joint Planning Committee on Housing. Retrieved from http://www.homelesshub.ca/Library/View.aspx?id=34829

Goering, P., Veldhuizen, S., Watson, A., Adair, C., Kopp, B., Latimer, E., … Aubry, T. (2014). *National final report: Cross-site At Home/Chez Soi project.* Calgary, AB: Mental Health Commission of Canada.

Haldenby, A. M., Berman, H., & Forchuk, C. (2007). Homelessness and health in adolescents. *Qualitative Health Research, 17*(9), 1232–1244.

Kidd, S. A., Thistle, J., Beaulieu, T., O'Grady, B., & Gaetz, S. (2019). A national study of Indigenous youth homelessness in Canada. *Public Health, 176*, 163–171. doi:10.1016/j.puhe.2018.06.012.

McCay, E., Langley, J., Beanlands, H., Cooper, L., Robinson, P., Howes, C., … Rigatti, M. (2006). Quantitative and qualitative approaches to understanding the mental health needs of transitional street youth. Poster session presented at the International Research Congress Focusing on Evidence-Based Practice, July 26, 2006. Montreal, Quebec, Canada.

Morton, M. H., Dworsky, A., Matjasko, J. L., Curry, S. R., Schlueter, D., Chávez, R., & Farrell, A. F. (2017). Prevalence and correlates of youth homelessness in the United States. *Journal of Adolescent Health, 62*(1), 14–21.

Narendorf, S. C., Cross, M. B., Santa Maria, D., Swank, P. R., & Bordnick, P. R. (2017). Relations between mental disorders, mental health treatment and substance use in homeless youth. *Drug and Alcohol Dependence, 175*(1), 1–8.

Padgett, D. K., Gulcur, L., & Tsemberis, S. (2006). Housing First services for people who are homeless, with co-occurring mental illness and substance abuse. *Research on Social Work Practice, 16*(1), 74–83.

Polvere, L., MacLeod, T., Macnaughton, E., Caplan, R., Piat, M., Nelson, G., … Goering, P. (2014). *Canadian Housing First toolkit: The At Home/Chez Soi experience.* Toronto, ON: Mental Health Commission of Canada and the Homeless Hub.

Reid, S., Berman, H., & Forchuk, C. (2005). Living on the streets in Canada: A feminist narrative study of girls and young women. *Issues in Comprehensive Pediatric Nursing, 28*(4), 237–256.

Tolomiczenko, G., & Goering, P. (2001). Gender differences in legal involvement among homeless shelter users. *International Journal of Law and Psychiatry, 24*(6), 583–593.

Tsemberis, S., Gulcur, L., & Nakae, M. (2004). Housing First, consumer choice, and harm reduction for homeless individuals with a dual diagnosis. *American Journal of Public Health, 94*(4), 651–656.

Wong, C. F., Clark, L. F., & Marlotte, L. (2016). The impact of specific and complex trauma on the mental health of homeless youth. *Journal of Interpersonal Violence, 31*(5), 831–854.

Author Biographies

Heather Atyeo, RN(EC), BScN, is a Nursing Practitioner with the Thames Valley Family Health Team working in primary health care with a clinical focus in mental health. Heather previously worked as crisis counsellor for a community-based crisis service and as nurse case manager in both emergency room and out-patient mental health settings. She is currently completing her MScN degree through the Arthur Labatt Family School of Nursing at Western University.

Sarah Benbow, RN, MScN, PhD, is a Professor in the School of Nursing at Fanshawe College, as well as an Adjunct Professor in the Arthur Labatt Family School of Nursing, Western University. Her program of research focuses on housing and homelessness in Canada, social inclusion/exclusion and health, mothering in marginalized contexts, and poverty reduction policies. Her work is guided by critical feminist intersectional approaches, with expertise in qualitative research methods. She has published and presented nationally and internationally on topics including social exclusion and health for mothers experiencing homelessness, a critical discourse analysis of Ontario's Poverty Reduction Strategy, intersections of exclusion and trauma, and surveillance in the lives of mothers.

Helene Berman, RN, PhD, is a Distinguished University Professor in the Arthur Labatt Family School of Nursing in the Faculty of Health Sciences at Western University and a Fellow in the Canadian Academy of Health Sciences. Her program of research has focused on the subtle and explicit forms of violence in the lives of girls and young women. In recent years, she has extended that work to include boys and young men. With a lengthy history of community-based research, Helene played a lead role in the establishment of the Centre for Research on Health Equity and Social Inclusion and currently serves as the Centre's founding Academic Director.

Mirella Bryant was Manager, Transition Services for Youth Opportunities Unlimited in London, Ontario, during the period of the CURA on poverty and social inclusion. Her programs reached out to at-risk youth who were often out of school, out of work, and homeless. She was also co-chair of the Collaboration Advisory Group (CAG) for the Street Level Women at Risk initiative, a collaboration of 24 organizations working to provide housing and supports to street-level sex workers.

Fatima Bukair received her Master of Science in Health Promotion from Western University. She is a Research and Knowledge Exchange Specialist at Thunderbird Partnership Foundation, a non-profit organization committed to working with First Nations to further the capacity of communities to address substance use and addiction. Fatima previously worked and volunteered at the Mental Health Nursing Research Alliance as both a Research Assistant and Coordinator.

Bethany Butzer, PhD, currently lives in Prague where she teaches and does research as a Lecturer in the psychology department at the University of New York in Prague. Bethany received her PhD in psychology from Western University in London, Ontario, and completed her postdoc research fellowship at Harvard Medical School.

Miriam Capretz is a Professor in the Department of Electrical and Computer Engineering at Western University. Before joining Western University, she was with the University of Aizu, Japan. She received her BSc and MESc degrees from UNICAMP, Brazil, and her PhD from the University of Durham, United Kingdom. She has been working in the software engineering area for more than 35 years. She has been involved with the organization of workshops and symposia and has served on program committees in international conferences. Her current research interests include cloud computing, Big Data, machine learning, service-oriented architecture, privacy, and security.

Robin Coatsworth-Puspoky received her diploma in Nursing from Fanshawe College in 1989. At the University of Western Ontario, Robin earned her BA in Sociology in 1987, her BScN in 1997, and her MScN with specialty in nursing education in 2001. Robin is an advanced practice nurse in geriatric mental health and is currently a Professor in the first year of the BScN Program in the School of Health Sciences at Lambton College in Sarnia, Ontario. Robin is currently completing her doctoral studies in the Faculty of Nursing at the University of Alberta.

Benita Cohen, PhD, is a public health researcher and educator. The focus of her work is on strengthening the integration of an equity/social justice lens in public health education, research, policy, and practice. Benita's research activities have included an exploration of the role of public health nurses and public health agencies in addressing child and family poverty, an equity scan of Canadian provincial/territorial tobacco control programs, an equity-focused health impact assessment of a proposed parenting program, the development of a conceptual framework of organizational capacity for public health equity action, and a scoping review of the role of advocacy for health equity in public health practice. She has also worked as a co-investigator on research teams that explored the use of research in public health networks and developed health equity performance indicators for Ontario's local public health agencies.

Martha Connoy, RPN, is currently the Director at Mission Services of London's Community Mental Health Programs. The Community Mental Health Programs provide a variety of emergent crisis intervention programs for those experiencing mental illnesses, addiction, and homelessness. Her work experience has provided a variety of opportunities to work within the community mental health sector, community development, system navigation, and system change while working collaboratively with municipal, provincial, and federal governments and educational institutions. Martha is a member of numerous committees that advocate for responsible, equitable, and accessible mental health services; decent affordable housing; addiction harm reduction and treatment services; and necessary systems change for vulnerable and at-risk adults.

Rick Csiernik, BSc, BSW, MSW, PhD, CCAC, RSW, Professor, School of Social Work, King's University College, is a White settler currently living on Dish With One Spoon Treaty Territory. He has written and edited 16 books, including *Homelessness, Housing, and Mental Health*, *Practising Social Work Research: Case Studies for Learning*, and *Responding to the Oppression of Addiction*. He has authored over 200 peer-reviewed articles and book chapters and has presented at over 200 conferences, workshops, and seminars. He has been part of research teams that have received over $4.5 million in funding and has been recipient of both the King's University College and McMaster University Continuing Education Teacher of the Year awards, as well as the Hugh Mellon Excellence in Research Award and the Ontario Volunteer Service Award.

Samantha Davie works as a Decision Support Associate at Unity Health Toronto. There, she works with clinicians and managers to help ensure that decisions affecting patients are rooted in sound data and rigorous analysis. She is passionate about using Big Data to understand and improve the health-care experience, quality improvement, and translating local findings into scholarly materials that facilitate knowledge translation. However, Sam is passionate not just about understanding and improving care but ensuring that health service organizations are regularly measuring equity and engaging in quality improvement efforts that have an embedded equity lens. This involves using data in creative ways to ensure that overall improvements are not unfairly disadvantaging patient subgroups.

Kevin Dickins is the City of London's Manager of Employment and Income Support Services and the Ontario Works Administrator. Kevin considers working to address and eradicate poverty a key priority of his, and he believes that all persons with the right support have the ability to find and maintain successful and sustainable employment, ultimately improving their quality of life and social inclusion. Kevin has and continues to serve on several local, provincial, and national working groups and planning committees. Kevin has an MBA and previously worked as the Manager of Community Programs with the Canadian Mental Health Association-Middlesex and participated in multiple research initiatives surrounding social enterprise, mental health, and employment and social determinants of health. Kevin was involved as a contributing author on projects related to the Community University Research Alliance (CURA).

Mark Dolson completed his PhD in Sociocultural Anthropology with Regna Darnell (Distinguished Professor of Anthropology) at the University of Western Ontario. His current research interests revolve around issues of marginalized youth cultures and the state, as well as the dynamic between affect, social structures, and subjectivity. He is also interested in the intersection between continental philosophy, critical theory, ethnographic writing, and issues of representation.

Lorie Donelle, PhD, is an Associate Professor at Western University in the Arthur Labatt Family School of Nursing and a Scientist with the Lawson Health Research Institute in London, Ontario. She holds the Arthur Labatt Family Chair in Nursing focused on digital health. Lorie's research addresses issues of health literacy, social justice, and digital health. Her research investigates technology-enabled models of homecare and the relationships between health information technologies and health practices, as well as the impact of multiple literacies with respect to access of health information, services, and support. Lorie sits on international (World Health Organization—WHO) and national advisory committees for health literacy and digital health and is a co-author, with Dr. Hoffman-Goetz and Dr. Ahmed, of a recently released book entitled *Health Literacy in Canada.*

Betty Edwards obtained her Master of Education in Counselling Psychology in June 1991. She became a Marital and Family Therapist in 1994 and worked as a

Family Therapist for ten years. She then worked five years as a Children's Counsellor in a women's shelter. Betty works at Can-Voice as a Peer Support Specialist. This involves working with adults 16 years of age and older who have mental health challenges, providing social and therapeutic groups. In addition, she is also the housing advocate for Willow Creek House, the Can-Voice eight-bedroom facility. She worked as a Peer Support Counsellor at The Mental Crisis Service, which provides interviews for individuals with mental health challenges who are in crisis. Betty was the research co-chair on the CURA that examined homelessness, poverty, and mental health, and co-chair of the follow-up CURA that examined mental health, poverty, and social inclusion.

Sandra Fisman, MD, is a psychiatrist practising in child and adolescent psychiatry at the Parkwood Institute, St. Joseph's Health Care—London. Sandra began her education at the University of Witwatersrand in Johannesburg, South Africa, and worked previously at the Children's Psychiatric Research Institute, also located in London, Ontario.

Cheryl Forchuk, PhD, is the Beryl and Richard Ivey Research Chair in Aging, Mental Health, Rehabilitation and Recovery at the Parkwood Research Institute in London, Ontario. She is a Distinguished University Professor at the Arthur Labatt Family School of Nursing, Western University. She is also a Scientist and Assistant Director for the Lawson Health Research Institute, the research arm of both London Health Sciences Centre and St. Joseph's Health Care—London, as well as Group Leader of Mental Health/Health Outcomes Research at Lawson. She has published on many topics including transitional discharge, technology in mental health care, and poverty, housing, and homelessness. She has been honoured with numerous awards, including the Order of Ontario, an honorary life membership in the Registered Nurses' Association of Ontario and the Canadian Association of Advanced Practice Nursing, and a Research Pioneer Award from Psychosocial Rehabilitation Canada.

Mike Godin worked during the CURA on poverty and social inclusion as Team Leader at the London/Middlesex branch of the Canadian Mental Health Association in the Housing Advocacy division. He played a key role in assisting with the preventing discharge to homelessness program. He is currently working in London at the Salvation Army's Recovery Community Centre, a holistic program supporting individuals with substance use and mental health instability issues.

Carolyn Gorlick, PhD, is a Professor Emerita at King's University College. Among Carolyn's career highlights are her work on the Community-University Research Alliance on Mental Health and Housing and being the Principal Investigator of the nationally funded *Welfare to Work in Canada: Policy Intentions and Program Realities* project.

Sebastian Gyamfi is a PhD candidate in Leadership in Health Promotion and Advanced Practice in Mental Health and Stigma, Faculty of Health Sciences, Western University, London, Ontario. He currently works at Parkwood Institute of Research with Mental Health Nursing Research Alliance in London, Ontario, as a Graduate Research Assistant. Sebastian has engaged in various scholarly activities in Ghana and Canada, including teaching psychiatry and mental health nursing at the College of Community Health Nursing, Winneba, and the University of Cape Coast. In 2016, he authored *Comprehensive Psychiatry for Nurses in Ghana*, making him the first person to be the sole author of a textbook on psychiatry in Ghana. In 2019, Sebastian was given the Irene Nordwich Graduate Student award in Canada, in recognition of his academic excellence.

Laura Hall, PhD, is currently an Assistant Professor with Laurentian University's Indigenous Social Work program. Her mother's family are Mohawk, while her father's family are English-Canadian. Laura's work with Indigenous communities looks at research as embodied, land-based practice and reciprocal learning, combining ecological and social justice goals. Her work asks how Indigenous culture-based learning can move us further towards ending violence against Indigenous women, Two-Spirited people, and youth. Laura's doctoral research explored Indigenous women's knowledge as temporal and spatial, embodying cycles of renewal and reciprocity.

Peter V. Hall is a Professor of Urban Studies at Simon Fraser University in Vancouver, BC. Peter's research seeks to understand the role of institutions and institutional change in shaping patterns and outcomes of local and regional economic development. His wide-ranging areas of exploration include seaports, logistics, social enterprise, and community development. He is interested in research practice and the role of research in public discourse, and he served on SFU's Research Ethics Board. He previously directed the SSHRC-funded Partnership Development Grant on "Reclaiming the New Westminster Waterfront," and between 2010 and 2016, he co-led an initiative to study the impact of the social enterprise sector in Canada. His publications include the co-edited *Integrating Seaports and*

Trade Corridors (Ashgate, 2011), *Community-University Research Partnerships: Reflections on the Canadian Social Economy Experience* (Victoria, 2012), *Cities, Regions and Flow* (Routledge, 2013), and, as co-author, *Proposal Economy* (UBC, 2015).

Jeffrey Hoch, PhD, is a Professor and Chief, Division of Health Policy and Management, Department of Public Health Sciences at the University of California, Davis. He is also the Associate Director, Center for Healthcare Policy and Research. Jeffrey's experience is in health services research related to cancer, mental health, and other health issues affecting poor and vulnerable populations. An award-winning teacher, Jeffrey has taught health economics and economic evaluation classes in the United States and internationally.

Momodou S. Jeng (Mo), PhD, is a Public Servant, Researcher, and an Adjunct Assistant Professor at Western University. He has spent a great deal of time trying to understand and advocate for vulnerable populations. He holds a Diploma in Statistics, a Graduate Diploma in Demography, a Master of Arts in Demography, and a PhD in Social Demography. Dr. Jeng has published numerous peer-reviewed articles in relation to social issues, population, and development.

Elsabeth Jensen, PhD, is an Associate Professor and Director of the Graduate Program, School of Nursing, York University, Toronto. Elsabeth has authored 17 book chapters, 22 peer-reviewed papers, and 3 technical reports, and has co-edited *Homelessness, Housing, and Mental Health: Finding Truths—Creating Change* with Dr. Cheryl Forchuk and Dr. Rick Csiernik. She has given 8 invited addresses and presented 66 papers at conferences all over the globe. Dr. Jensen has been on 26 research projects, representing over $911,000 worth of funding. She was involved with the SSHRC-CURA project that led to the creation of a new housing initiative, a restructuring of homelessness services in London, Ontario, and new policies regarding hospital discharges to "no fixed address." More recently, she led a team in the first Canadian evaluation of a community-based model of discharge service. Implementation of the model resulted in a 40% reduction in readmission rate in an acute care mental health program.

Libbey Joplin, BA, MTS, CAPPE, is a citizen development researcher. She was involved in the CURA on Housing, Homelessness, and Mental Health as an active community representative participating in numerous committees and team research projects.

Chandell Kelly graduated from Western University with a Bachelor of Science in Nursing and has worked for Dr. Cheryl Forchuk. She started off as a Research Assistant working on the Youth Matters in London: Homelessness, Mental Health and Addiction project. Chandell went on to be one of Dr. Forchuk's Research Coordinators, managing various studies. She has worked in many areas of nursing, including the medical surgical field, nursing in Australia working with individuals in the criminal justice system, a rural hospital in northern Canada serving largely Indigenous populations, and community health and homecare. She has obtained a certificate in critical care nursing and is currently working in a cardiac surgery intensive care unit in Vancouver.

Melissa Kersey has worked in social services, in the Ontario Disability Support Program since 2001. As a Caseworker and now a Manager, she is passionate about the relationship between mental health and social inclusion.

Shani Kingston-MacClure, who was born in Ireland, received her BSW degree from King's University College and her MSW from Wilfrid Laurier University in Waterloo, Ontario. Since 2000, Shani has been a social worker in the Adult Mental Health Care Program, London Health Sciences Centre, London, Ontario. She has also worked for the Canadian Mental Health Association, Paramed Health Services, and the Children's Aid Society of London and Middlesex.

John Kok, MPH, MD, was born in the Sudan during the first Sudanese Civil War, fought during the 1970s, and became a refugee escaping to Ethiopia in 1984 during the nation's second civil war. From 1986 to 1997, John received secondary and university education in Cuba. Upon graduation as a Medical Doctor from Higher Institute of Medical Sciences of Havana in 1997, he resettled in Canada. From 2009 to 2014, John worked as Program Director for Primary Healthcare Delivery with Sudan Medical Care, an NGO, and as Director of Planning and Coordination with Jonglei State Ministry of Health & Environment in the Republic of South Sudan. John is multilingual, writing and speaking Arabic, English, French, and Spanish. Discovering that his true passion is in public health, John trained in this area and was awarded a master's degree at Western University in 2016. He also holds a graduate certificate in Project Management from Fanshawe College. Currently, he is a Project Coordinator at Centre Communautaire Régional de London (CCRL), for francophones and ethno-cultural communities, with a goal to achieve health through physical activities and ethno-cultural activities and ultimately have a sense of identity, belonging, and self-confidence.

Pam Lahey is a social policy analyst and policy researcher. She holds a PhD from McMaster University. Her area of research focuses on (re)integration of people with mental illness into mainstream employment. She is currently a research associate with the Centre for Research on Work Disability Policy. Pam has published in peer-reviewed journals on approaches to strengthening disability income support programs to enhance the employment experiences for workers with disabilities.

Justin Langille is a documentary photographer and anthropology doctoral candidate at the University of Toronto. His images and ethnographic research examine human relationships with regional environments in Canada, with a focus on water stewardship. His work has been featured by the CONTACT Photography Festival, Greenpeace Canada, and the Royal College of Physicians and Surgeons of Canada, among others. Justin is currently based in Guelph, Ontario, and you may find other examples of his work at www.justinlangille.com

Karen Laverty is a Direct Support Worker at Craigwood Youth Services in London, Ontario, a fully accredited children's mental health centre, with more than 60 years' experience helping youth to overcome their challenges.

Bryanna Lucyk is a Research Coordinator at Lawson Health Research Institute. She works for Dr. Cheryl Forchuk on her team, the Mental Health Nursing Research Alliance. She received a BA Honours in Psychology, as well as a BA Honours in Thanatology and English, both from King's University College at Western University in London, Ontario, Canada.

Grant Martin attained his Honours Degree in Social Work from King's University College in London, Ontario, in 2005. He is the former Managing Director of London CAReS, and, over the past decade, his professional experience includes working with street-involved and at-risk youth and adults living with the effects of poverty, addiction, and mental illness in various direct service and management roles.

Amanda Meier, MSW, RSW, was a Research Coordinator for the Lawson Health Research Institute, London, Ontario, playing a key role coordinating the CURA on Poverty and Social Inclusion. She currently works as a psychotherapist in Mississauga, Ontario.

Beth Mitchell, PhD, C.Psych., was born in Mississippi. Beth completed her undergraduate degree at the University of Mississippi and her MA and PhD in

Psychology at Ohio State University. She has pursued further learning through the Rotman Advanced Health Leadership Program, University of Toronto, and the Ross School of Business at the University of Michigan. She worked for 30 years with the London Health Sciences Centre as a clinical psychologist, Director of Psychology, Director of the Mental Health Care Program, and Director of Organizational Effectiveness, concluding her professional career as CEO of the Middlesex branch of the Canadian Mental Health Association.

Phyllis Montgomery, PhD, is a Professor at Laurentian University's School of Nursing with a long-standing interest in psychiatric mental health nursing. Drawing on a broad array of theoretical and empirical knowledge, her research focuses on individual, social, and structural factors shaping health. A major thrust of her work is to help advance greater equity and positive social change for persons living with mental health challenges.

Sharolyn Mossey, MScN, a Registered Nurse, is an Assistant Professor at Laurentian University. Sharolyn's areas of expertise include Indigenous/cultural awareness, clinical/preceptor evaluation, chronic illness, and mental health. She has worked extensively with communities on housing issues for persons with mental illness.

Denise Newton-Mathur is an Assistant Professor in Laurentian University's School of Nursing. She is of Métis heritage and was instrumental in the development of *A Nursing Student's Guide to Cultural Competence and Cultural Safety.*

Tony O'Regan was a Research Coordinator at the Lawson Health Research Institute's Mental Health Nursing Research Alliance, Canada. He holds a Bachelor of Science in Nursing Studies and a Master of Science in Mental Health Studies. He has practised as a registered nurse and nurse educator in both the United Kingdom and Canada.

Abe Oudshoorn, PhD, is an Assistant Professor in the Arthur Labatt Family School of Nursing at Western University, the Department of Psychiatry Schulich School of Medicine & Dentistry, and Associate Scientist with Lawson Health Research Institute. Having worked as a nurse with people experiencing homelessness, Abe's research focuses on health, homelessness, housing policy, and poverty. Outside of the university, Abe has the privilege of chairing the London Homeless

Coalition, is a board member with the United Way of London & Middlesex, and serves on the Mayor's Advisory Panel on Poverty.

Chantelle Perreault is a Shelter Diversion Worker at Rotholme Women's and Family Shelter, part of Mission Services of London, Ontario. In this role, she helps families avoid coming into shelter by helping to improve their current living situation or helping them obtain alternate housing. Chantelle has always had a passion for helping people to advocate for their needs. Chantelle is a graduate of the Police Foundations program and has worked in social services for over 15 years.

Stewart E. Perry, PhD, has been engaged in community activism for half a century. His work has involved him in education and leadership activities with the National Institute of Mental Health, Washington School of Psychiatry, Boston University School of Medicine's Psychiatric Home Treatment Center, Institute for New Enterprise Development, and Centre for Community Economic Development. He concluded his career working as an independent consultant fostering community economic development initiatives in both Canada and the United States.

Major Steven Pirie, CD, MSc, RN, CHE, is Health Services Operations Officer, Royal Canadian Medical Service. He has served on the Joint Theatre Trauma System Team at Kandahar Air Base, Afghanistan, where he delivered point-of-injury training to medics in the field. He also served with Air Force medics, helping coordinate care across coalition forces.

Liz Puddy was employed by the Canadian Mental Health Association (London) during the CURA on Housing, Homelessness and Mental Health. She was instrumental in developing the program to prevent discharge to homelessness. Liz has also worked as a resource worker for Lennox and Addington Family and Children's Services, a counsellor for Tri-Light Counselling Services in Deseronto, Ontario, and for the Sudbury/Manitoulin CMHA.

Jan Richardson, MBA, retired as the City of London's Manager of Strategic Priorities, Homeless Prevention and Housing. Jan's priority and commitment was to solve homelessness in London and beyond, and to do so she served on a number of local, provincial, and national advisory groups and committees, including the Law

Society of Ontario. Jan remains an Adjunct Faculty Member at the Arthur Labatt School of Nursing, Western University.

Abraham (Rami) Rudnick, MD, PhD, CPRP, FRCPC, CCPE, DFESPCH, FCPA, CSLI, CPRRP, is a psychiatrist and a philosopher. He is a Professor in the Department of Psychiatry and School of Occupational Therapy at Dalhousie University and the Clinical Director of the Nova Scotia Operational Stress Injury Clinic, Canada. Rami is a Canadian Certified Physician Executive and the Editor-in-Chief of the *International Journal of Mental Health*. He is a recipient of national and international awards and other recognitions, such as the pioneer award in recovery research granted by Psychosocial Rehabilitation/Réadaptation Psychosociale Canada and a Distinguished Fellowship and Gold Medal of the European Society for Person Centered Healthcare.

Gordon Russell works at the Men's Mission and Rehabilitation Centre in London, a branch of Mission Services of London. The Men's Mission is an emergency and transitional to long-t erm shelter for men 16 years of age and older. Gordon has worked at the Men's Mission as the Branch Director, participating in a number of community initiatives over that time, but most recently with the No Fixed Address Committee of the CURA, the London Homeless Coalition, and the Evangelical Fellowship of Canada's Roundtable on Homelessness and Poverty.

Ruth Schofield, RN, MSc(T), is an experienced nursing professor in community health nursing (CHN) at McMaster University and Western University. Her 23 years of nursing practice in public health result in an expertise in health promotion programs, including with marginalized populations. Further capabilities include leading national competency development and revisions to standards of practice. Ruth's research endeavours in community health nursing, nursing education, and mental health and housing have resulted in several peer-reviewed publications and chapter co-authorship in several nursing textbooks. Other leadership roles have included former President of Community Health Nurses of Canada (CHNC) and Community Health Nurses Initiatives Group (CHNIG) of the Registered Nurses of Ontario (RNAO); former Board of Directors member of RNAO and Ontario Public Health Association (OPHA); Chair and Co-chair of the national research projects and founding leader of a national CHN leadership institute.

Michelle Solomon is a Registered Nurse, PhD student, and Research Assistant at Western University and Lawson Health Research Institute in London,

Ontario. Her area of research is mental health system reform, supporting access to community mental health services through incorporating community members into the delivery framework via peer support and self-help. Michelle previously founded and was Executive Director of Connect for Mental Health for ten years, from 2007 to 2017, a consumer-survivor peer-support organization providing support, education, and outreach to individuals affected by mental illness. Michelle has been involved in the implementation of the Transitional Discharge Model, helping individuals being discharged from psychiatric inpatient units into the community. Michelle's clinical experience is in acute care mental health and community care, supporting individuals with chronic health conditions.

Wafa'a Ta'an, RN, PhD, has international experience studying and working in the field of psychiatric mental health nursing in Jordan, the United Kingdom, and Canada. After completing her doctoral studies at Western University, she accepted a faculty position within the Department of Community and Mental Health Nursing at the Jordan University of Science and Technology in Irbid, Jordan.

Katherine Turner, BA, LLB, Dipl. CED, was the Community-Director of the inaugural London, Ontario, Community University Research Alliance that examined issues of mental health and housing. At that time, she also served as the Chair of the London Homeless Coalition and as the Director of Margaret's Haven Non-Profit Housing, a non-profit, charitable corporation that provided housing to women with psychiatric challenges and a history of serious housing difficulties. Katherine is currently the Regional Manager for Innovation, Science and Economic Development Canada in Thunder Bay, Ontario.

Rebecca Vann, BSW, MSW, RSW, has worked in the field of Psychiatric Social Work for over 30 years. An experienced Dialectical Behaviour Therapist with a passion for working with those who struggle with mental illness and their families, Rebecca is a strong advocate for those who are homeless: "It is a basic human need that should be met for all." She is also a part-time professor at King's University College in London, Ontario, and a student practicum supervisor. Rebecca has won awards for student mentorship and leadership in her work.

Catherine Ward-Griffin, RN, PhD, Professor Emerita, earned her doctorate in Community Heath at the University of Toronto in 1998. She spent 25 years at the University of Western Ontario teaching family nursing, health promotion, and research to both undergraduate and graduate students. Working in the areas of gerontology, gender, and community health, her research program focused on the experiences of elders and their families living with a variety of health challenges, such as dementia, cancer, and mental illness. Using a variety of methodological approaches, she investigated the health effects of providing and receiving care in light of social, economic, and political contextual factors that promote or undermine health.

Laura Warner earned her Bachelor's in Health Sciences from Brock University and her Master's in Epidemiology from Western University. She has worked as a Research Coordinator at Western University, an Epidemiologist at the Lawson Health Research Institute in London, Ontario, and is currently employed at the South West Regional Cancer Program as a Data and Evaluation Specialist.

Amanda Wright has worked for Lawson Health Research Institute for over ten years and was previously the Poverty and Social Inclusion Research Coordinator, and the Coordinator of the Youth Matters in London research project. Along with her work at Lawson, Amanda practices as a Youth Development Counsellor with Youth Opportunities Unlimited in London, Ontario.

Annie Yang, BSc, completed her Bachelor's in Psychology at Western University and is currently completing her Master's in Counselling Psychology. Her thesis examines how symptoms of developmental trauma present in children and adolescents across different ages. She has worked as a Research Assistant in the Mental Health Nursing and Research Alliance team at Parkwood Institute since 2016. During this time, Annie has been involved in several research projects that examined mental health issues and homelessness, as well as program evaluations that assessed the effectiveness of systemic interventions for marginalized groups.

Copyright Acknowledgements

Chapter 5: Forchuk, C., & Meier, A. (2014). The article idea chart: A participatory action research tool to aid involvement in dissemination. *Gateways: International Journal of Community Research and Engagement*, *7*(1), 157–163. UTS ePRESS, http://dx.doi.org/10.5130/ijcre.v7i1.3393.

Chapter 6: Forchuk, C., O'Regan, T., Jeng, M., & Wright, A. (2018). Retaining a sample of homeless youth. *Journal of the Canadian Academy of Child and Adolescent Psychiatry*, *27*(3), 167–174. Used by permission of the Canadian Academy of Child and Adolescent Psychiatry.

Chapter 7: Meier, A., Csiernik, R., Warner, L., & Forchuk, C. (2015). The stigma scale: A Canadian perspective. *Social Work Research*, *39*(4), 213–222. Reprinted by permission of Oxford University Press.

Chapter 8: Forchuk, C., Montgomery, P., Rudnick, A., Lahey, P., Cohen, B., Schofield, R., Perry, S.E., Coatsworth-Puspoky, R., Edwards, B., Butzer, B., & Meier, A. (2017). Poverty trajectories experienced by persons with mental illness. *Journal of Poverty*, *21*(3), 247–264. Reprinted by permission of the publisher (Taylor & Francis Ltd, http://www.tandfonline.com).

Chapter 9: Benbow, S., Rudnick, A., Forchuk, C., & Edwards, B. (2014). Using a capabilities approach to understand poverty and social exclusion of psychiatric survivors. *Disability & Society*, *29*(7), 1046–1060. Reprinted by permission of the publisher (Taylor & Francis Ltd, http://www.tandfonline.com).

Chapter 10: Benbow, S., Forchuk, C., Gorlick, C., Berman, H., & Ward-Griffin, C. (2019). "Until you hit rock bottom there's no support": Contradictory sources and systems of support for mothers experiencing homelessness in southwestern Ontario. *Canadian Journal of Nursing Research*, *51*(3), 179–190. Used by permission of SAGE Publishing.

Chapter 11: Montgomery, P. B. S., Hall, L., Newton-Mathur, D., Forchuk, C., & Mossey, S. (2014). Sheltering Aboriginal women with mental illness in Ontario, Canada: Being "kicked" and nurtured. *Journal of Nursing and Care*, *3*(3), 1–6. © 2014 Montgomery P, et al.

Chapter 12: Pirie, S. D. (2015). The mental health of those who serve Canada. *Canadian Journal of Nursing Research*, *47*(3), 2–6. Used by permission of SAGE Publishing.

Chapter 13: Forchuk, C., Richardson, J., & Atyeo, H. (2016). Addressing homelessness among Canadian veterans. In N. Nichols & C. Doberstein (Eds.), *Exploring* *effective systems responses to homelessness* (pp. 368–377). Toronto, ON: The Canadian Observatory on Homelessness Press.

Chapter 15: Reprinted from *Work*, *52*(1), Hall, P. V., Montgomery, P., Davie, S., Dickins, K., Forchuk, C., Jeng, M. S., Kersey, M., Meier, A., Lahey, P., Rudnick, A., Solomon, M., & Warner, L., "Seeking and securing work: Individual-level predictors of employment of psychiatric survivors," 91–101, Copyright (2015), with permission from IOS Press. The publication is available at IOS Press through http://dx.doi.org/10.3233/WOR-141973

Chapter 16: Forchuk, C., Donelle, L., Capretz, M., Bukair, F., & Kok, J. (2018, July). Evaluating iris scanning technology to link data related to homelessness and other disadvantaged populations with mental illness and addiction. In M. Mokhtari, B. Abdulrazak, & H. Aloulou (Eds.), *Smart homes and health telematics, designing a better future: Urban assisted living* (pp. 171–178). Springer International Publishing. Reprinted by permission of Springer Nature.

Chapter 18: Forchuk, C., Godin, M., Hoch, J. S., Kingston-MacClure, S., Jeng, M. S., Puddy, L., Vann, R., & Jensen, E. (2013). Preventing psychiatric discharge to homelessness. *Canadian Journal of Community Mental Health*, *32*(3), 17–28. https://doi.org/10.7870/cjcmh-2013-028. Reprinted by permission of the publisher.

Chapter 20: Forchuk, C., Richardson, J., Laverty, K., Bryant, M., Rudnick, A., Csiernik, R., Edwards, B., Fisman, S., Mitchell, B., Connoy, M., Dolson, M. S., & Kelly, C. (2013). Service preferences of homeless youth with mental illness: Housing first, treatment first, or both together. In S. Gaetz, B. O'Grady, K. Buccieri, J. Karabanow, & A. Marsolais (Eds.), *Youth homelessness in Canada: Implications for policy and practice* (pp. 95–110). Toronto, ON: Canadian Homelessness Research Network Press.

Index